PERFORMANCE MEASUREMENT & CONTROL SYSTEMS FOR IMPLEMENTING STRATEGY

Robert Simons

Harvard Business School, Boston

Contributors:

Antonio Dávila
IESE, University of Navarra, Barcelona

Robert S. Kaplan
Harvard Business School, Boston

Prentice Hall
Upper Saddle River, New Jersey 07458

Executive Editor:	Annie Todd
Editorial Assistant:	Fran Toepfer
Editor-in-Chief:	PJ Boardman
Executive Marketing Manager:	Beth Toland
Production Editor:	Marc Oliver
Manufacturing Buyer:	Lisa DiMaulo
Senior Manufacturing Supervisor:	Paul Smolenski
Senior Manufacturing/Prepress Manager:	Vincent Scelta
Designer:	Jill Little
Design Manager:	Patricia Smythe
Cover Illustration/Photo:	Tony Stone Images
Composition:	Progressive Information Technologies

Copyright © 2000 by Prentice-Hall, Inc.
Upper Saddle River, New Jersey 07458

ISBN 013-021945-2

Prentice-Hall International (UK) Limited, London
Prentice-Hall of Australia Pty. Limited, Sydney
Prentice-Hall Canada, Inc., Toronto
Prentice-Hall Hispanoamericana, S.A., Mexico
Prentice-Hall of India Private Limited, New Delhi
Prentice-Hall of Japan, Inc., Tokyo
Pearson Education Asia Pte. Ltd., Singapore
Editora Prentice-Hall do Brasil, Ltda., Rio de Janeiro

Printed in the United States of America

10 9

To Judy

CONTENTS

PREFACE

New accounting and control tools are needed to implement strategy in the 21st century. Rapid innovation, entrepreneurial competitors, and increasingly demanding customers have radically altered competitive dynamics. This book integrates the latest performance measurement and control techniques with the new realities of competition, strategy, and organization design. Anyone interested in running a business—either experienced managers or students—will benefit from understanding these new concepts and approaches to implementing strategy.

All the materials in the book have been rigorously pre-tested both in and out of the classroom. Students enrolled in Harvard Business School's MBA course, *Achieving Profit Goals & Strategies,* have used early versions of the book for three years. Selected chapters have been used in executive education programs at Harvard Business School and in a variety of corporate training programs. Case studies have been classroom tested at Harvard and many other business schools. Well-known U.S. and international companies have successfully implemented these new concepts. The result of this pre-testing and refinement is a coherent body of practical theory coupled with the latest application techniques.

The book is divided into four parts. Part I sets out the foundations for strategy implementation. Part II teaches quantitative tools for performance measurement and control. Part III illustrates the use of these techniques by managers to achieve profit goals and strategies. Part IV offers action-oriented case studies to illustrate key ideas and management techniques.[1] Throughout the book, concepts are illustrated with current, real-life examples. The reader is encouraged to refer to the glossary at the end of the text to gain a further overview of the broad range of concepts and techniques covered. An extensive bibliography is provided at the end of the book for those interested in additional references for specific topics.

Chapter 1 sets the stage for Part I—Foundations for Implementing Strategy—by highlighting the *tensions* that are the essence of successful strategy implementation. We discuss the challenges of balancing profit, growth, and control; the tensions between short-term results and long-term capabilities; the differing expectations of a firm's constituents; and the motives of human behavior.

Chapter 2 explores the basics of formulating and implementing *business strategy.* We discuss how to analyze competitive dynamics and the capabilities of a business. We then view strategy from four different angles: strategy as perspective, strategy as market

---

[1] Part IV is included only in the Text & Cases format of this book (ISBN 0-13-234006-2)

position, strategy as goals and plans, and strategy as patterns of emerging activities. We demonstrate that each of these approaches to strategy implementation requires distinct performance measurement and control techniques.

Chapter 3 introduces the essentials of *organization design.* In this chapter, we explore the implications of grouping business units by function as opposed to grouping business units by geography, products, or customers. We introduce key concepts that are essential to the effective design of performance measurement systems such as span of control, span of accountability, and span of attention.

Chapter 4 rounds out the introductory part of the book. In this chapter, we study how managers use *information* to control critical outputs. We discuss the technical feasibility of monitoring and measurement, the cost of information, and the effects of performance measurement and control on innovation. We end the chapter by discussing how managers use information not only for decision-making and control, but also for signaling, learning, and external communication.

Part II of the book—Creating Performance Measurement Systems—begins with Chapter 5, in which we show how to build effective *profit plans.* Using a profit wheel model, we illustrate how to develop accurate estimates for sales, profit, cash flow, investment in new assets, return-on-equity, profitability, and asset turnover. We illustrate how to gather and analyze data and assumptions, and demonstrate the effects of sensitivity analysis on predictions. We end this chapter by illustrating how to use a profit plan to test a strategy's validity.

Chapter 6 shows how to use *strategic profitability analysis* to calculate profit from competitive effectiveness and profit from operating efficiencies. Formulas and examples are provided for variance calculations related to profit plans, market share, revenue, and efficiency and costs.

Chapter 7 provides tools for *allocating resources.* For assets that enhance operating efficiencies or increase revenue, we review well-known techniques such as discounted cash flow and internal rate of return. For assets designed to enhance competitive effectiveness, we review the necessary analyses to ensure that resources are aligned with strategic initiatives.

Chapter 8 shows how to link profit plans and other performance measurement systems to internal and external *markets.* We discuss how to design an internal transfer pricing system. In addition, we discuss how to create financial and nonfinancial measures to link corporate performance to capital markets, supplier markets, and customer markets. Finally, we illustrate how to use residual income techniques such as economic value added.

Chapter 9 completes Part II by describing how to build a *balanced scorecard.* Using an internal value chain model, we discuss how the balanced scorecard can support and enable innovation, operations, and post-sale service processes. We describe how to build performance indicators to monitor the achievement of financial goals, customer goals, internal process goals, and learning and growth goals.

Part III of the book—Achieving Profit Goals and Strategies—focuses on how managers actually use these techniques to achieve business goals.

Chapter 10 introduces *diagnostic* and *interactive* control systems. We illustrate how managers use these systems to implement top-down intended strategy and guide bottom-up emergent strategy. In addition, we explore the special risks that are introduced through the use of performance measurement and control systems.

Chapter 11 focuses on *goal setting* and the aligning of *incentives*. We learn how to use goals to communicate strategy, the importance of targets and benchmarks for motivation, and the multiple purposes for which goals are used, including planning, coordination, motivation, and evaluation.

Chapter 12 provides the tools to identify *strategic risks*. We illustrate how performance measurement and control systems can be used to monitor operations risk, asset impairment risk, competitive risk, and franchise risk. We introduce the risk exposure calculator—a tool to measure the type and magnitude of pressures that can lead to failures or breakdowns. Finally, we consider the possibility of misrepresentation and fraud.

Chapter 13 provides an overview of the design and use of business conduct and strategic *boundaries* to control risk. We present a framework for designing *internal control systems* to safeguard information and assets. We review the behavioral and motivational assumptions that underlie these systems.

Chapter 14 ends the book by pulling together key concepts into an integrated model—the *levers of control*. The power of this approach is illustrated in two contexts: the introduction of performance measurement and control systems over the life cycle of the business, and the use of the levers of control by managers taking charge of a new business.

As I look back over the scope of the book, I realize that I could not have completed such an ambitious project without the help of many people. Robert Kaplan, my friend and colleague for the past 15 years, contributed Chapter 9 on the balanced scorecard. An acknowledged expert and one of the innovators of this important performance measurement tool, Bob was generous to allow me to include this chapter as well as several of his cases in the book. Antonio Dávila, a former doctoral student at Harvard Business School and now an assistant professor at the University of Navarra in Spain, worked closely with me on this project during his four years at Harvard. Tony helped write Chapters 5 and 6 (Building a Profit Plan and Strategic Profitability Analysis), prepared initial drafts of the bibliography, provided detailed commentary and suggestions on many of the chapters, and was a joint author for several of the case studies. Ken Koga, another doctoral student now at Waseda University in Japan, provided helpful comments and input. My colleagues Thomas Piper, who teaches *Achieving Profit Goals & Strategies* with me in the MBA program, William Bruns, the author of a number of cases in the book, and Marc Epstein and John Waterhouse, both of whom visited Harvard while I was developing the manuscript, helped me work through ideas and approaches. Professor William Fruhan generously allowed me to include one of his cases in the book.

I also gratefully acknowledge the willingness of Harvard Business School Press and Harvard Business School Publishing to allow me to use material from my book *Levers of Control* and to reproduce the Harvard case studies. Audrey Barrett, permissions editor at Harvard Business School Publishing, was especially helpful in researching all the cases and granting the necessary permissions.

I have benefited from comments on early drafts provided by Michael Alles (University of Texas at Austin), Shahid Ansari (California State University, Northridge), Howard Armitage (University of Waterloo), Jacob Birnberg (University of Pittsburgh), Len Brooks (University of Toronto), Clifton Brown (University of Illinois, Urbana-Champaign), Kung Chen (University of Nebraska, Lincoln), Chee Chow (San Diego State University), Kenneth Euske (Naval Postgraduate School), Neil Fargher (University of Oregon), Severin Grabski (Michigan State University), Harriette Griffin (North Carolina State University), Sanford Gunn (SUNY at Buffalo), Susan Haka (Michigan State University), Raffi Indjejikian (University of Michigan), Christopher Ittner (University of Pennsylvania, Wharton School), Stephen Jablonsky (Penn State University), Douglas Johnson (Arizona State University), Charles Klemstine (University of Michigan), Laureen Maines (Indiana University), Steve Reimer (University of Iowa), Alan Richardson (Queen's University), Toshi Shibano (University of Chicago), Michael Shields (Michigan State University), and John Vogel (Lockheed Martin).

Students in Harvard Business School's *Achieving Profit Goals & Strategies* course responded with good humor and perceptive suggestions as I tested and revised various versions of the manuscript. Many students, including Nicole DeHoratius, Timothy Dornan, Kenneth Gonzalez, Uchechi Orji, Yungwook Shin, and Kirsten Steward, made substantive suggestions that are reflected in the current text. Special mention must go to Michael Mahoney, who worked with me over several months revising and refining the manuscript prior to publication. Mike made many suggestions, drafted the initial version of the glossary, prepared clarifying paragraphs to the text, and identified many of the business examples.

Research associate Indra Reinbergs also made important contributions finding company examples to support the text material, as did Jeff Cronin, information analyst at Baker Library. Luz Velazquez, my assistant for the past two years, coordinated the submission of the manuscript and cases, and was characteristically efficient and cheerful in the face of deadline pressures. Jenny Tsoulos also provided invaluable assistance in checking page proofs and managing the submission of final changes.

At Prentice Hall, I am indebted to Annie Todd, executive editor, who has patiently and professionally shepherded the project to completion, PJ Boardman, editor-in-chief, who gave critical support throughout the project, and Marc Oliver, production editor, and Fran Toepfer, editorial assistant, both of whom kept the flow of the project on schedule. Ann Koonce made helpful suggestions in copyediting the manuscript. Beth Toland, executive marketing manager, provided the skill to communicate the essence of these new ideas to potential readers.

Developing the concepts, cases, and course upon which this book is based has filled my professional life over the past three years. I hope that you, the reader, will find the effort worthwhile.

Robert Simons
Boston

PART I

Foundations for Implementing Strategy

1

Organizational Tensions to be Managed

I magine that you are the owner of a small clothing chain in suburban Boston. You started with one small store and a novel idea: to offer cheap but fashionable clothing, along with a selection of decorative merchandise, to college students who attend Boston's many universities.

By focusing on the college market and staying in tune with youthful fashion and lifestyle changes, you have successfully built up a company with six stores. Your business now employs more than 100 employees. Innovation—focusing on the local youth market—differentiates your merchandise from the big department stores in the area. The key to success is your employees—young and in tune with the college clientele. They experiment continually with new products and fashion fads and recommend changes in merchandising mix.

However, as the company has grown larger, unanticipated problems have surfaced. Profitability among the six stores has been uneven. Two of the units are especially profitable, but it is not clear what causes them to be more profitable than the others. Another store seems to consistently underperform. Moreover, if you are not always in a store, you suspect that sloppy financial controls may be eroding profits.

Other issues have absorbed a lot of your time. You worry about missing the next fad. In one store, employees began experimenting with nontraditional products such as vegetarian foods. Some of the new products sold briskly, but overall store sales declined.

You are considering expanding into New York state, but you worry about how much to invest in new facilities and inventory. As the business becomes larger and more dispersed, you wonder how to set direction and ensure common goals for the business. The strength of your business has been in letting employees suggest new products to meet their local customers' needs. They know their customers best. On the other hand, some of their ideas have been failures. As the number of stores increases—especially in other states—greater geographical distance will make it harder for you to communicate your vision for the business and to get information to allow you to manage the business effectively.

To resolve these issues, effective managers rely on **performance measurement and control systems** to set direction, make strategic decisions, and achieve desired goals. Setting direction and achieving desired goals is relatively easy for a small business in which all employees work together in one location. Informal discussions and direct supervision can be used to ensure that the business is being managed effectively. As businesses become larger and more dispersed, however, these techniques become more difficult.

At the heart of the problem is a series of tensions—between innovation and control; between profitability and growth; between your goals and those of your employees (and others who have an interest in the business); and between the various opportunities to create value in the marketplace and the scarce amount of time and attention available to you.

This book describes the techniques that effective managers use to set direction and achieve desired strategic goals for the organizations they lead. The issues to be addressed in succeeding chapters can be broken down into the following questions:

1. How can managers leverage the potential for innovation in their businesses and, at the same time, ensure adequate control and protection from unpleasant surprises by employees?

2. How can managers drive growth that enhances, rather than dilutes, profitability?

3. How can managers communicate business strategy and performance goals effectively to all employees?

4. How can managers organize and dedicate various kinds of resources to support the implementation of business strategies?

5. How do managers measure and track performance toward strategically important goals?

6. How can managers ensure that their businesses are not exposed to unacceptable levels of risk?

7. How can senior managers move information from employees, who are in day-to-day contact with customers, back up the hierarchy to those who are responsible for formulating and supporting new strategies?

Throughout the book, we focus primarily on performance measurement and control systems for business organizations. However, the principles and techniques discussed are applicable to all goal-oriented organizations whose managers are interested in maximizing performance. Such organizations include non-profit educational institutions, charities, government departments and agencies, the military, and many others.

SYSTEMS FOR PERFORMANCE MEASUREMENT AND CONTROL

This book focuses on performance measurement and control systems, which are the *formal, information-based routines and procedures managers use to maintain or alter patterns in organizational activities.*[1] Four aspects of this definition are important:

1. The purpose of any performance measurement and control system is to *convey information.* These systems focus on *data*—financial and nonfinancial information that influences decision making and managerial action.

---

[1] Robert Simons, *Levers of Control* (Boston: Harvard Business School Press, 1995): 5.

2. Performance measurement and control systems represent *formal routines and procedures*. Information is written down or entered into computer systems and captured in standard formats, either on paper documents or in computer-based systems. The recording, analyzing, and distributing of this information is embedded in the rhythm of the organization, and is often based on predetermined practices and at preset times in the business cycle.

3. The performance measurement and control systems that we study in this book are designed specifically to be *used by managers*. Organizations create massive amounts of information, not all of which is directly relevant to managers in their day-to-day work. A profit statement for a division or data on customer satisfaction is part of a manager's control system; information received by shipping clerks to allow them to pick merchandise from inventory for specific customers is not.

4. Managers use performance measurement and control systems *to maintain or alter patterns in organizational activities*. Desirable patterns of activity may relate to efficiency and error-free processing, such as yield rates in a manufacturing process. In other instances, they may relate to patterns of ongoing creativity and innovation in products or internal processes, such as the percentage of sales from new products or year-over-year improvement in processing speed.

We can think of performance measurement and control systems in a business in much the same way that we think of controls in a car. The steering, accelerator, and brakes allow the driver to control direction and speed; instrumentation on the dashboard provides critical information about actual speed and early warning about potential problems with the car's key operating systems. Like a racing car operating at top speed, high-performance organizations need excellent performance measurement and control systems to allow managers to operate their organizations to their highest potential.

In the next section, we introduce profit planning systems. These systems are the foundation for performance measurement and control in all high-performing businesses, and we will refer to them repeatedly throughout the book.

Profit Planning Systems

Every business seeks to make a *profit*. For a business to survive and prosper over time, the inflow of resources must exceed the outflow. Revenue from goods and services provided to customers must be greater than the expenditures needed to manufacture and supply those goods and services on an ongoing basis.

Accounting systems collect information about the transactions of a business. Accounts (such as the T accounts that you studied in financial accounting classes) are ultimately summarized in financial statements such as balance sheets, income statements, and cash flow statements. **Internal control systems**—the set of procedures that dictate how and by whom information should be recorded and verified—provide the checks and balances to ensure that assets are safeguarded and the information collected and processed by the accounting system is accurate.

Accounting systems report actual, or historical, data. In addition to understanding how a business has performed in past accounting periods, however, managers must *plan* how much profit the business will (or needs to) make in future accounting periods. A **profit plan** is a summary of future financial inflows and outflows for a specified future accounting period. It is usually prepared in the familiar format of an income statement (similar to the one used in financial accounting). Managers must plan in order to (1) determine the quantity and type of resources that should be committed to a business and to (2) estimate the resources that will be provided by the business. Analyzing resource requirements—such as cash needs, machinery and equipment, and distribution facilities—is necessary because funding for resources must be lined up in advance and the acquisition and installation of resources may take considerable lead time. Estimating the level of resources that will be provided by the business—accounts receivable, cash flow, inventory stocks—is necessary to predict the business's ability to cover its obligations and invest in future productive capacity.

Profit planning involves analyzing past trends, making assumptions concerning cause and effect (e.g., what is the effect of advertising on revenue growth?), and predicting expected outcomes. In a seasonal ski-manufacturing business, for example, past trends might include looking at how revenues expanded and contracted each month over the past three years. Assumptions need to be made about anticipated interest costs and the availability and cost of purchased materials and services. Predictions must also be made about customer demand and the effects of competitor pricing.

Profit plans are supported by **planning systems**—recurring procedures to routinely disseminate planning assumptions, gather market information, provide details about relevant analyses, and prompt managers to estimate resource needs and performance goals and milestones. These systems are essential in providing the frameworks or templates for complete and careful trend analysis, consistent assumptions, and thoughtful predictions. In subsequent chapters, we will study how managers use these systems to implement their objectives.

Performance Measurement Systems

Profit is earned by success in a competitive marketplace. Firms compete for customers by offering goods and services that customers are willing to buy after comparing available alternatives. Profit is an outcome of successful performance against competitors. Thus, the starting point in our analysis must be understanding how a business chooses to compete in its market—that is, the strategies and goals that managers set for the business. It is the successful implementation of these strategies and goals that provide profit.

Business strategy refers to how a company creates value for customers and differentiates itself from competitors in the marketplace. Strategy necessarily involves decisions about how a company will compete and what types of opportunities employees should be encouraged to exploit. The clothing store in Boston, described at the beginning of this chapter, may choose to compete on fashion and selection, drawing customers away from competitors because of a superior array of up-to-the-minute fashion clothing. In this store, employees are encouraged to keep in touch with the latest fashions and adjust retail displays to ensure that they attract fashion-conscious shoppers. Alternatively, a competing store several blocks away may choose to attract customers by offering lower prices. In this store, fashions are less current. The store is still profitable, however, because the customers attracted to this outlet are more price conscious.

Employees are constantly reminded of how to keep the store's costs to a minimum to ensure adequate profits in spite of low prices.

Business goals are the measurable aspirations that managers set for a business. Goals are determined by reference to business strategy. Goals may be financial, for example, achieve 14% return on sales; or nonfinancial, for example, to increase market share from 6% to 9%. The business goals for the clothing store following a fashion strategy will be different than the goals of the store following the low-price strategy. As we will discuss in later chapters, goals can be set for any entity that can be held accountable for performance: individual managers, departments, divisions, and stand-alone businesses.

Performance measurement systems assist managers in tracking the implementation of business strategy by comparing actual results against strategic goals and objectives. A performance measurement system typically comprises systematic methods of setting business goals together with periodic feedback reports that indicate progress against those goals. Performance goals may be either short-term or long-term. Short-term performance usually focuses on time frames of one year or less. Longer-term performance goals include the ability to innovate and adapt to changing competitive dynamics over periods of several years. Successful competitors are able to recognize or create opportunities and turn them into advantage over both the short term and long term. Performance measurement systems can play a critical role in helping managers adapt and learn.

Two types of decisions must be made by the designer of a performance measurement system. The first decisions are about *design features:* What types of information should be collected and with what frequency of feedback? Second, decisions must be made about how to *use* the performance measurement systems. Who should receive the data and what should they do and not do with it?

How to make each of these types of decisions will be covered in subsequent chapters. First, we must acknowledge briefly the inherent challenge of employing performance measurement and management control systems in any complex organization.

BALANCING ORGANIZATIONAL TENSIONS

Organizations are complex entities in which managers must balance a variety of forces. There are five major tensions to be balanced in implementing performance measurement and control systems effectively:

1. Balancing Profit, Growth, and Control

Managers of high-performance companies constantly seek profitable growth. To do so, they are continually innovating. Innovation may take many forms. It may be in developing new products or services, or it may appear as new ways of doing internal tasks related to order-processing and manufacturing. Over time, successful innovation finds its way into sustained profitability and growth.

However, an excessive emphasis on profit and growth can lead to danger. Employees may engage in behaviors that put the business at risk. They may misconstrue management's intentions and "innovate" in ways that present unnecessary risks to the business. Recent debacles at Barings Bank, Kidder Peabody, and other financial institutions are chilling examples of employee behavior putting the entire organization in jeopardy.

A wise manager knows that control is the foundation of any healthy business. Only when adequate controls are in place can managers focus their energies on creating profit. Only when a business is profitable can managers focus on growing the business.

In all businesses, there is a constant tension between profit, growth, and control (see Figure 1-1). A profitable business that lacks adequate controls can quickly collapse. Control weaknesses inevitably allow error and risk to creep into operations and transaction processing. Managers can fool themselves into thinking that because the business is profitable, controls must be adequate. (Over the next month, make a point of looking at the front page of *The Wall Street Journal* for stories that describe businesses that have gotten into trouble because managers ignored the adequacy of controls and focused their attention elsewhere.)

Similarly, attempting to grow a business that is not profitable can only be described as foolhardy. Adding incremental revenues that do not generate profits can only lower the returns to stockholders. Managers in a poorly performing business might ask, "What is worse than 20% market share?" (Answer: 30% market share!)

Thus, as we consider how to design and use performance measurement and control techniques to implement strategy, it is important that we constantly assess whether or not managers have struck the right balance between profit, growth, and control. So far, we have alluded to several types of formal management systems: accounting systems, internal control systems, profit planning systems, and performance measurement systems. There are others to be covered later in the book that are important for managers in achieving profit goals and strategies. Collectively, these systems and techniques allow managers to balance the organizational tensions created by striving for profit and growth.

FIGURE 1–1   Tension of Profit, Growth, and Control

Source: Robert Simons, "Templates for Profit Planning," Boston: Harvard Business School Case 199-032, 1998.

Tension of Profit and Growth at America Online

When America Online (AOL) went public in 1992, it pursued an aggressive growth strategy. AOL "rained diskettes" by direct mail to millions of computer owners, offering them free trials of AOL. It distributed free disks in music CDs, in boxes of Rice Chex cereal, with video rentals at Blockbuster Video, and even with meals on United Airlines. Membership soared from 155,000 in 1992 to more than 4.6 million in 1996.

However, this growth came at the expense of profitability and control. Subscriber-acquisition costs soared to $400 per new subscriber. AOL decided to treat these enormous marketing costs as capital expenses, amortizing them over 12 to 18 months. However, after negative publicity over its accounting practices, AOL abandoned its amortization policy and wrote off $385 million, an amount that exceeded the sum of all prior earnings. Then, when AOL changed its pricing policy from an hourly charge to a flat-rate plan, its systems could not handle the explosive growth in subscriber demand, leading to well-publicized outages and breakdowns in service access.

AOL's refocus on profitability started in 1997. Having established a well-recognized brand name for Internet access, managers slashed marketing costs. AOL's subscriber-acquisition costs were reduced to $90 per new subscriber and more than 3 million new subscribers were added to the system. It leveraged its scale to cut access costs by nearly 50%. AOL exploited its dominant market position by signing lucrative advertising deals with online retailers such as N2K music, 1-800-FLOWERS, Preview Travel, and CUC International. For example, Tel-Save paid AOL $100 million to become the exclusive retailer of telecommunication services on AOL. By 1998, AOL reported profits once again. It even increased monthly subscriber charges, a clear sign that it did not intend to sacrifice profitability for growth in the future.

Source: Adapted from Marc Gunther, "The Internet is Mr. Case's Neighborhood," *Fortune,* March 30, 1998, 69–80.

---

2. Balancing Short-Term Results Against Long-Term Capabilities and Growth Opportunities

Businesses must deliver financial performance—not tomorrow, or the year after, but today. The stock market, representing shareowners, rewards managers who can produce earnings in the current period. However, producing earnings consistently—period after period—is often difficult, especially in cyclical businesses, or when significant up-front investment is necessary to launch a new product or invest in a new plant.

Managers must also manage for the long term. They must renew production facilities, enter new markets with new products, and invest in research and development to stay current with competitors and meet changing customer needs.

Performance measurement and control systems play a critical role in managing the tension between short-term profit demands and the necessity for long-term investment in capabilities and growth opportunities. These systems do this by serving the following objectives:

- communicating to the organization the strategic goals of the business and the performance drivers critical to achieving those goals
- providing a framework for ensuring that adequate resources are available for the achievement of long-term goals and strategies
- specifying the cause-and-effect relationship between business goals and profit
- providing a yardstick for systematic growth in key performance indicators
- establishing and monitoring short-term profit goals
- establishing a framework for allocating resources to build long-term organizational capabilities

We will say more about each of these objectives in later chapters.

3. Balancing Performance Expectations of Different Constituencies

Managers strive to achieve a variety of goals: financial, nonfinancial, short-term, and long-term. However, we must stop and ask the question, "Whose goals are we seeking to achieve?" A business entity is comprised of many different constituencies. Different parties may have different stakes in the success of a business and desire different things from the people who manage it. Important constituencies might include:

- owners, including both small and large stockholders
- managers and employees of the business
- customers
- suppliers
- lenders such as banks
- government agencies (e.g., the Internal Revenue Service) and regulators such as the National Labor Relations Board

Each of these constituencies may be interested in different aspects of performance. *Owners and stockholders* may seek growth in earnings or stability in dividend payments. *Managers,* in addition to profit, may value growth in the size of the business to allow the opportunity for promotion and advancement. *Employees* may desire steady earnings and employment and the opportunity to participate in the business's success. *Customers* will be interested in product quality, service, and price. *Suppliers* appreciate ease of doing business and reliability in order and payment processing. *Lenders* will look for indicators of financial strength and liquidity to pay debt obligations as they become due. *Government agencies* will be interested in compliance with laws and regulations.

Thus, when managers design and use performance measurement and control systems, they must be aware of the different interests of each of these constituencies.[2] Managers must strike a balance between these expectations because they will sometimes collide. For example, customers may want high quality and low prices; managers may want

---

[2] For further elaboration of this argument, see Anthony A. Atkinson, John H. Waterhouse, and Robert B. Wells, "A Stakeholder Approach to Strategic Performance Measurement," *Sloan Management Review* (Spring 1997): 25–37.

to increase prices and profit margins, but pay low taxes; employees may be interested in salary increases and generous post-retirement benefits. Well-designed performance measurement and control systems provide a fundamental way of recognizing and balancing these trade-offs.

4. Balancing Opportunities and Attention

Another tension in organizations relates to having too much of one thing and too little of another. What do managers today have too much of? The answer is "opportunity." Think of all the things that any modern business might choose to do: new products, new services, branching into other industries, striking alliances, and opening global markets. Consider MCI Communications Corporation, started by a young Harvard M.B.A. in 1968 to compete with AT&T's monopoly in long-distance telephone communications. MCI's managers recognized many untapped opportunities to create value for customers, and they have created many opportunities themselves. Today, MCI has entered into a long-term alliance with Microsoft Corporation to develop an array of on-line and Internet services. MCI is also collaborating with News Corporation to deliver satellite television using high-powered orbital satellites. Recently, MCI agreed to merge with World-Com, another communications company. What is the limit to the opportunities that MCI WorldCom might pursue?

To answer that question, think about what businesses have too little of. The answer is management time and attention. Think of all the constraints facing a modern business: financial constraints, production constraints, information constraints, and technology constraints. Still, the most critical constraint is *management attention.* If enough smart people focus their attention on a set of problems, there are very few opportunities that cannot be turned to advantage and very few problems that cannot be solved. However, there are only 24 hours in a day. Yet, there are so many things to do, and so many issues to focus on, that managers must ration their time and attention wisely. There is too little to go around.

Thus, an important issue in designing performance measurement and control systems is ensuring that these systems are valuable tools in leveraging scarce management time and attention. In the chapters that follow, we will be focusing on various types of measurement techniques and financial ratio measures such as Return on Assets (ROA) and Return on Investment (ROI). We should note, however, that we need to pay attention always to how performance measurement and control systems can enhance **Return on Management (ROM),** which we can define as:

$$\text{Return on Management} = \frac{\text{Amount of productive organizational energy released}[3]}{\text{Amount of management time and attention invested}}$$

Effective managers have learned how to leverage this scarcest of all resources. In this book we will study how managers can use performance measurement and control systems to maximize their ROM by driving up the numerator (amount of productive

---

[3] Robert Simons and Antonio Dávila, "How High is Your Return on Management?" *Harvard Business Review* 76 (January–February 1998): 70–80.

organizational energy released) and driving down the denominator (amount of management time and attention invested).

5. Balancing the Motives of Human Behavior

One of the principal reasons that managers use performance measurement and control systems is to influence the behavior of subordinate managers and other employees of the business. To do so successfully, managers (and designers of performance measurement and control systems) must have a clear sense of what motivates people to work effectively toward the goals of any business. Every manager—and each of us—makes assumptions about how people in organizations will act in particular circumstances. These assumptions are critical in determining the best designs for performance measurement and control systems.

What are your assumptions about human nature? One possibility is that people are fundamentally self-interested and put their own interests ahead of the interests of the firm. Individuals calculate what will make them personally better or worse off and act accordingly to maximize their personal utility. In most cases, they can be expected to *minimize effort* devoted to achieving business objectives that do not pay off for them

---

Values at Allied Signal

Lawrence Bossidy helped Jack Welch turn around General Electric Company. Then in 1991, he became CEO of AlliedSignal, a $13 billion supplier of aerospace systems and automotive parts. When he arrived at AlliedSignal, the company was facing a severe cash drain. Bossidy approached the problem with his "burning platform" theory of change—he believed that employees would be willing to change only if top management was open with employees about the company's situation so they could see the problem for themselves. To this end, he spoke to 5,000 employees in his first 60 days.

The company's cost problem stemmed from a bloated bureaucracy of 58 strategic business units, with managers of each business unit protecting their own turf. Once the organization had been slimmed down, Bossidy described how he attempted to achieve cohesion of values throughout the business. "I think that you coach people to win. Basically, people want to be successful. They want to go home at night and feel that they've made a contribution. . . . But we had to unite ourselves with vision and values. And that effort begins with the team at the top. In November 1991, we had an off-site meeting with the top 12 managers of the company. We spent two days arguing—and I mean arguing—about values. That was helpful because, at the end of the meeting, we not only had the values, we also had a specific definition of each of those values. The seven values we settled on are simple: customers, integrity, people, teamwork, speed, innovation, and performance."

Source: Noel M. Tichy and Ram Charan, "The CEO as Coach: An Interview with AlliedSignal's Lawrence A. Bossidy," *Harvard Business Review* 73 (March–April 1995): 68–78.

personally. This is the view that is prevalent in economic models of organization: Employees and managers are viewed as rational, calculating, maximizing individuals who dislike work, attempt to do the minimum that is demanded of them, and can be expected to act in opportunistic ways to enhance their own well-being at the expense of the organization to which they belong. To the extent these assumptions are true, performance measurement and control systems must be designed to ensure that people will work hard and do what managers expect of them.

Although these assumptions are undoubtedly true in specific circumstances for all of us, they can sometimes be too limiting. For example, they fail to explain people's sense of commitment and responsibility to others—why people often try to help someone else without inducement or possibility for future payoff. They fail to explain why people join organizations in which they think that they can make a difference, such as charities and benevolent organizations that help the poor and indigent. They fail to explain the importance of deeply held convictions about values, core beliefs, and religion. They fail to explain the role of conscience in personal decisions. They fail to explain the sense of pride and accomplishment that is often a sufficient reward for a job well done.

To design a performance measurement and control systems effectively, therefore, managers need a more holistic and rounded view of human nature. In this book, we make the following assumptions about the nature of human activity in organizations operating in modern economies.[4]

1. People in organizations *want to contribute* to an organization of which they can be proud. All of us have a need to contribute. We want to feel that we are making a difference. The organizations to which we belong can be vehicles to express that need. Many of us join churches and synagogues or work for volunteer organizations. In our work life, as well, we want to feel that "our business" is doing something worthwhile and that we are playing a productive role in that mission. In many businesses, our value is easy to appreciate. We can see our contribution and how we make a difference. In other circumstances, however, employees may be unsure of the mission of the business or its value to society. (The *New York Times* recently carried a feature story on the personal turmoil that is presented to executives of cigarette manufacturing firms.)[5]

2. People employed by business organizations know the difference between right and wrong and generally *choose to do right*. Our society has complex mechanisms for teaching people the difference between right and wrong, such as social groups, churches and synagogues, benevolent associations, and scouting. These organizations transmit norms of acceptable behavior. Also, educated citizens are aware of the laws that govern behavior and generally act accordingly. Our actions become guided by our conscience.

3. People *strive to achieve*. All of us work for a variety of reasons. In many instances, we work to capture extrinsic rewards such as money, promotion, and praise. These are always valuable and must be considered carefully in the design of reward and compensation systems. However, there are also innate drives in all of us to feel a sense of satis-

---

[4] A modern economy is one in which there is both economic freedom and institutions to effectively legislate and enforce laws. See S. H. Hanke, "The Curse of Corruption," *Forbes,* July 29, 1996, 103 for a summary of countries that satisfy these requirements based on a 1996 report *Economic Freedom of the World* by Transparency International.

[5] J. Goldberg, "Big Tobacco's Endgame," *New York Times Magazine,* June 21, 1998.

faction from personal achievement. Even in the absence of external inducements, people often set a personal goal for themselves, whether it be sailing around the world or learning a new skill.

4. People *like to innovate.* The basic urge to experiment is a powerful human instinct that has allowed mankind to continually improve our standard of living over time. Men and women in organizations also have innate desires to experiment by creating new technologies and new ways of doing things. In many companies, the so-called "bootleg project" refers to the secret experiment by employees who are trying something new without the express consent or knowledge of senior management. This is a powerful inner force that can successfully be harnessed by organizations.

5. People *want to do competent work.* Many, if not most, individuals take pride in their abilities. A job well done allows us to exercise our skills and receive satisfaction from our competence. In addition, people would rather do something right than have to go back later to fix it.

Now that we have made these somewhat heroic assumptions—that people want to contribute, achieve, innovate, and do competent work—we must confront reality. Although we can find examples of these behaviors in many circumstances, oftentimes people do not act like this in businesses that we know. What are the reasons?

Organizations—especially large ones—often make it hard for people to reach their potential. To understand why, we must examine the **organizational blocks** that organizations unwittingly create for the men and women who work in them.

First, business organizations often make it *difficult for people to understand* how they can contribute and make a difference. Employees may not understand the strategy and direction of the business. They may not be sure of the larger purpose—or mission—of the business, or how they can fit into that purpose.

Second, businesses often create *pressure and temptation* for employees. Performance pressures ("If you can't do it, I'll find someone who can!") may cause people to bend the rules or hide information, even though they know what they are doing is wrong. Also, temptation in the form of lucrative bonuses and performance awards—as well as access to company assets—may cause employees to step over the line between what they know to be right and wrong.

Third, achievement can be difficult either because individuals *lack resources* to get the job done, or because they face so many *competing demands* that they are unable to focus on any single objective with enough intensity to achieve the desired outcomes. Productive energy becomes scattered and diffused, making it difficult to achieve strategically important goals.

Fourth, people may fail to innovate because they *lack the resources* or are *afraid of the risk* of challenging the status quo. How many times do we hesitate when attempting to voice opinions that may seem novel or radical and may not be supported by our superiors and colleagues?

The qualities of human nature are inextricably bound up in the organizational tensions that affect all of us who work in organizations. Performance measurement and control systems cannot be designed without taking into account both human behavior and the causes and effects of these organizational blocks.

In the following chapters, we will study how effective managers utilize performance measurement and control systems to balance the organization tensions that are the keys to unlocking profitable growth through the successful implementation of business strategy.

CHAPTER SUMMARY

Performance measurement and control systems are essential tools used by all effective managers in achieving their desired profit goals and strategies. These systems comprise profit planning and a variety of performance-management techniques that we will discuss later. These systems also allow managers to balance the tensions between: profit, growth, and control; short-term versus long-term performance; expectations of different constituencies; opportunities and attention; and the differing motives of human behavior. Properly applied, performance measurement and control systems can be used to overcome the organizational blocks that impede the true potential of all people who work in modern organizations.

C H A P T E R

2

Basics for Successful Strategy

This chapter reviews the underpinnings for a successful business strategy. Some readers may have already studied parts of this material in a business-strategy or business-policy course. For others, the ideas and concepts will be new. Whatever your level of familiarity with this topic, we recommend that you review this chapter because the remainder of our analysis in the book builds on concepts that we introduce here.

Business strategy is at the root of effective performance measurement and control for two reasons. First, performance measurement and control systems provide the analytic discipline and communication channels to formalize business strategy and ensure that strategic goals are communicated throughout the business. Second, performance measurement and control systems are the primary vehicle to monitor the implementation of these strategies.

The techniques and systems that we discuss in this book help managers of all organizations answer two critical questions:

1. How can we be sure that people understand what we are trying to achieve?
2. How can we ensure that we are reaching our strategic goals?

CORPORATE STRATEGY AND BUSINESS STRATEGY

Strategy is a word that is used in many different ways in business and other organizational settings. The first distinction that is important for our purposes is the distinction between corporate strategy and business strategy.

Corporate strategy defines the way that a firm attempts to maximize the value of the resources it controls. Corporate strategy decisions focus on *where* corporate resources will be invested. Questions such as "What businesses should we compete in?" or "What level of resources should we invest across our portfolio of businesses?" are typical of corporate-level resource allocation decisions. For example, managers at Boston Retail can choose to compete in women's clothing or in some entirely different product category. They may wish to branch out into men's clothing, or even to home furnishings. In time, it may be possible to leverage existing distribution resources to enter an entirely unrelated business, such as apparel manufacturing or wholesale distribution. These decisions—which businesses and segments of the market to compete in—are necessary whenever a corporation decides to expand its scope beyond a single product market.

Business strategy, by contrast, is concerned with *how* to compete in defined product markets. Once managers have decided to compete in the women's clothing market in Boston, they must attract customers and build market share. How will they differentiate themselves from competitors to create value in the marketplace? How can they offer something unique and valuable to their targeted customers? These are the questions that we tackle in this chapter.

Figure 2–1 illustrates the distinction between corporate strategy and business strategy.

Performance measurement and control techniques are important for the successful implementation of both corporate strategies and business strategies. The majority of topics in this book focus on creating value in specific product markets, which is the major issue for managers who run businesses. However, for firms operating in multiple markets, special measurement and control systems are needed to implement corporate-level strategy effectively. We cover these techniques and systems as well in later chapters.

The formal processes for formulating and implementing business strategy can be captured in the cascading hierarchy illustrated in Figure 2–2. Strategy formulation and implementation are multifaceted concepts. The cascading hierarchy of Figure 2–2 illustrates that a mission—the broad purpose for which an organization exists—guides the formation of business strategy. Business strategy, in turn, determines performance goals and measures, and, ultimately, patterns of action.

FIGURE 2–1   Corporate and Business Strategy

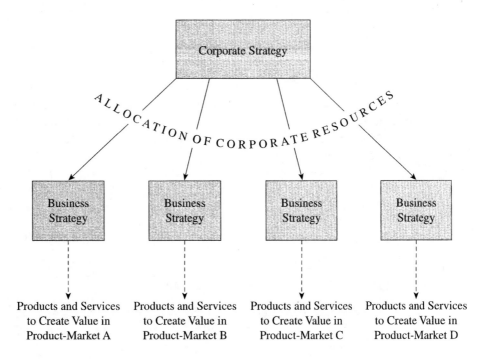

FIGURE 2–2   Hierarchy of Business Strategy

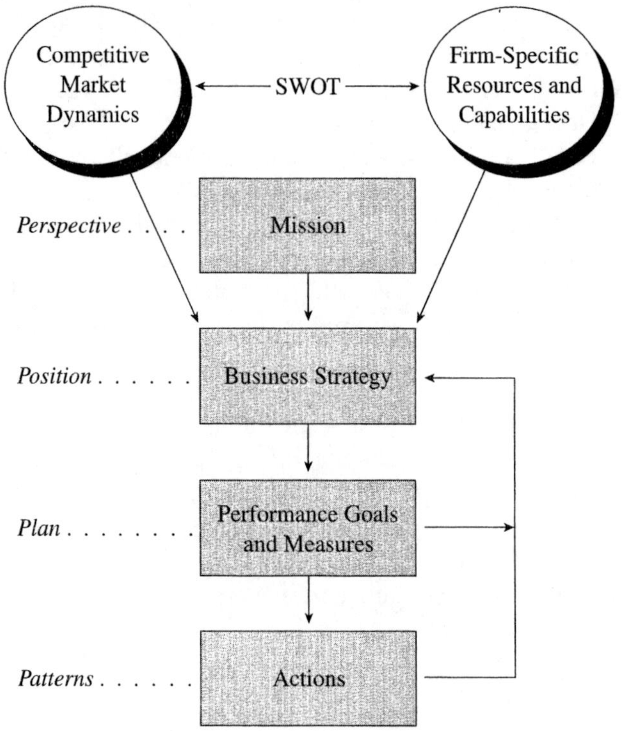

Before they develop specific business strategies, managers must analyze and understand (1) the competitive market dynamics in their industry and (2) their own firm's resources and capabilities. Thus, the first stage of our analysis must relate the *internal* strengths and weaknesses of the firm to *external* opportunities and threats in the marketplace. These two inputs to the strategy process are illustrated as ovals at the top of Figure 2–2.

SWOT is a useful acronym to remember the purpose of this analysis. SWOT stands for: **S**trengths, **W**eaknesses, **O**pportunities, and **T**hreats. The purpose of a SWOT analysis is to relate firm-specific strengths and weakness back to the industry opportunities and threats. Only then can we understand the context within which successful strategies can be formulated.

COMPETITIVE MARKET DYNAMICS

What is the nature of the market? Who are the major competitors? What are the rules of the game? How great is the potential for profit? These are questions that all managers must answer as they seek to create competitive advantage in specific markets. The "five-forces" analysis provides a useful framework and checklist for analyzing the competitive dynamics of any given industry.[1]

The **five forces** that determine the degree and nature of competition (as shown in Figure 2–3) are (1) customers, (2) suppliers, (3) substitute products, (4) new entrants, and (5) competitive rivalry. In any industry, these forces individually and collectively influence competitive dynamics and potentially create opportunities for or constraints to effective competition.

In attempting to understand market dynamics at the industry level, the following questions must be analyzed in detail to fully understand opportunities and threats:

Customers

- Who are our customers? How much does each buy from us? Would they be willing to buy more? Under what circumstances?
- Is any customer or customer group particularly important to us?
- How do we appeal to different segments of the market? Why do they buy our product or services? What advantages does it offer them?
- How sensitive are they to price? To quality? To service? To other factors?

FIGURE 2–3   Five Forces of Competitive Markets

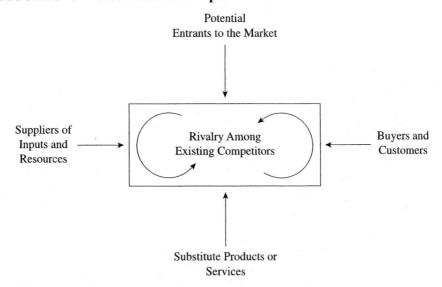

Source: Adapted from Michael E. Porter, *Competitive Strategy* (New York: The Free Press, 1980), 4.

---

[1] For a complete treatment, see Michael E. Porter, *Competitive Strategy* (New York: The Free Press, 1980).

Suppliers

- Who are our major suppliers? How much do we buy from each? Would we be willing to buy more or less? Under what circumstances?
- Is any supplier or supplier group particularly important to us?
- What supply factors are critical to us—quality, price, reliability, service, and so forth?
- How costly is it for us to switch to alternate suppliers or sources?

Substitute Products

- What substitutes for our products or services exist in the market?
- How are they different from our offerings in terms of price, quality, and performance?
- How likely are our customers to switch to competitors' products or services?

New Entrants

- What are the barriers to entry to deter new competitors from entering our markets?
- How strong is our brand franchise?
- How difficult would it be for a new competitor to imitate the way we do business?

Competitive Rivalry

- Is the industry growing or shrinking?
- Are there few or many competitors?
- Is there overcapacity?
- What are the switching costs for customers who might consider purchasing goods and services from competing firms?
- What is the ownership structure of competing firms? How important is our market to each of them?

At Boston Retail, managers have targeted a specific customer segment: young, fashion-conscious students. However, because of limited incomes, many of these customers are price sensitive, so merchandise must be both up-to-date and price competitive. To reach this goal, Boston Retail has found non-traditional suppliers—some of whom are themselves start-ups—who are willing to supply fashionable goods at reasonable prices. These suppliers are critical to Boston Retail's strategy.

There are many substitutes in the market and competition is intense. To prosper, managers at Boston Retail have decided to follow a niche strategy and expand only to regions that have similar customer demographics, but they must choose their battlefields carefully. Fortunately, the failure of a competitor—a business that offered a full line of women's and men's clothes throughout New England—has opened up the possibility for enlarging the business.

Armed with insight about *opportunities* and *threats* in a specific market, managers are ready to set strategy. However, before they can make definitive recommendations for a successful strategy, they must assess the internal *strengths* and *weaknesses* of the business. It is useless to enter a competitive arena unless a firm has the resources to fight for market share and a reasonable chance of earning profit.

RESOURCES AND CAPABILITIES OF A BUSINESS

Accordingly, the next stage of a SWOT analysis, shown at the top of Figure 2–2, is to analyze the *resources and capabilities* of the firm to determine what a business does well and what it does not do well.

As a first step in analyzing internal strengths and weaknesses, we can look at a firm's balance sheet to learn more about the resources that are available for competition. (In this discussion, we focus only on the asset side of the balance sheet, leaving consideration of the debt and equity side of the balance sheet to finance and financial-statement-analysis courses.) As we perform this analysis, we need to remember that accountants apply a series of tests to determine which resources can be recorded on the balance sheet. In accounting, an **asset** is defined as *a resource, owned or controlled by the entity, that will yield future economic benefits.* Examples include plant, equipment, cash in the bank, and inventory. For purposes of strategy formulation, a **resource** is more broadly defined as *a strength of the business embodied in the tangible or intangible assets that are tied semipermanently to the firm.*[2] As we shall see, a resource may or may not appear as an asset on the balance sheet.

Balance Sheet Assets

The following assets are customarily recorded on the balance sheet. These accounting assets are employed by the firm to generate revenues and will be the focus, in later chapters, of analytic techniques for performance measurement and control of strategy.

Current Assets

The first category on the balance sheet is current assets. **Current assets** include cash and other assets that will be turned into cash during the course of an accounting cycle— normally one year. Current assets include:

- cash
- marketable securities
- accounts receivable
- inventory
- prepaid expenses

Any strategy requires sufficient cash flow to fund it. Cash is needed to pay bills, purchase inventory, pay service providers, and meet current debt obligations. Cash flows, based on sales and the conversion of inventory to cash, must be planned carefully in advance to ensure that cash levels will be adequate, especially in a growing business. A large cash reserve may provide the freedom to fund growth or acquisition strategies. Our profit planning and performance measurement techniques must, therefore, include analysis of cash flows, cash reserves, and forecasts of the cash needed to fund specific strategies.

---

[2] B. Wernerfelt, "A Resource-Based View of the Firm," *Strategic Management Journal* 5 (1984): 171–180.

Productive Assets

The second major category of assets on the balance sheet is **productive assets.** These assets are used to produce goods and services for customers. Productive assets represent the technology, machinery, and infrastructure necessary to compete. Some of these assets contribute directly to production—such as a machine in the manufacturing process. Other productive assets contribute indirectly to production—such as the computer hardware and software used to support gate agents at an airline terminal.

Examples of productive assets include:

- computers and information-technology equipment
- buildings
- manufacturing equipment

Productive assets must be sufficient—both in quantity and type—to support a business's strategy. As part of our performance measurement and control toolkit, we will discuss techniques to analyze the acquisition of productive assets and measure their effective utilization.

Intangible Assets

The final category of assets on the balance sheet is **intangible assets.** These include:

- copyrights, patents, and trademarks
- goodwill
- valuable licenses (e.g., broadcast rights)
- leases

For any asset—either tangible or intangible—to be recognized on the balance sheet, accountants impose two tests. First, an asset must have *future value* to the firm. Second, that value must be *quantifiable with reasonable precision.* Tangible assets, such as buildings and equipment, or financial assets, such as cash and notes receivable, easily pass these tests and, therefore, are included on a firm's balance sheet. For intangible assets, however, the second condition—the ability to quantify value with precision—is typically met only when that value is priced independently through a third-party transaction. Examples of arm's length transactions that implicitly price the value of an intangible asset include the purchase of a broadcast license, the signing of a lease agreement, the granting of a patent based on past investment in proprietary research, or the creation of goodwill on the purchase of a subsidiary. Other intangible assets that may build up over time, such as reputation or dealer contacts, are much more problematic for accounting purposes. Their monetary value is difficult to measure, so these resources rarely appear on a firm's balance sheet.

Intangible Resources

Intangible resources are often among a business's most valuable assets. These intangible resources may include, for example:

- distinctive internal capabilities
- market franchises
- networks and relationships with suppliers and customers

In highly competitive markets, it is these three categories of resources that provide the essential difference between success and failure. They are critical to achieving profit goals and strategies, yet they are not recognized on a firm's financial statements. Because intangible resources are a central focus of management's attention, our analysis of performance measurement and control systems must take into account the quality and nature of these intangible resources. Let's review briefly the nature of these three categories of resources.

Distinctive Internal Capabilities

Distinctive business capabilities—sometimes called **core** or **distinctive competencies**—refer to the *special resources and know-how possessed by a firm that give it competitive advantage in the marketplace.* **Distinctive capabilities** include the ability to perform world-class research (e.g., Merck & Company), excellence in product design (e.g., Apple Computer), superior marketing skills (e.g., Coca-Cola Company), the ability to manage costs (e.g., Vanguard Mutual Funds), proprietary information technology (e.g., American Airlines), proprietary manufacturing skills (e.g., Intel Corporation), and so on. Distinctive capabilities are of three types: functional skills, market skills, and embedded resources.

Functional skills refer to strengths (and weaknesses) in the major functional areas of a business, such as research and development, information technology, production and manufacturing, and marketing and sales. Each of these functions can be an important source of opportunity in the marketplace. Research and development creates value at Minnesota Mining & Manufacturing (3M), manufacturing quality allows differentiation in the marketplace for many Japanese automobile companies, and marketing skills at consumer packaged-goods companies such as General Mills allow successful competition. As the name suggests, functional skills reside in the internal functions of a business. Functional vice presidents—such as vice presidents of marketing or manufacturing—are usually responsible for managing these critical competencies.

Market skills refer to a business's ability to respond quickly and effectively to market needs. Rather than analyzing resources and competencies by function, the appropriate unit of analysis is the customer or market segment. Here, the analysis focuses on (1) understanding what attributes of a product or service create value for a customer and (2) assessing the business's ability to provide those attributes. Responsiveness is key—to demands of price, quality, flexibility, reliability, service, or whatever else may be important in creating value in the eyes of a defined customer or market segment. Examples of well-known companies with strong market skills include American Express Company (travel and financial services), Johnson & Johnson (health care products), and Nordstrom (fashion retail).

The final category of distinctive capability is **embedded resources**—tangible resources that are difficult to acquire and/or replace. Physical plant, distribution channels, and information technology are all embedded assets that represent potential strengths and weaknesses. Although their historical transaction prices may appear on a balance sheet, these assets are far more valuable than a balance sheet would suggest because of the distinctive capability that they provide. A plant may be new or old—efficient or inefficient—yielding a competitive strength or weakness in the market. Similarly, information-technology advantages over competitors may be strengths (or weaknesses if old and outdated), as may a long-standing network of dealer contracts.[3]

Distinctive business capabilities—whether from functional skills, market skills, or embedded resources—often build up over long periods of time. Think of the firms listed above and ask yourself how long it took these firms to acquire their distinctive capabilities. How long did it take Merck to build up its world-class research capabilities? Or Coca-Cola to acquire its awesome marketing prowess?

Note also how difficult these capabilities are to copy. How difficult would it be to imitate any of these firms in what they do so well? Imagine attempting to "out-market" Coca-Cola, or to beat Merck at developing the next generation of hypertension drugs? Possessing distinct capabilities is a unique resource that often gives a business substantial competitive advantage (and puts competitors at a substantial disadvantage).

In some instances, capabilities are created by being first at something—a "first-mover"—and locking out competitors. For example, many U.S. airlines built efficient distribution networks in the early 1980s by creating regional hubs to serve as gateways for all their connecting domestic routes. By obtaining contractual rights to the majority of gates in these hubs, major airlines were able to gain significant first-mover advantages over regional competitors in the same markets. Thus, Delta Air Lines has a 72% market share in Atlanta, Northwest has an 80% share in Minneapolis, and United has a 70% market share in Denver.[4]

Business capabilities are the lifeblood of any firm operating in a competitive market and are among its most valuable assets. Although business capabilities sometimes appear on the balance sheet—such as large-scale distribution centers or investments in proprietary information technology—most business capabilities represent intangible assets that are not normally valued on a firm's balance sheet. They are "invisible assets."[5]

Managers must understand the existence and nature of these invisible resources if they are to measure their effectiveness in achieving profit goals and strategies. Performance measures must focus on the key drivers of success. Moreover, these capabilities are dynamic; they are constantly changing. New capabilities are developed, previous competencies atrophy, people and skills come and go, new technologies emerge, and new alliances are formed. Performance measurement and control systems provide the essential feedback to allow managers to monitor the health of these distinctive resources.

---

[3] For a complete treatment of this topic, see Pankaj Ghemawat, *Commitment: The Dynamic of Strategy* (New York: The Free Press, 1991).

[4] Michael J. McCarthy, "Major Airlines Find Their 'Fortress' Hubs Aren't Impenetrable," *Wall Street Journal*, February 6, 1996, A1.

[5] Hiroyuki Itami, *Mobilizing Invisible Assets* (Boston: Harvard University Press, 1987).

Unilever vs. Mars

Since the late 1980s, Unilever plc, the Anglo Dutch consumer-goods company, and Mars, the U.S. company, have been battling over the Irish market for impulse-bought ice cream. Mars entered the Irish market in the late 1980s, at which time Unilever had 85% market share. Unilever's commanding market share was due to its ownership of freezers in retail shops. Most retailers were willing to carry only one ice-cream freezer because of limited floor space, so Unilever had the power over retailers to tell them which products to carry (either directly or by filling the freezer with Unilever ice creams). To protect its market share, and preempt Mars' entrance in the Irish market, Unilever tried to exclude Mars products from its freezers. As a result, Mars was able to sell its products through only 400 of a possible 1,920 outlets.

Mars interpreted this policy as an anti-competitive use of market power and successfully petitioned for an investigation on the "freezer exclusivity" issue by the European Commission. Mars' objective was to gain freezer space in Unilever's freezers to allow it to compete on an equal footing.

Source: J. Willman, "Seized Unilever Papers Show Strategy to Freeze Out Mars," *Financial Times,* June 22, 1998, 22.

Market Franchises

Market franchises is the second category of intangible resources. The term franchise is used two ways in business. In a strict sense, a franchise is a *contractual agreement that allows an independent party to use a trade name or to sell a specific product owned by someone else.* A franchise agreement names the *franchisor*—the owner of the brand name—and the *franchisee*—who purchases the right to use the brand name under conditions set out in the franchise agreement (e.g., standards related to quality control, pricing, etc.). The ubiquitous North American fast food restaurants, such as McDonald's and Burger King, are typically operated as franchises. So too are auto repair centers (e.g., Midas) and rental car agencies (e.g., Budget Group). In each of these instances, an independent owner/operator of the retail unit is the franchisee who has purchased the right to sell products or services under the brand name of the franchisor.

A franchisee is willing to pay a fee and be bound by the strict terms of the franchise agreement because he or she is receiving something valuable in return—a recognized brand name and set of products or services ("a franchise") that can be expected to draw in customers.

Thus, the more general use of the term **franchise** among business managers refers to a *business's distinctive ability to attract customers who are willing to purchase the business's products and services based on marketwide perceptions of value.* A business is said to "own a franchise" when a brand name itself is an important source of revenue and value to the business. For example, consumers may seek out and be willing to pay a premium for an IBM computer, Johnson & Johnson Band-Aids, a Citibank credit card, Cheerios breakfast cereal, a Coke, Calvin Klein perfume, or any number of products that have created market franchises through customer awareness and brand loyalty.

Needless to say, franchises are among the most important and valuable assets of a business. Healthy franchises produce long-lived streams of revenue and profitability. As a result, the stock of companies with strong franchises often trade at high price/earnings multiples. Managers jealously guard their brand franchises and invest heavily in their brands to ensure a continuing perception of value in the eyes of current and potential customers. Accordingly, it is common in consumer companies for the highest levels of management—often the CEO—to personally review all new brand advertising to ensure that misguided advertising does not dilute or harm the brand image.

Unfortunately, a balance sheet, which is based on the accounting for historical cost transactions, is of little help in determining the value of a company's brand franchise. Because the value of a brand cannot be measured with precision, financial accounting standards in North America do not allow the recognition of franchise value on a firm's financial statements. How much is the L. L. Bean brand name worth? It clearly has great value, but you won't find its value reported in its financial statements.[6]

The exception to this rule occurs when businesses are bought and sold by corporate owners. When one firm buys another, it is buying more than the physical assets of the business, such as its buildings and equipment. It is also buying its franchise—the brand name, the customer base, and the goodwill in the marketplace. Thus, the purchase price of an acquisition is often significantly higher than the assessed value of its tangible assets. To make the debits equal the credits, accountants must somehow reconcile the difference between the purchase price of the business, which includes franchise value, and the historical cost shown on the balance sheet, which omits it. This residual—the difference between purchase price and the value of identifiable assets—is classified as "goodwill," an intangible asset recorded on the balance sheet to be amortized against income over some arbitrary period.

Notwithstanding the limitations of financial accounting, effective performance measurement and control systems must monitor the effective use of *all* significant business assets. Accordingly, as we think about techniques for achieving profit goals and strategies, we must pay special care to ensure that our performance measurement and control systems capture and protect the value of brand franchises.

Relationships and Networks

In addition to distinctive capabilities and market franchises, successful businesses must also create and nurture long-term relationships with important suppliers and customers. These relationships are critical intangible resources for successful strategies.

Suppliers of factor inputs—raw materials, technical services, parts, and administrative support—are essential to the success of any business. Relationships with suppliers can be especially important if:

---

[6] In countries such as Britain that depart from the cost-based accounting model favored in North America, the value of a franchise can be estimated and shown explicitly on the balance sheet.

- there are few suppliers from which to choose
- there are few substitutes for the product or service that the supplier provides
- the supplier's product or service is important to the competitive success of the business
- switching to alternative sources of supply is expensive[7]

In these situations, good relations with suppliers is an essential resource to be monitored and managed carefully.

Similarly, relationships with buyers become important to competitive success if:

- a customer buys large quantities relative to the business's total sales
- products or services are standard or undifferentiated (allowing customers to easily purchase from someone else)
- a buyer can switch to alternative suppliers with little cost[8]

In many industries, distribution access is a prerequisite for success. Products are sold to wholesalers who warehouse and deliver products to retail stores; retailers in turn sell the product to customers. This is true in the brewing industry, for example, where Miller Breweries sells beer in large quantity to regional wholesalers. Sales representatives who are employees of the wholesaler visit retail establishments (restaurants and liquor stores) on a weekly basis to deliver product, stock shelves, and take orders for later delivery. Without these distributors, the nature of Miller's competitive position would be severely damaged. In industries such as this, access to efficient distribution channels that facilitate the flow of goods and services from the producer to the end consumer is an extremely valuable resource.

Like everything else in our modern world, electronic media has changed dramatically the nature of customer relationships. It is now commonplace to electronically link producers, distributors, and customers so that orders can be instantly transmitted from buyer to seller, with real-time updating of purchase orders, inventory records, and shipment dates. These electronic linkages can be extremely valuable intangible resources providing competitive advantage.

THE 4 Ps OF STRATEGY

Look back at Figure 2–2. Our SWOT analysis has now considered the strengths, weaknesses, opportunities, and threats created by the interplay of competitive market dynamics and firm-specific resources and capabilities. This is the background or context for the formation and implementation of business strategy. Next, to formulate and implement strategy effectively, we must understand the design implications of each of the four cascading boxes shown in Figure 2–2. Understanding these different views of strategy will be essential to the performance measurement and control techniques developed later. In the remainder of this chapter, we analyze strategy from these four different angles: strategy as perspective, strategy as position, strategy as plan, and strategy as patterns of action. These are the four Ps of strategy.[9]

---

[7] Porter, *Competitive Strategy,* 27–28.

[8] *ibid,* 24–26.

[9] Henry Mintzberg, "Five Ps for Strategy," *California Management Review* (fall 1987). The fifth "P," not covered in this chapter, is strategy as ploy.

Information Technology at Wal-Mart

Wal-Mart, the $100 billion U.S. retailing giant, continually searches for ways to boost its profits through advanced use of information technology. With 65 million retail transactions a week, even incremental improvements can have a significant impact.

Wal-Mart keeps information-technology spending lean (0.5% of sales as compared with competitors' 1.0% to 1.4% of sales) and develops applications in-house. Wal-Mart typically has 350 new IT applications in the pipeline, requiring retraining of 600,000 cashiers every two weeks. For example, Wal-Mart's SMART information system, (Store Merchandising through Applied Retail Technology), encompasses more than 1,000 applications that store employees can access through hand-held units.

Wal-Mart's proprietary "Store Manager Workbench" system provides up-to-the-minute profitability analysis and "what-if" scenarios for store-based decision making. These systems enable headquarters to calculate profitability down to the individual shopping-cart level and combine it with data on weekend sales, gross margins, and payroll—all available for its 3,017 stores in seven countries by 6 a.m. on Mondays.

To maintain profitability under its "Everyday Low Prices" strategy, Wal-Mart uses its purchasing power to extract favorable terms from vendors. In turn, it integrates them into its information-technology systems. With the promise of lower inventory costs, Wal-Mart provides weekly sales forecasting data to more than 3,500 of its 5,000 suppliers.

Source: Bruce Calwell, "Wal-Mart Ups the Pace," *Informationweek,* December 9, 1996, 37–51.

Creating a Mission—Strategy as Perspective

Mission is the starting point for our analysis of the formulation and implementation of business strategy. **Mission** refers to the broad purpose, or reason, that a business exists. At the most basic level, a firm's mission is recorded in its legal charter or articles of incorporation. However, senior managers usually draft their own versions of the business's mission to communicate their personal views of ideals and core values to employees throughout the organization.

Good missions supply both inspiration and a sense of direction for the future. Sony Corporation, for example, was founded in 1945 with the following purpose:

- To establish a place of work where engineers can feel the joy of technological innovation, be aware of their mission to society, and work to their heart's content.
- To pursue dynamic activities in technology and production for the reconstruction of Japan and the elevation of the nation's culture.
- To apply advanced technology to the life of the general public.[10]

---

[10] James C. Collins and Jerry I. Porras, *Built to Last* (New York: Harper Business, 1994), 50.

Sony's mission is intended to inspire employees to patriotic effort and make each employee proud of his or her association with the company and its values.

Missions are often written down in formal documents known as **mission statements** that are circulated widely throughout a firm. A mission statement communicates the core values of the business. Some firms may adopt different names for their mission statements such as *credo,* or *statement of purpose,* but they all serve the same objective: *to communicate the larger purpose of the organization and inspire pride in participants.*

Johnson & Johnson's Credo is reproduced in Exhibit 2–1. Note that in both the Sony and Johnson & Johnson examples—as well as the missions of most high-performance companies—maximizing profit is *not* the principal reason for existence. Earning profit is never a sufficient definition of a firm's mission; higher ideals are necessary to instill pride and motivate productive effort from employees. Of course, every company has to earn profit—just as each of us needs oxygen and water to survive. However, breathing and quenching our thirst are not the primary purposes by which we define our human existence. Like profit, they are necessary, but not sufficient, conditions for success.

A firm's mission provides an overarching *perspective* to all its activities. Rooted in a business's history, its culture, and the values of its senior managers, a mission statement provides the guideposts that allow all employees to understand how the firm responds to the opportunities that surround it. Can you imagine Jaguar introducing a low-priced entry level car to compete with Hyundai Motor Company? Or McDonald's Corporation opening a fashionable French restaurant? Or Rolex Watch Company producing cheap plastic watches? Or Swatch Group AG offering a $5,000 watch? Of course not. In each of these firms, an overarching perspective frames the opportunities that managers pursue and the types of decisions they make when faced with competing choices. This perspective is the lens through which business strategy is defined.

The mission of Boston Retail is reproduced in Exhibit 2–2. What do you think of it? What are its strengths and weaknesses? (Remember, its purpose is to inspire, instill pride, and give an overarching sense of direction and perspective to employees at all levels of the business.)

Choosing How to Compete—Strategy as Position

With the mission of the business providing overall perspective—a backdrop for formulating strategy—the next step is to focus on two key questions about the **position of a business** in its competitive marketplace: (1) How do we create value for our customers? and (2) how do we differentiate our products and services from those of our competitors?

Managers of competing firms might answer these questions in very different ways. Some firms may choose to create value by offering their goods and services at *low cost,* hoping to draw customers who are price sensitive; other firms may compete by *differentiating* their products and services in a way that adds unique benefits for customers, or by *customizing* product offerings to respond to the specialized needs of specific customer segments. In the mutual fund industry, for example, Fidelity Investments has suc-

EXHIBIT 2–1
Johnson & Johnson Credo

Our Credo

We believe our first responsibility is to the doctors, nurses and patients,
to mothers and fathers and all others who use our products and services.
In meeting their needs everything we do must be of high quality.
We must constantly strive to reduce our costs
in order to maintain reasonable prices.
Customers' orders must be serviced promptly and accurately.
Our suppliers and distributors must have an opportunity
to make a fair profit.

We are responsible to our employees,
the men and women who work with us throughout the world.
Everyone must be considered as an individual.
We must respect their dignity and recognize their merit.
They must have a sense of security in their jobs.
Compensation must be fair and adequate,
and working conditions clean, orderly and safe.
We must be mindful of ways to help our employees fulfill
their family responsibilities.
Employees must feel free to make suggestions and complaints.
There must be equal opportunity for employment, development
and advancement for those qualified.
We must provide competent management,
and their actions must be just and ethical.

We are responsible to the communities in which we live and work
and to the world community as well.
We must be good citizens—support good works and charities
and bear our fair share of taxes.
We must encourage civic improvements and better health and education.
We must maintain in good order
the property we are privileged to use,
protecting the environment and natural resources.

Our final responsibility is to our stockholders.
Business must make a sound profit.
We must experiment with new ideas.
Research must be carried on, innovative programs developed
and mistakes paid for.
New equipment must be purchased, new facilities provided
and new products launched.
Reserves must be created to provide for adverse times.
When we operate according to these principles,
the stockholders should realize a fair return.

Johnson & Johnson

EXHIBIT 2–2
Boston Retail Mission

Boston Retail Clothing was founded to offer young-at-heart customers
the best in fashion, value, and fun. Our employees work together as a team
to listen, learn, and serve to the very best of our ability.
We will not sell products that we would not be proud to own and wear
ourselves.
We anticipate fashion trends and ensure that our products lead the way.

cessfully differentiated itself by providing high levels of service and excellent invest-ment returns on its actively managed funds. The ability of its fund managers to outper-form market indexes is critical to its differentiation strategy. Because of its history of su-perior returns and high service levels, many customers are willing to pay Fidelity a fee that is higher than some other competitors in the industry. By contrast, Vanguard Mutual Funds competes on the basis of price and attracts its customer by offering the lowest possible management fees. Vanguard does not attempt to outperform the market, but in-stead specializes in index funds that mirror the rise and fall of the stock market. Finally, some specialized mutual funds target their offerings only at specified customer groups, such as the Teachers Income and Annuity fund, which tailors its services to college pen-sion funds.

Perspective and Position at British Petroleum

John Browne, CEO of British Petroleum, described the key aspects for success in his business:

A business has to have a clear purpose. A clear purpose allows a company to fo-cus its learning efforts in order to increase its competitive advantage. What do we mean by purpose? Our purpose is who we are and what makes us distinctive. It's what we as a company exist to achieve, and what we're willing to do to achieve it. We are in *only* four components of the energy business: oil and gas exploration and production; refining and marketing; petrochemicals; and photovoltaics, or solar. We're a public company that has to compete for capital, which means that we have to deliver a com-petitive return to shareholders. But, in our pursuit of exceptional performance and sus-tained growth, there are certain financial boundaries we will not cross and values we will not violate. The values concern ethics; health, safety, and the environment; the way we treat employees; and external relations.

Source: Steven E. Prokesch, "Unleashing the Power of Learning: An Interview with British Petroleum's John Browne," *Harvard Business Review* 75 (September/October 1997): 146–168.

Setting Performance Goals—Strategy as Plan

After determining the mission and desired strategic position for the business (by analyzing competitive dynamics and resources and capabilities), the preparation of plans and goals represents the formal means by which managers (a) communicate a business's strategy to the organization and (b) coordinate the internal resources to ensure that the strategy can be achieved. When managers are asked, "What is your strategy?," they will often refer to their strategic plans—the documents where strategy is written down.

A major purpose of preparing plans is to communicate **intended strategy.** With agreement among top managers about how to compete in the marketplace, it is essential that they communicate this direction to the organization at large. Plans and goals can be used to communicate strategies and coordinate action. The linkage can be visualized as shown in Figure 2–4.

Goals, as reflected in profit plans and operating plans, are the *ends or results that management desires to achieve in implementing the business strategy.* Examples of goals for Boston Retail might include:

- increase market share
- open new stores
- launch a new product line
- reduce expenses
- develop information-technology capabilities
- improve customer satisfaction

However, goals become actionable only when time frames and quantitative indicators of success are added. Without performance indicators and time frames, managers cannot track progress and evaluate their success in achieving goals. For example, to be actionable, the performance goals listed above could be rewritten as follows:

- increase market share by 4% within 18 months
- open two new stores during the next year
- launch a new product line by July 1
- reduce expenses by 5% over the next year
- install a new automated inventory system in the next six months
- improve customer satisfaction by 12%

FIGURE 2–4   Linking Strategy with Action

Mission
↓
Intended Strategy
↓
Goals and Plans
↓
Performance Measure
↓
Actions

The final requirement for effective communication and implementation of goals is a *measure or scale* that can be used by managers to monitor progress toward these goals. For example, when driving your car on a long trip, you may set a goal of covering 100 more miles before stopping for gas. However, without an odometer and fuel gauge, you have no way of tracking your success in achieving that goal. Measures are equally important for every business. For the business goals and objectives listed above, we might measure:

- number of units of product shipped
- number of new store openings
- number of new product launches
- spending levels in dollars
- customer satisfaction ratings on a scale of 1 to 10

Plans can be used to communicate strategy, set goals, and coordinate resources. In subsequent chapters we will discuss the nature of information used for performance measurement and control, and then we will study in detail how to: build profit plans, evaluate performance against those plans, ensure that adequate resources are on hand to support successful implementation of strategies, link performance goals with markets, and design balanced measurement systems to communicate and monitor the achievement of strategic goals.

Feedback and Adjustment—Strategy as Patterns in Action

The hierarchy of *mission* → *strategy* → *goals* → *measures* → *action* (shown in Figure 2–4) illustrates a cascading concept—from a general inspirational mission to specific quantitative measures of success. As we have discussed briefly, this hierarchy is supported by strategic plans based on a series of analytic techniques such as SWOT. However, this is an incomplete picture of the strategy process. Not all successful strategies are planned. Many arise spontaneously. Consider the following story:

Robert Stage, president of Hamilton Bank, was addressing a group of M.B.A. students at Harvard Business School. Hamilton Bank was an important competitor in the private banking industry. The bank specialized in meeting the personal and corporate banking needs of wealthy individuals who owned their own businesses.

A student raised her hand and asked, "Mr. Stage, you've told us that your private banking strategy is new. Where did it come from? Whose idea was it?"

Stage responded, "Denise, that's an excellent question. You probably think that a group of us—Hamilton's executive committee—got together and worked it out based on market opportunities and an assessment of our own capabilities. But it didn't happen like that. As I explained to you, our earlier strategy was much broader . . . and not very successful. We had scheduled a series of performance review meetings with key managers around the world—country heads of major markets. Each came to the meeting to review their profit plans for the coming year and discuss year-to-date performance.

"What surprised us was how many country managers described profitable niches they had created catering to wealthy business owners in their local countries. During the meetings, we started to question how much of this type of business we had around the world. No one had a clue. So we commissioned a study to find out.

"After a couple of months' hard work, we were stunned to discover that, in country after country, our local managers had built up very solid and profitable franchises catering to this market segment. After digesting this for a time, and looking at the momentum that had already been built, we decided that this could be the key to a successful strategy in the future. After further analysis and a lot of thought, we threw out the old strategy and adopted this new one. We're still in the process of rolling it out. This strategy didn't come from the top—it emerged from the bottom of the organization as local managers independently figured out how to create value in their markets."

This story is not unusual. Many successful strategies arise from local experimentation and replication. New approaches are tried—and many fail. However, some initiatives work in unexpected ways and suggest new ideas to managers about how to reposition the business. Experiments, trial and error, and sometimes just plain luck lead to new tactics and ways of competing. If these innovations are replicated, managers can learn over time how to change and/or improve their strategy. This "bottom-up" strategy is illustrated in Figure 2–5.

The importance of **emergent strategy** and learning is as true in life in general as it is in business. Read the biography of any successful business person (or any person, for that matter) and ask yourself how much of their success was planned and how much was due to serendipity and a willingness to embrace new circumstances that were emerging around them.

Thus, strategy can be planned—as we have discussed at length in our analysis of strategy as position and plan—but it can also emerge in unexpected and unanticipated ways. At Boston Retail, the decision to focus on college students was not planned. The company's first store stocked a wide variety of merchandise: clothing for both men and women, as well as an assortment of household goods. However, the female college students who worked in the store attracted friends who enjoyed mixing unusual fashion accessories to create bold statements. Over time, the store became known among local college women as a unique source of fashion accessories. Without a lot of forethought by

FIGURE 2–5   Bottom-Up or Emergent Strategy

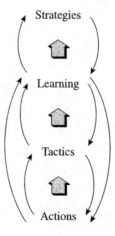

the owners, volume in this category grew steadily. In time, a decision was made by the owner/president to specialize in the college-fashion niche and eliminate other product lines. Replicating this formula, the business prospered and additional stores were opened.

Professor Henry Mintzberg describes how this can happen in other unpredictable ways:

> Out in the field, a salesman visits a customer. The product isn't quite right, and together they work on some modifications. The salesman returns to his company and puts the changes through; after two or three more rounds, they finally get it right. A new product

---

Emergent Strategy at 3M

Innovation is the driving force in 3M's strategy. In 1997, 30% of sales came from products less than four years old, up from 26% in 1994. However, innovation, by its nature, cannot be planned in advance. Over the years, 3M has created a unique culture and set of processes that promote its prolific inventiveness.

All 3M employees are trained in risk-taking, and all scientists are expected to devote 15% of their time to projects outside of their current responsibilities. If a project fails to win approval within a business unit, scientists routinely find funding outside of their own organization. 3M is determined to follow where its scientists and customers lead them. 3M scientists work closely with major-customer teams to address expressed requirements and to identify and solve unarticulated needs. 3M promotes cross-fertilization of knowledge and ideas by frequent job changes. For example, when the "Post-It Note" product was being launched, 3M temporarily assigned the Post-It note product manager to develop a new fly-fishing line.

3M pursues a corporate program of investing in emerging technologies with limited current commercial application but with the potential for changing the basis of competition in an industry. In 1961, for example, 3M developed a technology called "microreplication" for covering surfaces with millions of precisely made structures such as cubes or spheres. By 1981, microreplication was used in one small 3M business for making lenses for lighting systems, but many more business units were experimenting with this technology for new applications. Recognizing its broader applicability, 3M made substantial investments in the technology. Microreplication is now responsible for more than $1 billion in sales, with explosive growth predicted.

Being a patient investor is not without its risks. For example, 3M continued to invest in innovation in its magnetic-storage business while the technology followed steep downward cost curves that quickly turned the high-tech product into a commodity. In 1994, 3M wrote off $600 million, laid off thousands of workers, and spun off operations related to this investment.

Source: Adapted from Thomas A. Stewart, "3M Fights Back," *Fortune,* February 5, 1996, 94–99; 3M 1997 Annual Report Chairman's Letter.

emerges, which eventually opens up a new market. The company has changed strategic course.[11]

The potential for new strategies to emerge in unexpected ways requires managers to be constantly aware of changing *patterns of action* in their businesses. For example, in the 1980s, Intel Corporation changed its strategy from a manufacturer of commodity computer memory to a manufacturer of high-value-added microprocessors. This change was not planned from the top; instead it was driven by mid-level managers and operations people who were making day-to-day decisions aimed at maximizing the value of scarce production capacity. However, top managers were ready to *learn*. They were alert for changing patterns in the business and were able to embrace the new strategy when it became evident from the actions of lower-level employees that this new approach could pave a profitable pathway to the future.[12]

To capture the benefits of emerging strategy, managers must foster **organizational learning**—the ability of an organization to monitor changes in its environment and adjust its processes, products, and services to capitalize on those changes. They must use their performance measurement and control systems to encourage employees to constantly innovate and search for signs of change in the business. Managers must encourage employees to experiment, to find new opportunities, and test new ideas. And, perhaps most importantly, they must ensure that performance measurement and control systems create effective communication channels to move this information up the line from employees to senior managers at headquarters. Feedback becomes critical for learning: it allows managers to fine-tune and, sometimes, radically change their business strategies.

CHAPTER SUMMARY

Getting strategy right is not simple—if it was, top managers would not command the high salaries and bonuses that are the rewards of success. Implementing successful strategies requires the ability to conduct SWOT analysis of market dynamics and internal capabilities. Then, managers must be able to control the multiple dimensions of strategy reflected in the four Ps of strategy implementation (see Figure 2–6).

Ideals, values, and history must be woven together into an overall perspective that provides a lens through which to view the opportunities that surround the business. This is strategy as *perspective*. Managers must also have a deep understanding—a gut-level intimacy—of the market dynamics in their industry. They must use a five-forces analysis to understand customers, suppliers, products, and competitors. Based on a SWOT assessment of their own business's strengths and weaknesses, they must choose how to create value for customers. Will they compete on price? On quality? On service? On product features? This is strategy as *position*. Once strategy is set, managers must possess the tools to implement it. They must prepare plans, communicate goals, coordinate

---

[11] Henry Mintzberg, "Crafting Strategy," *Harvard Business Review* (July–August, 1987).

[12] Robert Burgelman, "A Process View of Strategic Business Exit: Implications for an Evolutionary Perspective on Strategy," *Strategic Management Journal* 17 (Summer 1996): 193–214.

FIGURE 2–6   Basics for Successful Strategy Implementation

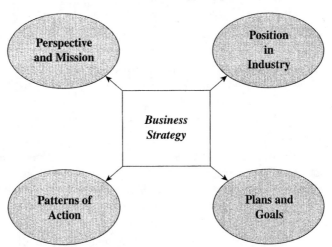

resources, motivate people, and measure and monitor implementation. This is strategy as *plan*. Finally, to succeed over the long term, managers must keep their eyes focused on customers and competitors and their ears to the ground. They must listen and learn. They must encourage employees to experiment and constantly challenge subordinates to share their ideas and successes so this information can be used to realign strategy over time. This is strategy as emerging *patterns* of actions.

The remainder of this book is devoted to learning how to use performance measurement and control systems to achieve profit goals and strategies. To do so, we introduce the tools and techniques that allow managers to take charge of *all* the aspects of successful strategy.

3

Organizing for Performance

After business strategy has been set, managers must decide how to organize people and resources to achieve that strategy. As we shall see, there are many potential ways of organizing a business, but some ways are preferable to others. In this chapter, we tackle the questions, How do managers organize people and resources into work units? and What are the implications of this choice for implementing strategy?

We start by looking at the basic building block of organization design—the work unit. Then we explore different accountability structures and the criteria by which managers can choose one structure over another. Understanding organization design is important because performance measurement and management control systems must be aligned with the underlying structure of organizations.

Organizations are comprised of individuals who work together in groups. Groups may be large or small, including teams, task forces, shifts, departments, functions, plants, divisions, business units, and so on. Each of these groups performs specific functions that support the strategy of the firm.

PURPOSE OF STRUCTURE

A dictionary defines structure as the way in which individual parts or elements are arranged or put together to form a whole. When designing **organizational structure,** the "parts" are the basic building blocks of the organization—that is, the groupings of people into work units—and the "whole" is the working relationships among these groups that collectively comprise a business.

In organizations, managers seek to impose structure for two principal reasons: (1) to facilitate work flows and (2) to focus attention. The former relates to the physical flow of materials and information, the latter to where people focus their time and energy.

Patterns in work flows are achieved by the structuring of *activities.* For example, managers must choose what assembly steps to put in a specific production line and in what order. They must also decide where information about new orders should be routed as it is received from salespeople. In both of these cases, the design of work flows—in one case the flow of products down an assembly line; in the other case, the flow of information through a networked computer system—determines how value will be added at each specific stage of the production, billing, and collection processes.

Managers must also structure the *attention* of the people who work in their organizations. In this case, rather than dealing with work flows per se, managers attempt to influence what people think about, worry about, gather information on, and make decisions about. This aspect of organization structure recognizes that the creativity and energy of managers and workers throughout the business must be channeled so that all energy can be as productive as possible.

Structuring of attention is achieved by three primary levers: the design of work units, span of control, and span of accountability.

DESIGN OF WORK UNITS

The basic building block for organizational design is the clustering of related work activity in a work unit. A **work unit** represents *a grouping of individuals who utilize the firm's resources and are accountable for performance.* A maintenance facility, a production team, and a university history department are all examples of work units.

Individuals are grouped into work units to perform specific tasks. On the machine floor of a factory, for example, clusters of workers are organized around a production line; in the controller's department of a gas utility, accounting staff are grouped together to provide transaction processing and accounting services; in an international consumer-products firm, separate business units are created to produce and deliver products into specific geographic markets.

Accountability defines (1) the outputs that a work unit is expected to produce and (2) the performance standards that managers and employees of that unit are expected to meet. Most firms create a picture, or diagram, of their accountability units called an **organization chart.** Organization charts are useful visual reference tools because they allow members of the organization to understand how people and resources are grouped and who is responsible for directing activities and receiving accountability information—that is, information for performance measurement and control.

As we move from the smallest work unit (a team) to the largest work unit (a business), we see a hierarchy of organizing that reflects the foundation of organization design. Small work units are grouped together into larger work units; team-based production lines are grouped together into a plant; three plants are grouped together into a production division; the production division is grouped with marketing and sales into a geographic unit serving the Canadian market; the Canadian unit is grouped with other international units to form the international division; the international division is grouped with the U.S. division to form the highest level grouping—the entire business.

BASIC DESIGN CHOICES

There are two basic types of work units: (1) groups of people and resources engaged in a similar *work-process,* and (2) groups of people and resources focused on a specific *market.* The former is often called a function; the latter is often called a division or business unit.

Units Clustered by Work-Process

When new organizations are created, and are therefore quite small, employees typically work as "jacks-of-all-trades." When the first Boston Retail stores opened, for example, each employee pitched in to do whatever needed to be done with little regard for titles or specialization of duties. Think of anyone you know who has started his or her own business. At first, they have to do everything themselves—from selling, to purchasing, to record keeping, to negotiating contracts and obtaining permits. As the business grows and employees are hired, however, this approach becomes increasingly inefficient for two reasons. First, some people are better at certain tasks than others. This means that efficiencies can be gained by **specialization**—matching specific individuals with tasks that they enjoy and at which they can excel. It does not make sense to ask talented salespeople to spend their time bookkeeping, and vice versa. To maximize their productivity and contribution, certain people should spend all their time selling; others should spend all their time keeping records. Second, the constant switching back and forth between different tasks can result in wasted time and a **diffusion of attention** as employees refocus on a new set of activities. With employees frequently changing their attention to the latest demand or crisis, no single activity receives the full attention and expertise it deserves.

Accordingly, as businesses grow, it is common for managers to streamline work flows and focus attention by clustering workers by work-process or function. A **function** is the most basic organizational component, comprising a group of managers and employees who specialize in a specific work process.

Examples of functions based on work-process include:

- a marketing and sales unit
- a controller's department
- an information technology department
- a production unit

In a "functional" organization—where work units are grouped by activity—specific groups of individuals specialize in ordering merchandise and maintaining adequate inventory, others specialize in selling to customers, and others specialize in accounting and keeping records. In each case, the work unit performs a specialized function (hence the name) needed by the business: generating revenue (sales and marketing), designing new products (research and development), providing transaction processing and accounting services (the controller's department), supplying networked computing power (information technology), or manufacturing goods for sale (production department).

Managers organize by function to leverage the benefits of specialization and thereby create economies of scale in production, research and development (R&D), and marketing. With specialization, large-scale resources can be effectively deployed to maximize efficiency and effectiveness. Specialized resources, specialized knowledge, and dedicated support functions can all focus on achieving maximum outputs for predetermined levels of inputs.

In cases where specialization is carried to an extreme, organizations often group work processes by knowledge.[1] In hospitals and universities, for example, highly trained experts are organized by specialty. In a hospital, each medical specialty is clustered as a separate work unit: obstetricians are organized together; cardiologists are grouped separately, and so on. Similarly, in a university business school, the finance faculty are clustered as a unit, as are the accounting and control faculty. In these cases, professional postgraduate training and apprenticeship (of a physician or a professor) impart specific specialized knowledge that can be best exploited by clustering experts who work together on common sets of tasks using similar methods and techniques.

Functional work units typically receive both financial and nonfinancial goals and are held accountable for specific lines on a business's profit and loss statement. For example, the marketing and sales organization may be held accountable for successfully launching a new product (a nonfinancial goal) and the amount of sales revenue that it

---

PSA Rationalizes Manufacturing

On October 1, 1997, Jean-Martin Folz became CEO of PSA Peugeot Citroën, the French car company formed in the 1970s when Peugeot and Citroën merged to create one of Europe's largest car makers. For more than 20 years, the company had kept manufacturing for the two brands virtually separate. Folz believed that the company could reduce costs by combining production for the two brands. Folz's aim was to reduce the number of platforms (groups of similar components) from seven to three for cars and one platform for car parts. At the same time, Folz intended to differentiate the marketing, sales, and style autonomy of each brand.

Peugeot and Citroën already shared such functions as finance, information systems, engineering, purchasing, and manufacturing of major components including engines. Furthermore, a precedent for rationalizing manufacturing facilities existed among PSA's competitors like Volkswagen and Fiat. To implement his new strategy, Folz reorganized the company into three functional divisions: one group manufacturing operation (in charge of all of the group's factories) and two separate sales divisions, one for Citroën and the other for Peugeot.

The full corporate reorganization, completed six months later, created three additional divisions to support PSA's product-development strategy: a new innovation and quality division to revamp and separate the Citroën brand identity from Peugeot, a platform division with responsibility for managing costs and quality, and an engineering and purchasing division.

Sources: Stephane Farhi, "PSA Managers to Enter the Folz Era," *Automotive News Europe,* March 2, 1998, 8; "Peugot Starts Revamp to Boost Image and Sales," *Wall Street Journal Europe,* January 22, 1998, 3; "France's Peugot Merging Production of Core Auto Brands," *Dow Jones Online News,* January 21, 1998.

---

[1] Henry Mintzberg, *The Structuring of Organizations* (Englewood Cliffs, N.J.: Prentice Hall, 1979), 108.

generates (a financial goal representing the top line of the income statement). The manufacturing department is held accountable for product quality indexes (nonfinancial goals), as well as cost of goods sold and relevant production variances on the income statement. Even in hospitals and health maintenance organizations (HMOs), physicians are held accountable for indices of patient care as well as expense control and resource utilization.

Units Clustered by Market Focus

The second principal way of clustering individuals and firm resources is by market. Market-focused work units are normally found in one of three basic configurations: units clustered by product, units clustered by customer, and units clustered by geography.

Units Clustered by Product

At the level of the firm, companies that have only one product are already clustered by product: All the energies of the organization—both people and resources—are focused on producing and marketing a single product category. Boston Retail, for example, competes in only one market segment—young women's fashion clothing.

However, the strategy of many companies leads them to produce products for multiple market segments. These multiproduct companies often choose to cluster workers and facilities according to a defined subset of products so employees in each unit focus their attention exclusively on their range of products. Thus, IBM Corporation has created a separate unit for its mainframe computer products, another unit for its personal computer products, another unit for its networking products, and so on. In such cases, each work unit, comprising dedicated production facilities and employees, is called a **product division.**

Firms choose to organize by product for two reasons. First, product specialization can create *economies in production* (for example, by allowing dedicated and specialized plant facilities for personal computer products), *economies in R&D* (scientists and engineers can spend all of their time working on enhancing existing software products or creating new products for defined target markets), and *economies in distribution and marketing* (distribution channels and marketing campaigns can be focused on meeting the needs of defined retail customer segments). These economies may be due to either **economies of scale**—allowing the business to utilize efficient large-scale resources to drive down unit costs—or **economies of scope**—utilizing the same resources (such as distribution channels) across multiple products or activities to increase the throughput for a given fixed amount of that resource. Economies of scale are achieved when Ford Motor Company builds all its Windstar minivans in one plant and can therefore install and dedicate efficient, high-volume production equipment to this single purpose. Economies of scope can be seen in the distribution trucks that bring fresh stock to convenience stores. Companies like PepsiCo are able to use their vast and highly efficient distribution networks to deliver multiple product categories (such as soft drinks and potato chips) in one truck. Because of these potential economies, many firms reorganized their businesses around product lines during the wave of "downsizing" that occurred in the 1990s.

The second reason for product-based clusters is to increase *return on management* when product knowledge and specialization are key to competitive success. Without undue distraction, managers can devote their full attention to understanding the competitive threats and opportunities related to a narrow, defined set of product-market opportunities and work to create value in the eyes of target customers. They can devote all their energy to understanding customers and competitors and implementing strategies with the utmost effectiveness and efficiency.

Thus, even though Fidelity Investments owns a limousine service—Boston Coach—and a large portfolio of community newspapers, these operations are segregated into separate product divisions that do not distract the attention of investment managers from Fidelity's primary mutual fund business. Similarly, many U.S. auto manufacturers have moved away from functional organizations that emphasized efficiency to product division structures to ensure adequate focus on differentiated product markets (for example, small front-wheel drive, rear-wheel drive, and recreational trucks).

Unlike a function, where managers are held accountable only for those revenues or costs relating to their specific activities—typically a single line on the income statement—a product division manager is held accountable for an entire profit and loss statement. Often, product divisions are also responsible for managing assets on their balance sheet.

Units Clustered by Customer

A second common clustering based on market focus occurs when a business is grouped according to customer or customer type. This type of organizational arrangement is found most often when firms have a small number of large, important customers, each

---

Reorganization at Compaq Computers

In 1991, Compaq was losing market share due to its inability to compete in a new, price-sensitive market for personal computers (PCs). In the third quarter, it reported a loss of $70 million and its CEO was fired. A new management team, lead by Eckhard Pfeiffer, had to turn the company around and bring costs back under control. Pfeiffer changed Compaq's structure from a functional structure (based on manufacturing, sales, etc.) to a product division structure to focus each business on its key competencies. Each product division was given profit and loss responsibilities. PC operations, where low cost was paramount for success, became one of the new divisions. The objective for the PC division was to cut costs by 35% to 50%. Pfeiffer sent this message again and again to ensure that people understood clearly the new strategy. Products with higher technological content were grouped in another division. When expertise was not available within the organization, partnerships were formed, including the server division's union with Corollary, whose software enabled eight processors to run simultaneously.

Source: C. Arnst and S.A. Forest, "Compaq: How It Made Its Impressive Move Out of the Doldrums," *Business Week,* November 4, 1992, 146 and E. Nee, "Compaq Computer," *Forbes,* January 12, 1998, 90.

with distinct needs and attributes. Businesses like General Electric Corporation that sell to both industrial and government customers often organize their people and resources so that one organizational unit specializes in production and sales to the government, and another specializes in production and sales to industrial customers. Similarly, textbook publishers cluster their activities into separate customer-focused business units that specialize in producing and marketing books for elementary schools, four-year colleges, graduate schools, and so on.

Customer-based work units can take two forms. The first is a separate sales and marketing organization dedicated to serving the needs of large, important customers. IBM has followed this approach by creating a separate unit of "Client Executives" who receive specialized training and are dedicated to meeting the needs of the specific, large corporate customers to whom each is assigned. The second, and larger scale, approach is to carve out an entire organization—from procurement, to production, to sales and marketing—that is dedicated to a single customer or category of customer. This is most often encountered in businesses like General Dynamics that do a substantial amount of work with the U.S. government and set up dedicated business units to serve the specialized needs of this important customer. Similarly, the Internal Revenue Service is changing from an organizational structure based on region to one based on serving its three main constituencies: individual filers, small businesses, and big corporations.[2]

Firms cluster by customer type when the market needs of each customer segment are sufficiently unique that *specialized expertise and knowledge* about that customer are essential to competitive success in the marketplace. To serve a large customer effec-

---

Structuring for Customer Service at Ford Motor Company

Customer demands are forcing managers of traditional hierarchical, functional organizations to group units horizontally around key customer-oriented processes. At Ford Motor Company's Customer Service Department, managers realized that they were behind both American and Japanese competitors in customer satisfaction ratings. Accordingly, the 6,200-employee division was reorganized around four key processes: (1) fixing it right the first time on time; (2) supporting dealers and handling customers; (3) engineering cars with ease of service in mind; and (4) developing service fixes more quickly. Changes in dealer relations were especially dramatic. Through the introduction of field teams, the number of Ford people a dealer had to contact to resolve a customer problem dropped from 25 to three—a divisional operations manager, a field engineer, and a customer service representative.

Source: Rahul Jacob and Rajiv M. Rao, "The Struggle to Create an Organization for the 21st Century," *Fortune,* April 3, 1995, 90–99.

---

[2] Richard W. Stevenson, "Senate Votes 96–2 On Final Approval for Changing I.R.S.," *New York Times,* July 10, 1998, A1.

tively may require a dedicated sales forces, specialized distribution channels, or special attention to laws and regulations that only a separate and distinct organizational unit can provide. Customer-focused work units provide this attention and specialization. Managers who wish to increase revenue growth (particularly after a cost-driven downsizing) often reorganize their businesses to create customer-based units. By focusing work units around various customer segments (by industry, customers size, etc.), the organization becomes more knowledgeable about the needs of specific customers and the strengths and weaknesses of its competitors in each market segment. This customer intimacy can lead to more opportunities to do business with these customers (but often at the cost of corporate efficiencies previously described).

Units Clustered by Geography

The final type of market-focused cluster occurs when firms organize by region or geography. Businesses venturing abroad for the first time often do so by creating regionally-based work units that focus on specific regions. For example, a U.S.-based firm may set up separate organizations to serve Canada, Europe, and Asia-Pacific. The task of each of these business units, often referred to as a **regional business,** is to market and sell (and sometimes produce) the company's products in their defined geographic territory. Again, specialization is necessary to understand and respond to local languages, tastes and

---

Organizing for Global Service

When expanding outside their "home countries," service firms often adopt different organizing approaches depending on management's analysis of competitive industry dynamics and SWOT. Managers in these firms generally employ three types of organizing structures or "networks":

- Brand networks — Used when the brand is relatively strong, customer needs are local, and strategy can be customized to specific geographies. Units are organized by geography with core operational systems copied from the home country. Examples: McDonald's and Blockbuster Video.
- Distribution networks — Used when customers who travel to different regions or countries desire the same products or services in each of those locations with the same consistently high standards. Units are organized with centralized services providing global consistency. Examples: British Airways and Marriott Hotels.
- Knowledge networks — Used when the firm competes by its ability to transfer knowledge globally and to offer best-practice solutions to clients around the world. Global organization structures require significant coordination on two dimensions: lines of business and geography. Organizational practices and policies such as recruiting and compensation are centrally determined. Example: McKinsey & Company and Citibank.

Source: Gary Loveman, "The Internationalization of Services: Four Strategies that Drive Growth Across Borders," Boston: Harvard Business School, Note 897–081, 1996.

preferences, packaging laws, and business regulations. In addition, unique arrangements are often necessary to support product distribution in countries where the firm has no infrastructure of its own. As with all market-focused units, all the energies of the cluster are focused on serving the defined geography and its local markets.

A HIERARCHY OF ACCOUNTABILITY

From the previous discussion, it should be clear that the grouping of people and resources into work units entails choice. Managers must choose, for example, whether to cluster business activities by function, by customer, or by geography. However, this question is complicated because it is typically embedded in a hierarchy of organization design. At one level in any organization, units are grouped by function; at another level, they are grouped by market focus.

The most basic design is the functional organization, with distinct work units that are accountable for marketing, sales, production, accounting, R&D, and so forth. For example, the organization chart in Figure 3–1 for a medium-sized business that produces consumer radios reflects its functional groupings.

Inside this functional organization, however, the marketing function may in turn be grouped into three distinct units, each serving a different geographical area. Thus, separate units may be accountable for North American sales and marketing, European sales and marketing, and Asia-Pacific sales and marketing. The organization chart now looks as shown in Figure 3–2.

Figures 3–1 and 3–2 represent a stand-alone business. However, in a larger, more diversified firm, this business might be one of several businesses, each organized around discrete products or sets of products. Thus, the organization chart in Figure 3–3 depicts a company with three product divisions (consumer radios, avionics, and cellular telephones), each of which is organized functionally. Within each organization, the sales and marketing function is further subdivided as before into separate units focusing on distinct geographic regions.

FIGURE 3–1   Organization Chart for a Functional Organization

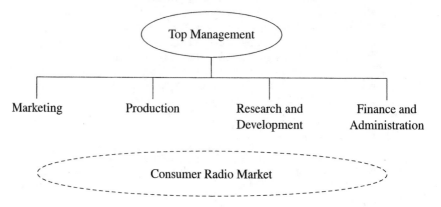

FIGURE 3–2   Functional Organization with Expansion of Sales and Marketing

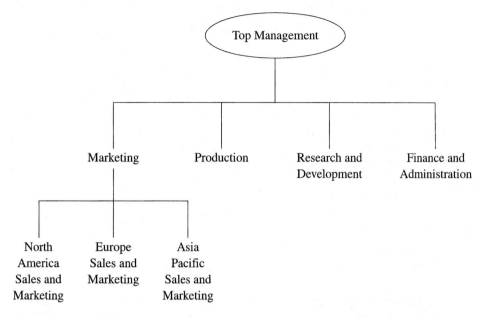

Hybrids on these basic designs are also possible. For example, Ford Europe has organized to create a national sales company in each separate country (market-focused), but it retains one large, centralized manufacturing division that produces cars and trucks for all European markets (functional specialization).

After a brief review of the design possibilities in terms of clustering organizations—by function or market focus—and the hierarchy of work units, the question

FIGURE 3–3   Organization Chart of Product Division Organization

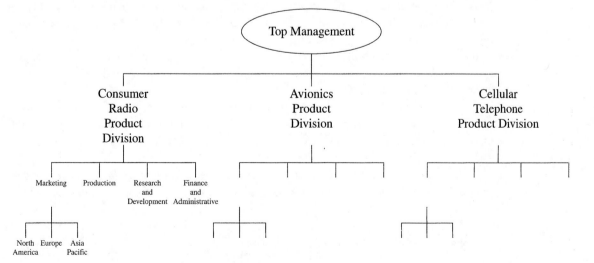

arises, "How do managers decide on the optimal organizational design?" As these examples illustrate, there are many different ways of grouping people and resources. Yet, there are systematic ways of evaluating these choices.

SPECIALIZATION AND MARKET RESPONSIVENESS

As a starting point in our analysis, there are two generalizations about work-unit design that are true in virtually all cases. First, any firm—whatever the structure—*when taken as a whole* is a market-focused entity. As discussed in the previous chapter, a firm's mission and strategy focus on creating value for customers and differentiating products and services in a defined market. Thus, the consumer radio company illustrated in Figure 3–1 is organized by function, but, at the firm level, all its activities focus on producing and selling radios to consumers. As a total firm, it is market focused.

Second, it should also be clear that, at the lowest organizational level, all activity is grouped by function to allow specialization. This is true in even the largest firms. For example, at the center of any billion-dollar diversified firm you will find dedicated functions for production, research, accounting, and so on. Thus, the basic choices for managers relate to the structuring of intermediate organization levels—those between the top of the organization and the bottom. For these intermediate levels, we must ask: when do managers choose to group people and resources based on *work-process,* and when do they choose groupings based on *market focus*?

Each choice—clustering by function or clustering by market focus—brings different benefits and costs. The benefits of grouping by work-process derive primarily from the benefits of specialization: economies of scale and scope in production, R&D, and marketing and distribution. These economies can bring improved effectiveness and efficiencies that are reflected in lower costs and/or higher quality.

The benefits of clustering by market derive from increased responsiveness to customers and competitors. Many consumer products companies such as Colgate–Palmolive Company are extremely responsive to changing market conditions and can launch new products and adjust pricing, promotion, and packaging extremely quickly to defend market share. If everyone in a unit—regardless of function—is focusing only on one type of product, one type of customer, or one geographic region, then all energy in the unit can be devoted to gathering information about that product, customer, or region. This information can then be used to deploy resources rapidly and respond quickly to changing threats and opportunities.

However, there is an important trade-off to be made here. *A unit can be either as efficient as possible or as responsive as possible—but, unfortunately, not both.* Except under the difficult circumstances of a matrix organization, managers must choose one over the other.[3] How do they choose?

Managers cluster units by function when the benefits of specialization are greater than the benefits of market responsiveness. If the strategy of a firm relies on economies

---

[3] Readers interested in the workings of a matrix organization can refer to Chris Bartlett and Robert Simons, "Asea Brown Boveri," Boston: Harvard Business School, Case No. 192–139, 1992.

of scale and scope—to drive such critical performance variables as low price, high quality, capital-intensive R&D, or standardized distribution—then managers will choose a functional organization. Thus, major pharmaceutical companies such as Merck are invariably organized by function to obtain economies of specialization in R&D, production, and marketing. This specialization is critical to the success of their strategy.

We can generalize and apply this rule to all organizations: *Working from the core of any organization outward, work units are grouped by function as long as the benefits of specialization are greater than the benefits of market responsiveness.* In general, the benefits of specialization outweigh the benefits of market-focused feedback at the lowest organizational levels. Thus, most manufacturing plants are organized as functional units—the benefits of bringing specialized knowledge and resources together in one group outweigh the benefits of focusing on market intelligence and responsiveness. Individuals in the core of the organization do not generally interact directly with customers and markets. Instead, everyone in the manufacturing division can focus their full attention on producing the highest quality goods for the lowest cost. Imagine what would happen if the assembly line supervisors were required to spend 50% of their time meeting with customers and research scientists: The benefits of specialization would be lost, and the potential gains in customer responsiveness would be slight. Instead, other units are better suited to the task of interacting with customers and scientists. The trade-off in favor of the relative importance of specialization is true also for staff functions. Because the benefits of specialized knowledge and training outweigh the benefits of market responsiveness, staff units such as accounting, legal, and human relations are invariably clustered by work activity.

At some point as we move higher in any organization, however, the demands of market forces must prevail. *Managers cluster work units by market focus (i.e., products, customers, or geography) when the benefits of market responsiveness outweigh the benefits of specialization.* (For this reason, the overall firm itself—the organization that interacts with its competitive environment—is always a market-focused unit.) The benefits of grouping by market derive principally from enhanced focus on the customer and the ability to create value through product and service differentiation. Market-focused units devote all their energies to aligning internal resources to respond to customer needs and changing competitive conditions. For example, worldwide food companies such as Nestlé are organized by geography because the taste and packaging requirements for food products differ widely around the world. Managers of these businesses must be able to respond to local market demands. Market-focused units are designed to scan and process competitive market information quickly—and to act on that information.

The benefits of each of these choices—specialization and market responsiveness—are not without corresponding costs. These costs accrue primarily from the need to create and use information for coordination, control, and learning. For units that are clustered by function, specialization creates the need to integrate highly interdependent processes: sales forecasts must be integrated with production plans; R&D expenditures must be coordinated with production prototypes; marketing programs must be coordinated with inventory levels to ensure that surges in demand can be handled. Literally thousands of day-to-day decisions and actions must be coordinated between functional work units that each focus primarily on performing their specialized work processes with maximum efficiency. In these businesses, higher level managers must ensure that performance measurement and control systems can effectively coordinate inputs and outputs between the different specialized units inside each business.

Also, with separate functions managed as stand-alone units, cross-fertilization of ideas and innovation may be stifled. Creativity and learning may be sacrificed in the pursuit of efficiency.

Coordination of the inputs, outputs, and information flows of independent functions is achieved primarily through formal *operating plans and budgets.* Performance targets—both financial and nonfinancial—are set by senior managers to define acceptable levels of performance. Because the outputs of marketing, R&D, procurement, and production departments are transferred internally and cannot easily be translated into corresponding market prices, managers must monitor expense levels to gain assurance that each functional unit is delivering value in accordance with the resources consumed. These monitoring systems are costly, however, both in terms of the cost of creating information, and in the management attention consumed to ensure that the units are working effectively in support of the business strategy.

For units that are clustered by market, there is less need to invest in systems for internal coordination. Performance standards are created naturally by selling goods or services into the market (for example, market share, revenue growth, gross margins), so performance evaluation can be based on achieving acceptable levels of profit from the assets employed in running the business. Instead of monitoring line-by-line expense statements, managers can review overall profit plans and accomplishments to assure themselves that the business is producing adequate returns.

However, market-focused units make performance measurement and control costly in two ways. First, there is a critical need to transmit market intelligence and best-practice information to other units within the firm so they can learn from it. If there is no possibility for learning or transferring best practice from one market-based unit to the next, there is little reason for these units to be in the same firm. Accordingly, an investment must be made in transferring information vertically—to higher management levels—and horizontally to other organizational units.

Second, to the extent there are product flows between market-focused units (i.e., the outputs of one unit are inputs to another), a system of internal transfer prices must be created and administered. (These transfer-pricing mechanisms are described in Chapter 8.)

ACCOUNTABILITY AND SPAN OF CONTROL

So far in this chapter, we have discussed the organizational arrangements that are depicted in a business's organization chart—how the parts are put together to form the whole. These reporting relationships are illustrated by solid lines connecting functions or business units. However, we have not yet introduced the most important part of organization structure—the *managers* who are responsible for achieving profit goals and strategies. After all, we must remember that we are talking about groupings of people. It is important, therefore, to understand that the solid vertical lines represent *accountabil-*

ity of individual managers—those who have the formal authority to direct subordinates in their activities and who are ultimately responsible for the success of their efforts in creating value for the firm.

Thus, instead of focusing on functions or business units, we can redraw these diagrams to show more precisely the reporting relationships of individual managers. For example, Figure 3–4 shows that the regional director of the European Sales and Marketing unit reports to the vice president of marketing, who in turn reports to the company's president.

Hidden within any organization chart are three related "spans" that are important in understanding the role of performance measurement and control systems. They are span of control, span of accountability, and span of attention. As we shall see, unit grouping (discussed in the pervious sections), span of control, and span of accountability are the key levers that influence a manager's span of attention (i.e., what he or she pays attention to).

Span of Control and Span of Accountability

When organization charts are drawn on the basis of the reporting relationships of individual managers, the solid lines connecting individuals depict the **span of control** for each manager in the organization chart. Span of control indicates how many (and which) subordinates and functions report to each manager in the organization. Span of control, in effect, describes the resources—in terms of people and work units—*directly* under a manager's control. Span of control can be broad, with many people and a wide range of resources reporting to a manager, or narrow, with few people and a narrow range of resources under a manager's direct control (see Figure 3–5).

However, span of control as shown on an organization chart is only part of the story. It outlines reporting relationships—*who* is accountable to whom—but span of control does not tell us *what* they are accountable for. For this, we need another

**FIGURE 3–4   Organization Chart Showing Accountability of
                     Individual Managers**

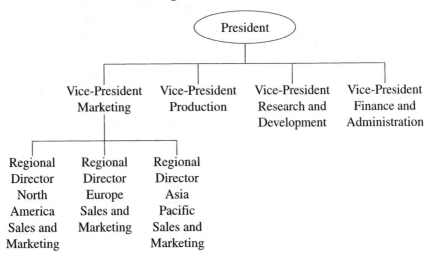

FIGURE 3–5   Comparison of Two Different Spans of Control

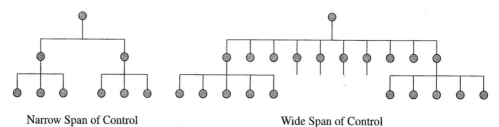

Narrow Span of Control   Wide Span of Control

concept—**span of accountability.** *Span of accountability describes the range of performance measures used to evaluate a manager's achievements.* At its most basic level, span of accountability defines the financial statement items for which a manager is accountable.[4] For example, managers can be held accountable for various combinations of their business's income statement and balance sheet. Some managers may be held accountable for revenues only (a sales and marketing manager), for costs only (a manufacturing plant manager), for net profits before interest and taxes (a product division manager), or for return on assets (the manager of a stand-alone business that controls its own balance sheet). We now consider the two most common configurations of financial accountability—**cost center accountability** and **profit center accountability.**

Cost Center Accountability   A cost center represents the narrowest span of work-unit accountability encountered in most firms. Managers of cost centers are accountable only for their unit's level of spending. Typically, cost center managers are given cost budgets

---

Span of Control at GE

In 1981, John Welch assumed control of General Electric. Five years later, he had reorganized its 14 businesses into three "strategic circles": core manufacturing, technology-intensive products, and services. Under Welch's leadership, GE also achieved its target of first or second place in almost all markets worldwide.

The next, more difficult, step was to streamline the company's communication and decision making processes. Welch first dismantled a layer of middle management so the 14 separate businesses would report directly to him and a few vice chairmen. "Layers hide weakness," claimed Welch. "Layers mask mediocrity. I firmly believe that an overburdened, overstretched executive is the best executive because he or she doesn't have the time to meddle, to deal in trivia, to bother people."

Source: Nichy, Noel and Charan, Ram, "Speed, Simplicity, Self-Confidence: An Interview with Jack Welch," *Harvard Business Review* (September–October 1989): 112–120.

---

[4] The concept of span of accountability is equally applicable to nonfinancial goals and performance measures, but we postpone this discussion to later chapters.

and asked to deliver the desired level of goods or service within those spending constraints. To do so, cost center managers need only monitor specific expense lines of their business's profit and loss statement. Most functional units—the mail room, a production plant, R&D labs, or an internal audit staff group—are set up as cost centers.

Profit Center Accountability   A profit center manager has a broader span of accountability than a cost center manager. He or she is not only accountable for costs, but also for revenues and, often, for assets as well. Any function or business unit that accounts for its own revenue and expenses on an income statement can be a profit center. For example, an information systems (IS) function can be a profit center if it charges other units for its services, as can a processing plant—as long as it receives revenue for the goods and services provided.

The important implication—one that we explore in detail in Chapter 5—is that the manager of a profit center is asked to make *trade-offs* between costs and revenues to achieve his or her profit goals. Whereas a cost center manager need only focus on minimizing costs (or maximizing outputs for a given level of inputs), a profit center manager with a broader span of accountability must consider the impact of spending levels on revenues and profit. For example, a profit center manager may decide to increase expenses to boost revenue (e.g., by increasing advertising).

Although all profit center managers, by definition, are responsible for an income statement, the span of accountability can differ quite dramatically across different companies and different profit centers. In some profit centers, managers are responsible only for managing revenues, costs, and net profits. In others, managers are also accountable for efficient utilization of assets as recorded on their units' balance sheets. These managers have the widest span of accountability.[5] In essence, they are being held accountable to operate their unit as an integral business. As such, they must not only make trade-offs between costs and revenues, they must also make trade-offs between the costs of the assets they employ and the value that those assets deliver to the business.

SPAN OF ATTENTION

We have introduced the three structural design levers that senior managers use to organize their businesses: (1) work units—groupings by function or market to drive specialization or market responsiveness, (2) span of control—the subordinates and resources under a manager's direct control, and (3) span of accountability—the range of performance measures for which a manager is accountable to superiors. Now we are ready to make a critical point. These three mechanisms are employed for one primary purpose: to influence **span of attention.** *Span of attention refers to the domain of activities that are within a manager's field of view.* Span of attention defines what an individual will attempt to gather information on and influence. In simple terms, it's what people care

---

[5] Some textbooks refer to balance sheet accountability as an "investment center" to denote accountability for return on investment. This nomenclature is rarely found in practice. Instead, managers use the term profit center as we have defined it above.

about and pay attention to. As we will see in later chapters, managers must be able to influence span of attention at all levels of an organization if they are to have any success in achieving their profit goals and strategies.

Like span of control and span of accountability, span of attention can be narrow or broad. For example, a plant manager with a narrow span of attention may have little interest in any part of the business outside the factory walls. Alternatively, he or she may care very deeply about the level of customer satisfaction associated with products produced in his plant. Similarly, an R&D manager with a narrow span of attention may care little about the growth of the firm—focusing instead only on specific research programs—or, he or she may be very interested in knowing how customer demand is likely to shape technology demands over the next year.

Span of attention is fundamentally different in nature than either span of control or span of accountability. Span of control and span of accountability are top-down concepts. They are determined by superiors. It is, after all, a boss who determines the reporting relationships for his or her subordinates and performance dimensions on which those subordinates will be evaluated. Span of attention, by contrast, comes from *within an individual manager,* because all employees and managers must form their own judgments about what they believe to be important. Span of attention, however, can—and must—be influenced by superiors.

The span of attention for any individual manager is determined by the three levers that we have introduced so far: (1) the work unit to which the manager belongs, (2) the people and functions under the manager's direct control, and (3) the performance measures for which the manager is held accountable to superiors. Let us consider briefly how each level influences span of attention.

Work Unit Design $\Rightarrow$ ***Span of Attention***   In general, people pay a great deal of attention to the work of their own unit, but relatively little attention to work that is outside their field of view. As we have discussed, work units are groups of people brought together to concentrate on functional specialization or market responsiveness. People in the unit work toward shared goals. These goals may be to introduce the latest and best technology for radio products worldwide (functional specialization), to serve government customers in Eastern Europe (market focus), or to process accounting transactions for the entire business as efficiently as possible (functional specialization). Attendance at trade shows, meetings, reports, and hallway discussions are all determined by the type of work and goals assigned to the unit to which an individual belongs.

Span of Control $\Rightarrow$ ***Span of Attention***   Span of control is a powerful determinant of the range of activities that is within a manager's field of view. Managers use the resources under their direct control—people, functions, and business units—to achieve their business goals. They must think carefully about how to deploy those resources effectively. To do this, managers are forced to devote attention to the needs of subordinates who report to them. Goals must be set, resources must be allocated, performance must be monitored, and progress must be evaluated. These activities, and the many face-to-face meetings, telephone calls, and e-mails that are necessary to support a superior-subordinate relationship, require a significant amount of attention.

Span of Accountability $\Rightarrow$ ***Span of Attention***   Span of attention is influenced by span of accountability because of one simple fact: managers pay attention to what they are measured on. As the old saying goes, "What gets measured, gets managed." If senior managers want a subordinate to devote all his energies and attention to increasing sales, they will make that manager accountable only for achieving revenue goals. If senior managers want attention directed at making trade-offs between marketing expenditures and increased revenues, then a manager will be held accountable for net profit as defined on an income statement. If senior managers want subordinates to focus their energies on the most productive use of assets, then a return-on-net-assets measure will be employed, holding the unit managers accountable for performance on both the income statement and balance sheet.

Span of Attention and Organizational Design

Shaping span of attention is one of the key objectives of organizational design. Structure is one of the primary tools that managers use to ensure that people are concentrating on the right things—day-in and day-out—as they face many competing demands for their time. Span of attention determines who worries about what. Profit goals and strategies can only be achieved if managers are able to motivate subordinates to devote sufficient time and attention to critical tasks. Span of attention—as determined by work unit assignments, span of control, and span of accountability—is a critical ingredient in the formula of success.

Span of attention is at the core of the concepts of centralization and decentralization. A **centralized organization** is designed so that unit managers have narrow spans of attention. Why? In centralized organizations, senior managers want to ensure that subordinates do not become distracted by information and events that could pull their attention away from maximizing efficiency through specialization. Units are typically grouped by functional specialty, and unit managers are accountable for narrow subsets of the income statement as defined by their cost center responsibilities. The coordination of individual functions and business activities is reserved for higher level managers. Thus, in a centralized organization, accountability for trade-offs among income statement and balance sheet accounts rests at the top of the organization, where the individual functions come together to form profit centers.

Decentralized organizations, by contrast, are designed so that managers have wide spans of attention. Decentralized organizations are essential when business strategy demands quick and agile responsiveness to customers and markets. In a decentralized organization, business units are market-based, with employees of the unit interacting directly with customers and markets. Accountability for trade-offs among key income statement and balance sheet accounts is delegated low in the organization. Low-level unit managers run profit centers. They make trade-offs to maximize competing objectives across a wide array of activities. Spans of control are also wide, with many individuals and a broad resource base reporting to individual managers.

CHAPTER SUMMARY

Managers must decide how to organize their businesses to achieve profit goals and strategies. The functioning of an organization depends on work and information flows. The design of work units, spans of control, and spans of accountability are the main structural tools to influence and direct organizational attention to ensure that everyone is working toward shared goals.

However, organization structure—as discussed in this chapter—is a static concept until we introduce the information flows that are necessary to support work flows and accountability. Information about plans, goals, and results must be created and transmitted. Information about customers, markets, competitors, and best practices must be collected, stored, and disseminated. Above all, managers must ensure consistent and reliable information channels to allow everyone in the business to work together and learn together as they strive to achieve shared business goals. This is the topic of the next chapter.

C H A P T E R

4

Using Information for Performance Measurement and Control

Information is essential to all well-managed businesses and nonprofit organizations. The amount and quality of information available to managers of any organization is a good barometer of organizational health. Managers of organizations that have too little information do not have the means to effectively communicate goals and are forced to make decisions on the fly—by intuition. Managers of organizations that are capable of processing relevant information quickly can plan for the future, communicate direction efficiently, and capitalize more effectively on emerging problems and opportunities.

One of the primary purposes of performance measurement and control is to allow **fact-based management**—management that moves from intuition and hunches to analysis based on hard data and facts. (As Sherlock Holmes said, "It is a capital mistake to theorize before one has data.") In Part II of this book, which follows this chapter, we study the techniques and analyses that allow managers to use performance measurement and control information as a tool for fact-based management.

Information can be defined in many ways. A dictionary definition would refer to information as the *communication or reception of intelligence or knowledge.* An entire field of knowledge known as **cybernetics** is devoted to the study of information and its use in feedback processes. Feedback information of various types is used to control animate and inanimate systems, including biological, mechanical, electrical, and organizational systems. It is on this last category—control of organizational systems—that we will focus in this chapter and the remainder of the book.

In terms of achieving profit goals and strategies, Figure 4–1 outlines key information flows that are required for effective management.

Inside an organization, we usually think of information flowing *to managers* to inform them about the operations of their businesses. For example, budget variances are reported to managers for follow-up and action; productivity data is collected and reported to managers to allow the monitoring of significant trends; and order backlogs are reported to give managers assurance that key goals are being met. In terms of implementing strategy, the information is of two types: information about progress in achieving goals, and information about emerging threats and opportunities. Both of these types of information provide **feedback**—information about actual events or outcomes that

FIGURE 4–1   Information Needs of Top Managers in Achieving Profit Goals and Strategies

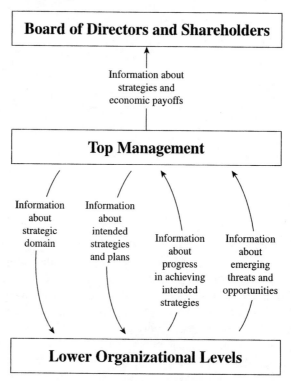

Source: Adapted from Simons, *Levers of Control*, 6.

can be compared with expectations or standards. This information is essential to allow managers to conduct and update SWOT analyses based on changing competitive dynamics and internal capabilities.

In addition to feedback, however, information must also flow from managers *to employees* to serve a number of purposes. First, managers must inform employees throughout the organization about the market segments and types of activities to which they are willing to commit resources. Will Boston Retail expand into men's clothing? Will a music recording company focus on classical music, new age, or both? Will an auto supply business cater to original-equipment manufacturers or repair centers? Second, managers must communicate clearly the intended strategy of the business. How it will create value and differentiate itself from competitors? What is the nature of the value that will be created for customers? Will it compete by price or differentiate itself on some other dimension? Employees must have a clear understanding of how top managers have made these choices.

Third, managers must communicate plans, goals, and milestones. How much profit must be generated in the third quarter? What are management's expectations in terms of revenue and market-share growth? How many new stores must be opened next year to hit the business plan goals? This information flow is critical to give employees a clear understanding of the short-term goals of the business so they can contribute to achieving these goals.

Finally, managers must communicate these same strategies and performance goals to *superiors and external parties* whose support is needed to implement the strategy of the business. These external parties may include banks or other lenders who supply capital on a short-term basis, stockholders and investment analysts who provide long-term equity capital to the firm, and suppliers and partners who play important roles in the manufacture and distribution of products and services. We also must not forget the board of directors. Managers must communicate their plans and strategies to their boards for approval and ratification.

In the remainder of this chapter, we introduce three important topics related to the choices that managers must make in using information effectively for performance measurement and control:

1. Trade-offs inherent in choosing to measure either organizational inputs, processes, or outputs as defined by the organizational process model
2. Implications in choosing to use management information for decision making, control, or learning
3. Conflicts in the use of this management information for achieving profit goals and strategies

ORGANIZATIONAL PROCESS MODEL

Performance measurement and control information can be understood only by reference to some model of underlying organizational processes. In other words, managers must understand the processes by which inputs are converted to outputs. All organizational processes can be decomposed into (1) inputs such as information, material, energy, labor, and support services that are needed to create a product or service, (2) a transformation process that consumes these inputs to create or sustain something of value, and (3) outputs in the form of intermediate or final products or services. This chain is pictured in Figure 4–2.

Consider these examples:

- A clerk at Boston Retail opens a box of incoming sweaters, applies price tags, updates inventory records, and arranges the merchandise on display racks. The *inputs* to her work are the sweaters, tags, and her effort, as well as the storeroom and physical display space. The transformation *process* includes the application of tags, updating of records, and movement of goods from the storeroom to the store shelves. The *output* is the availability of fresh, sorted, and priced merchandise ready for sale.
- An automobile assembly line accepts parts, energy, and computer instructions as *inputs* and transforms these inputs through a *process* as each automobile proceeds down the

FIGURE 4–2   Inputs-Process-Outputs Model

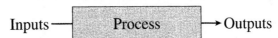

line to have fixtures and engines installed. At the end of the line, a complete automobile emerges as *output*.

- A division manager studies an income statement for the past month. She focuses on the *inputs* or resources consumed by her division (such as materials, depreciation—as a proxy for capital utilization—and overhead costs), the efficiency of the *processes* by which these resources were transformed into product (e.g., gross margin ratio), and the *outputs* (such as sales and inventory).

This basic inputs→process→outputs model is generic, so we could easily create examples for a machine, a factory, an individual worker, a team, or an entire business. The principles are the same: absorb inputs, transform them through productive processes, and create outputs of value (either as inputs to downstream organizational processes or as products or services delivered to customers).

In all of these cases, managers are responsible for ensuring that (1) inputs are appropriate to the tasks at hand and are adequate in quality and quantity, (2) the transformation process is efficient, and (3) the outputs meet specifications. To meet these responsibilities, managers can measure and monitor inputs, processes, and outputs in both nonfinancial and financial terms. Examples of some nonfinancial and financial internal measures are shown in Table 4–1 for:

- development of a new product (inputs include customer ideas, engineering designs, prototyping, and production setups)
- order processing (inputs include sales and marketing campaigns, order-entry clerical labor, and computer processing)
- parts manufacture (inputs include externally sourced components, energy, machine processing capability, and direct and supervisory labor)

For a manager to gain control over any of these processes, however, knowledge about inputs, processes, and outputs is often not enough. How would you respond if

TABLE 4–1 Examples of Nonfinancial and Financial Measures

	INPUT MEASURES	PROCESS MEASURES	OUTPUT MEASURES
Non-Financial Measures for:			
(a) New Products	# of engineering hours	# of product delivery milestones achieved	# of new products introduced
(b) Order Processing	# of telephone answering staff	Order completion time	# of orders processed
(c) Parts Manufacture	# of components meeting specifications	Setup time	% of units meeting standard
Financial Measures for:			
(a) New Products	Labor and material $	$ cost of prototyping	% of sales $ from new products
(b) Order Processing	Clerical labor $	$ cost of backorder handling	$ cost per order processed
(c) Parts Manufacture	$ cost of components	Setup $ cost, cost of rework	$ cost per unit

someone said that production for the week was 11,642 units? Was this good or bad? You could not tell, of course, unless you had a standard or benchmark as a point of reference. Your answer would differ depending on whether the performance expectation was 11,000 units or 12,750 units.

To *gain control* through a cybernetic process, therefore, we must add two additional ingredients beyond an understanding of inputs, processes, and outputs. We also must have (1) a standard or benchmark against which to compare actual performance and (2) a feedback channel to allow information on variances to be communicated and acted upon. These two critical additions to the cybernetic control model are illustrated in Figure 4–3.

An output **standard** or **benchmark** is a formal representation of performance expectations. **Ex ante** performance standards (those set in advance) may be created by reference to efficiency or effectiveness criteria for any measurable data—cost accounting data, quality specifications, budgets and profit plans, productivity data, and so on.

With preset standards at hand, a manager can assess how well inputs have been transformed into outputs. The Boston Retail store manager may compare the 162 items that the sales clerk stocked on the shelf during a two-hour period against a standard of 75 items per hour. This comparison indicates either a high level of effort (relative to past experience) or an unusually efficient worker. The shift supervisor in the auto assembly plant may look at a report that shows the number of automobiles produced on his shift as compared with the number produced during each shift over the past week. A shortfall will cause him to investigate further to understand the reasons. Similarly, the division manager compares the actual profit performance of her division against budgeted profit to ascertain the magnitude of any deviations.

However, having a performance standard or benchmark is, in itself, not sufficient. There must be a way of *using* the data—comparing outputs with standards and using the resulting **variance information** to change the inputs or process to ensure that performance standards will be met in the future. Thus, the second ingredient is a feedback channel coupled with an understanding of how adjustments to inputs and process are likely to influence outcomes.

Feedback is the return of variance information from the *output* of a process to the *input* or *process* stages so that adjustments can be made to maintain desired levels of performance or control the stability of a system (Figure 4–3). We all use feedback systems when we watch the speedometer of our cars (output information) and compare this

FIGURE 4–3   Cybernetic Feedback Model

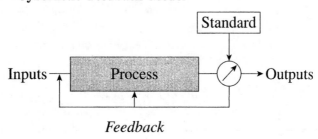

Feedback

information with posted highway speed signs (pre-set standards) to determine whether we need to accelerate or slow down to keep the car moving at our desired speed (process adjustment). An automatic speed control equipped on many automobiles automates this process and frees our attention from having to constantly monitor the speedometer. The thermostat in our homes, or any number of automatic controllers in a production line, operate in similar ways. (Anticipating a discussion later in the book, what do you think the effect of these cybernetic feedback systems is on return on management effort?)

Feedback information—the backbone of performance measurement and control systems—can be used in many ways. The manager at Boston Retail can use feedback information about one clerk's superior performance to learn how other clerks may do their jobs better; the assembly line's shift supervisor can discuss information about production shortfalls with the foremen to understand what remedial steps have been taken; and the division manager can order cuts on maintenance spending to try to meet profit-plan targets.

THE CHOICE OF WHAT TO CONTROL

If you look again at the diagram in Figure 4–3, you will notice that a manager might choose to gather information about (1) inputs, (2) the process itself, or (3) outputs. In fact, a manager can, and must, choose among these three categories to determine *where* he or she will devote attention in attempting to ensure that goods and services are produced in accordance with expectations.

For example, to satisfy herself that the sales clerk is working diligently in stocking the shelves, the Boston Retail store manager has two options: she can actually watch the clerk work to see if she is working at an appropriately energetic level, or she can later monitor the outcome of the clerk's efforts—by counting the number of sweaters placed on the shelves and observing if quality of the display meets expectations.

The assembly plant supervisor also has two choices: to count the number of finished automobiles as evidence that the process is proceeding according to plan, or to continually monitor the inputs and the process itself to ensure that automobiles are being assembled without delay. The choice between gathering information on inputs, process, or outputs is fundamental to the performance-control process. How, then, should managers choose?

As a starting point, we can state that *information about inputs is necessary, but rarely sufficient, for control.* For example, managers pay a great deal of attention to the quality of people who are hired and trained, to the nature and quality of material inputs, and to the level of parts inventories. This is especially true when inputs are costly relative to the value of outputs, such as the use of rare metals in electronics or diamonds in jewelry products. However, having high-quality inputs will not guarantee a good product or service. To ensure that these valuable inputs are transformed into high-quality outputs, *managers must focus their performance measurement and control activities on either the transformation process itself or the outputs being produced.*

Assuming that a manager knows the nature of desired outputs (as we shall discuss shortly, this is not always the case), there are four criteria that must be considered in making this choice: (1) technical feasibility of monitoring and measurement, (2) understanding of cause and effect, (3) cost, and (4) desired level of innovation.

1. Technical Feasibility of Monitoring and Measurement

In considering the *technical feasibility* of monitoring and measurement, managers must determine whether it is even possible to monitor a process directly or, alternatively, to measure its outcomes. In some cases it is possible to observe processes; in others, it is not. Watching an assembly line worker is not difficult. Nor is visiting a McDonald's location to ensure that service and cleanliness standards are being met. However, watching a mid-level manager as she goes about her tasks—attending meetings, answering telephone calls, visiting with customers, preparing plans and budgets—is impractical. Similarly, some outputs—production units, invoices processed, linear feet of pipe—are possible to quantify and measure. Others, such as goodwill or research productivity, are much more difficult to measure.

A manager can choose to monitor process directly only if it is possible to observe production or service processes in action. Watching a sales clerk stock the shelves of a retail store is easy and will lead to the desired outcome of a fully stocked merchandise array. The retail store manager can easily observe the work of the store clerk to ensure that it is progressing satisfactorily. However, the division manager reading an income statement cannot observe the many intricate processes that go into creating the inflows and outflows reflected on the income statement. It is just not possible to be everywhere at once—observing supplies being ordered, products being created, bills being paid, facilities being used, and all the myriad activities that underlie the financial statements. Instead, because she cannot physically observe processes, she must focus on outputs.

The flip side of the same coin is that *a manager can choose to monitor outcomes only if it is possible to measure production or service outputs accurately.* For example, a daily sales report provides accurate quantitative data about the success of each salesman. The sales report is a sufficient indicator of the efforts and contribution of individual salespeople. However, what would the daily output report look like for a research scientist? In this case, it is not possible to measure outputs accurately (at least on a daily timetable), and other approaches must be adopted.

Thus, in some instances, managers may not have a choice about what types of information to receive. They may be forced to focus on either processes or outputs because information on the other variable is simply unavailable.

2. Understanding of Cause and Effect

The second criterion relates to the *understanding of cause and effect* in the chain of activities that leads to outputs. Even if it is possible to monitor processes directly, a manager may not understand the actions that lead to the desired outcomes. In a parts-assembly operation for electronic test equipment, for example, the relationship between cause and effect is clear. If parts are supplied in the proper quantity and quality, and if workers install and test those parts according to carefully laid-out procedures, a fully functioning piece of electronics equipment will be built. Based on engineering drawings, development of test procedures, the training of workers, and the successful manufacture of many similar units, managers can have high confidence that following the specified process will lead to the desired outcomes. Thus, managers can easily gather information to ensure that processes are operating according to instructions.

Consider, by contrast, attempts to secure a major construction contract to build a large commercial building. A team of salespeople work on the deal for more than a year—developing relationships, compiling cost and bid data, and working with architects and mortgage brokers. The complexity of the project precludes a complete ex ante understanding of the actions and behaviors that will lead to the desired outcome—winning the bid. Too many possibilities are uncertain. Managers and employees of the construction firm must decide how to increase the chance of winning the bid as circumstances unfold. Procedure manuals specifying the exact steps to be undertaken for each contingency are not possible. In this case, even though gathering information about actions and behaviors may be feasible, senior managers cannot have any confidence that following a set of prespecified activities will lead to success. Gathering information in attempts to monitor process, therefore, is wasted effort if the causal link to desired outputs is not well understood.

The same problem occurs in monitoring any creative work—that of a research scientist, software programmer, architect, or orchestra leader. *If a manager does not understand the cause-and-effect relationship between the transformation process and desired outcomes, monitoring processes is not feasible as the primary means of control.* Thus, even though it may be possible to directly observe the work of a research scientist in his lab, it is not feasible to monitor that behavior to ensure successful discovery efforts. The cause-and-effect relationship between the researcher's efforts and the discovery of new products is not well understood and cannot, therefore, be modeled or predicted with any degree of accuracy.

3. Cost

Notwithstanding the limitations described above, in many situations managers may reasonably choose to monitor *either* processes *or* outputs. Often, both are observable. In these circumstances, we must analyze the *relative cost* of generating information about processes or outputs. Cost in this instance has two components: (1) the costs of generating and processing information and (2) lost opportunity or damages resulting from *not* generating information. The latter cost depends on the importance of securing the desired outcomes.

As an example, consider the plight of a sales manager who wishes to gather information on the activities of a sales representative. He can choose to gather information on the adequacy of the sales process by accompanying the sales rep on all his weekly visits or he can review outputs by perusing a weekly sales report. Which of these two options will he pick? In this instance, using the sales report is much more economical of the manager's time, and this alternative will be chosen. This example is typical—monitoring outputs is usually less time consuming than monitoring process. *All things being equal, therefore, managers will choose to monitor outputs to conserve their time and attention.*

In some instances, however, the important cost is not the cost of monitoring; it is related to the cost of *not monitoring* a critical process. Consider NASA managers responsible for the launch of a space shuttle. They may choose to monitor either the process of launch controllers working step-by-step through authorized procedures or they may measure only the output—whether or not the launch was successful. In this instance, because of the high cost of a launch failure to the space program, it is a safe bet that managers will choose to measure processes very carefully. As a general principle, *whenever safety or quality is a critical criterion of effectiveness, managers will choose to gather information about, and monitor directly, the transformation process itself.*

4. Desired Level of Innovation

After analyzing relative cost, there is one last consideration—often the most important from a managerial perspective—in choosing whether to monitor process or outputs: the effect on innovation. Which choice—monitoring process or monitoring outputs—yields the most innovation? The least innovation?

Start with the choice that yields the least innovation. Standard operating procedures, job descriptions, and manuals specify in great detail how a task is to be performed. Supervisors can look over their employees' shoulders to ensure that they are doing what is expected, and information on conformance to policies and procedures can be collected regularly. By telling people *what to do* and ensuring that they do just that, we limit freedom of action. People are precluded from experimenting; they cannot innovate and try new things. Therefore, *if managers desire to limit innovation, they will choose to control processes carefully by standardizing work procedures.*

Why would managers want to limit innovation? There are often important reasons related to quality, efficiency, and safety. When quality is an important consideration, there is always the risk that employees may introduce poor quality inputs, or service may not be conducted at the desired level of performance. Thus, fast-food franchisors like Burger King always insist on detailed written policies that specify minimum quality levels for key ingredients and standardized procedures and cooking times for preparing food. Corporate managers do not want to leave it up to local employees to experiment with these critical ingredients of competitive success.

When we think of efficiency in a large-scale semi-automated plant, we can understand why it may sometimes not be optimal to have assembly line employees tinkering with parts of the production line. In the absence of specialized training and/or specialized structures (autonomous teams or cells), managers leave this task to engineers and production-control specialists who can optimize across the entire line. Henry Ford, who invented the moving assembly line, used standardization of process to transform the production of automobiles from a craft industry into the highly efficient, mass-production industry that we know today.

Similarly, when speed—time to market—is an important competitive variable, managers may wish to standardize development processes to drive efficiency in the roll-out of new products. Thus, in many high-technology businesses, internal processes are standardized around product "platforms" for a full range of products. Enhancements and next-generation products can be rolled out quickly by minor modifications to the standardized product platforms.

Finally, the control of process becomes important where safety is critical to success—and the costs of failure are high. We have mentioned already the potential cost of failure at a NASA space shuttle launch. The same principle holds, for example, in the operation of a nuclear reactor. How significant are the costs of failure and a reactor meltdown? How much leeway for innovation and experimentation would you want managers to give nuclear plant operators? For this reason, where safety is critical, managers always limit discretion and innovation by installing very tight process controls.

Total Quality Management (TQM) is a popular approach that represents the standardization and streamlining of key operating processes to ensure high levels of quality and/or low defect rates. Under TQM methods, prescribed steps are followed to streamline and routinize key processes. By following TQM methods (the seven steps of quality), the potential for error and waste can be minimized.

Controlling process tightly assumes that senior managers know best—or at least have a broader perspective than the workers whose discretion is being limited. However, this is not always the case. The more competitive and fast moving the marketplace, the more important it becomes to give employees the freedom to experiment. If, instead of constraining initiative, managers wish to empower employees to exercise their energies in creating value, then managers must give workers the freedom to experiment. *For maximum innovation, managers do not focus on process, but instead focus on monitoring outputs.*

By controlling output rather than process, subordinates are free to create solutions and opportunities that managers had not previously contemplated. Employees are held accountable for output goals, but they are encouraged to experiment with inputs and processes to configure the transformation process in a way that best meets local market conditions. As a result, services can be tailored to meet the needs of specific customers. Process flows can be redesigned to streamline the transformation process.

Of course, there is risk in innovation. If people are to experiment, they must be allowed to make mistakes. Yet, some errors can be extremely costly. Employees may fail to meet customer expectations; they may squander resources; they may damage the business's reputation for quality. An important agenda for later chapters of this book, therefore, is understanding how to capture the benefits of innovation while, at the same time, controlling these inevitable strategic risks.

When All Else Fails

In rare circumstances, it may not be possible to obtain reliable information on *either* process *or* outputs. Processes may be poorly understood or unobservable. Outputs may be ill-defined or created at remote locations that are not easily susceptible to information gathering and oversight. In these exceptional cases, a manager must rely on other—mostly informal—means of control. For example, forest rangers commonly work alone in the wilderness areas for periods of several months. It is neither possible to observe their behavior nor to measure the value of their outputs as they engage in activities to further the mission of the Forest Service.

In these rare instances, managers have no choice but to rely primarily on the *control of inputs,* coupled with a high degree of training and indoctrination. Employees must be carefully selected, trained, and indoctrinated with the values and objectives of the organization. In some religious orders, for example, missionaries work in remote geographic locations. Because their work cannot be directly monitored or measured, they are sent out to the field only after careful selection, training, and indoctrination at the seminary. The same is true for expatriate managers of large multinational firms. These individuals are often selected because of their understanding and allegiance to the goals of the home office and then sent abroad—away from the direct oversight of their bosses—to supervise the activities and instill core values in foreign-based subsidiaries.

Table 4–2 summarizes the factors that managers must consider in determining whether to devote their attention to controlling inputs, processes, or outputs.

USES OF INFORMATION

Having discussed how managers choose among alternatives for collecting information on inputs, processes, or outputs, we must now consider what they should do with it. What is the purpose for gathering and analyzing this information? Management information can be used for a variety of purposes—planning, coordination, motivation, evaluation, and education. For our purposes, these differing uses can be categorized into five broad categories.

Information for:

- Decision making
- Control
- Signaling
- Education and learning
- External communication

We examine each of these uses in turn.

TABLE 4–2 Factors in Determining Whether to Control Inputs, Processes, or Outputs

CONTROL INPUTS WHEN:	CONTROL PROCESSES WHEN:	CONTROL OUTPUTS WHEN:
• It is impossible to monitor processes or outputs (i.e., monitor inputs as a last resort)	• Processes can be observed and/or measured	• Outputs can be observed and/or measured
• Cost of input is high relative to value of outputs (e.g., precious metals in computer chips)	• Cost of measuring/monitoring process is low	• Cost of measuring/monitoring outputs is low
• Quality and/or safety is important	• Standardization is critical for safety and/or quality	
	• Cause-and-effect relationships are understood	• Cause-and-effect relationships may not be well understood
	• Proprietary processes or process enhancements can result in strategic advantage	• Freedom to innovate is desired

Information for Decision Making

Managers routinely rely on information to *improve decision processes.* For example, a request for an increase in head count may cause managers to study profit plans and other performance data to ascertain what the effects are likely to be on the cost structure of the business. Before making their decision, managers are interested in understanding how additional employees (an increase in the level of inputs) will affect service processes and outputs. Similarly, a decision to add a new line to a production facility may hinge on an analysis of performance data that provides insight into the economics and profitability of the business. In each of these cases, information about cause-and-effect relationships is used to bring economic facts to bear on the decision.

Managers use information for decision making in two broad categories: (1) information for planning and (2) information for coordination. **Planning** is the process of setting aspirations through performance goals and ensuring an adequate level and mix of resources to achieve those goals. In simple terms, **plans** are a road map for the business.

Dell Computers

Dell Computer Corporation was founded in 1984 by 19-year-old Michael Dell, with the innovative concept of selling custom-built PCs directly over the telephone. After going public in 1988, Dell Computer's revenue grew at 67% and earnings at 63% annually. By 1992, the company posted $2 billion in sales, and sales for 1993 were expected to reach $3 billion. However, in the second quarter of 1993, the company announced its first loss.

What happened? The astounding growth had outpaced performance measurement and control systems. The turn of bad luck began in November 1992 with the abrupt resignation of the chief financial officer. Then, Dell Computer lost $38 million in the second quarter of 1992 due to aggressive foreign exchange dealings. Finally, in May 1993, the launch of a series of new laptop computers, based on the unexpectedly outdated 386 chip, was canceled. For fiscal 1993, Dell reported a net loss of $36 million, or $1.06 a share, despite a 42% increase in sales to $2.8 billion. The company took a $91.4 million charge to earnings for inventory writedowns, the laptop problems, and restructuring.

Explaining its loss to the financial markets, the company said that management control systems and infrastructure had not kept pace with the tripling in sales. Management was overextended, and coordination problems between marketing and production left overvalued inventory in the warehouse. Dell was forced to renegotiate its debt agreements with its bankers to avoid default.

An analyst commented on Dell's problems: "Without [performance management and control] systems behind you, you can grow yourself into bankruptcy."

Sources: A. Osterland, "Dell: Nice Quarter, but . . . ," *Company Watch,* March 15, 1994, 20; and L. Kehoe, "Dell Stock Hit by Gloomy Second Quarter," *Financial Times,* July 15, 1993, 24; Palmer, Jay, "Dell Computer: Goodbye, Buzzards," *Barron's* 74, Issue 42, October 17, 1994, 22–24.

As we shall see in Part II of the book, performance measurement and control systems play a central role in mapping future direction by giving managers quantitative information for setting goals and the ability to price out their plans.

Coordination refers to the ongoing ability to integrate disparate parts of a business to achieve objectives. As businesses become more complex, coordination becomes both more important and more difficult. The outputs of one unit are often the inputs to another unit (for example, when the output of the customer order department is input to the purchasing department). In any customer-focused business, the work of marketing, sales, production, and distribution must be coordinated like a complex jigsaw puzzle. Customers must receive current information about new product offerings; manufacturing capabilities must be sufficient to fulfill demand; and internal administrative functions must be structured and staffed to adequately support the business. Information on inputs, processes, and outputs for many different work units and functions is critical to line up and coordinate these resources.

Information for Control

Managers use information for **control** when they use feedback to ensure that inputs, processes, and outputs are aligned to achieve organizational goals. Managers most commonly use feedback information for control purposes to motivate and evaluate employees. (The principles are equally applicable to inanimate objects such as a machine.)

Profit plans and variance information play a critical role in the **ex post evaluation** of performance by comparing actual effort and outcomes against expectations. Profit plans and performance goals often provide important benchmarks of accomplishment. Income statements and performance reports provide the actual data on performance. These feedback data can be used to evaluate the performance of individuals and the businesses for which they work.

Information in the form of output goals, such as profit plan goals or performance targets, can be a powerful tool to motivate employees to adjust inputs, processes, and outputs to achieve organizational goals. Such motivation may be either **extrinsic**—the anticipation of tangible rewards such as money or promotion as an incentive for performance—or **intrinsic**—internally generated inducements for performance arising from such feelings as personal accomplishment. As we shall discuss later, both extrinsic and intrinsic motivation are influenced directly by performance measurement and control techniques.

We must remember, however, that the use of information for control is inextricably linked to assumptions that managers make about human behavior in organizations. In Chapter 1, we set out assumptions that guide the analysis of this book. We assume that people are multifaceted in their response to the opportunities that are offered by organizations: they want to contribute and achieve, be rewarded and recognized for their accomplishments, do what is right, and have some opportunity to innovate and exercise their creative capacities.

Yet, these same opportunities that release human potential create risk. Some employees may not share the goals of management, or they may actively work in their own self-interest to the detriment of the firm. Others, although well meaning, may be ill-equipped to make the correct choice when faced with difficult trade-offs and unyielding pressures for performance.

Managers need to be aware of the risks that they are creating so they can adequately control and manage these risks. Assessing and calibrating these danger signals relies on special information and risk analysis techniques. Information is needed to diagnose potential risks and highlight problem areas. Information about operations risk, asset impairment risk, business risk, and franchise risk must be collected and reported regularly to managers. We will examine this further in later chapters.

Information for Signaling

Information is used for **signaling** when managers send cues throughout the organization about their preferences, values, and the type of opportunities that they want employees to seek and exploit. The use of information for signaling is predicated on a simple fact that we will rely on later in the book: everyone watches what the boss watches. Employees throughout the organization are looking for cues as to what is important and where they should be focusing their energy and attention. To avoid embarrassment and ensure that their actions are those desired by top management, employees will try to understand what information is important to their superiors. What pieces of information and what types of reports do their bosses focus on? What do they do with this information? What types of information do superiors ignore, even though it is routinely produced?

By focusing systematically on certain types of information, and ignoring other information, all managers send strong signals to their employees about their preferences and values and the types of opportunities that they want people to focus on. A manager's behavior in studying and processing information—as observed by subordinates who are challenged to explain data and discuss its meaning—becomes a powerful indicator of what is important and what will be rewarded.

Information for Education and Learning

Information is also used for *education and learning*—to train individual managers and employees and to enable the entire organization to understand changes in the internal and external environment that might affect it. For example, the information contained in performance measurement and control systems is important in educating managers on the economics of their business and the drivers of revenue, cost, and performance. All managers progress through developmental stages in which they become increasingly skilled in managing their businesses. Working with performance measures and control data—to plan and coordinate the business, to motivate and evaluate subordinates, and to signal preferences and priorities—is a powerful way for employees to learn how to leverage scarce resources to achieve their objectives. Employees are forced to study the relationship of outputs to inputs, and to understand the key drivers of the firm's profit goals and strategies.

Information can also be important in supporting organizationwide learning. Profit plans and performance measurement data, for example, can inform managers about the effects of changes in the competitive environment. This information may be used subsequently for planning and control, or it may be used to alert managers of pending opportunities or problems in the business and the need to remain vigilant.

Ritz-Carlton: Using Information Systems to Better Serve the Customer

The Ritz-Carlton Hotel Company and Four Seasons Hotels are the two dominant brands in luxury hotels in North America. Ritz-Carlton senior executives believed that it would be extremely difficult to grow through geographic expansion or by competing head-on with Four Seasons. Therefore, Ritz-Carlton managers decided to focus on finding new ways of using information to differentiate their service. The aim was to build seamless, customer-driven service systems that could anticipate a guest's needs and preferences and, at the same time, react instantly to correct any service error or satisfy any complaint.

Ritz-Carlton developed a systematic process for capturing the unique preferences of each of its customers. When staff members engage in conversations with guests, they listen for comments such as, "I really appreciate it when the beds are made and the bathroom is clean when I come back from breakfast." Staff members also note when guests like extra pillows or an unusual beverage. The guest service coordinator collects the guest preferences and enters this information into a database for all Ritz-Carlton guests. Any service problem experienced by a guest is also entered into the database.

The Ritz-Carlton guest information system enables Ritz-Carlton to provide a unique level of personalized service—consistent across its properties—which is a distinct competitive advantage for this luxury hotel.

Source: Norman Klein, W. Earl Sasser, and Thomas Jones, "The Ritz-Carlton: Using Customer Information Systems to Better Serve the Customer," Harvard Business School Case No. 395–064, Rev. May 4, 1995.

Information for External Communication

The previous discussion has focused on the use of performance measurement and control information inside the firm. There is one important additional use of this information—for **external communication** to constituents who have a vested interest in the direction and success of the firm.

These constituents fall into three groups: providers and potential providers of capital (lenders, stockholders, and investment analysts), providers and potential providers of goods and services (suppliers and business partners), and existing and potential customers. Each of these groups wants to know about the future prospects of the firm for different reasons. Lenders, owners, and analysts want to understand the business strategy so they can evaluate the likelihood of its success and the amount of economic value that the firm is likely to generate. Suppliers and business partners are interested in the ability of the firm to honor its commitments—both in the short and the long term. Customers want to know if the firm will be able to support its products and services in the future.

Managers use profit plans and performance information to communicate this information externally. Numbers speak louder than words to investors, suppliers, and customers. In meetings with stockholders, lenders, analysts, business partners, and important customers, managers refer to and share business plans and current performance data.

We discuss how managers use profit plans and performance information to communicate externally in later chapters.

CONFLICTS IN THE USE OF MANAGEMENT INFORMATION

As we move through the analyses of this book and learn how to use information effectively for performance measurement and control, we must be sensitive to the unit of analysis. The same information may be used quite differently for different accountability units. As described in the previous chapter, an accountability unit might be a machine, an individual, a department, a division, or a business.

Imagine that a manager is working with productivity numbers—say number of units produced per week. He or she might take weekly production data related to an individual machine and use it for *decision making* (Do we have enough excess capacity to accept this new order?), *control* (Is the machine operating within specifications?), or for *learning* (Have the new resin pellets allowed us to increase the throughput on this

---

Communicating Profit Plan Targets at Guidant

Guidant Corporation was created in 1994 when pharmaceutical giant Eli Lilly & Company decided to spin off all its medical-devices divisions into one stand-alone company. Guidant designs, produces, and distributes medical products, including pacemakers, defibrillators, catheters, and devices for minimally invasive surgery. In December 1994, Lilly sold 20% of Guidant's stock in the market in an initial public offering, and in September 1995, the remaining 80%.

Guidant top managers believed that communicating and meeting profit-plan targets was critical to build their reputation in the capital markets. Top managers wanted to demonstrate that they understood the competitive forces and could outperform their industry. They believed that the best way to show that they had mastered the situation was to share very specific profit plans with the investment community that detailed expected performance for each line of the plans, including sales, cost of goods sold, operating expenses, R&D expenses, and expected profits.

In each quarterly presentation to analysts, top managers compared actual results to date and expected year-end figures with their original profit plan. Any difference was thoroughly explained to demonstrate their control of the situation and build their reputation as a team that delivered on their promises. Investors have handsomely rewarded Guidant's capability to meet its profit plan by doubling its stock price in less than a year, ahead of its competitors.

Source: Robert Simons and Antonio Dávila, "Guidant Corporation: Shaping Culture Through Systems," Harvard Business School Case No. 198–076, 1998.

machine?). In this example, because the machine is inanimate, there is no conflict between the various uses of information.

Now take exactly the same productivity information—weekly production data—and relate it to an individual worker. Now—when the accountability unit is a human being—we must separate how the information is used by the individual for decision making and how the same information is used for control by the manager responsible for that person's performance. Focus first on the employee. The production worker can use weekly productivity information for decision making (When should the line be stopped to change over to a new run?), for control (How should I budget my time to increase my productivity?), for education (Which parts of this information should I share with others to teach or compare?), and for learning (How does the output of this new production technique compare with previous periods?).

The picture is complicated, however, because the same productivity information will also be used by superiors for motivation and control of the employee's work effort. In this case, the performance information will be used for setting goals, communicating expectations, and judging performance. For the first time, there is a serious potential for conflict.

Conflict arises because of the different biases introduced into information by the manager as he or she attempts to use it to achieve multiple purposes. To motivate workers, the manager may desire to *inflate* performance goals to challenge workers and thereby ensure that they exert maximum effort. However, the workers may know that any improvements in production methods created by workers, through innovation or hard work, may cause their performance goals to be ratcheted upward—more effort will be expected in the future. Therefore, the workers may have an incentive to *understate* actual performance. At the same time, the boss will want to use the information for early warning if key processes go out of control. To be effective as early warning, however, the manager will want to receive variance information based on relatively *low performance standards* to ensure that feedback information is sent early. The manager will also want to use this same performance information for decision making (Should this machine be overhauled?) and learning (Has this worker created a new way of configuring the machine that reduces scrap?). For these uses the manager would like the information to be as *accurate* as possible—with no distortion for motivational or early warning purposes.

This simple example illustrates that when information is applied to the control of an individual or a team, inevitable conflicts are introduced because information has the potential to affect individual and team performance goals and rewards. A fundamental distinction must be made, therefore, between the use of information for the measurement and control of *people* and the use of the same information for the measurement and control of inanimate objects or *business units*. The same information (for example, productivity figures) can be used to assess the performance of a department (a work unit) or of the manager who is responsible for running that work unit. However, whenever information is used to evaluate the performance of individuals, it is subject to distortion.

TABLE 4–3 Potential Distortion and Bias in Performance Information Use

PURPOSE OF PERFORMANCE INFORMATION	INFORMATION BIAS DESIRED BY MANAGERS
Decision making	None. Attempt to gather most-accurate information for planning and control purposes.
Motivation	Inflate performance expectations to create stretch targets for employees.
Early warning	Lower minimum-acceptable performance standards to expose variables that may require remedial action.
Evaluation	Adjust reported performance for factors outside a subordinate's control.
External communication	Lower performance expectations to be sure that goals can be achieved and credibility maintained.

Table 4–3 summarizes some of the conflicts and biases that are inherent in the use of management information for differing purposes. We will discuss this topic more fully later.

CHAPTER SUMMARY

Information for performance measurement and control is essential to the effective functioning of organizations. Managers use this information to communicate goals up, down, and across their organizations, and later to monitor performance against those goals.

Using information requires choices about what to monitor and measure. Managers can focus their attention on inputs, processes, and outputs based on factors such as measurability, cost, understanding of cause and effect, and desired levels of innovation. Management information can be used for various purposes: decision making, control, signaling, education and learning, and external communication. As we shall see in later chapters, these different uses require different techniques and design principles.

In the past, performance measurement and control information has suffered from a number of deficiencies: Information was often too limited in scope; information was too aggregated and general to be of much use for effective decision making and control; information was late; and information was unreliable.[1]

Today, with better information technology and a better understanding of how to use performance measurement and control systems effectively, these limitations have been largely overcome. In the remainder of the book, we outline the tools, techniques, and processes that allow effective managers to use performance measurement and control information to implement strategy.

---

[1] Henry Mintzberg, *Impediments to the Use of Management Information* (New York: National Association of Accountants, 1975).

PART II

Creating Performance Measurement Systems

C H A P T E R

5

Building a Profit Plan

Profit plans are the principal tools that managers use to price their business and operating plans, make trade-offs between different courses of action, set performance and accountability goals, and evaluate the extent to which business performance is likely to meet the expectations of different constituents.

The terms profit plan and budget are often used interchangeably. A **budget** refers to the resource plans of any organizational unit that either generates or consumes resources. The term profit plan is reserved for units that generate profits—stand-alone business units that generate and are held accountable for both revenues and expenses. Thus, managers might refer to the budget of the maintenance department (which generates expenses, but no revenues), or to the budget of the sales-order department (which generates revenues without full accountability for expenses), or to the profit plan of a financial services business (which has full accountability for sales, operating expenses, and profit).

Regardless of terminology, the preparation of profit plans and budgets follows a consistent pattern in most organizations. Several months before the beginning of each fiscal year (the normal twelve-month operating cycle of the business), managers develop their profit plans or budgets. The objectives of this planning process are threefold:

- *To translate the strategy of the business into a detailed plan to create value.* This process requires managers to agree on assumptions, evaluate strategic alternatives, and arrive at a consensus regarding a business strategy and its ability to satisfy the demands of different constituencies.
- *To evaluate whether sufficient resources are available to implement the intended strategy.* Companies need resources to finance their current operations (operating cash) and to invest in new assets for future growth (investment cash).
- *To create a foundation to link economic goals with leading indicators of strategy implementation.* To implement strategy successfully, financial goals must be linked with key business input, process, and output measures.

To build a profit plan, managers need to answer three different questions relating to the economics of their business.

First, managers must ask, does the organization's strategy create economic value? Strategies may sound attractive when described by proponents in bright words and colorful phrases, but strategies need to be translated into accounting numbers to evaluate how they actually create value. Does it pay to invest in a new strategic opportunity? How attractive are different strategic alternatives? Boston Retail has been successful with its line of clothing for women college students. However, the fashion market continually evolves, creating new opportunities and eliminating ideas that move out of fashion. The strategy has to adapt to these changes if the firm is to continue to create economic value and survive.

Second, managers must ask, does the organization have enough cash to fund the strategy and remain solvent throughout the year? All companies need cash to pay their suppliers, but cash may be in short supply if there is a lag between the sale of goods or services and the collection of cash from customers. In some industries, supermarkets for example, companies collect cash from customers before they need to pay their suppliers; however, this is the exception. Most companies need to plan cash flow carefully to estimate cash reserves and potential borrowing requirements.

Finally, managers must ask, does the organization create enough value to attract the financial resources that it needs to fund long-term investment in new assets? Growth requires productive assets, and acquiring those assets requires investors who are willing to lend resources to a company. Investors will only commit their money to a company if they are likely to receive an adequate return. Boston Retail is expanding and it needs to attract additional financial resources to grow. Before it can convince investors to provide capital to the company, Boston Retail needs to show an attractive return on investment.

THREE WHEELS OF PROFIT PLANNING

To answer the above questions and design a profit plan, three distinct analyses must be performed. Figure 5–1 shows the three cycles that managers must analyze to build a profit plan: the **profit wheel,** the **cash wheel,** and the **ROE wheel.** In the following sections we look in detail at each of these "wheels." Although we introduce each wheel separately, Figure 5–1 illustrates that these wheels are interlocking like a set of mechanical gears—all three wheels turn simultaneously. Adjusting or changing any assumption or number on any of the wheels causes a change in all the other variables. The wheels move in lockstep like the gears of a mechanical clock.

The foundation of profit planning is built upon **assumptions** about how the future will look. Will the market grow over the next year? How will customers respond to our new product offering? What will competitors do to try to capture market share? Will we be able to expand our manufacturing capabilities to support new growth opportunities? What if we increase our level of advertising? Managers need to agree on assumptions such as these to create a profit plan.

Sometimes, top managers already possess most of the relevant information needed to prepare a profit plan. If so, assumptions can be established at the top and communicated down the organization. However, information is usually dispersed more widely throughout the organization: Sales people often know best what specific customers desire; production managers have information on how to reduce costs and increase quality; the purchasing department is in the best position to understand suppliers' relationships; top management has the organizational and industry perspective to assess opportunities and threats. Accordingly, to incorporate all this information, the *profit planning process* must span the whole organization and involve frequent interactions among different hierarchical levels and departments.

FIGURE 5–1   Three Wheels of Profit Planning

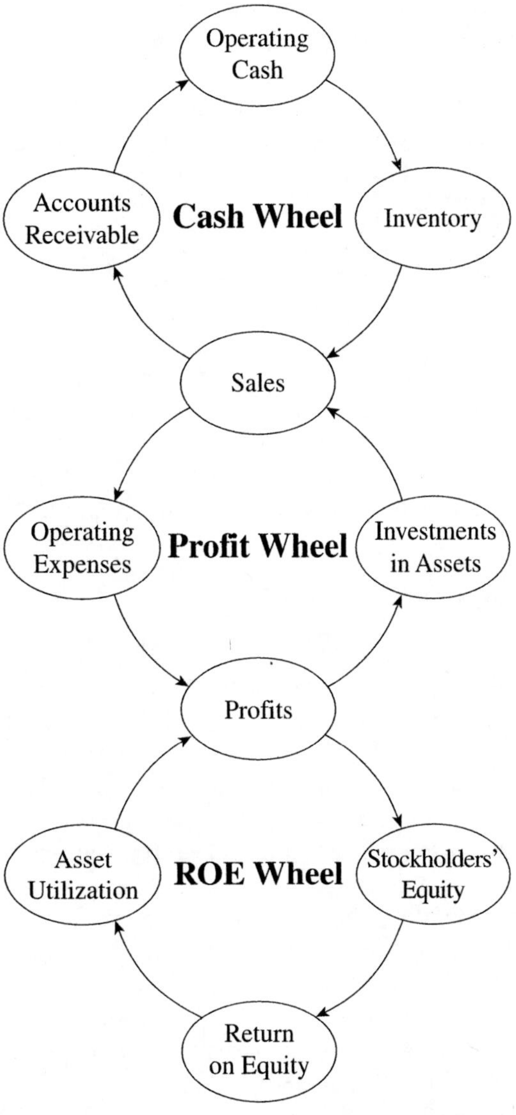

Source: Robert Simons, "Templates for Profit Planning," Boston: Harvard Business School Case 9-199-032, 1998.

The profit plan provides information on the economic resources available to the company and helps managers evaluate the trade-offs facing them. Different strategies require different investments. For Boston Retail, the investment plan for opening new clothing stores in New York is not the same plan needed to add furniture to the product line. Perhaps managers would like to invest in all of these alternatives, but resources are limited and managers are forced to make trade-offs. It is not easy to choose: Some managers at Boston Retail may favor geographical expansion, whereas others may prefer to diversify into furniture.

By the end of the profit planning process, people throughout the organization have agreed on the direction of the company. Knowing where the company is going facilitates coordination among the various departments. For example, if the profit plan reflects the introduction of a new product line, employees know that they must include the necessary resources in their own plans to support the success of the new initiative.

In many instances, the profit plan is also used to set performance goals. Managers are held accountable for the achievement of targets defined in the profit plan. As discussed briefly in the previous chapter, when the profit plan is later used for performance evaluation, a tension emerges. If the manager knows that the information disclosed as part of the profit planning process will be used for ex post evaluation, he or she may attempt to build slack into profit plan targets to increase the probability of a favorable evaluation. The undesirable side effect of this biasing behavior is distorted information, which may impede strategy implementation. Because of the inherent conflict between information sharing and performance evaluation, some companies tend to downplay the role of the profit plan as a performance evaluation tool, especially when lower-level managers possess important market and competitive information that must be shared to allow the business to adapt to changing conditions.

THE PROFIT WHEEL

As all students of accounting know, value creation is measured by profit.[1] Without building a profit plan, managers cannot evaluate whether their intended strategy will generate value for shareholders. Moreover, without a profit plan, managers cannot estimate the economic impact of different strategic alternatives and, as a result, lack adequate information to decide among different courses of action.

The profit plan *summarizes the expected revenue inflows and expense outflows for a specified future accounting period* (typically one year). The outcome of this planning process is a financial document that uses the familiar format of an income statement. To build a profit plan, managers must analyze the profit wheel for the upcoming operating period. Usually, managers go back and forth, iteratively projecting sales, operating expenses, profits, and required investment in assets before the profit plan is acceptable (see Figure 5–2). Then, they work on the cash wheel and the ROE wheel to make sure that sufficient resources will be available to implement the profit plan. If there are not enough resources, they must go back to the profit wheel and repeat the planning process all over again.

Foundations of a Profit Plan

The starting point for any profit plan is a set of assumptions about the future. These assumptions describe the consensus among managers about how various markets—customer, supplier, and financial—will evolve in the future. The profit plan also reflects

---

[1] We defer to Chapter 8 a discussion of the relationship between economic value added and accounting income. For the purposes of this chapter, we consider accounting income as a measure of economic value created by the firm.

FIGURE 5–2   The Profit Wheel

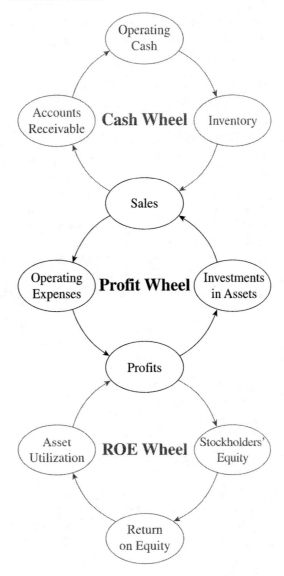

managers' beliefs about *cause-and-effect relationships*. For example, managers may decide to increase the level of advertising if they believe that it will cause a significant increase in the level of sales. Similarly, they may invest in training for their employees if
they believe that this expenditure will improve customer service or increase quality. Finally, the profit plan captures the commitment of managers to an intended strategy. For
example, the merger between Chemical Banking Corporation and Chase Manhattan
Corporation reflected the belief of managers in these two businesses that the banking industry had untapped economies of scale that the new company could capture.

Arriving at consensus often requires intensive interaction among managers. Different perspectives on market competition require sharing information and building a common view about the future of the company. Exhibit 5–1 shows the foundations for building Boston Retail's profit plan for 20X2: actual results of 20X1 with key assumptions for 20X2.

We next review the five steps in creating a profit plan using the profit wheel as illustrated in Figure 5–2.

Step 1: Estimate the Level of Sales

Most companies start building their profit plan by estimating the level of future sales. This is a logical starting point for two reasons: revenue growth is a major determinant of profit, and the level of operating expenses is often a function of sales volume. Projecting sales is a mixture of art and science; estimating sales volume accurately requires predictions about the impact of external factors and estimates of the effect of internal decisions, such as R&D spending, advertising, and investment in new assets. Sales forecasts are typically generated from sales force estimates, customer surveys, or from a jury of executives or other experts.[2] A good forecast also includes some measure of forecast error, perhaps in the form of a range. For both external and internal factors, a great deal of judgment is required.

To predict sales accurately, companies need to consider many of the external variables that we reviewed in Chapter 2 as part of the analysis of competitive market dynamics, including:

- Macroeconomic factors
- Government regulation
- Competitor moves
- Customer demand

External factors are often outside management's control, but estimating their impact is critical to all companies. For example, estimated car sales depend on predicted prospects for the economy. If potential car buyers are confident about their future income, they are more likely to purchase a new car. Similarly, projected sales for highly regulated European gas and electric utilities depend very much on the prices that are likely to be allowed by the government. The significant influence of macroeconomic factors and political decisions on the level of sales explains why managers pay so much attention to this information.

Competitors' actions and changes in customers' needs are also largely outside managers' control. However, understanding both factors are critical to defining the strategy of the company and designing the profit plan. Managers spend a lot of time evaluating competitors' actions, predicting changes in customers' demands, and judging how the company can capitalize on these events to gain competitive advantage in the marketplace.

In addition to these external factors, internal decisions also have a major impact on the expected level of sales. This is why we illustrate a circular **profit wheel:** sales

---

[2] Steven Nahmias, *Production and Operations Analysis,* (Chicago: Irwin, 1997), 60.

EXHIBIT 5–1
Boston Retail
20X1 Operating Results with Key Assumptions for 20X2

	20X1 ACTUAL (IN THOUSANDS OF DOLLARS)	KEY ASSUMPTIONS FOR 20X2
Income Statement		
Sales	$9,200	10% sales growth
Costs of goods sold	4,780	same % of sales as 20X1
Gross margin	4,420	
Wages and salaries	1,530	4% growth
Rent and facilities	840	5% growth
Advertising	585	same % of sales as 20X1
Administrative expenses	435	same % of sales as 20X1
Interest	72	estimated at 65
Depreciation	57	add depreciation of new assets
Training	38	2.5% of wages and salaries
Other	54	4% growth
Profit before taxes	809	
Income tax	283	35% of profit
Net profit	$ 526	

KEY BALANCE SHEET FIGURES	DECEMBER 31, 20X1	KEY ASSUMPTIONS FOR 20X2
Assets		
Cash	$ 208	Cash will stay at same % level of cash expenses
Accounts receivable	255	Accounts receivable at same % level of sales
Inventory	985	Inventory at same % of cost of goods sold
Property, plant, and equipment	1,854	Property, plant, and equipment increases by new investment
Other assets	325	Other assets up by 50%
Total assets	$3,627	
Liabilities		
Accounts payable	$ 209	Accounts payable at same % of cost of goods sold
Bank loan	1,180	Pay back debt of $100,000
Stockholders' equity	2,238	
Total liabilities and stockholders' equity	$3,627	

generate profits that are reinvested in assets to generate more sales. Over time, almost every decision in a company impacts the level of sales. However, managers consider most carefully those decisions that have direct influence on sales during the current planning period, such as:

- Mix and pricing of product categories
- Marketing programs
- New-product introductions and product deletions
- Changes in product quality and features
- Manufacturing and distribution capacity
- Customer service levels

Managers have discretion—indeed the responsibility—to set these variables to reflect the agreed strategy. In fact, strategy provides the criteria for consistency in all these decisions.

Based on their analysis of the above factors, managers at Boston Retail estimate that sales volume will grow by 10% in the next year. Exhibit 5-1 illustrates that they are estimating 20X2 sales to be $10,120,000 ($9,200,000 × 110%).

Predicting Sales in an Uncertain World

With rapid product introductions and a proliferation in the number and variety of products offered, manufacturers and retailers are finding it increasingly difficult to accurately predict which of their products will sell and which will not. The accuracy of these estimates affect production plans and the level of expenditure for support functions. If they predict that sales will be higher than actual demand, managers will be left with excess inventory that must be marked down and potentially sold at a loss. If actual demand exceeds sales estimates, then the business will lose potential revenue and damage customer satisfaction as customers are frustrated by an out-of-stock item.

Companies have responded to this challenge in a variety of ways. Dell Computer Corporation has successfully developed a capability to respond extremely quickly to actual customer demand. In 1997 it kept only 12 days' worth of sales in inventory. Other companies have taken steps to dramatically reduce the number of products they sell to simplify the forecasting process.

In the highly volatile fashion skiwear industry, Sport Obermeyer developed a new way to improve the accuracy of its sales forecasts. It had always relied on a committee of company experts to estimate demand and used the average of the committee's predictions to forecast sales volumes for each of its new parkas. Sport Obermeyer analyzed the forecasts for specific product items and found that the *variance* among the individual forecasts of committee members for a product was almost a perfect predictor of forecast accuracy. Using this new insight, it moved the production of the "accurate forecast" items (i.e., low variance among individual forecasts) to China, which required much longer lead times for production, and it delayed the production of its high-variance-forecast items until some initial sales data from early in the season became available. Sport Obermeyer's new forecast system significantly reduced excess inventory costs and stock-outs to retailers.

Source: Steven Nahmias, *Production and Operations Analysis* (Chicago: Irwin), 81.

Step 2: Forecast Operating Expenses

After the expected level of sales is determined, the next task for managers is to estimate operating expenses. To make this estimate, different categories of operating expenses must be analyzed differently.

The first category of operating expense is **variable costs.** As the name suggests, *variable costs vary proportionally with the level of sales or production outputs.* Variable costs are typically estimated as a percentage of sales. To do so, managers must assume that the cause-and-effect relationships between inputs and outputs are constant over the relevant range of sales. That is, an increase in sales volume is assumed to lead to a proportional increase in the usage of inputs. Raw materials is an example of a variable cost in a manufacturing firm. If sales volume of a particular product increases by 10%, we can expect the level of raw material inputs to increase by 10%. Interest expense to cover short-term loans in a bank is another example of a variable cost. The more short-term loans that the bank makes to its customers, the more interest it earns (revenue), but also the more interest it pays to borrow that money (variable costs).

In forecasting variable costs, managers must determine the actual percentage number that relates each category of variable costs to sales. For example, managers may determine that material costs can be set at 24% of sales, labor costs at 18%, energy costs at 4% of sales, and so on. In most cases, a lower cost percentage is preferred (unless reducing variable costs forces higher fixed costs). There are several ways in which variable costs can be reduced as a percentage of sales:

- Taking advantage of economies of scale (e.g., installing one large machine in place of three smaller, less-efficient machines) and economies of scope (such as combining distribution channels for different products to eliminate redundant or underutilized resources)
- Improving operating efficiencies (for example, **re-engineering** or streamlining work flows to do the same work with fewer resources)
- Bargaining with suppliers to negotiate lower prices
- Redesigning products to lower their cost of production
- Increasing prices[3]

The second category of operating expenses is **nonvariable costs.** As the name implies, *nonvariable costs do not vary directly with the level of sales.* However, it would be a mistake to think that they do not vary at all (thus, we avoid calling them fixed costs). These costs are typically large and have become a higher percentage of the operating expenses of most companies in recent years. Nonvariable costs are of three types:

- *Committed (or engineered) costs.* Some expenses are determined by previous management decisions and, therefore, are not subject to discretion during the current profit planning period. Depreciation is usually a committed cost because it depends on past investment decisions and company accounting policies. The salaries of managers, engineers, and long-term employees are normally also committed costs, as is the cost of a long-term lease.

---

[3] This alternative reduces variable costs in percentage terms because sales revenue—the denominator—goes up.

- *Discretionary costs.* In contrast to committed costs, the planned level of discretionary expenditures is open to significant debate during the planning process—and subsequent adjustment during the operating period. These are expenses that can be increased or decreased at will, almost without constraints. Advertising, employee training, and research programs are examples of discretionary expenses. Managers can invest as much as they wish if sufficient cash is available. However, managers usually use some guiding criteria to estimate level for these expenses. Some companies choose to set the level of discretionary expenditures by treating them as variable costs. For example, advertising expense is often set as a percentage of sales. Alternatively, managers may set expenditure levels based on industry practice or their assessment about the resource requirements needed to support the intended strategy or specific strategic initiatives. For example, if a business is differentiating its products based on exceptional service, it needs to invest more on employee training than a competitor that competes on low prices and minimal services.

- *Activity-based indirect costs.* The final set of operating expenses are *indirect costs.* Indirect costs cannot be traced directly to a product or service, but change with the level of specific underlying support activities. Examples of activity-based indirect costs include supervision, material handling, and billing costs. Traditionally, these types of cost have been described as "fixed." However, recent developments in cost accounting show that these expenses are not constant, as the word "fixed" implies. They may look fixed, especially if part of the expenses are committed, but their consumption varies with the level of some underlying activity. Most overhead costs, including administrative expenses, fall into this category. To estimate them, managers must identify indirect **cost drivers**—those activities that consume indirect resources. Increases in these cost drivers (for example, increases in customer order complexity or material handling) can be traced to growth in indirect expense levels, such as increased handling, setup, and shipping costs. If cost driver activities can be decreased, then managers can plan to save some money by using fewer resources to perform this activity. Using this approach—known as activity-based budgeting—managers authorize the supply of resources based on anticipated demand for cost driver activities.[4]

Step 3: Calculate Expected Profit

The difference between expected sales and expected operating expenses determines the amount of economic value that the company is expected to generate in the profit planning period. To assess this value, managers often estimate **NOPAT,** which stands for Net Operating Profit After Taxes, or **EBIAT,** which represents Earnings Before Interest and After Taxes.

These accounting estimates reveal the amount of resources generated during the accounting period that are potentially available for distribution to lenders and owners. Lenders, like banks, have a fixed claim on the profits of the business. They receive interest payments proportional to the amount of financial resources that they lend to the company. Given the expected levels of debt, managers can forecast the expected interest cost by multiplying the expected amount of debt on their balance sheet by the interest rates negotiated with the debt holders (adjusted for income tax effects).

Profit, also called **earnings** or **net income,** is the residual economic value *after* interest expense and income taxes (both of which are nondiscretionary payments).

---

[4] Activity-based costing is a topic covered in management accounting courses. It is outside the topic coverage of this book. For more information on activity-based budgeting, see Robin Cooper and Robert S. Kaplan, *Cost & Effect* (Boston: Harvard Business School Press), chap. 15.

Profit is the financial measure of the economic value that is available for distribution to the residual claimants—equity holders—or for reinvestment in the business. Profit is the most important number in evaluating the financial performance of any company.

Step 4: Price the Investment in New Assets

When managers have agreed on expected sales, operating expenses, and profit numbers, they have created the most important part of a profit plan: the expected income statement. However, the process of translating strategy into economic value does not end there. To finish the profit plan, managers must look at the required level of investment in new assets, including working capital such as inventory and accounts receivable.

As the recursive profit wheel shows, the predicted level of sales is itself determined by the level of assets available to generate those sales. Therefore, managers must decide the levels and types of investments that are required to support desired sales (and strategies). At this point in the process, assumptions about the levels and types of assets needed to support the profit plan must be backed up by an **asset investment plan.** The investment plan is another important tool to implement strategy.

There are two main types of assets for which managers must consider investment: *operating assets* and **long-term assets.** (The cash wheel that we study in the next section is used to determine the investment in operating assets needed by the company.) The proposed investment in long-term productive assets is called the **capital investment plan.** A capital investment plan must reflect and support the intended strategy because it often commits the company to a limited set of strategic alternatives. For example, in the late 1970s, Intel Corporation decided to invest resources in the design and production of microprocessors and to reduce its focus on commodity computer memories. Intel's capital investment plan included resources to develop microprocessors and to build manufacturing facilities. The plan reflected management's new strategy and ensured that sufficient resources would be in place to make that strategy a reality.

Exhibit 5–2 presents the 20X2 asset investment plan for Boston Retail, assuming no major changes in strategy. Anticipated growth in the business will require larger balances in accounts receivable ($26,000) and inventory ($98,000), although these requirements will be partially financed by an increase in accounts payable ($21,000). Some store displays also must be replaced and updated. Two capital initiatives are also planned: (1) a new computerized accounting system that will integrate purchasing, inventory record keeping, and SKU (stock keeping unit) management, and (2) an expansion of the warehouse to accommodate the increase in business.

Before we finish our brief introduction to the asset investment plan, we must mention how companies assess whether any single capital investment proposal is financially attractive. The most common investment evaluation technique is net present value. Finance books discuss this technique in depth because it is a basic tool in the finance toolbox. Any investment proposal that is included in the capital investment plan should meet these financial criteria or be included for compelling strategic reasons. We will have more to say about this in Chapter 7, when we discuss in detail how to create a capital investment plan.

EXHIBIT 5–2
Asset Investment Plan for Boston Retail

	NEW ASSETS NEEDED FOR 20X2 (THOUSANDS OF DOLLARS)
Working Capital	
Increase in accounts receivable	$ 26
Increase in inventory	98
Increase in accounts payable	(21)
Long-Term (Depreciable) Assets[a]	
New computerized management system	60
Store displays	80
Warehouse expansion	120
Total investment in new assets during 20X2	$363

---

[a] *For simplicity, assume that long-term assets have an average life of five years; all investments in long-term assets are made in January.*

Step 5: Close the Profit Wheel and Test Key Assumptions

The feedback loop among all the components of the profit wheel suggests that the profit planning process is not linear. Managers must go back and forth among the variables in the profit plan to ensure that it reflects the strategy and is attractive from an economic point of view. Of course, an electronic spreadsheet such as Excel can be used to link and integrate this process.

When managers have arrived at an acceptable expected profit, they usually perform a **sensitivity analysis** based on changes in sales or other key profit plan variables. The objective of a sensitivity analysis is to estimate how profit might change when underlying assumptions about the competitive environment or other predictions embedded in the base profit plan prove to be under- or overstated. Managers often develop three different scenarios: worst-case scenario, most likely scenario, and best-case scenario. Sales, operating expenditures, and capital acquisition plans are estimated for each scenario. For example, utility companies usually project at least three scenarios based on the severity of winter weather. The most likely scenario is an average winter based on typical temperatures for the region. The other two scenarios are based on the effects of an unusually mild winter and an unusually cold winter. For each scenario, utility companies build a profit plan, test its viability, and prepare action plans based on predicted outcomes of that scenario.

Exhibit 5–3 on pages 90–91 shows the profit plan for Boston Retail. Boston Retail managers have performed a sensitivity analysis by constructing two additional profit plans: one for a better-than-expected market growth rate of 15% (sales = $10,580,000), and another with a worse-than-expected market with no growth (sales = 20X1 sales = $9,200,000). These sales alternatives are illustrated at the top of the exhibit.

Sensitivity Analysis at Allied Signal

Lawrence Bossidy, CEO of Allied Signal, has strong opinions about profit planning: "One of the first things that struck me when I came here was that it was more or less accepted practice that you put a plan together and then missed it. We don't need meaningless targets. We need an operating plan that recognizes that underlying assumptions are often wrong and that provides options when that happens.

"Good finance people are the ones who can help give real meaning to operating plans. When you say you're going to get a 6% improvement in productivity, they're the ones who are supposed to ask where, What are the projects? When are they going to be done? How much money are they going to be providing? If we're going to grow by 5%, they ask the tough questions: Where are we going to grow? What products are going to grow by 5%? How are we going to get price increases? Good financial involvement is critical in constructing a sound operating plan; it really drives at the particulars."

Source: Noel M. Tichy and Ram Charan, "The CEO as Coach: An Interview with Allied Signal's Lawrence A. Bossidy," *Harvard Business Review* 73 (March–April 1995): 68–78.

CASH WHEEL

Before a profit plan can be accepted as feasible, managers must forecast whether the company will have enough cash to operate (cash wheel) and whether the return to investors is sufficiently attractive (ROE wheel). If either of these critical constraints is not met, then managers must go back to the drawing board and adjust the profit plan.

The cash wheel (Figure 5–3 on page 92) illustrates the operating cash flow cycle of a business: Sales of products and services to customers generate accounts receivable, which are eventually turned into cash; this cash is used to produce inventory, which in turn can be used to generate more sales. However, depending on the nature of the business, considerable time can elapse between the moment that the company disburses cash to purchase inventory and pay operating expenses until it receives cash from customers for goods and services received. During this period of time, the company may have to borrow from lenders to cover its ongoing operating and capital expenses.

Looking at the cash wheel, we can understand why a company may need more or less operating cash, depending on its industry and its strategy. High levels of inventory require more operating cash to finance the inventory. Similarly, if credit terms to customers are 60 days instead of 30 days, the company needs to borrow more from the bank to cover its cash outflows during the additional 30 days. Conversely, a company can reduce its operating cash by delaying payments to its suppliers, usually by negotiating better credit terms.

EXHIBIT 5–3
Boston Retail
Profit Plan for 20X2 Based on Existing Six Stores
(in thousands of dollars)

	20X1 ACTUAL	KEY ASSUMPTIONS FOR 20X2
Sales	$9,200	10% sales growth
Costs of goods sold	4,780	same % of sales as 20X1
Gross margin	4,420	
Wages and salaries	1,530	4% growth
Rent and facilities	840	5% growth
Advertising	585	same % of sales as 20X1
Administrative expenses	435	same % of sales as 20X1
Interest	72	estimated at 65
Depreciation	57	add depreciation of new assets
Training	38	2.5% of wages and salaries
Other	54	4% growth
Profit before taxes	809	
Income tax	283	35% of profit
Net profit	$ 526	

KEY BALANCE SHEET FIGURES	DECEMBER 31, 20X1	KEY ASSUMPTIONS FOR 20X2
Assets		
Cash	$ 208	Operating cash not less than 150
Accounts receivable	255	Accounts receivable at same % level of sales
Inventory	985	Inventory at same % of COGS
Property, plant, and equipment	1,854	Property, plant, and equipment increases by new investment
Other assets	325	Other assets same
Total assets	$3,627	
Liabilities		
Accounts payable	$ 209	Accounts payable at same % of COGS
Bank loan	1,180	Pay back debt of $300,000
Stockholders' equity	2,238	
Total liabilities and stockholders' equity	$3,627	

20X2 PROFIT PLAN	20X2 PROFIT PLAN (OPTIMISTIC SCENARIO 15% GROWTH)	20X2 PROFIT PLAN (PESSIMISTIC SCENARIO NO GROWTH)
$10,120	$10,580	$9,200
5,258	5,497	4,780
4,862	5,083	4,420
1,591	1,591	1,591
882	882	882
644	673	585
478	500	435
65	65	65
109	109	109
40	40	40
56	56	56
997	1,167	657
349	408	230
$ 648	$ 759	$ 427

DECEMBER 31, 20X2

$ 302	$ 361	$ 184
281	293	255
1,083	1,133	985
2,005	2,005	2,005
325	325	325
$ 3,996	$ 4,117	$3,754
$ 230	$ 240	$ 209
880	880	880
2,886	2,997	2,665
$ 3,996	$ 4,117	$3,754

FIGURE 5–3   The Cash Wheel

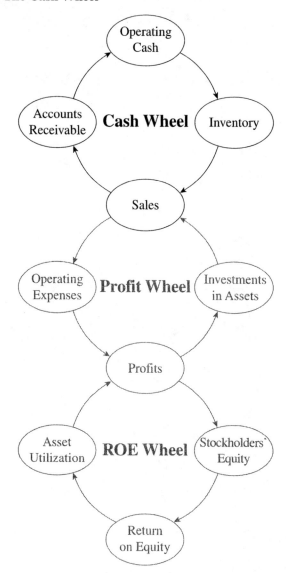

Forecasting cash needs is important for all businesses because companies have limited cash reserves and borrowing capacity. If managers project that the cash needed to operate the business exceeds cash reserves and maximum borrowing capacity, then the *profit plan is not feasible* and must be reworked. For example, fast-growing companies need a lot of cash to finance increases in working capital (inventory and accounts receivable) and the purchase of new productive assets such as machinery and equipment. However, existing debt may limit their borrowing capacity. If a company's borrowing capacity is limited to $500,000 and its profit plan requires $700,000 investment in new assets, then the profit plan is not feasible. To overcome this constraint, managers must choose to either revise their profit plan by reducing growth or, alternatively, they can consider issuing new equity to increase their cash reserves.[5]

The basic technique for computing the cash wheel is quite simple. The most intuitive way to estimate cash requirements is to forecast cash inflows and cash outflows for each specific time period. To estimate the operating cash required during a period of time, managers project the cash that they will receive—in most cases, from customers—and the cash that they will disburse—in paying suppliers, operating expenses, and for committed costs such as interest and lease payments. The basic formula is the following:

$$\text{Operating cash needed during a period} = \text{Cash received from customers} - \text{Cash paid to suppliers and operating expenses}$$

This is the method that most of us employ when budgeting our personal finances to determine whether we have sufficient cash flow to support our rent and car payments.

You may remember from your financial accounting course the name of this cash flow method: it is the **direct method.** Companies often use the direct method to estimate cash requirements for short periods of time—a day, a week, or a month. For each period, managers estimate cash that will be collected (cash inflows) and cash that will be paid out (cash outflows). If cash inflows are larger than cash outflows, then the cash on hand increases. If, however, the opposite holds—cash outflows exceed inflows—the company's cash position gets worse. Sometimes, companies must make very detailed cash forecasts—even daily—if managers project that they may hit or exceed their fixed borrowing limit.

Exhibit 5–4 shows Boston Retail's cash plan for 20X2 broken down by the four quarters of the year. The analysis indicates a small cash shortfall in quarter one, which must be covered by bank borrowing.

To estimate cash needs over longer periods of time—to tie in with the monthly, quarterly, or yearly profit plan projections—companies generally use the **indirect method** (this method should also be familiar from your financial accounting class). To use the indirect method, managers start with their projected income as shown on the profit plan and follow four steps to estimate their cash needs.

Step 1: Estimate Net Cash Flows from Operations

A simple technique to estimate *operating cash flow* is to use a measure known as **EBITDA,** which stands for Earnings Before Interest, Taxes, Depreciation, and Amortization. It is a rough calculation of nonaccrual—or cash-based—operating earnings that

---

[5] The sustainable growth rate of any business is defined as

$$\text{Sustainable growth rate} = \text{ROE} \times (1 - \text{Dividend payout ratio})$$

where the dividend payout ratio is

$$\text{Dividend payout ratio} = \frac{\text{Cash dividends paid}}{\text{Net income}}$$

Interested readers can refer to any standard finance textbook for a full discussion of the implications and use of this formula.

EXHIBIT 5–4
Boston Retail
Quarterly Cash Plan for 20X2
(Prepared by estimating cash inflows and outflows)

	FIRST QUARTER	SECOND QUARTER	THIRD QUARTER	FOURTH QUARTER	TOTAL
Cash at the beginning of the quarter (cash balance at least 200)	$ 208	$ 200	$ 200	$ 200	$ 208
Cash Inflows					
Cash received from customers	1,470	2,631	2,400	3,594	10,095
Borrowing required	288	(58)	(100)	(130)	—
Total cash inflows	$1,758	$2,573	$2,300	$3,464	$10,095
Cash Outflows					
Cash paid to suppliers	818	1,359	1,274	1,885	5,336
Cash expenses	526	1,052	864	1,315	3,757
Investment in new assets	260	—	—	—	260
Tax payments	87	87	87	87	348
Pay back debt	75	75	75	75	300
Total cash outflows	$1,766	$2,573	$2,300	$3,362	$10,001
Total cash flows	$ (8)	—	—	$ 102	$ 94
Cash at the end of the quarter	$ 200	$ 200	$ 200	$ 302	$ 302

can be computed readily from an income statement. The calculation starts with accrual-based profit—taken directly from the profit plan—and adds back (1) depreciation, which does not require an outlay of cash, and (2) interest and tax expenses, which represent nonoperating expenditures.

Step 2: Estimate Cash Needed to Fund Growth in Operating Assets

EBITDA is a rough measure that ignores any changes in working capital needed to operate the business. For example, cash may be used up (or provided) by changes in inventory levels and accounts receivable balances. These changes in working capital will either reduce (or increase) cash balances on hand.

Experience in any business will provide good data on the level of working capital needed to fund a business. From past experience, Boston Retail managers know that they must invest approximately $165,000 in inventory, $40,000 in accounts receivable, and $25,000 in store displays for each store. They also know that suppliers will finance approximately $35,000 of this amount through accounts payable. Therefore, adding a new store will mean an investment in working capital of almost $200,000, which will require cash either from cash reserves on hand or from borrowing.

For 20X2, managers anticipate that the increasing scale of operations will require an additional $103,000 of working capital. This amount must be subtracted from operating cash flow calculated as EBITDA. At Boston Retail, the calculation of operating cash flow using EBITDA for 20X2 is shown in Exhibit 5–5.

We can see that managers expect to have approximately $1,068,000 of operating cash flow available to fund growth, repay debt, pay financing costs and taxes, and distribute any dividends to shareholders. If opening a new store requires approximately $200,000 in working capital, the business will have enough free cash from operations (after tax payments and interest) to open three new stores, assuming it does not use its cash for debt repayment, dividends, or other types of investment.

Step 3: Price the Acquisition and Divestiture of Long-Term Assets

Different strategies and initiatives will require different levels of investment and cash. At Boston Retail, the investment plan for 20X2 (Exhibit 5–2) suggests that the new computer system, warehouse expansion, and store displays will require $260,000. This

---

EXHIBIT 5–5
Boston Retail
Cash Plan for 20X2
(Prepared using EBITDA)

	20X2
Cash at the beginning of the year	$ 208
Cash from Operating Activities	
Profit after taxes	648
Tax payments	349
Interest payments	65
Add: depreciation and other noncash expenses	109
EBITDA	1,171
Changes in Working Capital	
Decrease (increase) in accounts receivable	(26)
Decrease (increase) in inventory	(98)
Increase (decrease) in accounts payable	21
Cash flow from operating activities	1,068
Cash from Investment Activities	
Investment in new assets	(260)
Cash from Financing Activities	
Pay back debt	(300)
Additional borrowing required	—
Tax payments	(349)
Interest payments	(65)
Total cash flows	94
Cash at the end of the year	$ 302

anticipated need for cash will reduce the increase in cash on hand from $1,068,000 to $808,000.

Step 4: Estimate Financing Needs and Interest Payments

The final step in the calculation of cash flow by the indirect method is to subtract the amount of cash needed for (or generated by) financing and income tax. Financing demands on cash flow include dividends, interest expense, and repayment of debt principal. In 20X2, managers at Boston Retail plan to repay $300,000 of their debt and anticipate paying $349,000 in estimated tax payments. In addition, they will pay $65,000 in interest costs. These deductions reduce estimated cash flow as follows:

Operating cash flow (from Exhibit 5–5)	$1,068
Asset purchases	(260)
Tax payments	(349)
Debt repayment	(300)
Interest payments	(65)
Increase in cash	94
Cash on hand—beginning of year	208
Cash on hand—end of year	$ 302

When all is said and done, the indirect method yields exactly the same result as the direct method (compare Exhibits 5–4 and 5–5 as a quick check). The primary difference lies in the fact that the indirect method can be calculated quickly from existing monthly, quarterly, or yearly financial-statement estimates. The direct method requires a detailed, and often laborious, estimate of cash inflows and outflows.

Cash flow analysis often will indicate the need for external funds in the form of either debt or equity to support the proposed profit plan. Managers must choose among available sources of external financing (equity, short-term debt, long-term debt, or some combination of these instruments) and choose funding sources that match financial risk with business risk.

Ensuring Adequate Cash Flow

In contrast to the profit plan, in which the time horizon is typically one year, cash flow projections often focus on much shorter time periods. The difference between cash inflows and cash outflows during the operating cycle is estimated for most businesses at least monthly. For highly seasonal industries such as ski manufacturing or boat building, cash flow balances must be calculated weekly or even daily during critical periods when available cash may not be sufficient to keep the business solvent. In these industries, a bank may be willing to lend the *average* cash requirements for a business, but the important question is whether the bank will advance the *maximum* cash shortfall that the company needs over the business cycle.

For example, ski manufacturers receive most of their cash from customers — retail ski stores — during the winter ski season when retail customers are purchasing new equipment, however, manufacturers disburse most of their operating cash for the production and distribution of skis at least five months earlier. As a result, these businesses need the most borrowing at the beginning of the season, when they have used up all their cash to manufacture inventory but have not yet received any cash from customers. Estimating the *aggregate* or average difference between cash inflows and cash outflows over the entire year will not reveal the shortfall that occurs before the ski season begins. Managers in these companies may pay a lot of attention to weekly cash requirements during the few critical months before the start of the season.

The cash wheel highlights the fact that all businesses have a significant amount of resources tied up in accounts receivable, inventory, and other working capital accounts. As a result, managers must work diligently to accelerate the flows around the cash wheel, thereby freeing up cash for investment, financing, or operations growth.

CFO Magazine conducted a survey of large public companies in 32 industries to learn how effectively managers were able to turn working capital into cash. In their sample, the average company earned $4.2 billion in revenue and generated roughly 9 cents of cash flow for every dollar of sales. On average these companies collected from customers every 50 days, paid suppliers every 33 days, and turned inventory 11 times per year. For the largest companies in the sample, the authors of the survey noted a "rule of 30": they collect bills in 30 days, pay bills in 30 days, and turn inventory in 30 days.

Although all companies can benefit from managing the cash wheel more efficiently, the savings for large companies can be truly significant. For example, Owens Corning recovered $175 million from managing its working capital more effectively; General Motors set a goal for 1997 to find $10 billion in working capital savings.[6]

ROE WHEEL

Businesses that earn the most profit will be better off: They will have more resources to invest in future opportunities; they will be able to pay higher dividends to investors; their stock price will be higher; and their cost of debt will be lower. Thus, profit can be considered both a constraint and a goal: A minimum level of profit is necessary for survival (a constraint), but more is always better than less (a goal).

Both stock price and dividend payments depend on a business's ability to generate profits from the investments that stockholders make in the business. In the most basic sense, when a stockholder invests $100 in a firm, the managers of the firm use the $100 to purchase assets, which are then deployed to earn profit for the benefit of the stockholder. The critical measure, therefore, is the amount of profit that managers are able to generate from the $100 investment entrusted to them. If the business generates $20, profit can be measured in two ways. First, the business could report a $20 profit—an absolute measure of success. Alternatively, managers could calculate the return on shareholders' investment by comparing the profit output ($20) with the investment input ($100). In this case, the return on the stockholder investment of $100 would be 20%—a ratio.

---

[6] S. L. Mintz and C. Lazere, "Inside the Corporate Cash Machine," *CFO Magazine,* June 1997, 54–62.

Cash Flow Analysis at Chicago Central & Pacific Railroad

Chicago Central & Pacific Railroad was a privately held, highly leveraged regional freight railroad. In 1987, when revenue growth did not keep up with capital spending, the company declared bankruptcy under Chapter 11 legislation. The company was rescued when the senior lender agreed to provide additional operational funding.

The new management team decided to focus attention throughout the business on cash flow by developing a simple direct-cash-flow report according to *Statement of Financial Accounting Standards 95.* Direct-cash-flow reporting would, managers believed, show the company's ability to service debt, quantify the consequences of operating managers' decisions, and simplify variance analysis.

Chicago Central already had a daily cash balance report, but more information was required to understand the sources of cash inflows and outflows for investing, financing, and operating activities. For example, determining direct cash flows from costs related to track improvement was difficult because there was a timing difference between when costs were charged to a project in the books and when actual cash was disbursed. Another challenge was accounting for services that a wholly-owned subsidiary purchased from Chicago Central, as well as for the revenue that this subsidiary collected from other railroads through an "interline accounting" system used in the industry.

With the new system, managers were better aware of the capital spending limits imposed upon them by loan obligations. They also learned that cash collected through interline accounting was 1.5 times greater than regular customer revenue but twice as slow in arriving as cash collected directly from customers.

Source: Kevin R. Trout, Margaret M. Tanner, and Lee Nicholas, "On Track with Direct Cash Flow," *Management Accounting* (July 1993): 23–27.

Investors in a firm monitor their investment returns carefully—and hold top managers accountable for these returns—so it is not surprising that the single most important measure for investors is **return on investment** (or **ROI**). ROI is a *ratio measure* of the profit output of the business as a percentage of financial investment inputs. This accounting measure is one of the single best surrogates for overall financial performance.[7]

If we adopt the perspective of managers—those entrusted by shareholders to generate profit—then the appropriate internal measure for return on investment is **return on equity (ROE).** The shareholders' equity portion of the balance sheet shows the total original investment by stockholders, plus accumulated business profits that accrue to stockholders' benefit (less, of course, any dividends paid out). Thus, the objective for any manager is to use the equity investment of the firm wisely—for the benefit of stockholders.

---

[7] We introduce alternative measures, such as EVA, in Chapter 8.

As with the profit wheel and the cash wheel, we can work systematically around the ROE wheel to determine if the profit plan is adequate to meet expectations (see Figure 5–4).

Step 1: Calculate Overall Return on Equity

Return on equity (*ROE*) is calculated as follows:

$$ROE = \frac{\text{Net Income}}{\text{Shareholders' Equity}}$$

FIGURE 5–4   The ROE Wheel

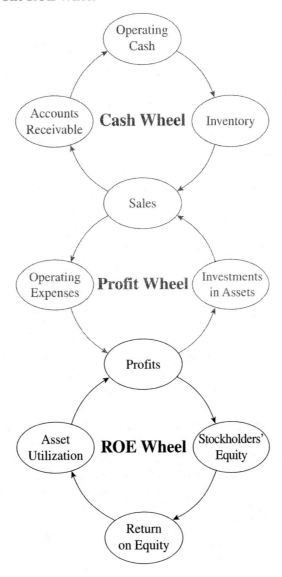

If we assume that senior managers wish to maximize this measure (which is a safe assumption because top managers' performance bonuses are often tied either directly or indirectly to this measure), we must ask ourselves how senior managers cascade this measure down to the organization hierarchy so that lower-level employees will also work to increase ROE.

To answer this question, we can decompose ROE into its component parts. The basic arithmetic decomposition of this measure was devised by Donaldson Brown, who developed his techniques as chief financial officer at Dupont about 1915 and later introduced the techniques to General Motors.[8] ROE can be broken as follows:

$$ROE = \frac{\text{Net Income}}{\text{Shareholders' Equity}}$$
$$= \frac{\text{Net Income}}{\text{Sales}} \times \frac{\text{Sales}}{\text{Shareholders' Equity}}$$

The first term (net income ÷ sales) is a ratio measure of **profitability.** It answers the question, How much profit will we generate for each dollar of sales? This information comes directly from the profit wheel. The second term (sales ÷ stockholders' equity) is a ratio measure as well, but one that is useful only for senior managers, because middle- and lower-level managers do not manage stockholders' equity per se. Rather, managers lower in the business are allocated funds to acquire *assets,* which in turn are used to generate sales and profits. Thus, it is helpful to expand the second term of the equation one step further as follows:

$$ROE = \frac{\text{Net Income}}{\text{Sales}} \times \frac{\text{Sales}}{\text{Assets}} \times \frac{\text{Assets}}{\text{Shareholders' Equity}}$$
$$= \text{Profitability Ratio} \times \text{Asset Turnover Ratio} \times \text{Financial Leverage Ratio}$$

The first term (net income ÷ sales) remains the same—a profitability measure. The second term (sales ÷ assets) is now a ratio measure of **asset turnover.** This ratio answers the question, How many sales dollars will we generate for each dollar that is invested in assets of the business? The objective for any manager is to maximize the sales created by the firm's asset base (assuming, of course, that incremental sales generate profits—not losses). The final term (assets ÷ stockholders' equity) focuses on **financial leverage** by asking, What percentage of total assets employed are to be funded by stockholders and what percentage by debt? To the extent that the asset-to-equity ratio is greater than 1, assets will be funded by debt extended by bondholders, banks, and other creditors of the business. A **leveraged business** is one that relies on a high percentage of debt to fund the productive assets employed in the business.

[8] H. T. Johnson and R. S. Kaplan, *Relevance Lost: The Rise and Fall of Management Accounting* (Boston: Harvard Business School Press, 1987), 86, 101.

For Boston Retail, we can plug profit plan numbers from Exhibit 5–3 into the formula to assess projected profitability, asset turnover, and leverage.

$$ROE = \frac{\text{Net Income}}{\text{Sales}} \times \frac{\text{Sales}}{\text{Assets}} \times \frac{\text{Assets}}{\text{Shareholders' Equity}}$$

$$= \frac{648}{10,120} \times \frac{10,120}{3,996} \times \frac{3,996}{2,886}$$

$$= 0.064 \times 2.5 \times 1.4 = 0.225*$$

$$= \text{Profitability Ratio} \times \text{Asset Turnover Ratio} \times \text{Financial Leverage Ratio}$$

(* difference due to rounding)

We can see that the business is projected to earn 6.4% net income on sales with asset turnover of 2.5 and a leverage ratio of 1.4. The combination of these three indicators yields ROE of 22.5%.

Step 2: Estimate Asset Utilization

Within a business, unit managers (division or profit center managers) are often accountable for a variant of ROE known as **ROCE,** which stands for **return on capital employed.** The breakdown of *ROCE* follows the same pattern as above:

$$ROCE = \frac{\text{Net Income}}{\text{Sales}} \times \frac{\text{Sales}}{\text{Capital Employed}}$$

In the ROCE ratio, **capital employed** refers to the assets within a manager's direct span of control. (See Chapter 3 for a discussion of span of control.) Some companies define capital employed as total assets controlled by a manager minus noninterest-bearing liabilities (for example, accounts payable). These assets typically include accounts receivable, inventory, and plant and equipment. In other cases, some corporate-level assets, such as unamortized goodwill, are also allocated to profit centers to be included in the "capital" that is employed to generate revenue and profit. Different businesses define ROCE in different ways, so care must be taken in using this ratio to understand precisely what managers are including in the denominator.

The detailed decomposition of ROCE provides important additional information about the effective utilization of capital and assets. We can decompose ROCE into a systematic view of many parts of the business's operations. Figure 5–5 depicts this decomposition. Like branches of a tree, we can pursue each component of the ratio to obtain greater detail and potential insight.

At Boston Retail, managers can take the asset-utilization ratios shown and break them down into more detailed projections relating to individual parts of the business.

Some of the more popular asset-utilization measures that are derived from the ROCE Tree are (using 20X1 asset balances for simplicity):

$$\text{Working Capital Turnover} = \frac{\text{Sales}}{\text{Current Assets} - \text{Current Liabilities}}$$

$$\text{Accounts Receivable Turnover} = \frac{\text{Net Sales on Credit}}{\text{Average Net Receivables}}$$

$$\text{Inventory Turnover} = \frac{\text{Cost of Goods Sold}}{\text{Average Inventory}}$$

$$\text{Fixed Asset Turnover} = \frac{\text{Sales}}{\text{Property, Plant, and Equipment}}$$

These turnover ratios show how efficiently managers have used each category of asset (working capital, accounts receivable, inventory, and fixed assets) to generate sales

FIGURE 5–5   ROCE Tree

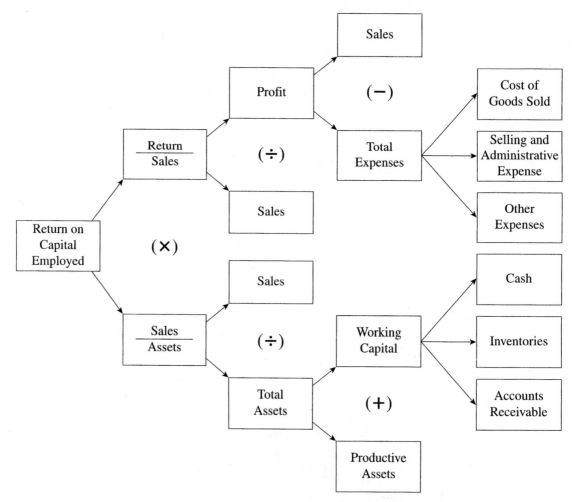

and, ultimately, profit. Generally, a higher number is preferred, indicating that managers have used the assets entrusted to them to maximum advantage. Once ROCE and detailed asset-utilization ratios have been estimated, managers assess the use of the resources under their stewardship.

Step 3: Compare Projected ROE with Industry Benchmarks and Investor Expectations

Once overall expected ROE is calculated, managers must compare it to some benchmark or standard to see how it stacks up against competitors and investor expectations. Managers are sensitive to the ROE expected by investors, analysts, and others who monitor the financial performance of their firm. High returns on investment lead to high stock prices and to the willingness of investors to commit additional financial resources to support the growth of the firm. Low returns cause the opposite result. Therefore, managers typically know—through discussion with analysts and company directors—the ROE that is anticipated from the performance of their business. The returns generated by other similar businesses provide an easily calibrated yardstick.

For Boston Retail, managers might compare their ROE with other publicly traded fashion retailers such as The Limited, GAP, and Nike, whose comparative figures for 1997 are as follows:

	ROE	PROFITABILITY	ASSET TURNOVER	FINANCIAL LEVERAGE
The Limited	10.6%	2.4%	2.1	2.1
Gap	33.7%	8.2%	1.9	2.1
Nike	25.2%	8.7%	1.7	1.7
Boston Retail	22.5%	6.4%	2.5	1.4

As with the cash wheel, if the expected ROE is not sufficiently high to meet expectations, it is back to the drawing board to find ways to increase profit or make better use of existing assets.

Key Financial Measures

Based on our analysis of the principal components of the profit, cash, and ROE wheels, we can summarize the primary financial measures for any business:

- sales
- profit or net income
- cash flow
- investment in new assets
- return on equity (or ROCE)
- net income ÷ sales = profitability
- sales ÷ assets = asset turnover

For Boston Retail, we can recap the profit plan calculations for 20X2 as follows:

- sales = $10,120,000
- profit or net income = $648,000
- cash flow = $1,068,000 operating; $94,000 net (after interest, taxes, new investment, and debt repayment)
- investment in new assets = $260,000
- return on equity = 22.5%
- profitability = 6.4%
- asset turnover = 2.5

USING THE PROFIT WHEELS TO TEST STRATEGY

Boston Retail is contemplating two different strategies for the future. One strategy is to expand into New York state. The increase in sales volume needed to support this strategy will force the company to move to mass production. The other strategy is to limit geographical expansion but diversify into furniture. The profit plan will change depending on which of these strategies is followed because each strategy has different underlying economics. Exhibit 5–6 shows the assumptions underlying both strategies.

Managers must use the three wheels to evaluate the economics and internal consistency of each of these strategies. Implementing either strategy requires the allocation of scarce resources among the various business opportunities open to a company. Resource allocation decisions commit the long-term future of an organization, so they are important decisions to determine the competitive position of the organization. Therefore, resource allocation decisions are often hotly debated inside companies. Agreement is not an easy task because different division managers will often champion different investment opportunities. If a company invests in a certain product line, it is simultaneously deciding not to invest in alternative product lines. This is always difficult for managers who believe in the prospects of the alternatives that are turned down.

The first step is to use the profit wheel to prepare a profit plan for each of the alternatives, based on the assumptions in Exhibit 5–6. Each alternative generates different levels of profit.

The next step is to use the cash wheel analysis to ensure that cash will be adequate to fund these initiatives. In this case, both strategies generate cash over a one-year period. However, the expected cash inflow from sales might lag the cash outflows linked to the increase in operating and long-term assets. Therefore, Boston Retail managers should estimate cash requirements for periods shorter than a year. For geographical expansion, if most of the investment in new assets were to happen early in the year, Boston Retail might need to borrow money from the bank.

Exhibits 5–7, 5–8, and 5–9 present the profit plans and cash flow analyses for each of the competing strategies.

The final step is to compare the ROE for each of the alternatives. For Boston Retail, ROE (using average equity) is 27% for the geographical expansion ($701 ÷ $2,588) and 29.5% ($775 ÷ $2,625) for the product-line expansion strategy.

EXHIBIT 5–6
Boston Retail
Assumptions Underlying Alternative Strategies

ALTERNATIVE 1: GEOGRAPHICAL EXPANSION INTO NEW YORK STATE

Description of Intended Strategy

Open three stores in New York state at the beginning of the year

Additional Investment in New Assets

$120,000 in fixed assets per new store (five years' straight-line depreciation schedule)
Same investment in working capital as existing stores
$20,000 in advertising per new store

Operating Results

Sales per store expected to be the existing average
Cost structure as in existing stores (% of sales)

ALTERNATIVE 2: ADDING A NEW PRODUCT LINE

Description of Intended Strategy

Introduce premium outdoor furniture product line in Boston Retail's three biggest stores

Additional Investment in New Assets

$25,000 per store (five years' straight-line depreciation schedule)
Same investment in working capital as existing product line
$10,000 in advertising per store carrying furniture

Operating Results

Expected increase in sales per store with furniture of 20%
Expected gross margin as clothing line
Administrative costs up by 15%
Wages and salaries up by 10%
Additional cost structure as existing business (% of sales)

However, economic criteria alone are not enough to fully assess each strategic alternative. Recall our discussion in Chapter 2. Profit plans may look attractive but actually deplete the core competencies of the firm, or be at odds with the current market position of the company. During the 1980s and early 1990s, for example, Apple Computer showed impressive economic performance, but the company was using up its advantage built over the previous years without creating new competitive advantage. The result was continuous economic problems in the 1990s. For Boston Retail, we could ask ourselves: Are both of these strategic alternatives consistent with Boston Retail's competencies? (We cover performance measurement and control systems related to this question in Chapter 10.)

EXHIBIT 5–7
Boston Retail
Profit Plan for 20X2 Based on Alternative Strategies
(in thousands of dollars)

	20X1 ACTUAL	20X2 PROFIT PLAN	20X2 PROFIT PLAN (GEOGRAPHICAL EXPANSION)	20X2 PROFIT PLAN (PRODUCT-LINE EXPANSION)
Sales	$9,200	$10,120	$13,800	$11,132
Costs of goods sold	4,780	5,258	7,170	5,784
Gross margin	4,420	4,862	6,630	5,348
Wages and salaries	1,530	1,591	2,387	1,750
Rent and facilities	840	882	1,322	882
Advertising	585	644	704	673
Administrative expenses	435	478	718	550
Interest	72	65	97	72
Depreciation	57	109	181	124
Training	38	40	59	43
Other	54	56	84	62
Profit before taxes	809	997	1,078	1,192
Income tax	283	349	377	417
Net profit	$ 526	$ 648	$ 701	$ 775

KEY BALANCE SHEET FIGURES

	12/31/20X1		12/31/20X2	
Assets				
Cash	$ 208	$ 302	$ 200	$ 255
Accounts receivable	255	281	382	309
Inventory	985	1,083	1,478	1,192
Property, plant, and equipment	1,854	2,005	2,293	2,065
Other assets	325	325	325	325
Total assets	$3,627	$3,996	$4,678	$4,146
Liabilities				
Accounts payable	$ 209	$ 230	$ 313	$ 253
Bank loan	1,180	880	880	880
Additional borrowing			546	
Stockholders' equity	2,238	2,886	2,939	3,013
Total liabilities and stockholders' equity	$3,627	$3,996	$4,678	$4,146

EXHIBIT 5–8
Boston Retail
Quarterly Cash Plan for 20X2 for Alternative Strategies
(Prepared by estimating cash inflows and outflows)

STRATEGIC ALTERNATIVE 1 GEOGRAPHICAL EXPANSION INTO NEW YORK	FIRST QUARTER	SECOND QUARTER	THIRD QUARTER	FOURTH QUARTER	TOTAL
Cash at the beginning of the quarter (cash balance at least 200)	$ 208	$ 200	$ 200	$ 200	$ 208
Cash Inflows					
Cash received from customers	1,911	3,588	3,273	4,901	13,673
Borrowing required	758	15	(24)	(203)	546
Total cash inflows	2,669	3,603	3,249	4,698	14,219
Cash Outflows					
Cash paid to suppliers	1,136	1,930	1,844	2,649	7,559
Cash expenses	752	1,504	1,236	1,880	5,372
Investment in new assets	620	—	—	—	620
Tax payments	94	94	94	94	376
Pay back debt	75	75	75	75	300
Total cash outflows	2,677	3,603	3,249	4,698	14,227
Total cash flows	(8)	—	—	—	(8)
Cash at the end of the quarter	$ 200	$ 200	$ 200	$ 200	$ 200

STRATEGIC ALTERNATIVE 2 PRODUCT-LINE EXPANSION INTO FURNITURE	FIRST QUARTER	SECOND QUARTER	THIRD QUARTER	FOURTH QUARTER	TOTAL
Cash at the beginning of the quarter (cash balance at least 200)	$ 208	$ 200	$ 200	$ 200	$ 208
Cash Inflows					
Cash received from customers	1,591	2,894	2,640	3,954	11,079
Borrowing required	388	(77)	(93)	(218)	—
Total cash inflows	1,979	2,817	2,547	3,736	11,079
Cash Outflows					
Cash paid to suppliers	908	1,509	1,440	2,091	5,948
Cash expenses	565	1,129	928	1,411	4,033
Investment in new assets	335	—	—	—	335
Tax payments	104	104	104	104	416
Pay back debt	75	75	75	75	300
Total cash outflows	1,987	2,817	2,547	3,681	11,032
Total cash flows	(8)	—	—	55	47
Cash at the end of the quarter	$ 200	$ 200	$ 200	$ 255	$ 255

EXHIBIT 5–9
Boston Retail
Cash Plan for 20X2
(Prepared using EBITDA)

	STRATEGIC ALTERNATIVE 1 GEOGRAPHICAL EXPANSION INTO NEW YORK 20X2	STRATEGIC ALTERNATIVE 2 PRODUCT-LINE EXPANSION INTO FURNITURE 20X2
Cash at the beginning of the year	$ 208	$ 208
Cash from Operating Activities		
Projected income after taxes	701	775
Tax payments	377	417
Interest payments	97	72
Add: depreciation and other noncash expenses	181	124
EBITDA	1,356	1,388
Changes in Working Capital		
Decrease (increase) in accounts receivable	(127)	(54)
Decrease (increase) in inventory	(493)	(207)
Increase (decrease) in accounts payable	104	44
Cash flow from operating activities	840	1,171
Cash from Investment Activities		
Investment in new assets	(620)	(335)
Cash from Financing Activities		
Pay back debt	(300)	(300)
Additional borrowing required	546	—
Tax payments	(377)	(417)
Interest payments	(97)	(72)
Total cash flows	(8)	47
Cash at the end of the year	$ 200	$ 255

CHAPTER SUMMARY

The profit plan describes business strategy in economic terms. Because of the importance of the profit plan as a management tool to *test* and *communicate* strategy, managers typically invest substantial time and effort to develop, negotiate, and design the profit plan for the coming year. Managers use the profit plan to assess the ability of different strategies to generate value and to estimate whether sufficient resources will be available to implement the chosen strategy. Managers at Boston Retail are considering two alternative strategies. The first alternative is to diversify geographically into New

York state. Alternatively, the company may move into furniture. The profit plan depicts the economic implications of these alternatives and allows managers to assess the merits of each strategy.

The process of building a profit plan allows managers to share information about competitive market dynamics and internal strengths and weaknesses. Each person in the company may have different information about what is happening in the market and, accordingly, different beliefs about what is the best future direction for the company. By sharing information, managers *learn* from the experience of others and generate valuable additional insights.

Every profit plan is subject to the constraints imposed by the profit wheel, the cash wheel, and the ROE wheel. Within these constraints, managers still have freedom to design profit plans as they see fit. Building a profit plan is an exercise in creativity—testing ideas, testing assumptions, and testing strategy. Yet, even if everyone in the organization accepts the stated strategy, each person may understand it differently. The profit plan forces managers to make explicit their assumptions about what the company's strategy means.

As we will see in chapters to follow, the profit plan plays other critical roles in every business: in setting performance goals for employees, in communicating expectations to the investment community, and in allowing the evaluation of the performance of individual businesses and managers. A profit plan may look like a simple document, but it is an essential foundation for driving any high-performing business forward.

6

Evaluating Strategic Profit Performance

In the previous chapter, we studied how strategies are translated into profit plans. In this chapter, we review the analytic techniques that managers use to monitor their business's success in achieving those profit goals and strategies.

In any business, managers must go through a series of steps to gain an understanding of the sources of strategic profitability. This is essentially a diagnostic function—tracking the progress of organizational achievements against preset performance goals and strategies. To perform this analysis, we revisit many of the themes introduced previously in the book—strategy implementation, profit wheel analysis, span of accountability, and the use of information for decision making and control.

To analyze profit performance, we must consider two different types of measures: effectiveness measures and efficiency measures.

- **Effectiveness** refers to the extent to which an activity achieves desired outcomes. Effectiveness answers the question: Did we achieve what we set out to do? Thus, measures of effectiveness focus on the comparison of actual results with preset expectations or standards.

- **Efficiency,** by contrast, refers to the level of resources that were consumed to achieve a certain level of output. Measures of efficiency answer the question: How many resources were used to achieve the actual outputs? Thus, efficiency variances focus on ratios of inputs to outputs.

To analyze profit performance, the three conditions enumerated in Chapter 4 must be present:

1. Ability to measure outputs—Managers cannot evaluate how well a business unit or manager has performed unless they are able to quantify outputs. Therefore, the ability to measure outputs is a prerequisite for evaluating whether a business has achieved its objectives and efficiently used scarce resources in achieving those objectives.

2. Existence of a predetermined standard of performance—Having a measure of output is useless unless a standard or target exists against which to compare actual performance. Telling someone that a business generated $125,000 in weekly sales does not mean much without an appreciation of how much the business was expected to produce. Was the sales target $100,000 (in which case the business did well)? Or was it $200,000 (indicating a disastrous week)?

3. Ability to use variance information as feedback to adjust inputs and/or process—Measurement and comparison, by themselves, do little good unless managers can use this variance information to change inputs and processes to either bring operations in line with expectations (i.e., where performance is below expectations), or to attempt to capture and replicate unexpected successes (i.e., where performance exceeds expectations). This implies, of course, that managers understand the causal linkages between inputs, processes, and outputs.

Managers can measure countless outputs and processes in any organization. The key to evaluating *strategic* profit performance is focusing on those accounting variables that inform managers about the success of their strategy. In the remainder of the chapter, we outline the procedures for calculating a series of variances that, in total, yield a complete analysis of strategic profitability. These variances include:

- profit plan variances, in absolute and relative terms
- market share variances
- revenue variances
- product efficiency and cost variances
- variances for nonvariable costs

STRATEGIC PROFITABILITY

Strategic profitability analysis is a tool to evaluate the success of a business in generating profit from the implementation of its strategy. To illustrate the techniques of strategic profitability analysis, we will focus on the financial performance of Shade Tree Furniture—a manufacturer of teak and mahogany outdoor furniture.[1] Boston Retail considered acquiring Shade Tree when managers were debating a diversification move into furniture. Shade Tree follows a differentiation strategy supported by premium pricing. The company invests significant resources in advertising to illustrate the quality features that distinguish its products from competitors. The company sells expensive premium furniture through direct mail advertising in periodicals such as *Architectural Digest* and *The New York Times.* Exhibit 6–1 presents Shade Tree's profit plan and actual results for the year ended 20X1.

By examining Exhibit 6–1, we can see that the profit plan, prepared before the beginning of the fiscal year, estimated $413,000 profit for 20X1. Actual profit was $437,211. What are the implications of this difference for evaluating Shade Tree's strategy?

To answer this question, we must know something about Shade Tree's strategic goals. Assume that the key strategic goals established by senior managers at Shade Tree were the following:

- Market share—Managers estimated the size of the outdoor wooden furniture market to be $430 million (or, equivalently, 1,250,000 units of furniture). For 20X1, Shade Tree managers wanted to capture, in dollar terms, 1% of this market. Because Shade Tree Furniture products are premium priced, the 1% market share in dollar terms is equivalent to 0.80% market share in number of pieces of furniture.

---

[1] We have chosen to illustrate strategic profitability analysis techniques using a manufacturing firm so we can review variances that reflect manufacturing and operational efficiencies, in addition to those variances that would apply to a retail company such as Boston Retail.

EXHIBIT 6–1
Shade Tree Furniture
Profit Plan and Actual Performance for 20X1

	PROFIT PLAN 20X1	ACTUAL INCOME STATEMENT 20X1
Sales	$4,300,000	$4,450,050
Cost of goods sold		
Raw materials	1,595,000	1,686,672
Wages	505,000	514,696
Other manufacturing costs	480,000	490,650
Gross margin	$1,720,000	$1,758,032
Administrative and selling expenses	505,000	488,500
Advertising expenses	516,000	520,700
Interest expense	64,000	76,200
Profit before taxes	$ 635,000	$ 672,632
Income tax	222,000	235,421
Profit after tax	$ 413,000	$ 437,211

- Gross margin—Shade Tree's premium pricing strategy should be reflected in high gross margin. Gross margin targets for 20X1 were set at 40% of sales.
- Advertising—Budgeted at 12% of sales.
- Cash flow—Managers wanted to be able to generate $300,000 cash flow from operations.
- Return on equity—the goal for 20X1 was set at 18%.

To perform strategic profitability analysis, we revisit the profit wheel concepts that we used in Chapter 5. In our analysis, we pay particular attention to three of the four variables on the profit wheel—sales, operating expenses, and profit. The fourth variable—investment in new assets—is covered in the next chapter.

Computing Profit Plan Variances in Absolute and Relative Terms

The first step in all profitability analysis is to isolate significant deviations from expectations using **variance analysis.** A variance is the difference between (1) an item estimated on a profit plan or budget prepared prior to the start of an accounting period and (2) the actual income or expense as reflected on accounting statements prepared after the accounting period has ended. Variances are **favorable** (F) if actual profit is higher than planned profit. Conversely, variances are **unfavorable** (U) if actual profit is below planned profit.

The first level of analysis then simply computes the difference between actual profit for year 20X1 and the standards set out in the accountability unit's profit plan or budget that was prepared in late 20X0 (see Exhibit 6–2). In Shade Tree Furniture's case, the profit difference is $24,211 (favorable). Sales revenue is $150,050 over plan. Some other expenses are below plan, such as administrative and selling expenses, which is $16,500 under plan.

EXHIBIT 6–2
Shade Tree Furniture
Profit Plan Variances

	PROFIT PLAN 20X1 (IN DOLLARS)	PROFIT PLAN 20X1 (IN % OVER SALES)	ACTUAL INCOME STATEMENT 20X1 (IN DOLLARS)	ACTUAL INCOME STATEMENT 20X1 (IN % OVER SALES)	VARIANCE ANALYSIS (IN DOLLARS)	
Sales	$4,300,000	100.0%	$4,450,050	100.0%	$150,050	(F)
Cost of goods sold						
Raw materials	1,595,000	37.1	1,686,672	37.9	(91,672)	(U)
Wages	505,000	11.7	514,696	11.6	(9,696)	(U)
Other manufacturing costs	480,000	11.2	490,650	11.0	(10,650)	(U)
Gross margin	$1,720,000	40.0%	$1,758,032	39.5%	$ 38,032	(F)
Administrative and selling expenses	505,000	11.7	488,500	11.0	16,500	(F)
Advertising expenses	516,000	12.0	520,700	11.7	(4,700)	(U)
Interest expense	64,000	1.5	76,200	1.7	(12,200)	(U)
Profit before taxes	$ 635,000	14.8%	$ 672,632	15.1%	$ 37,632	(F)
Income tax	222,000	5.2	235,421	5.3	(13,421)	(U)
Profit after tax	$ 413,000	9.6%	$ 437,211	9.8%	$ 24,211	(F)

Managers often use this first level of analysis to describe variances in ratio or percentage terms. Thus, a manager might describe her revenue as "3.5% over plan" or administrative and selling expenses as "3% below budget."

Once simple profit variances are calculated, the business strategy must be tested and validated. The reason for variances must be ascertained so that profit plan performance can be evaluated, corrective action taken, and key insights applied to other aspects of the business.

What should managers at Shade Tree make of the additional $24,000 profit? Although the number is relatively small in both absolute and relative terms, it may conceal large offsetting variances. For example, it could be made up of a $124,000 gain due to growth and a $100,000 loss due to poor products. Further analysis may reveal unexpected changes in revenue, cost of raw materials, and a variety of other factors. Higher profits may be due to efficient use of resources, increased demand for goods and services, or changes in the competitive marketplace. Revenue might differ from expectations due to changes in selling prices or to a change in product mix. Cost savings may be due to a successful experiment in production technology. Even though the net profit change is small, each of these potential explanations must be tested and verified so that strategy can be affirmed or adjusted as necessary.

Strategic profitability comprises two components, as defined by the following formula:

$$\text{Strategic profitability} = \text{profit (loss) from competitive effectiveness} \\ + \text{profit (loss) from operating efficiencies}$$

These two terms—competitive effectiveness and operating efficiencies—drive sales and operating expenses, respectively, on the profit wheel. Thus, for purposes of our strategic profitability analysis, we can relabel the profit wheel categories, substituting *competitiveness effectiveness* for sales, and *operating efficiencies* for operating expenses (Figure 6–1).

Analysis of *competitive effectiveness*—did we achieve what we set out to do?—is applicable primarily to business units that set and implement product market strategy. This includes all stand-alone businesses, as well as any profit center or other unit whose managers are accountable for creating profit through market transactions. The analysis of *operating efficiencies*—how many resources were consumed to achieve the actual

FIGURE 6–1   Strategic Profitability Analysis Wheel

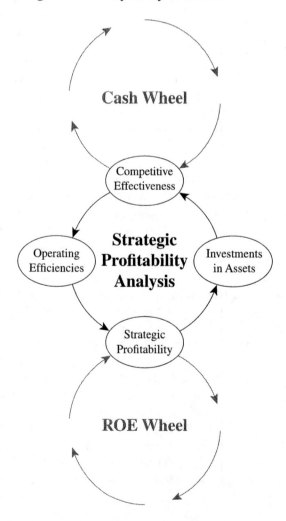

outputs?—is applicable to all accountability units that manage the flow of Inputs→Process→Outputs. This includes entire businesses and profit centers. It also includes those units that we discussed in Chapter 3 with narrower spans of accountability, such as functions and cost centers.

COMPETITIVE EFFECTIVENESS: MARKET SHARE VARIANCES

How well did Shade Tree Furniture implement its strategy? To answer this question, we must probe the effectiveness of the business in attracting customers, marketing its products, and differentiating itself from other competitors in the marketplace.

Effectiveness, by definition, focuses on outputs. *Profit* from competitive effectiveness focuses on how well a business fared against its competitors. It is gauged by two principal output indicators: market share growth and price premium. Market share growth reveals how customers reacted to a business's value proposition. Price premium, reflected in the revenue line of the income statement, reveals the success of a business in extracting value based on differentiation of its goods and services. In the next two sections, we compute market share and revenue variances to provide insight into how well the business performed on these dimensions of strategy.

Computing Market Share Variances

As part of any profit planning process, revenue goals are established based on analysis of market potential, SWOT, and intended strategies. These same market-based factors provide the foundation for analysis of market share growth.

Two key variables affect profitability attributable to market share:

- increase (or decrease) in profit due to changes in market *size* (i.e., changes in total unit or dollar volume sold in the entire market)
- increase (or decrease) in profit due to changes in market *share* (i.e., changes in percentage of total market served by the business)

Each of these variables is evaluated against the original expectations set out in the profit plan (see Exhibit 6–3).

The formula for unexpected profit due to changes in *market size* is:

Market size variance = Δ market size × planned market share × planned average contribution margin

= (actual market size in units − predicted market size in units) × planned market share × planned average contribution margin

From Exhibit 6–3, we find that the profit change due to increases in the size of the outdoor furniture market was:

$$= (1,268,293 - 1,250,000)$$
$$\times 0.80\%$$
$$\times \$220 = \underline{\$32,196} \text{ (F)}$$

EXHIBIT 6–3
Shade Tree Furniture
Revenue Assumptions in 20X1 Profit Plan

	ASSUMPTIONS REFLECTED IN 20X1 PROFIT PLAN	ACTUAL DATA FOR 20X1
Market size (in $)	$430,000,000	$436,280,000
Market size (in units)	1,250,000	1,268,293
Market share (in $)	1.00%	1.02%
Market share (in units)	0.80%	0.82%
Contribution margin per unit in $[a]	$ 220.00[b]	
Contribution margin per unit in %[a]	51.16%	

[a] *Only raw material and wages are variable costs*
[b] *Calculated from data in Exhibit 6–4*

Thus, this calculation reveals that Shade Tree's profit increased by $32,196 because of increases in overall market demand.

Next, we want to probe how successful the company was in capturing its share of this total demand. The formula for profit change due to increases or decreases in *market share* is:

A Common Way to Approximate Market Size Variance

Sometimes, managers do not have access to market size data expressed in unit volumes—that is, the number of pieces of furniture sold. In these cases, using market size expressed in *dollar terms* is usually a sufficient approximation to estimate a market size variance. For example, we can estimate the market size variance using the dollar value of the market as follows:

$$= (\$436,280,000 - \$430,000,000)$$
$$\times 1\%$$
$$\times 51.16\% = \underline{\$32,128} \text{ (F)}$$

For Shade Tree Furniture, estimating market size variance in dollars instead of number of units represents a difference in accuracy of less than 2%. Because this approximation fails to separate the effects of changes in market size (in units) and changes in unit prices, it is accurate only if the actual average unit market price (market size in dollars ÷ market size in units) is close to the expected average unit market price. A simple calculation reveals that the market for outdoor furniture meets this condition:

Expected average market price = $430,000,000 ÷ 1,250,000 = $344.00
Actual average market price = $436,280,000 ÷ 1,268,293 = $343.99

Market share variance = Δ market share × actual market size × planned average contribution margin

= (actual market share in units − planned market share in units) × actual market size × planned average contribution margin

From Exhibit 6–3 we can easily price the profit that was earned because of better-than-expected market share:

$$= (0.82\% - 0.80\%)$$
$$\times 1{,}268{,}293$$
$$\times \$220 = \underline{\$55{,}804} \text{ (F)}$$

By calculating these two market-based variances, we have ascertained that Shade Tree Furniture added $88,000 to its profit due to changes in the market. Part of this increase was due to unexpected growth in the size of the total market ($32,196), and part was due to an increased share of the larger pie ($55,804). Through our analysis, we have learned that the market for outdoor furniture grew more than expected during 20X1,

---

A Common Way to Approximate Market Share Variance

Again, however, market share data expressed as dollar sales (instead of number of units) may be more readily available. Therefore, managers sometimes estimate market share variance using data expressed in dollars instead of units sold. However, you must remember that this approach mixes the effects of changes in market share with changes in unit prices. Therefore, it is only an approximation—adequate in most situations—but an approximation nonetheless.

$$= (1.02\% - 1.00\%)$$
$$\times \$436{,}280{,}000$$
$$\times 51.16\% = \underline{\$44{,}640} \text{ (F)}$$

The difference that we get by using market share in dollars instead of units is $11,164. This approximation is accurate if actual average unit price (for both the overall market and the company's products) is close to the expected average unit price used to build the profit plan. For Shade Tree Furniture in 20X1, market prices were as expected, but the company's price was $2.11 below plan.[2] This lower-than-expected price makes the approximation of market share using dollars roughly accurate.[3]

---

[2] Expected average price = $4,300,000 ÷ 10,000 = $430 (see Exhibit 6–4 for volume data). Actual average price = $4,450,050 ÷ 10,400 = $427.89.

[3] We can reconcile the difference of $11,164 using the change in prices as follows:

$$\$11{,}164 = [(0.82\% \times \$2.11 \div \$430) - (0.80\% \times \$0.01 \div \$344)] \times 1{,}268{,}293 \times \$220$$

which indicates that Shade Tree Furniture is competing in a market with an attractive future. Moreover, the company captured a higher market share than expected. To understand the implications of this performance indicator, managers need to answer several questions: Did the premium market for outdoor furniture grow more than the rest of the market? Did the company cut prices to achieve growth? Did the sales and marketing department of Shade Tree Furniture perform up to expectations? We consider these questions next.

COMPETITIVE EFFECTIVENESS: REVENUE VARIANCES

With market share variances as a backdrop, we now evaluate managers' success in generating acceptable levels of revenue. Revenue is a simple accounting term; it equals sales volume in units multiplied by unit price. However, revenue is much more than that. Revenue is the unequivocal measure of the desirability of a value proposition. It is a key indicator of customer acceptance of products and services. In the long term, it is the ultimate measure of customer satisfaction.

Computing Revenue Variances

Managers are especially interested in two sources of revenue-based profit:

- increase (or decrease) in profit due to changes in prices
- increase (or decrease) in profit due to changes in product mix

Shade Tree Furniture sells both chairs and benches. Assume for simplicity that each type of product costs the same to manufacture—$210—but the chairs are priced at $400 and the benches sell for $500. In its profit plan, Shade Tree Furniture planned to sell 7,000 chairs and 3,000 benches (see Exhibit 6–4). Thus, in the original profit plan, total revenue was estimated at $4,300,000 (7,000 chairs × $400 + 3,000 benches × $500). However, the actual units sold differed from the number of units predicted in the

---

EXHIBIT 6–4
Shade Tree Furniture
Information Needed for Calculation of Revenue Variances

	ASSUMPTIONS REFLECTED IN 20X1 PROFIT PLAN	ACTUAL DATA FOR 20X1
Number of chairs (units)	7,000	7,050
Revenues from chairs	$2,800,000	$2,791,800
Number of benches (units)	3,000	3,350
Revenues from benches	$1,500,000	$1,658,250
Planned contribution margin per unit (chairs)	$190.00	
Planned contribution margin per unit (benches)	$290.00	
Average expected contribution per piece of furniture	$220.00	$222.21

profit plan. During the year, the company actually sold 7,050 chairs and 3,350 benches, and it generated revenues of $2,791,800 for chairs and $1,658,250 for benches, for a total of $4,450,050. We now have the information that we need to calculate basic revenue variances.

The first step in calculating revenue variances is to dig into the company records to find out how much of the profit variance was attributable to changes in selling prices. In our analysis of strategic effectiveness, it is critical to understand the ability of the business to receive price premiums for its products or services. Premium pricing results from effective differentiation and successful market positioning. Premium prices are possible for two reasons: (1) because customers believe that the value they are receiving is worth the higher price, and/or (2) competitive offerings or substitute products are not available at lower prices. Understanding these factors is essential for effective competition.

A favorable sales price variance, or **price premium** (selling prices are higher than profit plan estimates), indicates that managers have been successful in extracting value from the marketplace—either because of product superiority or weakness in competitors' product positions. An unfavorable sales price variance (selling prices are lower than profit plan estimates) suggests the opposite: the business had to lower price to meet competition or customers were unwilling to pay the planned price for the value they were receiving.

The formula for the *sales price variance* is:

Sales price variance = actual total revenue
- (product #1 standard selling price × product #1 actual volume)
- (product #2 standard selling price × product #2 actual volume)
- . . . .
- (product #n standard selling price × product #n actual volume)

For Shade Tree Furniture, the sales price variance is:

= $4,450,050 − ($400 × 7,050 chairs) − ($500 × 3,350 benches)
= 4,450,050 − 4,495,000
= $44,950 U

Through this calculation, we can see that lower prices reduced profits by just under $45,000. Managers must now investigate why prices had to be lowered. Did Shade Tree Furniture lower its prices to meet competitive pressures? Or, were discounts needed to compensate for weak demand?

The second revenue variance focuses on **product mix.** Product mix describes the percentage of total sales that is generated by each product in a business's product line. For example, a firm may generate 25% of its revenue from product A, 40% from product B, and 35% from product C. Product mix is important because selling prices and manufacturing costs often differ by product. If companies sell more or less of different products—each with different prices and contribution margins—then actual profit will differ from profit plan estimates.

To isolate the effect of product mix variances on profit, we must work with *standard contribution margins.* **Contribution margin** is defined as selling price minus variable costs. For our purposes, we are interested in isolating the profit effects of changes in product mix; therefore, we need to hold changes in variable costs and selling price constant. Thus, it is important to remember to compute product mix variances using standard (i.e., planned) variable costs per unit rather than actual variable costs per unit, which may reflect unanticipated changes in production efficiency. Similarly, we use planned selling prices in the calculation of contribution margin because the effects of changes in selling price changes have already been identified above as part of the sales price variance.

In its profit plan, Shade Tree Furniture planned to generate 65% of its revenue from chairs and 35% from benches. We know that chairs have a planned contribution margin of $190 per unit ($400 − $210), and benches have a planned contribution margin of $290 per unit ($500 − $210). We can calculate the total planned contribution margin as $2,200,000 (7,000 chairs × $190 + 3,000 benches × $290), and average contribution per unit as $220 ($2,200,000 ÷ 10,000 units). Assuming that costs to produce did not differ from the standards reflected in the profit plan (we will relax this assumption shortly), the restated "standard" contribution—using the actual sales mix—was $2,311,000 (7,050 chairs × $190 + 3,350 benches × $290). Average contribution per unit was $222.21 ($2,311,000 ÷ 10,400 units), reflecting a shift to higher-margin benches.

We can now use this information to compute the change in profit due to changes in product mix. The formula for **product mix variance** is:

Product mix variance = Δ average standard contribution × actual unit volume
    = (actual average standard contribution − planned average
       standard contribution) × actual unit volume
    = [($2,311,000 ÷ 10,400) − ($2,200,000 ÷ 10,000)] × 10,400
    = $23,000 (F)

The shift from chairs to benches generated $23,000 additional profit. With this information in hand, managers need to explore the implications of the switch to higher-margin products. Is this the start of a new trend? How can it be accelerated? What are the implications for production, sourcing, and advertising?

SUMMARY OF COMPETITIVE EFFECTIVENESS VARIANCES

To summarize, then, we have computed four variances related to competitive effectiveness:

Market size	$32,196	(F)
Market share	55,804	(F)
Sales price	44,950	(U)
Product mix	23,000	(F)
Total profit variances due to competitive effectiveness	$66,050	(F)

The picture that emerges from this analysis is generally favorable. Profit exceeded plan by $66,050 due to superior competitive effectiveness. Managers must next take this data and probe its implications. The market is growing ahead of expectations. (Q. What factors are causing this increase in overall market demand?) Managers have been able to shift the product mix from chairs to more profitable benches. (Q. How can the business capitalize on this unexpected shift?) Market share is also growing faster than expectations. (Q. What combination of advertising and promotion programs have contributed to this shift?) The one unfavorable variance is due to lower than planned selling prices. (Q. Are managers "buying" market share by lowering prices?) This pricing issue will have to be watched carefully by managers if they want to implement a differentiation strategy focusing on the high-end premium products in the market.

VOLUME-ADJUSTED PROFIT PLAN

In the previous section, we examined the reasons for changes in operating profit due to the success or failure of the strategy in attracting customers, extracting value, and building market share. Having completed this analysis, we can now take the level of sales volume as given and move on to the next steps in strategic profitability analysis—analyzing the extent to which managers were able to operate the business efficiently.

Calculating a Volume-Adjusted Profit Plan (or Flexible Budget)

To gain a full understanding of internal operating efficiencies and their effect on profit, it is necessary to recast the original profit plan to reflect the *actual volume* of sales. What we are trying to accomplish in this step is to set revised performance standards for internal efficiencies based on the realized level of production and sales. As discussed in Chapter 5, many of the profit plan estimates were based on forecasts of sales volume. To the extent that sales forecasts proved to be either too high or too low, managers must recalculate the profit plan standards so that variances can be computed accurately.

Exhibit 6–5 shows how this is done by inserting a new column for the *volume-adjusted profit plan* (or budget) between the original profit plan column and the actual profit column. The volume-adjusted profit plan is calculated by multiplying original estimates of sales-based cost variables (e.g., $159.50 of raw material for each chair or bench manufactured) by the *actual* sales volume (now 7,050 chairs and 3,350 benches instead of 7,000 chairs and 3,000 benches as estimated in the original profit plan) to yield a volume-adjusted estimate (in this example, $1,658,800). This new volume-adjusted profit plan is often called a *flexible budget.*

In our analysis of competitive effectiveness, we have already calculated variances due to market size, market share, sales price, and product mix that total $66,050 (F). This amount represents the difference between the original plan (column 1 of Exhibit 6–5) and the volume-adjusted profit plan (column 3). Now, the remaining profit variances due to internal operating efficiencies can be calculated. These are the variances between the volume-adjusted profit plan (column 3) and actual performance (column 5).

A quick look at the columns shows us that if managers had known a year ago that sales would actually be 7,050 chairs and 3,350 benches with lower selling prices, they

EXHIBIT 6–5
Shade Tree Furniture
Calculation of Volume-Adjusted Profit Plan

	ORIGINAL PROFIT PLAN 20X1	EFFECTIVENESS VARIANCES EXPLAINED	VOLUME-ADJUSTED PROFIT PLAN 20X1	ADDITIONAL VARIANCE TO BE EXPLAINED	ACTUAL INCOME STATEMENT 20X1
Sales	$4,300,000		$4,450,050		$4,450,050
− Cost of goods sold					
Raw materials	1,595,000		1,658,800	$(27,872)	1,686,672
Wages	505,000		525,200	10,504	514,696
Other manufacturing costs	480,000		480,000	(10,650)	490,650
Gross margin	$1,720,000	$66,050	$1,786,050	$(28,018)	$1,758,032
Administrative and selling expenses	505,000		505,000	$ 16,500	488,500
Advertising expenses	516,000		516,000	(4,700)	520,700
Interest expense	64,000		64,000	(12,200)	76,200
Profit before taxes	$ 635,000	$66,050	$ 701,050	$(28,418)	$ 672,632

would have budgeted a pretax profit of $701,050. Yet, actual profit was $672,632—$28,418 below revised expectations.

OPERATING EFFICIENCIES: VARIABLE COSTS

Next, we analyze the business's ability to manage variable costs. This analysis is used primarily in manufacturing firms. In Chapter 5, we distinguished between *variable costs* and *nonvariable costs*. You will recall that variable costs are resources (inputs) that vary proportionally with the level of sales (output). In simple terms:

$$\text{Variable costs} = \text{Input volume} \times \text{Cost per unit of input}$$

$$= \text{Output volume} \times \frac{\text{Input volume}}{\text{Output volume}} \times \text{Cost per unit of input}$$

This last expression reveals that variable costs change with (1) output volume, (i.e., sales volume), (2) an efficiency ratio of inputs to outputs, and (3) the prices of input factors. We have already recalculated output volume to reflect actual sales in the previous step, so we need only calculate two additional variances at this point:

- changes in the use of inputs in relation to outputs (*efficiency variance*)
- changes in the unit cost of those inputs (*production spending variance*)

These two variances will reveal why actual variable costs differ from those reflected in the original profit plan: either the costs of inputs are higher or lower than expected, or the efficiency with which inputs were converted to outputs is different from the profit plan.

Calculating Production Efficiency and Cost Variances (If Applicable)

Exhibit 6–6 gives us information on how changes in production efficiency and input prices affected the profit of Shade Tree Furniture.

First, let's analyze how well the manufacturing operation at Shade Tree Furniture utilized raw materials. As always, the reference point to analyze performance is managers' expectations as reflected in the profit plan. How much raw material did Shade Tree Furniture's managers expect to use to manufacture one piece of furniture? (We assume for simplicity that chairs and benches use the same amount of wood.)

Exhibit 6–6 tells us the answer. Managers expected to use 50 pounds of wood per piece of furniture at a cost of $3.19 per pound. The expected cost of raw material per chair or bench is $159.50. This expected cost is called the *standard cost of raw material.* This amount can be broken down into the *standard cost of wood* and the expected input/output relationship, or *standard efficiency.*

According to the assumptions that managers used to build the profit plan, the cost of materials required for each piece of furniture is $159.50. During 20X1, Shade Tree Furniture sold 10,400 pieces. Therefore, expected cost was 10,400 × $159.50 = $1,658,800 (you can check this number in the volume-adjusted profit plan, Exhibit 6–5). However, actual costs were $1,686,672. A variance of $27,872 must be explained.

EXHIBIT 6–6
Shade Tree Furniture
Data to Analyze Manufacturing Performance

	ASSUMPTIONS REFLECTED IN 20X1 PROFIT PLAN	ACTUAL DATA FOR 20X1
Raw Material		
Efficiency input/output (pounds per piece of furniture)	50.00	51.00
Cost of one pound of wood	$ 3.19	$ 3.18
Cost of raw material per chair/bench	50 × $3.19 = $159.50	51 × $3.18 = $162.18
Labor		
Efficiency input/output (hours per piece of furniture)	5.00	4.90
Wage per hour	$ 10.10	$ 10.10
Cost of labor per chair/bench	5.00 × $10.10 = $ 50.50	4.90 × $10.10 = $ 49.49
Total Variable Cost	$159.50 + $50.50 = $210.00	$162.18 + $49.49 = $211.67

We can analyze the difference between actual performance and expectations using an *efficiency variance* and a *spending variance*. The formula for the **efficiency variance** is:

Efficiency variance = actual units of output
$\times$ (planned volume of inputs per unit of output
     − actual volume of inputs per unit of output)
$\times$ planned cost of one unit of input

Thus, the efficiency variance for raw materials at Shade Tree Furniture is:

Efficiency variance = actual number of pieces of furniture produced
$\times$ (planned pounds of wood per piece
     − actual pounds of wood per piece)
$\times$ planned cost of one pound of wood
= 10,400 $\times$ (50 − 51) $\times$ \$3.19 = <u>\$33,176</u> (U)

The manufacturing operation at Shade Tree Furniture used more wood per piece of furniture than expected. In other words, the operation was *less efficient* than expected. This underperformance is reflected in an unfavorable efficiency variance of \$33,176. Were product designs more complex to manufacture than expected? Were workers less skilled and, therefore, used more wood for each piece of furniture? Did workers use more wood to meet increasing production demand? Did they have to use more wood because the purchasing department ordered cheaper wood, which resulted in more rejected pieces? These questions need further exploration by managers to understand the reasons for the efficiency variance. Analyzing additional variances may help in answering these questions.

The actual cost of one pound of wood was \$3.18 instead of the planned \$3.19. How did this change affect profits? Calculation of a **spending variance** answers this question. The formula is:

Spending variance = actual units of output
$\times$ actual volume of inputs per unit of output
$\times$ (planned cost of one unit of input
     − actual cost of one unit of input)

For raw materials at Shade Tree Furniture we have:

Spending variance = actual number of pieces of furniture produced
$\times$ actual pounds of wood per piece
$\times$ (planned cost of one pound of wood
     − actual cost of one pound of wood)
= 10,400 $\times$ 51 $\times$ (\$3.19 − 3.18) = <u>\$5,304</u> (F)

It appears that the purchasing department was able to obtain wood at a somewhat lower cost than expected. However, was it because a lower quality wood was purchased?

Or were market prices for wood lower than planned? Managers can explore the potential reasons for this variance if it appears to be significant to understanding the internal efficiencies of the business.

Efficiency variance and spending variance together explain the difference between the volume-adjusted profit plan and the actual raw material expense as shown on Exhibit 6–5: $33,176 (U) + $5,304 (F) = $27,872 (U).

We can apply the same tools to analyze the performance of Shade Tree's workers. The variance in wages to be explained is $10,504 (Exhibit 6–5).

$$
\begin{aligned}
\text{Efficiency variance} = \ & \text{actual number of pieces of furniture produced} \\
& \times \text{(planned labor hours per piece} \\
& \quad - \text{actual labor hours per piece)} \\
& \times \text{planned wages per hour} \\
= \ & 10{,}400 \times (5.00 - 4.90) \times \$10.10 = \underline{\$10{,}504} \text{ (F)}
\end{aligned}
$$

$$
\begin{aligned}
\text{Spending variance} = \ & \text{actual number of pieces of furniture produced} \\
& \times \text{actual labor hours per piece} \\
& \times \text{(planned wage per hour} \\
& \quad - \text{actual wage per hour)} \\
= \ & 10{,}400 \times 4.90 \times (\$10.10 - 10.10) = \underline{\$0}
\end{aligned}
$$

The planned labor cost is called *standard labor cost.* This amount can be broken down into planned wages, or *standard wages,* and labor hours per piece of furniture, called *standard labor efficiency.*

The efficiency variance was favorable; whereas, actual wages were exactly as planned (i.e., standard wages equal to actual wages). We have now analyzed the "wages" variance of $10,504 on Exhibit 6–5, indicating that Shade Tree Furniture workers produced more pieces per hour than expected (efficiency variance) and their wages were as expected (spending variance).

Production efficiency and cost variances are useful indicators to understand how efficiently any strategy was implemented. Revenue variances tell us about performance in the market, and spending and efficiency variances inform us about how well managers used the internal capabilities of the business.

Comparing this information with competitors can further enhance management's understanding of how they are using internal efficiencies as sources of advantage. This is especially important for businesses following a low-cost strategy. These businesses need lower input prices and/or higher efficiencies (achieved through process innovation, economies of scale, or economies of scope) than competitors. For such businesses, comparing efficiency costs against competitor benchmarks is critical. In some cases, companies have access to information on manufacturing efficiency through industry associations or independent **benchmarking** studies. When this information is not available, companies must rely on continuous improvement in profit plan indicators to ensure sustainable competitive efficiencies.

OPERATING EFFICIENCIES: NONVARIABLE COSTS

For service companies like Boston Retail, the concept of efficiency variance is rarely used because there are no manufacturing costs that vary directly with outputs. This does not mean that service companies do not care about efficiency in their processes. On the contrary, the profitability of service companies often depends significantly on how efficiently they use their resources. However, the critical resources in service companies tend to be *nonvariable* costs. For these resources—in both manufacturing and service firms—we calculate spending variances.

Calculating Variances for Nonvariable Costs

The formula for *spending variance* is simply:

$$\text{Spending variance} = (\text{Planned cost} - \text{Actual cost})$$

In Chapter 5, we identified three different types of nonvariable costs:

- committed (or engineered) costs
- discretionary expenses
- activity-based costs

We can apply spending variance analysis to each category.

Committed Costs

Companies commit to certain expenses for long periods of time. For example, depreciation of a fixed asset is determined for the life of the asset. Similarly, long-term contracts fix lease expenses over several years. Because committed costs are fixed over long periods of time, there should not generally be any variance between expected and actual costs. However, unexpected events can sometimes cause a variation. For example, a long-term lease contract indexed to inflation will show a *spending variance* if actual inflation is different from expected inflation.

For Shade Tree Furniture, the original profit planned reflected $150,000 for the depreciation of machines. This amount was included in "other manufacturing costs" under cost of goods sold. The actual depreciation was $155,000 because an old machine unexpectedly broke down and was replaced by a new one with higher depreciation. The spending variance was:

$$= \$150,000 - \$155,000$$
$$= \underline{\$5,000} \text{ (U)}$$

Discretionary Expenses

Discretionary expenses are also analyzed using spending variances to compare expected and actual levels of costs. Advertising expense is a discretionary cost because managers can adjust the level of advertising expense almost at will. Shade Tree Furniture planned to spend $516,000 on advertising, but the expense was $520,700. Using the spending variance formula, we can calculate the variance as

$$= \$516,000 - \$520,700$$
$$= \underline{\$4,700} \text{ (U) (Exhibit 6-5)}$$

Can we conclude that the company overspent in advertising? No. An unfavorable variance is not necessarily bad, because the additional advertising expense may have helped increase market share. As discussed in Chapter 3, managers of profit centers are responsible for making *trade-offs* to maximize profits. In certain circumstances, they may choose to increase spending if it will lead to higher profits.

Activity-Based Costs

Finally, some types of indirect resources are used in ways that vary with cost-driver activities other than manufacturing outputs. For example, if the quality control department checks the first 10 items of each new batch, then quality control expense will vary with the number of batches. Similarly, warehousing costs may vary with the number of shipping orders, or selling costs may vary with the number of customers or customer segments.

Traditionally, management accounting systems have interpreted these expenses as "fixed" and calculated only *spending variances.* However, recent developments in activity-based costing allow a more revealing analysis. In particular, we can now obtain *volume, efficiency,* and *spending variance* information about activity-based costs. The following example illustrates the analysis.

To maintain its premium prices, Shade Tree Furniture Company has a Quality Control Department to ensure that the furniture is of premium quality. For each batch of furniture, the quality department checks a sample to see if the batch meets its high quality standards. If the sample passes the control check then the batch is shipped, but if it fails the quality control check, then the whole batch is sent back for inspection and rework. For 20X1, the budget for the department was $120,000 (included in "other manufacturing costs"). Half of this amount was salaries and other committed costs; the other half was supplies used to perform the quality control tests. Exhibit 6–7 compares expected and actual performance.

For activity-based costs, we can estimate three variances that you should recognize as similar to previous calculations:

- impact on profits due to changes in cost-driver activity (i.e., number of batches)
- impact on profits due to changes in efficiency
- impact on profits due to changes in cost of resources

EXHIBIT 6–7
Shade Tree Furniture
Data to Analyze the Performance of the Quality Control Department

	ASSUMPTIONS REFLECTED IN 20X1 PROFIT PLAN	ACTUAL DATA FOR 20X1
Number of batches	500	490
Amount of supplies per batch (liters)	1.50	1.40
Cost per one liter of supplies	$ 80.00	$ 80.50
Total cost of supplies	$60,000	$55,223

The quality department planned to use $60,000 in supplies but it actually spent $55,223. Again, we can use variances to get more detail on how the quality department was able to "save" $4,777. The first variance that we compute is due to volume effects. The cost driver for the quality control process is the number of batches.

$$\text{Volume variance} = (\text{planned number of batches} - \text{actual number of batches})$$
$$\times \text{ planned liters of supplies per batch}$$
$$\times \text{ planned cost of one liter of supplies}$$
$$= (500 - 490) \times 1.50 \times \$80 = \underline{\$1,200} \text{ (F)}$$

Part of the difference between planned and actual costs comes from a lower number of batches. If the quality department processed 10 batches less than expected, then we should expect cost savings of $1,200.

The quality department also used fewer liters of supplies per batch than planned (1.40 liters versus 1.50 liters). The impact of this difference upon profits is an efficiency variance:

$$\text{Efficiency variance} = \text{actual number of batches}$$
$$\times (\text{planned liters of supplies per batch}$$
$$- \text{ actual liters of supplies per batch})$$
$$\times \text{ planned cost of one liter of supplies}$$
$$= 490 \times (1.50 - 1.40) \times \$80 = \underline{\$3,920} \text{ (F)}$$

Finally, the quality department paid a higher price for supplies than expected. This difference created a spending variance:

$$\text{Spending variance} = \text{actual number of batches}$$
$$\times \text{ actual liters of supplies per batch}$$
$$\times (\text{planned cost of one unit of supplies}$$
$$- \text{ actual cost of one unit of supplies})$$
$$= 490 \times 1.40 \times (\$80.00 - \$80.50) = \underline{\$343} \text{ (U)}$$

The difference in activity-based costs between planned and actual performance in the quality department is explained by:

Volume variance	$1,200	(F)	
Efficiency variance	3,920	(F)	
Spending variance	343	(U)	
Total	$4,777	(F)	($60,000 − $55,223 on Exhibit 6−7)

These variances allow managers to evaluate and perhaps further investigate the performance of the quality department. Managers may judge the efficiency variance to be somewhat high. Did quality people find a way to save on supplies to perform quality control procedures? Did savings jeopardize the quality of Shade Tree Furniture products?

SUMMARY OF OPERATING EFFICIENCY VARIANCES

To summarize, then, we have computed the following variances related to operating efficiencies:

Raw materials	Efficiency variance	$33,176	(U)
	Spending variance	5,304	(F)
Total variance for raw material		$27,872	(U)
Labor	Efficiency variance	10,504	(F)
	Spending variance	0	
Total variance for labor		$10,504	(F)
Other manufacturing costs			
Quality department	Volume variance	1,200	(F)
	Efficiency variance	3,920	(F)
	Spending variance	343	(U)
Other manufacturing costs	Spending variance	15,427	(U)
Total variance other manufacturing costs		$10,650	(U)
S&A expenses	Spending variance	16,500	(F)
Advertising expenses	Spending variance	4,700	(U)
Interest expense	Spending variance	12,200	(U)
Total variance for nonproduction costs		$ 400	(U)
Total Operating Efficiency Variances		$28,418	(U)

The objective of analyzing operating efficiency variances was to explain the difference between the volume-adjusted profit plan and the actual income statement (Exhibit 6–5). At this point, we know that the difference of $27,872 in raw materials is mainly due to the operation using more wood per piece of furniture than expected ($33,176). We also know that the savings of $10,504 in wages is related to higher productivity and not to changes in wages. The additional cost of $10,650 identified in other manufacturing costs (Exhibit 6–5) is driven by a spending variance of $15,427. Finally, the changes in administrative, selling, advertising, and interest expenses are described as spending variances.

The picture that emerges from this analysis is mixed. The efficiency in using the raw materials was much lower than expected and this reduced profit by $33,176. If this lower efficiency is due to using cheaper raw material (observe the favorable spending variance for raw material), the decision to use such material reduced efficiency more than it saved in raw material costs. Labor wages were lower than expected and people worked more efficiently than planned. Advertising expense was higher than expected; however, sales were also higher and, if any relationship exists between these two numbers, then the extra advertising was worth it.

INTERPRETING STRATEGIC PROFITABILITY VARIANCES

The analysis of profit performance due to competitive effectiveness and operating efficiencies is now complete. We can summarize the analysis in Exhibit 6–8.

We can see in Exhibit 6–8 that the sum of the variances is exactly the difference between the original profit plan and the actual performance. This is not an accident. In our review of effectiveness and efficiency variances, we systematically examined each of the profit plan assumptions in sequence. This is illustrated in Table 6–1. The left column lists all the variables that were estimated for the original profit plan: market size, market share, selling price, average contribution, input quantities, input prices, and nonvariable costs. Listed across the top of each column are the seven variances that can be computed by comparing the original profit plan with the actual profit as reported on the income statement. Four of these variances are the competitive effectiveness variances, which explain the difference between the original profit plan and the volume-adjusted profit plan. The remaining three variances are the operating efficiency variances, which explain differences between the volume-adjusted profit plan and actual performance.

As we worked across Table 6–1 from left to right and calculated the seven variances identified at the top of each column, we "flipped" one profit plan variable at a time, turning an assumption in the original profit plan from "plan" to "actual." By comparing the difference between plan and actual for that one variable—and holding all other variables constant—we were able to isolate the variance effects. Thus, for example, the market share variance is based on the change in market share (*plan versus*

TABLE 6–1 Strategic Profitability Analysis "Switches"

ASSUMPTION IN ORIGINAL PROFIT PLAN	ORIGINAL PROFIT PLAN	COMPETITIVE EFFECTIVE VARIANCES			
		MARKET SIZE	MARKET SHARE	SALES PRICE	PRODUCT MIX
Market Size	**Plan vs. Actual**		Actual	Actual	Actual
Market Share	Plan	**Plan vs. Actual**		Actual	Actual
Selling Price	Plan	Plan	**Plan vs. Actual**		Actual
Average Contribution	Plan	Plan	Plan	**Plan vs. Actual**	
Input Quantities	Plan	Plan	Plan	Plan	Plan
Input Prices	Plan	Plan	Plan	Plan	Plan
Nonvariable Costs	Plan	Plan	Plan	Plan	Plan

How to use this table:

The top row indicates the different variances that can be estimated. For example, "market size" is a competitive effectiveness variance, whereas "production efficiency" variance is an operating efficiency variance. The left column lists assumptions in the original profit plan that can adopt two different values (like a "switch"): plan or actual. Changing the "switches" sequentially gives the different variances.

To calculate a variance, choose the variance of interest from the top row and read down the column. The variance calculation focuses on the difference between "plan and actual" for one specific

EXHIBIT 6–8
Shade Tree Furniture
Strategic Profitability Analysis

Expected profit before taxes	$635,000	
Competitive Effectiveness Variances due to:		
Change in market size	32,196	(F)
Change in market share	55,804	(F)
Change in price	(44,950)	(U)
Change in product mix	23,000	(F)
Total competitive effectiveness	66,050	(F)
Expected profit before taxes (volume-adjusted)	$701,050	
Operating Efficiency Variances due to:		
Efficiency in raw materials	(33,176)	(U)
Spending in raw materials	5,304	(F)
Efficiency in wages	10,504	(F)
Spending in wages	—	(U)
Other manufacturing expenses	(10,650)	(U)
Administrative and selling expenses	16,500	(F)
Advertising expense	(4,700)	(U)
Interest expense	(12,200)	(U)
Total operating efficiencies	(28,418)	(U)
Actual profit before taxes	$672,632	

	OPERATING EFFICIENCY VARIANCES			
VOLUME ADJUSTED PROFIT PLAN	PRODUCTION EFFICIENCY	PRODUCTION SPENDING	NONVARIABLE SPENDING	*ACTUAL INCOME STATEMENT*
Actual	Actual	Actual	Actual	Actual
Actual	Actual	Actual	Actual	Actual
Actual	Actual	Actual	Actual	Actual
Actual	Actual	Actual	Actual	Actual
Plan vs. Actual		Actual	Actual	Actual
Plan	**Plan vs. Actual**		Actual	Actual
Plan	Plan	**Plan vs. Actual**		Actual

profit plan assumption and sets all other variables in the formula at either actual or plan according to the values shown in the table. For example, the product mix variance calculates the difference between planned contribution margin and actual contribution margin, while setting market size, market share, and selling price to "actual," and holding input quantities, input prices, and nonvariable costs at their "planned" values.

actual) times *actual* market size and *planned* contribution (i.e., selling price, average contribution, input quantities, input prices, and nonvariable costs all held at profit plan estimates). The next variance—sales price—holds market size and share at *actual* and computes the difference between actual and expected selling price (i.e., *plan vs. actual*); again, contribution margin and other variables on the profit plan are maintained at the *plan* values to isolate the effect.

One by one, we systematically covered all the variances, moving from the original profit plan in the left column—where all variables were estimates and/or standards (identified as "plan" in Table 6–1)—to the actual income statement at the far right of the table, where all variables reflect actual performance outcomes.[4]

Searching for Explanations and Initiating Action Plans

Variances in themselves do little to explain the reasons why performance was above or below expectations. Knowing that input prices fell, or that market share increased, is only the first step. We still do not know why. Managers must investigate the reasons for these changes and initiate actions to either rectify problems or take advantage of unforeseen opportunities. We have identified some of the possible causes earlier, but we can recap as follows:

Shade Tree Furniture's profits before income tax during 20X1 were $37,632 better than planned. The company was favored by a larger market and a higher market share, but it suffered a "cost" of $44,950 from reducing its prices. Did the company capture market share by reducing prices and putting its premium image at risk? The company sold a higher portion of benches, which have a bigger margin. Was this shift a one-time event in 20X1, or does it indicate a change in customers' tastes? The most significant variance on our analysis of operational efficiencies is an unfavorable $33,176 in raw material efficiency. Did the increase in sales volume affect production, or did the company hire low-skilled people to save on labor costs? Finally, administrative and selling expenses had a favorable variance. Was it caused by lower prices, or did the company manage its administrative systems differently?

USING STRATEGIC PROFITABILITY ANALYSIS

Managers formally compare actual performance to profit plan performance at least once a year and typically more often (e.g., monthly or quarterly). Effective managers *manage by exception.* In other words, they devote their scarce attention to understanding and acting upon variances that could imperil the strategy. Measures that are aligned with expectations receive little attention. By focusing on large or strategic variances, managers can quickly focus their attention on those issues that require follow-up action. Thus, strategic profitability analysis is an extremely important tool to increase ROM.

---

[4] John Shank and Neil Churchill introduced the genesis of this approach in their article "Variance Analysis: A Management-Oriented Approach," *The Accounting Review* 5 (1977): 950–57.

Managers use strategic profitability analyses for three purposes: strategic learning, early warning, and performance evaluation.

Strategic Learning

Variance analysis helps managers ask the right questions and calculate the costs or benefits of deviations from the norm. What was the effect on profits of higher input costs? What was the effect of a larger market share? Large deviations attract managers' attention.

The comparison between expected and actual performance leads managers to review:

- assumptions and standards
- cause-and-effect relationships
- the validity of intended strategy
- the effectiveness and efficiency of strategy implementation

Of course, the strategy of any particular business will influence which strategic profitability variances managers monitor. By way of example, Table 6–2 summarizes possible choices for two competing strategies: differentiation and low cost.

Managers of businesses following a *differentiation* strategy, based on high value-added products or services, will ensure that price variances and mix variances are being computed routinely and monitored carefully; these are key measures of strategic effectiveness for their businesses. By contrast, managers of firms competing by *low price* and high volume must ensure that they have accurate data to routinely calculate market share, internal efficiencies, and input prices. Regardless of strategy, all firms in competitive markets must monitor their discretionary spending habits (spending variances) and ensure that they are accurately informed about changes in the size of the market in which they are competing.

Strategy evolves as managers learn from their actions and incorporate new information revealed by analysis and follow-up. Variance analysis facilitates this learning process.

TABLE 6–2 Strategic Profitability Variances for Two Competing Strategies

	MARKET SIZE	MARKET SHARE	SALES PRICE	SALES MIX	PRODUCTION EFFICIENCY	PRODUCTION SPENDING	DISCRETIONARY SPENDING
Differentiation Strategy	✓	✓	✓	✓	❷	❷	❷
Low-Cost, High-Volume Strategy	✓	✓	❷	❷	✓	✓	❷

✓ = Primary strategic importance
❷ = Important, but not strategic (i.e., unlikely to cause strategy to fail)

Profit Planning in Magazine Production

In magazine production, advertising sales and revenue from reader subscriptions are the two major sources of profit. However, because so much production work is outsourced (e.g., prepress and printing), managing vendor costs is essential. In the 1980s, a midsized magazine publisher was losing money with 58 cents of every revenue dollar spent on manufacturing and distribution. Due to high indebtedness, the company was also cash-constrained.

To get a better understanding of the drivers of profitability, the publisher introduced a continual profit planning process that integrated financial income projections prepared by the advertising and circulation departments with cost budgets from manufacturing. For the first time, the manufacturing department based their budgets on layout and itemized vendor costs for a typical issue (e.g., number of pages, black and white versus color, editorial versus advertising content, and type of paper). Subsequent variance analysis between the budgets and actual profits revealed some important gaps.

The key problem was in advertising: Managers lacked a realistic sense of costs and revenues in making projections. The official advertising rates were set too low to generate profits; to make matters worse, advertising representatives were selling space in the magazine by discounting rates even further. Furthermore, production vendors essentially dictated their terms with the magazine. With these insights, new practices were introduced. The work supplied by vendors was opened to competitive bidding. Advertising rates were raised, causing advertisers to buy more-valuable ad space. Finally, changing the layout of the magazine with cost requirements in mind lowered the ratio of manufacturing costs to net revenues from 58% to 35%.

Source: Adapted from Bert Langford, "Take the Guesswork Out of Budgeting," *Folio: The Magazine for Magazine Management* (Special Sourcebook Issue for 1998 Supplement): 172.

Early Warning and Corrective Action

Strategic profitability analysis also warns managers about possible events that may derail intended strategy. Remember how many interdependencies existed among the variables on the profit wheel, cash wheel, and ROE wheel in Chapter 5? If one of those variables fails, it could mean a major threat to the company.

Unforeseen events continually affect any company. Without an early warning system, unexpected events may only be noticed when major consequences are unavoidable. Comparing the profit plan with ongoing performance facilitates early diagnosis of the potential consequences of these unforeseen events. If a particular item deviates from the value in the profit plan, managers can take actions to bring the indicator back on track. Managers can react early to avoid unpleasant "surprises." However, not all surprises are bad. Sometimes, early warning systems allow managers to take advantage of new opportunities in the market.

Performance Evaluation

Profit plans can also be used for performance evaluation. The comparison between expected and actual performance serves to inform managers about the effort that subordinates have put into achieving the goals described in the profit plan. Setting objectives and evaluating performance against objectives motivates people to put substantial effort into achieving the strategy of the organization. (We will cover this topic in depth in Chapter 11.)

For effective evaluation, managers must use strategic profitability analysis to get a true picture of the reasons for performance. Shade Tree's sales of $4,450,050 exceeded the profit plan estimate of $4,300,000 by a comfortable margin. Our initial reaction might be to praise the efforts of the sales manager and give him a positive performance evaluation. However, as we gather more information from our strategic profitability variances, we may temper or change our initial opinion. For example, as we saw earlier, sales have been favorably affected by growth in the overall market and possibly by favorable moves by competitors.

Strategic Profitability Analysis in the Banking Industry

A recent survey by the Bank Administration Institute showed that banks are struggling to keep pace with emerging needs for tactical and strategic performance information. As a result, they are spending substantial sums (on average $150,000 per $1 billion of assets) to replace or enhance aging information management systems.

The need for new performance measurement and analysis systems reflects the historic shift away from line-of-business management structures based on distinct legal entities (designed to meet banking regulations). Although many banks are executing new strategies that target specific customers and segments, fewer than one in 10 survey respondents generate either full or partial profitability analyses focusing on individual customers or customer segments. Similarly, only 25% of respondents generate product profitability reports.

An aging information systems infrastructure is at the root of the banks' problems. More than 60% of respondents said that their system platforms were more than five years old. Most older financial systems are based on traditional general ledger systems and cannot handle the complicated allocation algorithms and reports required for multidimensional performance analysis. Providing product and customer-segment profitability with these older systems is often next to impossible. Further complicating the picture is the lack of integration among the various components of each banks' performance management systems: general ledger, cost allocation system, funds-transfer pricing system, a reporting system, and a planning/budgeting system.

To address these challenges, banks are investing in new systems. One-third of survey respondents reported that significant new performance-measurement-systems enhancements were underway, with outlays averaging $2 million per bank.

Source: Adapted from Craig I. Coit and John Karr, "Performance Measurement: Miles Traveled, Miles to Go," *Banking Strategies* 72 (September/October 1996): 68–70.

CHAPTER SUMMARY

The discussion in this chapter has focused solely on evaluation of performance using financial accounting data. This is appropriate for our analysis of profit plan performance. However, we need to be careful not to forget the importance of intangible resources and nonfinancial measures. These will be covered in depth in later chapters.

The design of a profit plan is the first step in enabling managers to translate their strategy into action. During this process, managers are forced to make assumptions about the viability of the strategy and agree upon its details. Cause-and-effect relationships are hypothesized and strategies are communicated.

Successful strategy implementation requires managers to test their profit plan assumptions to validate strategy. The strategic profitability analysis tools described in this chapter provide that framework. Variance computations allow managers to understand the effectiveness and efficiency of strategy implementation.

Managers use strategic profitability analysis for three purposes:

- Strategic learning—Strategic profitability analysis allows managers to evaluate the adequacy of the intended strategy of the organization and the cause-effect assumptions that underlie the strategy.
- Early warning and corrective action—Analysis of strategic profitability gives managers either assurance that the strategy is on track or, alternatively, early warning that implementation is not proceeding according to plan.
- Performance evaluation—Strategic profitability analysis gives managers the tools to evaluate the success of individual managers in implementing strategy and the success of business units in creating value.

With strategic profitability data in hand, managers can redesign organizational processes or change the standards—even the strategy—to take advantage of changing developments in competitive markets and internal operations. Like all good performance measurement and control system tools, strategic profitability analysis should be used to enhance ROM. Techniques for using this information to enhance management effectiveness is the topic of Part III of this book.

7

Designing Asset Allocation Systems

I n previous chapters, we referred to the importance of developing a coherent plan for the acquisition and allocation of resources to support strategies underlying the profit plan. Procedures must be created to analyze and determine the appropriate level of investment in productive resources needed to support desired strategies.

We defined an asset in Chapter 2 as *a resource, owned or controlled by the business, that will yield future economic benefits.* At this point in our analysis, it is important to emphasize two aspects of this definition. First, managers must make a *decision* to acquire an asset. The right to own or control something of value is gained only for a price. Managers must make a conscious decision to acquire inventory, finance sales with a note receivable, prepay office rent, invest in research to develop a new drug, or acquire a new production machine. Each of these choices to create an asset requires the expenditure of working capital.

Second, the benefits from owning an asset — its value — are realized in the *future:* Inventory will be turned into cash in three months time, a note receivable will be collected in one year, prepaid rent will allow the future use of office space, a new drug will generate sales over the next 15 years, and a new machine will produce products over its 20-year useful life. In all these cases, expending resources today to build up or acquire an asset yields future benefits to the firm.

Two implications flow from this analysis. First, managers need a set of tools to help them decide when it makes sense to commit current resources to acquire assets (and when it does not). Second, these tools must incorporate estimates of the future economic value that an asset can provide and the degree to which future benefits support business strategies. These tools and analyses are the subject of this chapter.

ASSET ALLOCATION SYSTEMS

The impetus for acquiring new resources can come from many sources. For example, accounting or production data may suggest that cost, quality, or capacity shortfalls require investment in new assets. Emerging new technologies or markets may stimulate investigation of the benefits of acquiring additional productive assets to support new strategic initiatives. Table 7–1 illustrates some of the types of information that may cause managers to consider upgrading existing assets or investing in new assets. Managers in accounting, marketing, production, engineering, or division management may

TABLE 7–1 Sources and Types of Information That Stimulate Requests for Allocation of Assets

INFORMATION ABOUT	DISCREPANCY	EVIDENCE	SOURCE
Costs	too high	input costs have risen	accounting data
		prices have fallen	marketing
	may be lowered	analytic study or model	production or engineering
Quality	inadequate	competitive improvement	marketing
		customer need	marketing
		prices have fallen	marketing
	may be improved	analytic study or model	engineering
Capacity	insufficient	sales > capacity	marketing
		forecast > capacity	marketing
		planned new-product introduction	engineering development marketing division management

Source: Adapted from J. Bower, *Managing the Resource Allocation Process* (Boston: HBS Press, 1996; originally published 1970): 53.

obtain this information from customers, accounting data, analytic models, or production plans.

In small businesses, these types of information will be gathered and processed informally. As businesses grow larger, however, formal systems become critical in identifying the need for new assets and in helping managers decide how to allocate scarce financial resources. An **asset allocation system** is the set of formal routines and procedures designed to process and evaluate requests to acquire new assets. It is sometimes known as a **capital budget** or *capital investment plan*. These systems, like the profit plans to which they are linked, typically work on a calendar cycle—that is, formal proposals for asset acquisitions are created once a year. The timing of this process is designed to ensure that proposals are formally evaluated and approved prior to actually committing to spend any money.

Asset allocation systems provide a number of benefits. First, they provide a *framework* and set of categories into which asset proposals can be grouped. We can think of this framework as a set of buckets lined up according to defined categories. Sorting asset acquisition proposals into different buckets forces managers to be explicit about the type of value that they expect each asset to provide and the economic viability of the proposal. For example, the decision to install a new multimillion-dollar paper making machine would be put in a different category or bucket than the decision to replace the aging sprinkler system in a warehouse.

Second, asset allocation systems include *analytic tools* that can be tailored to different types of assets. The analysis of the net benefits of a sprinkler system is different than the analysis of the net benefits of a paper making machine. With proposals sorted into the correct bucket, decision makers can apply different decision tools to each category.

Finally, and most importantly, asset allocation systems provide *guidelines* that help managers throughout the organization understand how their proposals relate to the strategy of the business. Acquiring assets often involves the analysis and judgment of several, if not many, people. These systems can be used to communicate what types of assets are needed (and not needed) to support new and ongoing strategic initiatives.

The decision to allocate assets to a business can be extremely consequential. For example, a decision to build a plant in a new country, change core production technologies, or acquire a new distribution system can commit a business to a course of action for many years. Acquiring any asset involves choice, and future options may become more limited after choices are made.

Because of the sometimes large sums of money involved, and the often irrevocable commitments, there are few other decisions in organizations in which decision making authority is so carefully prescribed. Businesses invariably impose limits on the discretion of any individual manager to authorize or commit to the acquisition of assets. These limits are a function of span of accountability and position in the organizational hierarchy. The former affects the *type of assets* for which the manager has authority to commit; the latter affects the *amount of money* that a manager can commit.

Unlike double-entry bookkeeping systems, asset allocation systems are not designed according to generally accepted rules of practice. There are no GAAP (generally accepted accounting principles) for the design of asset allocation systems. Instead, managers must tailor these systems to their preferences, based on their performance measurement and control needs. Nevertheless, there are generalizable design principles that can serve as guidelines for any manager as he or she attempts to design systems to guide in the acquisition and allocation of assets.

Limits on Asset Allocations

Given the variety and unpredictability of requests for new assets, senior managers must provide some type of guidance to subordinates about what kind of assets to acquire. In practice, however, it makes little sense to specify in detail the types of assets that are desirable. In a large business, senior managers cannot know when machines should be replaced or when new technology indicates the need to upgrade equipment. There is too much that is unknown to senior managers, especially as unanticipated problems and opportunities emerge. Because senior managers can never possess the amount of specific knowledge that is known by lower-level managers, information about the need for new assets is typically gathered and created at lower organizational levels.

Therefore, rather than specifying in detail the types of assets that are desirable, senior managers typically specify limits on the types of capital expenditures that will be approved. Within these boundaries, managers are then free to exercise their initiative and judgment concerning the types of assets that they would like to acquire to achieve

---

Investment Strategy at Coke and Pepsi

Roberto Goizueta, the legendary CEO of Coca-Cola Company, left work at 4:30 most afternoons to spend time with his family. Yet, Coke's market value grew from $4.3 billion when he took over in 1981 to $180 billion by 1997. How did he do it? Goizueta delegated day-to-day management of most details of the business, except for resource allocation. Roberto Goizueta understood that resources had to be allocated to those investments that would enhance shareholder value, and he spent a good deal of his time evaluating how best to deploy Coca-Cola's assets.

During Goizueta's tenure, Coke invested heavily in soft drink infrastructure and brand building. The company divested the capital-intensive and low-return bottling operations into Coca-Cola Enterprises, which allowed Coke to remove these assets from its balance sheet while still retaining nominal control of these strategic assets through its 49% ownership of the company. Contrast Goizueta's investment strategy with PepsiCo, which continued to invest in its restaurant franchises (Kentucky Fried Chicken, Taco Bell, and Pizza Hut) and snack food businesses. In 1997 and 1998, Pepsi decided to embrace some of Coke's investment strategies. It spun off its capital-intensive and low-margin restaurant businesses and announced plans to do the same with its bottling operations.

Sources: Adapted from John Huey, "In Search of Roberto's Secret Formula," *Fortune,* December 29, 1997, 230–234, and Patricia Sellers, "How Coke is Kicking Pepsi's Can," *Fortune,* October 28, 1996, 70–84.

---

their business goals. Asset allocation constraints are especially important for expenditures that are large in magnitude or that relate to the strategic priorities of the business.

To create these boundaries, senior managers communicate limits on the type of assets that are suitable for potential acquisition. Senior managers do so by specifying *minimum constraints* that must be considered when proposing assets for potential acquisition. For example, a common means of specifying financial limits for potential new assets is to stipulate the *minimum* ROI that is acceptable. Asset allocation guidelines may stipulate that new asset proposals will not be considered unless they can generate *at least* 18% ROI. This guideline is not designed to tell managers what types of assets to acquire; instead, it tells them what types of assets should not be acquired—those earning less than 18% ROI.

Policies and Procedures

Understanding how to use asset allocation systems is important, both for those submitting proposals to acquire assets and for those responsible for approving proposals. Individuals making proposals must present information to communicate the need for the asset they wish to purchase. Resources are inevitably scarce, and each proposal will be competing against others for scarce funding resources. Thus, managers proposing to acquire specific assets must attempt to make the best possible case in support of their proposal.

Those responsible for ratifying asset acquisition proposals and allocating funding must also have a set of tools that will help them choose among competing alternatives. Some proposals should be accepted, but others must be rejected because of constraints in either capital or management attention. All proposals, whether good or bad, will have proponents—or champions—who may argue vigorously for the need to expend resources to support important initiatives. Good analysis is the key to responding to these requests in a way that reflects the intended strategy of the business.

Therefore, asset allocation procedures should specify a process by which proposals are evaluated and approved. These procedures typically set out:

1. the *analyses* needed to document a request,
2. the *process* by which proposals will be gathered together and reviewed by top managers, and
3. a *time frame* each year during which managers will consider formal requests for new assets. This time frame should dovetail with the approval of the profit plan to ensure that adequate resources will be available to support strategic initiatives. (See the "Investment in Assets" variable in the profit wheel diagram of Chapter 5.)

Span of Accountability

Senior managers should communicate policies regarding who has authority to approve the acquisition of assets. As mentioned above, the ability of a manager to acquire assets is directly related to his or her span of accountability. Managers with narrow spans of accountability—such as cost center or functional managers—are usually accountable for managing to a cost budget. Their performance measures do not typically encompass balance sheet assets (e.g., ROA or ROCE). Because cost center managers are not accountable for balance sheet assets, they are not given the authority to unilaterally acquire assets for their functional units without the approval of higher-level managers. For example, a cost center manager in charge of a function such as information technology is held accountable for delivering a specified level of information service utilizing a fixed level of resources. The chief information officer (CIO) is given a spending budget and held accountable for providing a satisfactory level of networked information services within those resources. Requests to purchase additional servers and network equipment to enhance this service must be approved higher in the organization by a manager with a wider span of accountability.

By contrast, business managers with wide spans of accountability will have relatively wide latitude and authority to acquire assets. Business unit managers are accountable for profit performance and, often, for managing the level of balance sheet assets to deliver that profit. Their performance measures can (and should) encompass balance sheet accounts such as working capital and ROCE. Therefore, profit center managers are often given the right—subject to defined spending limits—to acquire and dispose of assets to achieve these objectives.

Spending Limits

Spending limits, defined according to managerial position and span of accountability, are a common way of limiting discretion. When asset acquisition proposals fall outside a manager's spending limit and/or span of accountability, those proposals must be sent higher in the organization for approval. Thus, asset allocation spending limits may take some variation of the following form based on hierarchical position:

Asset Allocation Authority at SKF

SKF Ab, headquartered in Gothenburg, Sweden, is the world's largest manufacturer of industrial rolling bearings, accounting for a fifth of the $20 billion world market. Its production is organized worldwide, although 65% of its manufacturing still comes from western Europe. To reduce this imbalance, the group is investing $629 million in new plants in growth markets such as the United States, Poland, India, Malaysia and South Korea, as well as five joint ventures in China.

SKF's asset allocation structure has been designed to balance central control and local decision-making. Most capital investment decisions within existing country markets, such as plant extensions, require only the approval of the country manager and do not need to be referred to the financial director in Sweden. Within each local subsidiary, however, the project's economic value must be proven using standard cash flow and payback measures.

SKF's treasury function supports line management's decisions by providing access to capital for investments in specific geographical territories. Treasurers are located regionally, except for areas of high currency volatility (e.g., Asia and South America), which have been recentralized to the group treasury at the Swedish headquarters.

Source: Adapted from Tim Burt, "Own Words: Tore Bertilsson, SKF," *Financial Times,* November 5, 1997, and Peter Marsh, "Change of Culture at SKF," *Financial Times,* August 25, 1997, 17.

Hierarchical Position	Authority to Commit to Asset Acquisitions
Board of Directors	All asset acquisitions above $1 million must be approved by the Board
President and CEO	up to $1 million
Executive vice president	up to $500,000
Business unit president	up to $200,000
Functional vice president	up to $50,000

Under this type of spending limit rule, approval for increasingly large asset commitments is referred higher in the organization to those with wider spans of accountability. This decision rule ensures that all large, consequential, asset acquisition decisions are reviewed at senior-executive levels to ensure that they align with top management's strategy and do not commit the business to courses of action that are inappropriate or too risky.

Another approach, which often complements spending limits, stipulates different approval paths depending on the strategic implications of the investment. Under this approach, top managers define (1) asset investment categories into which proposals must be sorted and (2) a separate approval process for each category of investment. Usually, approval of strategic investments is reserved for top management; approval of investments to enhance existing operations is delegated to lower-level managers. We consider this approach next.

SORTING ASSETS BY CATEGORY

Consider the diversity of asset and capital expenditures that might be considered in any business: the purchase of new machinery, the renewal of existing computer equipment, the redesign and remodeling of a distribution facility, and the installation of a new telephone network. Managers responsible for allocating resources need some way to make sense of this diversity.

Managers must have a consistent way of categorizing projects so that the correct analytic tools and decision criteria can be applied to each bucket. Different businesses will create different classification schemes to meet their unique circumstances. The appropriate categories will be determined by the industry in which a firm competes and the types of technology that it employs. For example, the classification criteria will be different in a knowledge-intensive software developer as compared with a capital-intensive steel mill. In most businesses, however, the projects and/or initiatives fall into three general classes, each of which has different criteria for evaluation:

(1) Assets to Meet Safety/Health/Regulatory Needs   The acquisition of certain assets is necessary to protect the safety and health of employees, or to protect the local environment. Others are necessary to comply with new local, state, and federal regulations. These expenditures are either mandated by law or necessary to protect health and safety, so a formal cost/benefit justification is not required. These expenditures cannot be deferred or rejected—they are an unavoidable cost of doing business. Therefore, for this category of assets, analysis will focus on the most cost-effective way to comply with health, safety, or regulatory needs.

(2) Assets to Enhance Operating Efficiency and/or Increase Revenue   To compete successfully over time, production and information processing capacity must be maintained and overhauled, resulting in expenditures for replacement software and machinery, and the renewal and repair of existing capacity. Sometimes, new assets based on superior technologies can be acquired to reduce cost and/or improve reliability and quality (e.g., construction of a new state-of-the art manufacturing line). These types of expenditures are necessary to maintain efficient productive capacity but can often be deferred for limited periods if managers so choose.

Incremental investments in production, distribution, and internal processing capabilities may also offer the promise of increased revenue. For example, removing production bottlenecks in a manufacturing plant may allow the business to ship more product to meet excess demand. In a bank, faster turnaround of loan applications may allow more loans to be booked each quarter. Specialized techniques for economic analysis must be applied to this category of assets.

(3) Assets to Enhance Competitive Effectiveness   Certain assets must be acquired, or capital expenditures made, to fund the strategy of the business. For these assets, project proposals must be compared with strategic goals to determine how important each asset is to meeting the strategic imperatives of the business. These assets might include, for example, acquiring a new distribution network or constructing a new plant in a country where the business does not have any manufacturing capability. Also included in this category are ventures and acquisitions that take the business into new product markets.

Because of their strategic impact and substantial cost, these assets must be subject to a series of tests to ensure that they respond to the strategic and financial goals of the business. These decisions are typically reserved for the highest levels of management because the dollar magnitude can be large and the payoffs uncertain.

EVALUATING ASSET ACQUISITION PROPOSALS

In this section, we review the different analytic techniques for evaluating asset acquisition proposals. We begin with the most straightforward decisions—those relating to safety, health, and regulation—and work up to the most consequential decisions—those relating to major commitments that irrevocably set the strategic course of the business.

1. Evaluating Assets Acquired to Meet Safety/Health/Regulatory Needs

This is the most straightforward category. As noted above, there is little choice or decision regarding these assets. Reputable businesses, and managers of those businesses, must ensure that ongoing operations do not endanger the health or safety of employees and local communities. Ventilation systems, fire alarm and escape systems, emergency evacuation systems, and many other resources must be devoted to ensuring the welfare of employees. In addition, businesses must make all necessary investments to comply with laws and regulations—handicap access must be provided, toxic emissions must be cleaned, and waste chemicals must be disposed of safely.

The only analysis required for these expenditures is to ensure that (1) the assets being purchased are suitable to the task and (2) the business is receiving the best value relative to the features and/or benefits that are provided. Engineering studies and comparison of features versus cost will give managers the necessary information to make these decisions.

Pennsylvania Power and Light

In the early 1990s, Pennsylvania Power & Light Company was considering how to upgrade an antiquated, 1970s-era, fluorescent lighting system in a 17,775 square-foot drafting area. Not only was it expensive to maintain ($12,745 annually), but it was hurting employees' productivity and health through the glare and eyestrain that it produced. A new lighting system, more focused on lighting employees' individual workstations, would cost the company $48,882, but management estimated that it would be paid for in just 73 days and generate an average ROI of 501% annually. Under the new system, which had fewer components, maintenance costs dropped by 76%, drafter productivity percentage (measured in the days to complete a drawing) increased by 13.2%, and energy consumption dropped by 69%. The investment showed an annual cost benefit of $244,929. Worker morale also increased, with an initial 25% drop in sick leave.

Source: Adapted from Dana Dubbs, "Retrofit Chalks up 501% ROI Through Higher Productivity and Lower Costs," *Facilities Design & Management* (April 1991): 39.

Approvals for this category of investment can be delegated to individual business unit managers. Top-level corporate managers do not need to review or ratify these decisions unless the cost is unusually high, thereby affecting cash flow and/or profit plan and ROE estimates.

2. Evaluating Assets to Enhance Operating Efficiency and/or Increase Revenue

The decision to invest in upgrades and improvements for existing operations is usually discretionary. In other words, doing nothing is a viable option. This is the same type of decision many of us make in deciding whether or not to buy a new car. Should we trade up to a newer model with improved features and lower maintenance costs, or should we save our money and make do with our old car for one more year? For these types of decisions, choosing not to invest—at least in the short term—is a viable alternative.

In a business, this type of investment must stand on its own merits. The decision to acquire an asset to enhance efficiency or increase revenue can be delegated to individual business-unit managers. However, in delegating this decision, it becomes the responsibility of those managers to demonstrate that the economic benefits of acquiring the new asset exceed the cost. In essence, the question to be asked is, Will the increase in future cash flows justify the current outlay of resources to acquire or upgrade the asset?

Managers use three analytic techniques to estimate the benefits of investing in assets to improve operational efficiency: payback, discounted cash flow, and internal rate of return.

Payback

The most common and intuitive cash flow evaluation technique estimates the time period required for an investment to pay for itself from incremental cash flows. **Payback** is calculated as total acquisition cost (an outflow of cash) divided by the amount of the periodic inflow of cash (or cash saving) that the asset is expected to generate. For long-lived assets, the resulting ratio is usually expressed in years. Thus,

Payback in Years

$$= \frac{\text{Total Cash Outlay to Acquire Asset}}{\text{Annual Cash Inflow or Savings During Each Year of the Asset's Life}}$$

Recall from Chapter 5 that Boston Retail was planning to invest in a new computerized management system to integrate sales records, inventory management, purchase orders, and the accounting general ledger. The cost for this system was $60,000. Management estimated that the system would reduce bookkeeping and auditing costs by $10,000 a year and allow the business to lower inventory levels, which would save an additional $5,000 a year in financing costs. The payback for this investment can be calculated quickly as:

$$\text{Payback in Years} = \frac{\$60,000}{\$15,000}$$

$$= 4 \text{ years}$$

Thus, managers estimated that the investment would "pay for itself" in four years.

If cash flows are irregular—for example, if the annual cash savings were estimated to be $6,000, $12,000, $17,000, $20,000, and so on—then payback is calculated simply by adding up the yearly cash savings to determine the year (or month) in which the total savings eclipse the original outlay.

Break-Even Time in Product Development

In the early 1990s, companies such as Hewlett–Packard Company began to use break-even time to assess the performance of their new-product development efforts.[1] Break-even time revealed the number of months before a new product paid back the money that the company had invested in it. The "clock" was set to zero when the product development project was started. During development, the company invested money until the product was launched; then it began to earn profits that progressively paid back the investment. When the profits generated equaled the investment, the product reached its break-even time. (See figure.)

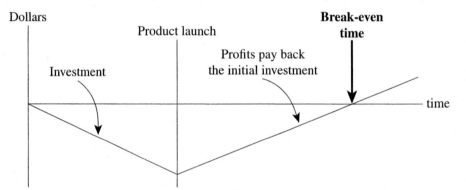

The break-even metric provided very useful information to evaluate the product development process. Long break-even times suggested that products were not as successful as expected and that the company was running the risk of not recouping its investment. Short break-even times provided a good indication that the product development process was efficient and effective.

However, in some companies, senior executives also used this information to evaluate the performance of product development managers. In these cases, product development managers were tempted to game the measure. To reduce break-even time as much as possible, for example, they could select new products that were simple modifications of existing products. These "new" products required very little investment and their success was assured if the original product was already established. Therefore, break-even time was minimized but, paradoxically, the company risked depleting its innovation capabilities as revolutionary products were avoided.

---

[1] For a complete description of the application of HP's break-even time measure, see Charles H. House and Raymond L. Price, "The Return Map: Tracking Product Teams," *Harvard Business Review* 69 (January/February, 1991): 92–100.

Payback calculations are quick and intuitive and are used in almost all businesses. This simple calculation tells managers when they will recoup their investment. Payback reveals the business's exposure to cash drain and the period of time for which it would have a cash deficit related to the project. When cash is scarce, this information is critically important.

A payback calculation, however, does not consider the time value of money. Thus, in dividing current dollars by future dollars, the numerator and denominator of the payback calculation may be stated in currencies of different values. In other words, managers may be dividing apples and oranges. Moreover, the payback calculation ignores the economic benefits received *after* the initial payback period. So, although payback provides important information in terms of *cash flow exposure,* it does not do a good job evaluating the true economic returns from the investment. For this, we need discounted cash flow analysis.

Discounted Cash Flow

A more sophisticated approach considers not only net cash flows over the entire life of the investment, but also recognizes that future cash flows are worth less than current cash flows. The basic starting point for discounted cash flow analysis is construction of a cash flow time line, as illustrated in Exhibit 7–1. If we stay with Boston Retail's analysis of a computerized reporting system, managers have estimated that the benefits will accrue over a seven-year period (with no residual value).

At this point, we could add up the cost savings over the seven-year period ($15,000 × 7 years = $105,000) and compare this with the initial cash outlay ($60,000) to discover that the project will save the business $45,000. However, this simple summation does not take into account the eroding effects of time on the value of future cash flows.

Therefore, the next step is to use a calculator or discount table to restate the future cash flows into their current dollar equivalents. If managers believe that money will decrease in value by 10% per year, a calculator or present value table can be consulted to find the discount factor for each of the next seven years (the current outlay of $60,000

EXHIBIT 7–1
Cash Flow Time Line

	COST SAVINGS						
INITIAL INVESTMENT JANUARY 1 20X2	YEAR 1 12/31 20X2	YEAR 2 12/31 20X3	YEAR 3 12/31 20X4	YEAR 4 12/31 20X5	YEAR 5 12/31 20X6	YEAR 6 12/31 20X7	YEAR 7 12/31 20X8
$-60,000	$15,000	$15,000	$15,000	$15,000	$15,000	$15,000	$15,000

EXHIBIT 7–2
Discounted Cash Flow Time Line

	INITIAL INVESTMENT JANUARY 1 20X2	COST SAVINGS						
		YEAR 1 12/31 20X2	YEAR 2 12/31 20X3	YEAR 3 12/31 20X4	YEAR 4 12/31 20X5	YEAR 5 12/31 20X6	YEAR 6 12/31 20X7	YEAR 7 12/31 20X8
	$−60,000	$15,000	$15,000	$15,000	$15,000	$15,000	$15,000	$15,000
Discount Factor	0	0.909	0.826	0.751	0.683	0.621	0.564	0.513
Current Value Equivalent	$ 60,000	$13,635	$12,390	$11,265	$10,245	$ 9,315	$ 8,460	$ 7,695

does not need to be restated because a dollar today is worth exactly one dollar). We can use this information to restate the cash flows for each future year into current-value equivalents (Exhibit 7–2).

By taking the sum of the seven discounted future savings ($13,635 + 12,390 + ... + $7,697 = $73,005) and comparing this amount with the initial investment of $60,000, we see that the true savings is not $45,000, as originally calculated, but instead a more modest $13,005. This summation of discounted cash flows is known as the **net present value** (NPV) of the investment. Stated in current dollars, Boston Retail will be better off by $13,000 if it goes ahead with the investment.

Obviously, the accuracy of a discounted cash flow analysis depends not only on the accuracy of cash flow estimates, but also on the assumed level of the discount rate. At a 10%

EXHIBIT 7–3
Calculation of Repayment of $60,000 Bank Loan
and Present Value of Future Cash Savings

YEAR ENDED DEC 31	(1) OPENING LOAN BALANCE	(2) ACCRUED INTEREST ON LOAN [(1) × 10%]	(3) CASH SAVINGS FROM INVESTMENT	(4) BANK PAYMENT
January 1, 20X2				
20X2	$60,000	$6,000	$15,000	$15,000
20X3	51,000	5,100	15,000	15,000
20X4	41,100	4,110	15,000	15,000
20X5	30,210	3,021	15,000	15,000
20X6	18,231	1,823	15,000	15,000
20X7	5,054	505	15,000	5,560
20X8		—	15,000	—
Net Present Value of Investment @ 10% interest				

discount rate, the project shows a positive NPV of $13,000. However, at a 17% discount rate, the NPV turns negative, showing that the value of cash outflows exceeds the present value of cash inflows by $1,150. Of course, if there is no time value to money—if the discount rate is set at 0—then the NPV of the project is $45,000, as we computed earlier.

Although it is intuitively appealing to think of discounting as a method for recognizing erosion in the purchasing power of money, in a business setting it is more theoretically correct to think of the discount rate as the rate that managers must pay for the use of the financial resources provided by shareholders and lenders (remember the ROE wheel?). By way of illustration, imagine that Boston Retail borrowed $60,000 from the bank to pay for the new computer system. Interest charges would accrue at 10% per year on the unpaid balance. The loan would be repaid in annual installments of $15,000 until the loan was paid in full. This, in fact, is exactly the cash flow that we worked with previously. The only difference is that we are now assuming that the money is being borrowed from a bank.

We have already calculated the NPV of this investment. Using Exhibit 7–2, we calculated that the value to the business of the $60,000 investment is $13,005. Let's calculate what the value would be if we borrowed the $60,000 from the bank. Exhibit 7–3 shows what happens. In year 1, all of the $15,000 cash savings is paid over to the bank to repay the loan and accrued interest. The business does not retain any of the savings. The same is true in years 2, 3, 4, and 5. In each of these years, none of the cost savings accrue to the business; they are all turned over to the bank. By year 6, however, the loan is almost paid off. Only $5,560 is needed to retire the loan. With this final payment, the remaining cash savings—$9,440 in year 6 and $15,000 in year 7—accrue solely to the benefit of the firm. What is the present value of these two amounts? The answer is revealed in column 8. The present value of the cash savings from the investment after the loan is paid off is $13,000 (with a small difference due to rounding).

(5) ENDING LOAN BALANCE [(1) + (2) − (4)]	(6) CASH SAVINGS RETAINED [(3) − (4)]	(7) PRESENT VALUE FACTOR	(8) PRESENT VALUE OF CASH SAVINGS RETAINED [(6) × (7)]
$60,000			
51,000	$ —		
41,100	—		
30,210	—		
18,231	—		
5,054	—		
—	9,440	0.564	$ 5,324
—	15,000	0.513	7,695
			$13,019

We can see, therefore, that the discount rate in our example represents the firm's cost of borrowing money—from both shareholders and lenders. The theoretically correct discount rate for asset acquisition calculations is equal to the business's **weighted average cost of capital (WACC).**[2] This discount rate represents the minimum rate that must be earned on any investment if it is to generate sufficient returns to pay capital providers (both shareholders and creditors) an amount equal to the returns that they expect to receive based on the risk of their investment and the opportunity cost of capital. Failing to return this amount to shareholders and lenders will cause them to cease investing in the firm, and managers will no longer have access to capital to purchase assets to implement their strategy.

In practice, the actual discount rate used in discounted cash flow calculations can be chosen in a variety of ways; it may be based on precise calculations of WACC or it may be based on a rough approximation of desired ROE. Regardless of how it is established, managers must communicate their chosen discount rate consistently throughout the organization so that everyone preparing asset acquisition proposals can work from the same set of assumptions. This consistency in approach allows managers to compare the NPV of different proposals, confident that the results are not biased by differing discount rate assumptions.

Internal Rate of Return

In calculating the discounted cash flow, we took the cash flows and discount rate as given and calculated the NPV of the investment—a net dollar amount. This amount represents the economic value of the project after consideration of the opportunity cost of the funds that were used to finance it. A related approach also takes the cash flows as given, but it sets the discounted cash flow (or net present value of the project) equal to zero. The computation then solves for the discount rate that equates these two. In other words, the calculation finds the discount rate where the value of cash inflows exactly equals the value of cash outflows. This technique is known as calculating the *discounted rate of return,* or **internal rate of return (IRR).** This is equivalent to asking: If I put $100 in the bank today and will be repaid $110 in one year's time, what rate of return will I be earning on my money? The answer in this simple example, of course, is 10%. A discount rate of 10% equates the present value of the future $110 cash flow ($110 × 0.909 = $100) with the current investment ($100). For business decisions with streams of multiple cash outflows and inflows, a computer or financial calculator is required to solve IRR problems. In the Boston Retail example, you can use a calculator to find the discounted rate of return for a $60,000 outflow that will repay seven annual payments of $15,000 as 16.3%. Using discount tables you can interpolate this result, because the NPV turns negative between 16% and 17%.

IRR is an appealing measure because it collapses the stream of cash flows into a single intuitive ratio that can readily be compared to ROI, ROE, and other commonly used ratio benchmarks. IRR, however, has several technical deficiencies that are covered in standard finance textbooks. For example, IRR calculations can yield multiple rates of return when cash flows change from inflows to outflows several times during the life of

---

[2] We will discuss weighted average cost of capital more fully in chapter 8.

the project. Also, IRR—because it is a ratio—does not take into account the scale of the investment and the size of the cash flows. Finally, IRR assumes that cash inflows can be invested in other projects that yield the same rate of return as the project under consideration.

Using IRR as an Investment Hurdle   Notwithstanding the limitations of IRR, senior managers often use a discounted rate of return or IRR target as a guideline to communicate minimum acceptable investment returns for proposed asset acquisitions. When used as a *communication tool,* the chosen IRR is called the **hurdle rate.** Managers are told in advance that projects not passing this financial hurdle—not earning at least this minimum internal rate of return—will not be approved. For example, a firm may set its hurdle rate at 18%, representing management's judgment of the rate of return that is necessary to maintain the financial performance of the business (based on cost of capital, riskiness of proposed projects, and any safety cushions that are built in to compensate for inaccurate or overly optimistic estimates of cash flows).

The effect of communicating this hurdle rate is to stipulate minimum boundary conditions that must be passed. That is, instead of specifying the desired ROI (e.g., "propose projects with a 20% ROI"), the boundary condition leaves it up to individual employees to find and select appropriate projects. Managers are implicitly saying, "I won't tell you what kinds of projects to propose. Higher returns are preferred to lower returns—find the best opportunities out there. But do not bring us projects with rates of return below 18%."

IRR at United Architects

High IRRs used by U.S. firms as thresholds for new investments (e.g., often above 20%) often penalize the evaluation of new technology projects, especially those with uncertain cash savings. An example of this is computer-aided design and drafting (CADD), which has been a revolution to the architectural and engineering industries. United Architects in Los Angeles was constantly losing bids to competitors, not because of the firm's qualifications or bids, but because of a lack of sophistication in the company's visual presentations. Fred Lake, a project manager, believed that a new CADD system would solve the problem, but he knew that management was under great cost pressure as lowest-bid contracts had replaced the traditional cost-plus contracts. Moreover, CADD systems were expensive—from $60,000 to $500,000. Lake could not convince management to invest in a CADD system because calculations revealed a negative NPV.

Lake finally convinced management to acquire a CADD system by including an estimate of lost contribution margin on failed bids in the NPV calculation. The lost margins were easily quantified as Lake's team had lost three bids in the latest quarter. Quantification of this intangible benefit helped management see the potential benefits of this new technology.

Source: Adapted from John Y. Lee, "The Service Sector: Investing in New Technology to Stay Competitive," *Management Accounting* 72 (June 1991): 45–48.

Managers can use any or all of these three analytic tools to communicate the types of projects that are likely to be supported for improvement of efficiency or for revenue enhancement. For example, they can stipulate that new projects for upgraded technology equipment must pay for themselves from internally generated funds within three years (payback), that all projects must have a demonstrated positive NPV when a discount rate of 13% is applied (discounted cash flow), or that no proposal will be considered if it cannot generate at least an 18% IRR. In addition, managers often provide other guidelines and "rule of thumb" constraints. For example, managers may impose a limit that cash outlays for productive assets (i.e., property, plant, and equipment) cannot exceed annual depreciation charges, or they may allocate funds for equipment upgrades only when the cost of maintenance exceeds the cost of annual depreciation.

3. Evaluating Assets to be Acquired for Competitive Effectiveness

We consider next those substantial assets that are acquired to enhance the competitive position of a business. These are notably different than assets acquired to promote efficiency or boost revenues. Assets for competitive effectiveness are needed to support the strategy of the business; as such, they are nondiscretionary if the strategy is to succeed. However, they are usually large and substantial and often commit the business to a direction that can only be altered with difficulty and at considerable expense. Approval of these projects is reserved for the highest level of management.

At Boston Retail, managers considered two strategic options. The first was to expand the business geographically into New York state. The second was to branch out into a new product line—furniture. In theory, the same cash flow techniques discussed previously—payback, discounted cash flow, and IRR—can be applied to asset acquisition proposals intended to improve competitive position. In practice, however, senior managers treat cash flow analysis for these types of assets with caution for two reasons.

First, the cash flows associated with the acquisition of strategic assets are usually extremely uncertain. The actual cash flows from new stores in New York and/or from a new line of furniture depend on management's success in implementing its strategy. Factors discussed in the SWOT analysis of Chapter 2—competitor tactics, acceptance by customers, the ability to find suitable suppliers, and a multitude of other variables (many of which are outside of management's control)—will determine ultimate cash flows. To put too much emphasis on the cash flow analysis techniques presented earlier would inevitably paint a false sense of reliability given the uncertainty inherent in cash flow estimates.

Second, the strategic value of newly acquired assets is often a function of an interaction or synergy with existing resources and capabilities in a way that makes complete analysis difficult. In strategic asset acquisitions, managers invariably hope to extract value because the whole is greater than the sum of its parts. For example, the acquisition of Medco Containment Services—a retail direct-distribution pharmaceutical network— by Merck & Company—a research pharmaceutical company—was based primarily on the perceived benefits of combining the resources and competencies of these two businesses. Managers at Medco and Merck believed that their businesses would be more valuable if they worked together than if they continued to work apart. Managers of the merged firms are betting that they can achieve economies of scale and scope, generate incremental revenues from cross-selling, and successfully eliminate the inevitable re-dundancies in bringing together two separate businesses. However, managers must rely heavily on their intuition and judgment about the ability of managers to work together, merge different cultures, and extract this extra value from the investment.

This is not to say that managers do not estimate payback, discounted cash flow, and rates of return (both discounted and undiscounted) for strategic acquisition propos-als. They do and, clearly, they should. The point to be made, however, is that they take this quantitative information—which is based on highly uncertain assumptions—and combine it with their best judgment about competitive market dynamics, the prospects for success, and the ultimate long-term payoff that may accrue as a result of the asset acquisition. Thus, intuition and hunch play as important a role as economic analysis.

Judgment is influenced by a variety of factors that we touched on in Chapter 2 as we discussed SWOT, distinctive internal capabilities, market franchises, and the value of relationships and networks. These factors include:

- Alignment of proposal with existing strategy and/or distinctive capabilities
- Risks in acquiring the asset
- Risks in deciding not to acquire the asset
- Quality of information supporting proposal
- Track record and ability of the people involved
- Feasibility and cost of reversing decision

Let's consider each of these factors in turn.

1. Alignment of Proposal with Existing Strategy and/or Distinctive Capabilities

The obvious point of departure for managers considering new assets to enhance compet-itive effectiveness is the extent to which proposals tie in with intended strategies. In businesses with smart, motivated people, there is never a shortage of ideas about new ways to create value. Some of these ideas will build on existing competencies, but many of these ideas will not fit well with management's intentions and strategy for the future, especially if managers have been at all unclear about their preferences or range of ac-ceptable investment options.

At Boston Retail, managers believed that expanding into a nearby geographic re-gion aligned well with their existing strategy and the capabilities of the business. A move into furniture did not appear to do so well on this dimension. Therefore, the decision to acquire a furniture line would require careful thought and judgment about the additional capabilities that they would need to build or acquire if the strategy were to succeed.

2. Risks in Acquiring the Asset

Every strategic decision creates risk. In acquiring an asset that affects the competitive effectiveness of a business, managers invariably alter existing business processes and ca-pabilities. At Boston Retail, the move into New York state would require substantially enhanced distribution facilities to serve a wider geographic area. Would the business be able to expand its distribution infrastructure quickly enough to respond? If not, the re-sources invested in expansion might be wasted. Managers need to assess the magnitude of the risk of failure.

Every investment also creates an opportunity cost. Managers must ask themselves: could funds be utilized more effectively in a competitive project? If no current proposals offer acceptable returns, should excess cash be returned to shareholders or held temporarily in money-market funds?

Market analysis gave Boston Retail managers some understanding of potential competitors in the New York market, but how would these competitors respond to the entry of Boston Retail? Would they retaliate? If so, by what means and how aggressively? Would their tactics change the profitability of planned expansion?

Managing these new stores would require a different organization structure. For the first time, stores would be situated outside Massachusetts. A new management team would have to be created and staffed. New reporting relationships and accountabilities would have to be created. Could they find the right people? Could they develop a good performance measurement and control system to ensure that the new managers worked toward the goals of the business?

Finally, a potentially serious risk in the acquisition of any asset outside the current domain of management expertise is distraction of management attention. Will managers be pulled away from what they know how to do best as they attempt to learn how to manage new types of operations? Managers can easily become stretched too thin and, inadvertently, fail to pay sufficient attention to the core business. Choosing to acquire assets that are outside the business's core competency may drive down ROM.

3. Risk in Deciding Not to Acquire the Asset

However, doing nothing also brings risk. A business that stands still will inevitably be overtaken by competitors. If Boston Retail managers choose not to expand into New York state, will another competitor take the opportunity to acquire prime retail space and begin building a competing market franchise? If managers fail to act, other competitors will surely take their place, and opportunities available today may no longer be available to those who follow. As we discussed in Chapter 2, first-movers can often create advantages that are difficult to replicate.

Even in relatively mundane matters, failure to act can ultimately harm the business. At Boston Retail, the current profit plan is predicated on the assumption that a $180,000 warehouse expansion will be approved to support the internal growth of the business. Without the expansion of warehouse capacity, however, predicted growth may be choked as the business struggles with inadequate storage and inventory management systems.

4. Quality of Information Supporting Proposal

Substantial amounts of information must be created and analyzed to support the acquisition of assets that affect competitive position. A market analysis, economic forecasts, estimates of cash flows and rates of return, and effects on strategic position can all be presented and analyzed. However, managers must assess, as part of their review, the degree of confidence that they have in the information that is presented to them. In some cases, they will have a great deal of confidence in the accuracy and reliability of the data. This is true, for example, of analyses of past trends based on historical accounting records. In other circumstances, they may have very little faith in the "crystal ball" ability of staff analysts to predict cash flows related to complicated acquisitions, or they may disagree with the assumptions (cash flow, asset value recoverability, discount rates) that underlie the analyses.

At Boston Retail, for example, managers have much more confidence in their ability to predict the economic value created by a move into New York state than they do in their ability to predict the long-term viability and benefit of the new furniture line. Furniture is an area where managers have no direct experience or internal data to draw upon to validate their assumptions. Therefore, they are forced to discount the reliability of information to a greater extent in the decision process.

Also, managers must evaluate the quality of the market analysis and supporting economics. Have staff analysts considered the right variables and interactions? Have they taken account of all the contingencies relating to market dynamics? Have they included brand value? Have they taken account of economies of scope? These and many similar questions must be probed by managers as they attempt to assess the quality of the information that is provided in support of the proposal.

5. Track Record and Ability of Champion

Throughout the technical analysis, we must remember that asset acquisition proposals are made by people—who have ambitions, skills, and weaknesses. Any proposal to acquire assets must be evaluated in light of the confidence that senior managers can place in the individuals making the proposal. Every substantial asset acquisition proposal has a *champion*—a person who believes that this asset is an important source of competitive advantage for the business and is willing to argue forcefully for the merits of acquiring it. Depending on the proposal, a champion may be a division manager, a functional vice president, or any other manager who believes that acquiring a resource will produce tangible strategic benefits for the business.

Does the champion have a good track record of achieving what he or she sets out to do? Does this person tend to be too optimistic? Too pessimistic? Do we believe that they will have sufficient resources to utilize the asset effectively? These questions, which can only be answered subjectively based on first-hand knowledge of people in the organization, are critical to establishing the confidence that underlies management judgment about the merits of acquiring a strategic asset.

6. Feasibility and Cost of Reversing Decision

Acquiring assets to enhance competitive effectiveness often commits the business to a course of action that will play out over many years. At Boston Retail, the decision to move into New York state or the decision to move into furniture will substantially influence the future course of the business. New facilities must be opened, contracts with new suppliers signed, new staff must be hired, and so on.

In deciding whether or not to make these commitments, managers should always imagine the worst. What if this turns out to have been a bad idea? Can we reverse it, and how much will it cost? One of the critical components of the analysis is a feasible exit plan that can be executed should the contingencies of market dynamics or other events force managers to reverse their decision.

PUTTING IT ALL TOGETHER

The asset acquisition process is both important and complex. Managers use the process to communicate guidelines, solicit proposals, and weigh and evaluate alternatives. The final decision for nonroutine asset acquisitions is often handled by a committee of senior managers who represent different businesses and functions. Over a series of meetings, proposals are presented, questions asked, and managers deliberate—often acting as judges—in deciding how to allocate scarce capital resources. Requests for large acquisitions—beyond the cash-generating ability of the business—must also be weighed against the availability and cost of financing. Here, the chief financial officer plays a critical role in crafting financing options and alternatives.

We can use the inputs → process → outputs model discussed in Chapter 4 to illustrate the approach that managers use in allocating assets to support competitive effectiveness (Figure 7–1).

The "inputs" are information, people, opportunities, threats, and available resources. These inputs are used by managers throughout the organization to create formal proposals to acquire and allocate new assets in support of strategy or to enhance operational efficiencies. The "process" of developing proposals should rely heavily on the techniques outlined in this chapter: analysis of cost effectiveness (for assets related to safety and regulation), calculation of payback, estimation of discounted cash flow, and computation of discounted rate of return or IRR. The "outputs" of this process—the formal proposals submitted to top managers—can then be separated into appropriate categories and compared against strategic plans and economic standards and criteria. Senior managers can allocate funding to support proposals that meet these criteria and reject or defer those that fail to pass the test. Some proposals may be sent back to subordinates with the request to reconsider, redraft, and alter their proposals and related action plans to meet strategic goals.

The asset acquisition process—although usually separate from the profit planning process—should be timed to support the allocation of resources to implement plans and strategies. Thus, "Investment in Assets" is included as a key variable in the profit wheel diagram of Chapter 5. Usually, profit plans are completed first. Soon after, asset acquisition proposals are reviewed by senior managers to ensure that resources will be sufficient to implement plans. When new proposals are approved or rejected, it is often necessary to go back to the profit wheel and rework profit plans. For example, profit plans

FIGURE 7–1 The Process of Allocating Assets

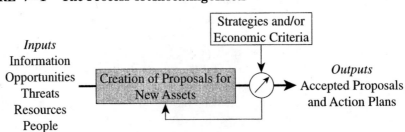

Investment Categories at a Medical Devices Firm

Deciding which new products to develop is a critical decision for many companies, but relying solely on financial analysis may lead a company down the wrong path. Why? New products are often very different from existing ones: They tend to show lower initial financial return; the required investment is higher; the expected levels of sales and costs are more uncertain; and the payback period is longer. Thus, companies may be tempted to underinvest in new products even if, over the long term, they are likely to shape the company's future. To avoid this trap, a medical devices company developed a unique way to analyze new-products decisions.

First, it classified new products into three categories: derivatives, platforms, and breakthroughs. *Derivatives* were new products that incorporated only minor design enhancements. Designing a new interface for a laboratory centrifuge was considered a derivative product. *Platforms* were totally new products that replaced existing ones. A new blood-glucose testing system based on an improved technology, which replaced the system currently being offered, was a platform product. *Breakthrough* products were radically new ideas that would start a new product concept. Syringes with retractable needles, for example, represented a revolutionary new product that would help nurses avoid accidentally hurting themselves.

Then the company allocated a certain amount of money for each category of product, regardless of whether derivatives looked more financially attractive than platforms and breakthroughs. Finally, within each category it then used financial and strategic criteria to decide which products would be funded.

---

that reflect growth in revenue and market share may stimulate asset acquisition proposals for enlarged facilities or new distribution networks. Alternatively, the decision to reject a proposal may require scaling back earlier profit plan goals that were based on the assumption that specific assets would be available to support the strategy.

At Boston Retail, managers worked carefully with the profit wheel analysis developed in Chapter 5 and the strategic considerations discussed in this chapter. On balance, they decided to pursue expansion into New York state. Concerns about ROM, alignment of core competencies, and risk made the acquisition strategy seem undesirable.

CHAPTER SUMMARY

Acquiring and allocating productive assets is an integral part of achieving profit goals and strategies. Asset allocation systems help managers throughout the organization make effective proposals and give top managers the tools to evaluate the relative merits of each proposal.

The first step in the process is to design a system that allows information about new asset proposals to be gathered, analyzed, and communicated to senior management for consideration. For systems to be effective, managers must:

1. Communicate limits on the type of assets that are suitable for potential acquisition
2. Specify a process by which proposals are evaluated and approved
3. Communicate policies regarding who has authority to approve the acquisition of assets
4. Categorize projects consistently so that the correct analytic tools and decision criteria can be applied to each bucket

Many firms categorize potential assets into three buckets: assets needed for health/safety/regulation, assets needed to enhance efficiency and/or increase revenue, and assets needed to support strategic initiatives and competitive effectiveness. Each category is subject to different types of analyses.

Designing and using asset allocation systems—like other performance measurement and control systems—is partly art and partly science. Analytic techniques related to cash flow analysis and rate of return analysis play an important role in understanding the economic effects of acquiring new resources. However, as the assets become larger and more strategic, management judgment becomes the determining factor.

8

Linking Performance
to Markets

The implementation of profit plans reflects the success of a business in creating value and implementing strategy in competitive markets. In this chapter, we explore how profit plans are linked to those markets and the implications of these linkages for performance measurement and control systems.

In the sections to follow, we discuss two types of markets that affect performance measurement and control systems: markets inside the firm and markets outside the firm. Markets *inside* the firm are created when goods and services are transferred between different business units or divisions of the same firm. In making these transfers, a value must be attached to the flow of these internal goods and services so that the profit plans of each division can properly reflect the value added at each stage of the process. To adjust profit plans appropriately, managers must develop a system of *transfer prices*. We can think of transfer prices as horizontal linkages between the profit plans of different business units in the firm.

Markets *outside* the firm include customer, financial, and supplier markets. These markets are critical to the long-term profitability of the firm. Therefore, measures must be developed to ensure that profit plans are adequately linked to these markets. We will discuss how managers link their profit plans to external markets in this and the next chapter. We can think of the linkage between the profit plan and these external markets as vertical linkages.

TRANSFER PRICES: MANAGING MARKETS INSIDE THE FIRM

All businesses produce goods and services for eventual sale to third-party customers. In some instances, however, business units sell their products or services to other divisions or business units within the same firm. In these cases, the outputs of one division are inputs for another. For example, an integrated oil company may have three different divisions: (1) exploration and extraction, (2) refining and processing, and (3) retail sales. The exploration and extraction division may choose to sell its crude oil on the open market or transfer it to its sister refinery division. Likewise, the petroleum products produced by the refinery division can be sold on the open market or transferred to the retail division for sale through its retail service stations. In each of these cases the outputs of one division (often called the selling or upstream division) can be transferred internally

FIGURE 8–1   **Horizontal Flow of Goods/Services Between Autonomous Divisions Within the Same Firm**

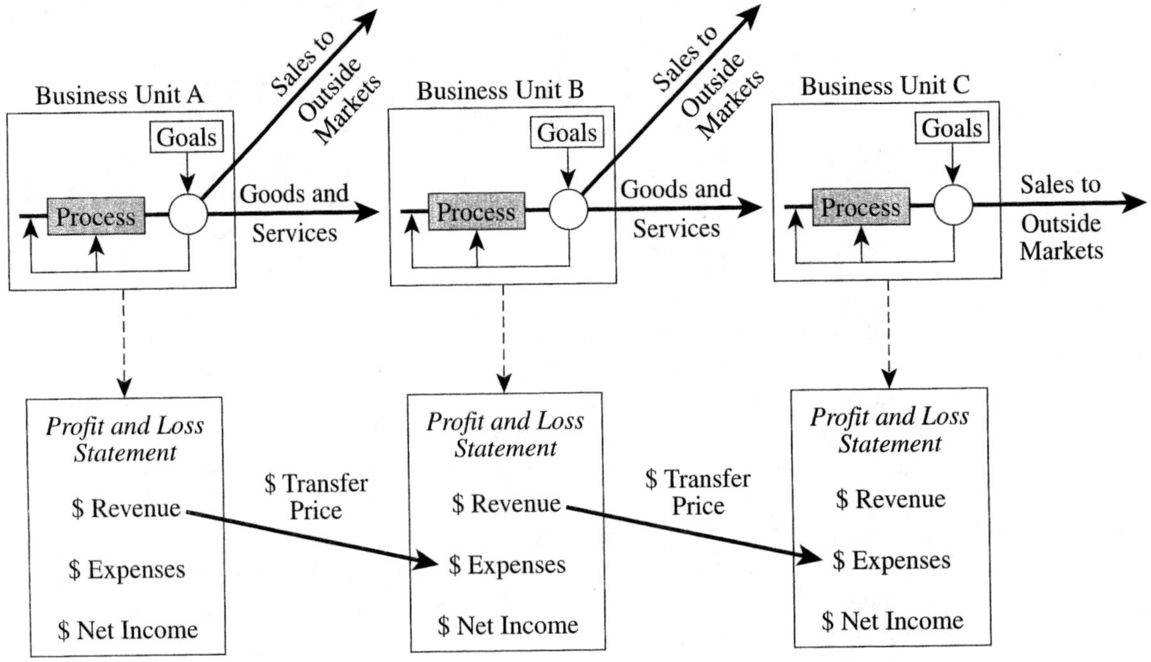

to become inputs for a second division (called the purchasing or downstream division). In these circumstances, managers must consider how to use transfer prices to link these operations through *internal* markets that are created by the horizontal flow of goods inside the firm (Figure 8–1).

A **transfer price** is an *internally set transaction price to account for the transfer of goods or services between divisions of the same firm.* Transfer prices are used to value and coordinate the work flows of interdependent organization units that are each held accountable for financial performance. For example, separate product divisions may each be held accountable for the profit of their respective products. The electronic components produced by one division may be sold to a sister division as inputs to the assembly of consumer radios. Alternatively, the components division may transfer goods to the marketing division for sales and shipment to outside customers. To the extent that the work flows of these separate divisions are interdependent—one transfers goods or services to the other—how should each account for performance?

As we have discussed at length in previous chapters, the profit plan for an individual business unit maps out the expected flows of revenues, expenses, and anticipated levels of profit. A problem arises, however, when the revenues and expenses shown on a business unit's profit plan include product flows to and from sister divisions of the same firm. The prices for these goods and services are not naturally determined by arm's length market transactions—as is normal between independent buyers and sellers—so distortions can be introduced into each business unit's reported revenue, expenses, and profitability.

These distortions can affect both performance evaluation and resource allocation. From the perspective of performance evaluation, the distortion of revenues, expenses, and profits can make it difficult to determine where value is actually being created. For example, if the upstream selling division is receiving too little revenue relative to the value of the products that it transfers to the downstream purchasing division, then upstream's profit will be too low, and downstream's profit will be too high.

This distortion can also be expected to affect resource allocation as individual managers in each of the divisions adjust their profit plans and business activities in response to any perceived distortions in performance evaluation. Managers at the upstream division, for example, will have little incentive to increase the level of sales to the downstream division if they are not receiving full credit for the value of their products. More generally, in cases where internal transfer prices are used, there is substantial risk that unit managers will make decisions that improve their division's profitability (or at least minimize the damaging effects of internal transfers) and, in so doing, lower the overall profit of the firm. To the extent that managers make decisions based on the level of internally set transfer prices, any distortions can affect the willingness of managers to buy goods from or sell goods to sister divisions, to source products internally versus purchasing from outside vendors, to make or buy products, and so on.

On the other hand, it is important to realize that the potential distortions of transfer prices can be mitigated if the profit plan anticipates the effects of these internal transfers and adjusts goals and targets accordingly. In other words, if managers adjust accountability targets based on an anticipated level of internal transfer at some agreed transfer price (even if it is too low or too high), managers will not be penalized for internal transactions at that level.

TRANSFER PRICING ALTERNATIVES

There are two basic ways of setting transfer prices: at market prices or at prices based on internally generated accounting data.

Transfer Prices Using Market Data

In many cases, transfers of goods and services between divisions of the same firm can be recorded at *external market prices*. In these cases, the upstream selling division records the transfer as a sale. The associated revenue is set equal to the price that would have been realized if the product (or, in some cases, service) had been sold to an arm's length customer on the outside market. Using the same market-based price, the downstream division records the transfer as an increase in its inventory (which ultimately flows to cost of goods sold). The recorded price is the same price that the division would have had to pay to purchase similar goods or services from an independent supplier on the outside market.

Using external market prices eliminates the potential for distortion resulting from non-arm's length transfers. Prices based on market data reflect the true opportunity cost and market value of the transfer. However, using market prices is possible only when (1) an active market exists for similar goods and services and (2) internal transfer prices based on comparable external market prices can be easily established. This poses little problem for the integrated oil company because highly efficient spot markets exist for all grades of crude oil and refined petroleum products (i.e., active buyers and sellers continually update market prices based on supply and demand). These spot market prices are easily obtained and can be used to set the prices of internal product flows between sister divisions. The same is true for intermediate products that can be purchased from outside vendors by reference to a published price list.

In many instances of internal transfer, however, active markets do not exist to easily price the value of intermediate products transferred between divisions of the same firm. Either the goods are specialized (such as uniquely designed electronic components) or prices cannot be established without obtaining bids from potential suppliers based on exact order quantities and product specifications (e.g., "please quote on this product in this amount").

The advantages—and major disadvantage—of market-based transfer prices are the following:

Advantages of Market Prices:
- By mirroring true market prices, prices based on market data allow accurate performance evaluation and minimize the potential for misallocation of resources based on faulty performance measures
- Simple
- Objective, and seen as valid by managers in all divisions
- Provides managers with the sense that they are running their own business

Disadvantage of Market Prices:
- For most intermediate goods and services transferred within a firm, market prices are typically not available

Transfer Prices Using Internal Cost Data

When market prices are not readily available (which is most often the case in practice), managers must rely on internal cost accounting data to establish transfer prices. Transfers among divisions using internal cost data can be priced by several methods: at variable cost, full cost, full cost plus a markup, or, if available, prices that approximate an arm's length market price. The hierarchy of transfer prices is illustrated in Figure 8–2.

Variable Cost

Variable cost of manufacture is the lowest accounting-based transfer price. A variable cost is one that can be traced directly to a product or service and varies directly with output quantities. Variable costs typically include materials, labor, and other direct costs of production. Administrative overheads incurred by the producing division as part of doing business (e.g., indirect costs such as supervision and office rent) are not included in the transfer price. Assuming efficient operations, **variable cost transfer prices** result in revenues (and profits) being understated for the upstream division relative to what

FIGURE 8–2   Hierarchy of Transfer Prices Using Internal Cost Data

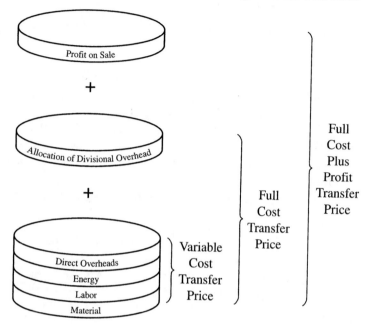

they could have received if they had sold the goods or services on the open market (presuming such a market exists). Correspondingly, the downstream division typically receives goods at a price significantly below a market-based competitive price. Thus, when products are ultimately sold to the customer, the gross margin and profits will reside disproportionately with the downstream division.

Advantages and disadvantages of using variable cost are:

Advantages of Variable Cost:
- Simple
- Allows pure marginal-cost decision analysis

Disadvantages of Variable Cost:
- Arbitrarily shifts profits from selling divisions to purchasing divisions
- Provides no incentives for the upstream division to manage overheads efficiently or for the downstream division to look elsewhere for sources of supply because of high costs at the upstream division
- Marginal cost may vary over a range of output levels due to economies of larger-scale production
- May limit profit of firm when selling division is at full capacity and is forced to sell its output to its downstream sister division
- The upstream division may refuse to sell to the downstream division in favor of sales to outside parties at prices that include overhead and a margin for profit

- May cause purchasing division to underprice products that are ultimately sold into final customer markets

Because of these limitations, variable cost transfer prices are rarely found in practice.

Full Cost

A somewhat higher accounting-based transfer price is a **full cost transfer price,** which includes direct costs plus an allocation for the divisional overhead that would normally be covered by the gross profit margin on goods sold to outside customers. Overheads include allocations for a representative portion of manufacturing overheads. Sometimes a portion of selling, general, and administrative overheads are included as well. Full cost is usually calculated using standard costs rather than actual costs to eliminate the possibility of passing along inefficiencies in manufacturing or processing. Full cost transfer pricing is quite common in practice for the following reasons:

Advantages of Full Cost:
- Simple—typically calculated by routine cost-accounting methods
- Allows upstream division to recover all its costs
- By charging downstream managers with the overheads that are generated by the upstream division, downstream managers have incentive to monitor the level of costs that are passed on and apply pressure to increase upstream efficiency if costs are excessive. (This pressure may be moderated, however, if the full cost charged by the upstream division is still lower than any alternative cost that the downstream division could obtain from third-party providers.)

Disadvantages of Full Cost:
- Subject to inaccuracies of internal cost-accounting allocations
- Fixed costs of the upstream division become variable costs to the downstream division, potentially resulting in the downstream division making decisions that reduce the profitability of the firm (e.g., investing in additional capacity to avoid having to buy from the upstream division even though the upstream division has excess capacity)
- The upstream division may refuse to sell to the downstream division in favor of sales to outside parties at prices that include a margin for profit

Full Cost Plus Profit

The highest accounting-based transfer price attempts to approach market price by including **full cost plus profit.** In this case the upstream division recovers not only direct costs and overhead, but also some profit on the sale. Markups are most simply calculated as a percentage add-on to the cost of transferred goods. Now, the upstream division and the downstream division share in the final profits on the ultimate sale of the goods in direct proportion to the value that each adds as calculated by the internal accounting system.

Advantages of Full Cost Plus Profit:
- Attempts to mirror market prices, which over the long run must include direct costs, overheads, and profits
- Allows upstream division to receive full credit for revenues and profits from sales to internal divisions

Disadvantage of Full Cost Plus Profit:

- Unless the downstream division has the right to refuse internal transfers in favor of purchasing from outside suppliers, it can result in the downstream division paying costs that are higher than the value of the products received

Negotiated Prices

Notwithstanding the virtues of each of these three methods—variable cost, full cost, and full cost plus markup—managers often choose in practice to negotiate among themselves some satisfactory transfer price—in effect, to "split the difference" to ensure that there is equity in the profit plans and results of each of the contributing divisions. This **negotiated transfer price** is usually based on standard direct costs plus some allowance for profit or ROCE.

Advantage of Negotiated Prices:

- Perceived fairness among managers who negotiate final prices

Disadvantages of Negotiated Prices:

- Time-consuming
- Profit and performance evaluation can be biased by the negotiating skills of the managers representing each of the various divisions

The academic literature has often tried to reconcile the advantages and disadvantages of these different approaches by arguing for the use of a "dual-pricing" system whereby the selling division is credited with market price and the buying division is charged with full cost. Thus, the selling division suffers no revenue disadvantage—and will make no uneconomic decisions—as a result of internal transfers, and the buying division will recognize the cost benefits of sourcing internally rather than going to outside markets. This approach is rarely found in practice. It requires elimination of the accounting profit that is counted twice (once by the selling division upon lateral transfer and once by the buying division upon ultimate sale to customers) and creates ambiguity about what the company is trying to achieve.[1]

Activity-Based Transfer Prices

Any method based on internal accounting data—variable cost, full cost, or full cost plus profit—is only as good as the data and allocations that support it. Recently, some companies have experimented with activity-based costing methods to develop more-accurate transfer prices. Under this approach, different cost standards are prepared for four different categories of cost: unit-based costs (e.g., direct material), batch-based costs (e.g., setup), product-based costs (e.g., package design), and plant-level costs (e.g., depreciation and insurance). Transfer prices are then charged using two separate approaches. Unit- and batch-level costs are charged based on unit volume—the quantities of products shipped between divisions and the number of batches it takes to produce those

---

[1] Robert G. Eccles, *The Transfer Pricing Problem: A Theory for Practice* (Lexington, Mass.: Lexington Books, 1985), 102–103.

products. Product-based and plant-level costs are charged annually based on planned levels of usage as reflected in profit plans and budgets.[2]

Proponents of this approach argue that it overcomes many of the shortcomings of traditional methods. Advantages and disadvantages are:

Advantages of Activity-Based Prices:
- Provides a more-accurate measure of profit performance in each division
- Separates short-term decisions based on batch-level and unit-level costs from long-term decisions based on product- and plant-level costs
- Motivates downstream managers to help selling division managers effectively manage capacity and other plant-level costs

Disadvantages of Activity-Based Prices:
- Relatively complicated
- Depends on the accuracy of cost-driven assumptions and availability of reliable data

As this new approach is implemented and tested, managers will be able to evaluate whether the potential benefits outweigh the increased complexity in recordkeeping and potential for disagreement about the reliability of the allocation assumptions.

TRANSFER PRICING EFFECTS AND TRADE-OFFS

Managers at different levels in a firm often attempt to achieve different objectives through their transfer pricing policies. For example, corporate managers, division managers, and financial staffs may desire the following:[3]

Corporate Managers Want Transfer Prices to
- encourage division managers to make decisions that maximize the long-run profitability of the overall firm
- provide information so that managers can make good short-term decisions (such as bids for orders) and long-term decisions (e.g., adding or deleting product lines)

Division Managers Want Transfer Prices to
- represent fairly the financial performance of their division
- reflect the impact of good business decisions within their division (e.g., product mix and improved efficiency)
- require downstream division managers to include the full costs associated with the products they are receiving from upstream divisions

Financial Staffs Want Transfer Prices That
- are simple and credible, so that they will be used and useful by division managers
- are easy to use and easy to explain

---

[2] For more information on activity-based transfer pricing, see Robert S. Kaplan, Dan Weiss, and Eyal Desheh, "Transfer Pricing with ABC," *Management Accounting* 78 (May 1997): 20–28, and Robin Cooper and Robert S. Kaplan, *Cost & Effect* (Boston: Harvard Business School Press, 1998), Chap. 15.

[3] Kaplan, Weiss, and Desheh, op. cit.

The effects of different transfer pricing policies are illustrated in Exhibit 8–1. Although the profits for the firm as a whole are the same, different transfer pricing methods allocate different amounts of profit between the selling and purchasing divisions.

Overlaid on the choice of transfer price is a decision whether or not divisions should be required to buy and sell from each other or whether either—or both—should have the option of rejecting internal transfers in favor of dealing with arm's length suppliers and customers in external markets. Exhibit 8–2 illustrates what can happen if one or both of the parties is allowed to opt out. In this illustration, the selling division is forgoing profit by selling to its sister division and, if given the chance, may choose not to sell to the purchasing division in favor of more-profitable sales to outside customers. As

EXHIBIT 8–1
Effect of Transfer Pricing Policies
on Divisional Profitability
Assuming Pricing Has No Effects on Decision Making

	SELLING DIVISION			
	VARIABLE COST	FULL COST	FULL COST PLUS MARKUP	MARKET PRICING
Revenue:				
Sales to outside customers [5,000 units @ $100]	$500,000	$500,000	$500,000	$500,000
Sales to Purchasing Division 2,000 units @ $50	100,000			
$70		140,000		
$84			168,000	
$100				200,000
	600,000	640,000	668,000	700,000
Cost of goods sold 7,000 units @ $70	490,000	490,000	490,000	490,000
Gross profit–Selling Division	$110,000	$150,000	$178,000	$210,000
	PURCHASING DIVISION			
Revenue from outside customers	$800,000	$800,000	$800,000	$800,000
Cost of goods sold				
2,000 units purchased from Selling Division	100,000	140,000	168,000	200,000
Additional value added by Purchasing Division	350,000	350,000	350,000	350,000
	450,000	490,000	518,000	550,000
Gross profit–Purchasing Division	350,000	310,000	282,000	250,000
Total gross profit for both divisions	$460,000	$460,000	$460,000	$460,000

EXHIBIT 8–2
Effect of Transfer Pricing Policies
on Divisional Profitability
Assuming Selling Division Chooses to
Sell 1,000 Fewer Units to Purchasing Division

	SELLING DIVISION	
	VARIABLE COST	FULL COST
Revenue:		
Sales to outside customers [6,000 units @ $100]	$600,000	$600,000
Sales to Purchasing Division		
1,000 @ $50	50,000	
1,000 @ $70	—	70,000
	650,000	670,000
Cost of goods sold		
7,000 units @ $70	490,000	490,000
Gross profit–Selling Division	$160,000	$180,000

	PURCHASING DIVISION	
Revenue from outside customers	$400,000	$400,000
Cost of goods sold		
1,000 units purchased from Selling Division	50,000	70,000
Additional value added	175,000	175,000
	225,000	245,000
Gross profit–Purchasing Division	175,000	155,000
Total gross profit for both divisions	$335,000	$335,000

---

a comparison of Exhibit 8–1 and Exhibit 8–2 reveals, if supply shortages affect down-stream sales this leads to higher profit for the selling division, but lower overall profit for the firm.

Robert Eccles, who conducted an in-depth study of transfer pricing policies, argues that firms following a strategy of vertical integration to achieve economies of scale and scope are likely to mandate that units within the firm buy and sell from each other—creating the need for a good system of transfer prices because the possibility of dealing with outside parties is removed. Firms following a strategy of unrelated businesses are more likely to leave the choice up to the managers of the individual profit centers.[4] Table 8–1 shows this breakdown in detail.

A special, but important, case arises when products are transferred between business units of the same company located in different countries. As described above, transfer pricing policies determine how much profit each business unit records in its books. If goods and services are transferred across national borders, tax authorities in

---

[4] Adapted from Eccles, pp. 8–9, 57.

TABLE 8-1 Profit Center Manager's Decision Authority to Choose Between Internal and External Vendors, by Strategic Type

AUTHORITY	SINGLE BUSINESS VERTICALLY INTEGRATED		DISTINCT BUSINESSES VERTICALLY INTEGRATED		UNRELATED BUSINESSES		TOTAL	
My decision	29%	(19)	35%	(43)	50%	(48)	39%	(110)
Two-person decision	20%	(13)	26%	(32)	22%	(21)	23%	(66)
Multiple-person decision	26%	(17)	18%	(22)	15%	(14)	19%	(53)
Corporate decision	20%	(13)	11%	(14)	3%	(3)	10%	(30)
Initiated by others	5%	(3)	10%	(12)	10%	(9)	9%	(24)
Total	100%	(65)	100%	(123)	100%	(95)	100%	(283)

Note: Number in brackets represents the number of respondents.
Source: Adapted from Robert G. Eccles, *The Transfer Pricing Problem* (Lexington, Mass.: Lexington Books, 1985), 114.

different countries take great interest in ensuring that the business unit domiciled in their country attracts a sufficient amount of profit for income tax purposes. Accordingly, any attempts by corporate or business executives to evade local income taxes by using transfer prices to shift profits out of high-tax jurisdictions into low-tax countries can result in civil and/or criminal legal action. Thus, when designing international transfer pricing policies, managers must take special care to ensure that their transfer prices fairly replicate the value that is created by each business unit situated in a foreign country.

Transfer Pricing Between Assembly Plants

A company that made hydraulic systems for dump and garbage trucks had two plants. Managers of each plant were measured on their plant's respective profits. One of the plants built the hydraulic systems and the second plant installed them on trucks. The first plant also sold its hydraulic systems to the spare parts market, as well as supplying them to its sister assembly plant. The transfer price for these hydraulic systems was set below the market price for spare parts, reflecting the fact that the original equipment was sold at a lower price than spare parts.

However, this arrangement had unexpected negative consequences. Managers of the hydraulic systems plant were more interested in selling parts to the external market and even competitors than in shipping products to its sister plant. The hydraulic plant manager was constantly praised for his plant's profitability. However, the late and irregular shipments of hydraulic systems to the assembly plant caused constant problems with its customers. Before top management discovered the source of the problem (the artificially low transfer price), the assembly plant manager was blamed for customer complaints.

Source: Adapted from James F. Cox, W. Gerry Howe, and Lynn H. Boyd, "Transfer Pricing Effects on Locally Measured Organizations," *Industrial Management* 2 (March 13, 1997): 20.

TABLE 8-2 Major Trade-Offs in Transfer Pricing Methods[5]

	TRANSFER PRICING METHOD				
OBJECTIVE	VARIABLE COST	FULL COST	FULL COST PLUS PROFIT	ACTIVITY-BASED	MARKET PRICE
Promotes rational decision making in Selling Division	Poor	Moderate	Better	Better	Best
Promotes rational decision making in Purchasing Division	Poor	Better	Better	Better	Moderate
Provides accurate product contribution measures	Poor	Moderate	Better	Better	Best
Easy to understand	Best	Better	Moderate	Worst	Best
Easy to apply	Easy	Moderate	Difficult	Difficult	Varies

Transfer pricing, as a response to the creation of artificial markets within firms, is inevitably a compromise. Transfer price information, like other information for performance measurement and control, is used for a variety of purposes—decision making, control, coordination, evaluation, and so on. Table 8-2 summarizes the trade-offs managers must make in designing transfer price policies.

Although the theory and mathematics of transfer pricing hold appeal for many academic economists and accountants, in practice, transfer pricing is not a serious problem for most managers to solve. As long as managers are aware of the potential distortions and incentive effects, profit plans can be adjusted ex ante and ex post to reflect internal transfers, and negotiations can easily be conducted between divisions so that no one is unfairly burdened by internal transfers of goods and services.

LINKING PROFIT PERFORMANCE TO EXTERNAL MARKETS

Now that we have discussed the horizontal linkage of profit plans within the firm, we next consider the vertical linkage of profit plans to external markets.

In Chapter 2, we drew a distinction between corporate strategy and business strategy. You will remember that business strategy is concerned with how to compete in defined product markets. Corporate strategy, by contrast, is concerned with decisions about how to maximize the value of resources controlled by the corporation. These decisions focus primarily on the *allocation* of resources inside the corporation. In single-business firms, all resources are devoted to only one business. In multibusiness firms— firms that are organized to compete in more than one product market—decisions must be made about how to allocate scarce resources across business units to maximize value creation.[6]

---

[5]Adapted from Eccles, p. 267

FIGURE 8–3   Corporate Performance Flows

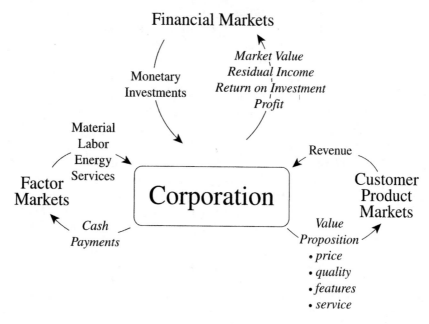

The success of any corporate strategy is reflected in **corporate performance.** *Corporate performance refers to a firm's level of achievement in creating value for market constituents.* Ultimately, corporate performance is determined by the achievement of business goals across the different business units of the firm. High-performing companies create value over time; low-performing companies do not. However, different market constituents seek different types of value. Thus, the creation of value—and corporate performance—can be assessed only from the perspective of major market constituents.

Figure 8–3 presents the flows that must be considered in assessing corporate performance. The key constituents of value creation from a corporate performance perspective are: (1) customers, (2) suppliers, and (3) owners and creditors. All three groups transact with the firm through markets. That is, customers buy (and sometimes resell) goods and services through product markets; suppliers sell products and services to the firm through factor markets; and, owners and creditors buy and sell ownership claims— shares of stock in the company—or debt instruments through financial markets.

Corporate Performance from the Perspective of Customer Markets

Customers in all competitive product markets face choices; they can choose among several different product or service offerings to meet their needs. Thus, managers of each firm that competes in a defined product market will attempt to develop a unique

---

[6] This section is reprinted from Robert Simons, "Corporate Performance," *Handbook of Technology* (Boca Raton, Fla.: CRC Press, 1999), Chap. 17.4.

value proposition to attract customers in given market segments and generate profitable sales. *A value proposition refers to the mix of product and service attributes that a firm offers to customers in terms of price, product features, quality, availability, image, buying experience, and after-sales warranty and service.* Customers and potential customers must perceive that a business's value proposition offers superior value and performance or they will choose to buy from a competitor.

To ensure an adequate flow of revenue and profit, managers must ensure that (a) their firm's products and services are meeting customer needs and expectations, (b) their value proposition is sufficiently differentiated from competitors, and (c) revenues exceed the cost of creating and delivering the value proposition. Managers monitor their value proposition in the marketplace by focusing on key customer-value measures. Customer-value measures can be either financial—expressed in monetary units such as dollars—or nonfinancial—expressed in units, counts, or quantities. Some of the more popular measures (to be covered in depth in the next chapter) are:

Financial Measures:
- Revenue, or Revenue Growth—This measure indicates customer willingness to purchase a firm's goods and services.
- Gross Profit Margin—Gross profit margin (sales revenue minus the direct and indirect costs of producing those goods or services) reflects the willingness of customers to pay premium prices in return for perceived value in the firm's products and services.
- Warranty Expenses and/or Product Returns—These measures provide insight into product quality and the extent to which products meet customer expectations concerning features and attributes.

Nonfinancial Measures:
- Market Share or Market Share Growth—Market share is a measure of customer acceptance relative to competitive offerings in the marketplace. Market share is calculated as the sales of the firm (revenue) divided by total sales of all competitors in a defined market.
- Customer Satisfaction—These measures reflect customer perceptions of value and the extent to which products or services have met expectations. These data are typically collected through survey techniques administered by telephone or mail after sales of goods and services.
- Referrals—This measure of customer loyalty is calculated by gathering data on the source of new business and maintaining a tally of new business generated by referrals.

Corporate Performance from the Perspective of Factor Markets

Any corporate strategy—strategy that attempts to maximize the value of resources controlled by the corporation—must rely on the resources provided by factor markets. These suppliers provide critical resources such as labor, contract services, materials, energy, and leased land and buildings.

However, suppliers think of value in a very different way than customers and owners. They are not investing in the firm or making a purchase decision that may have long-term consequences. Instead, they are selling their own goods and services to the firm in exchange for the promise of a cash payment under defined terms (such as net 30 days). Thus, the primary performance measure for suppliers is the promptness and reliability of payment for goods and services received.

In terms of supplier value, the applicable measures that managers monitor relate to liquidity—cash flow and days outstanding in accounts payable. As discussed in Chapter 5, managers of all businesses must project and manage cash balances carefully to ensure that cash on hand is sufficient to meet obligations as they become due.

Corporate Performance from the Perspective of Financial Markets

From stockholders' perspective, corporate performance is reflected in increases in the monetary value and financial return of their investment. For publicly traded companies, this value can be measured in daily changes in the stock price of the firm. For privately held companies, increases in value can only be assessed with certainty at the time when shares of the company change hands.

Managers must ensure that the financial returns created by the sustained profitability of their business are meeting the expectations of owners and potential owners. In competitive financial markets, there are always alternatives for investment funds. Thus, the economic performance of a firm—as reflected in its stock price—must be sufficient to attract new investment and induce existing stockholders to maintain their ownership position. To assess value creation from a financial market perspective, managers commonly monitor four financial measures of increasing aggregation that focus on corporate performance: profit, ROI, residual income, and market value.

Financial Value Measures

Profit   as disclosed on a firm's income statement is the cornerstone of business performance from an investor's perspective. Profit is the residual amount that is retained by the business after subtracting all expenses from the revenues earned during that accounting period.

$$\text{Accounting profit} = (\text{Revenues for the Period}) - (\text{Expenses for the Period})$$

Profit is a measure of how much of the revenue received from customers for goods and services is available for reinvestment in the business or distribution to owners. Note, however, that profit as a stand-alone measure does not take into account the level of investment needed to generate that profit. Thus, it is impossible to evaluate the economic performance of a business that earns $100 profit without knowing whether the investment needed to generate that profit was $500 or $1,000.

Return on Investment   remedies this problem by considering explicitly the underlying level of financial investment. ROI for any period is calculated as the ratio of accounting profit divided by the investment that was needed to create that income.

$$ROI = \frac{\text{Accounting Profit}}{\text{Investment in Business}}$$

ROI takes account of the investment made by owners to support profits, so higher levels of profit for a given level of investment can be expected to yield higher financial returns for investors and increased market values. As discussed in Chapter 5, common variations of this measure used within firms are ROE, ROA, and ROCE—all of which use internal balance sheet data to compute return measures.

In designing ROI- or ROCE-type measures, managers must make two decisions. First, they must decide what balance sheet items to include in the asset base, or denominator. At a minimum, working capital—cash, accounts receivable, and inventory—should be included. In addition, other productive assets such as buildings and equipment can also be included. This decision will depend on the use to which the measure is being put. If ROCE is being used to evaluate the performance of a *business,* then all productive assets should be included. If ROCE is being used to evaluate the performance of a *manager,* then only those assets within a manager's span of control will typically be included in the calculation.

The second decision concerns the best valuation method for depreciable assets. Should they be stated at net book value (net of accumulated depreciation), gross book value (before depreciation), or replacement cost? Choosing net book value is simple and ties in with generally accepted financial accounting policies. However, this approach suffers from the fact that ROI will increase monotonically over time as depreciation erodes the value of the denominator. Gross book value remedies this problem, but it may provide incentives for managers to shrink the denominator by shedding productive assets that are still useful but fully depreciated. Replacement cost is an effective alternative but is often difficult to compute with accuracy because of the estimates that are inevitably necessary.

Considerable care must be exercised in interpreting ratios that rely on balance sheet data. All readers of financial statements should understand that accountants are often forced to make trade-offs between accurate figures on the balance sheet and accurate figures on the income statement. For example, to measure performance in the income statement figures as accurately as possible, managers may adopt a LIFO inventory accounting policy. In so doing, however, there is no choice but to settle for out-of-date historical cost data on the balance sheet. (We will have more to say about this shortly.)

Residual Income   is a measure of value creation that goes one step further than ROI by considering how much profit investors *expect* to earn from their capital. **Residual income** is a measure of how much additional profit remains for (1) investment in the business or (2) distribution to owners after allowing for normal (expected) returns on investment. It is calculated by subtracting the normal cost of capital used in the business, calculated at current market rates, from accounting profit.

Residual Income = Accounting Profit − Charge for Capital Used to Generate Profit
= Accounting Profit − (Value of Assets Used to Generate Profit
× Expected Rate of Return on Those Assets)

Although residual income is an old concept, some firms have begun to make further refinements to transform residual income into a calculation known as *economic value added.* This technique is discussed in detail in the next section. Positive residual income correlates with increases in the market value of the firm because positive residual income indicates that a business is accumulating net resources at a rate greater than is needed to satisfy the providers of capital. The firm should, therefore, be in a position to grow and increase future cash flows (or pay out an abnormally high level of dividends to owners).

Market Value   represents the highest, most aggregate, measure of value creation because it represents the value of ownership claims in the business as priced by financial markets. **Market value** is the price at which shares in the company trade on the open market. For publicly traded companies, market value is priced daily on a per share basis and reported in the financial press. The total market value of a company, or **market capitalization,** is calculated as the product of the total number of ownership shares outstanding times the price per share.

Total market value = Number of Ownership Shares Outstanding × Price per Share

For example, the market value of The Gap is equal to $15.3 billion (calculated as 268 million shares outstanding × $57 per share).

Market value fluctuates with investor perceptions of the level and timing of expected future cash flows of the business. Market value can be expected to increase for companies in which investors believe that future cash flow growth will be positive. These expectations of value, as priced in current stock prices, are reflected in a calcula-

---

Top U.S. Market Value Added Firms

Fortune magazine published the following ranking by market value added of the 200 largest U.S. firms (as measured by market capitalization):

MVA RANK			COMPANY	MARKET VALUE ADDED ($ MILLIONS)	ECONOMIC VALUE ADDED ($ MILLIONS)	CAPITAL ($ MILLIONS)	RETURN ON CAPITAL (IN %)	COST OF CAPITAL (IN %)
1998	1997	1993						
1	2	5	General Electric	$195,830	$1,917	$59,251	17.3%	13.8%
2	1	2	Coca-Cola	158,247	2,615	10,957	36.3	12.1
3	3	12	Microsoft	143,740	2,781	8,676	52.9	14.2
4	5	4	Merck	107,418	1,921	23,112	23.2	14.5
5	4	24	Intel	90,010	4,821	21,436	42.7	15.1
6	8	9	Procter & Gamble	88,706	587	24,419	15.2	12.8
7	7	11	Exxon	85,557	(412)	88,122	9.4	9.9
8	11	16	Pfizer	83,835	1,077	15,220	19.9	12.1
9	6	3	Philip Morris	82,412	3,524	43,146	20.2	11.9
10	10	6	Bristol-Myers Squibb	81,312	1,802	14,627	25.3	12.5

Source: Adapted from Shawn Tully, "America's Greatest Wealth Creators," *Fortune,* (November 9, 1998): 194.

tion known as **market value added,** which is the excess of current market value over the amount of capital (i.e., adjusted book value) provided to the firm:

$$\text{Market Value Added} = \text{Total Market Value}$$
$$- \text{Capital Provided by Owners and Lenders}$$

ECONOMIC VALUE ADDED

The concept of residual income has been advocated by accountants for a long time, and its calculation is quite straightforward: the cost of capital is subtracted from accounting profit to determine how much is left over for reinvestment or distribution to owners. Recently, there has been a movement—especially in North America—to elaborate the concept of residual income into a calculation known as **economic value added** (EVA).[7] EVA adjustments attempt to transform accounting income (revenue minus expenses) into a number that more closely approximates economic income (cash flows in excess of the opportunity cost of capital). This calculation is similar to residual income but is distinguished by (1) a series of adjustments to eliminate potential distortions of accrual accounting and (2) the inclusion of both debt and equity sources of capital in the calculation of cost of capital.

Adjustments to Eliminate the Distortions of Accrual Accounting

Generally accepted accounting principles require managers to account for transactions on an *accrual basis*. Accrual accounting adjustments transfer costs and revenues between accounting periods. This is done for two reasons: (1) to better match costs with revenues and (2) to ensure a conservative calculation of profit when there is uncertainty about the timing of future revenues or costs.

For some categories of accruals—such as recording accounts payable for unpaid invoices—there is little dispute about the desirability of shifting costs to the correct accounting period. However, there are other accruals that accountants make for matching purposes or for reliability purposes that can potentially distort the economic income of a business. EVA calculations attempt to undo these adjustments to (1) generate a profit number that more closely represents economic cash flows and (2) restate the balance sheet to reflect the true value of resources used to generate income.

All accrual adjustments can be reversed for EVA calculations, but the following adjustments are the most common and capture most of the potential distortions of accrual-based accounting:

LIFO Inventory To match cost of goods sold with revenues, companies must choose an inventory accounting policy. Most U.S. companies choose LIFO (last-in, first-out) accounting to reduce income and thereby minimize income taxes. In this accounting method, the most recent product costs ("last in") are matched against current revenue

---

[7] Consultants Stern Stewart & Company have trademarked "EVA" as their name for residual income and "MVA" as their acronym for market value added.

(they are the "first out" for matching purposes), with the desirable result that cost of goods sold on the income statement most closely approximates current purchase prices. An unfortunate side effect of LIFO accounting, however, is the fact that the balance sheet inventory figure is often seriously understated, reflecting product costs that are many years out of date. (The "first-in" product costs can sit on the balance sheet until all inventory is liquidated — literally forever!)

Accordingly, for EVA purposes, the value of the inventory account on the balance sheet is adjusted to *current cost* to more accurately reflect the true value of working capital under the control of management. In addition, any distortion to income due to the reduction of inventory stockpiles and the consequent liquidation of LIFO "layers" (i.e., matching of current revenues with very old prices recorded on the balance sheet) is reversed.

Deferred Tax Expense   Many people think that "income tax expense" on a company's income statement shows the amount of income taxes a company is required to pay to the government. This is not true. Instead, accountants require companies to record a different — generally higher — tax expense based on *book income*. The difference between what a company records on its income statement as tax expense and what it actually pays the tax authorities reflects *a timing difference* — that is, accruals are recognized at different points in time for book and tax purposes. The most common timing difference is due to choices in depreciation accounting. For example, many companies choose a straight-line method of depreciation for their bookkeeping to best match revenues with expenses; however, for the calculation of taxable income, companies often adopt some method of accelerated depreciation to minimize taxable income and reduce current tax liabilities. Thus, accounting policies — and net income — differ under the book and tax calculations.

Accountants believe that the taxes saved today because of differences in depreciation policies will have to be paid tomorrow. As a result, *tax expense* on an income statement is based on *book income* (e.g., using straight-line depreciation), not on the income that is calculated on a company's income tax return (using accelerated depreciation). The difference between the taxes actually paid and the amount that would have been paid under the company's accrual assumptions is recorded as a deferred tax liability on the balance sheet. For EVA calculations, the current year's income tax expense attributable to the accrual of deferred taxes is added back to income. Similarly, deferred taxes payable on the balance sheet are considered part of the capital of the firm.

Amortization of Goodwill   Accountants account for the difference between the purchase price of a company and its identifiable net assets as goodwill. For example, if Company A purchased Company B for $400 million, and the net assets of Company B (assets minus liabilities) were valued only at $300 million, the balance of $100 million would be shown on the purchaser's balance sheet as an asset — "goodwill" — and amortized over some period up to 40 years. Over each of the future 40 years, some portion of the goodwill would be amortized against income, thereby reducing it. For EVA purposes, the goodwill accrual must be adjusted in two ways. First, the reduction in income due to the amortization of goodwill in the current period is added back to income.

Second, to the extent that accumulated amortization has eroded goodwill, the balance sheet is restated to reflect the full purchase price of the acquisition (not only the value of identifiable tangible assets) so that managers are held accountable for generating returns on the full value of the assets employed.

Research and Development Expense   Any asset, by definition, represents the present value of future cash flows. If it cannot generate future cash flows, it cannot be classified as an asset. One of the hotly debated issues in accounting over the years is how to account for R&D expenditures. Are they assets or expenses? Some argue that managers invest in research and development for the sole purpose of developing new products and processes that will generate future cash flows. According to this reasoning, R&D expenditures should be capitalized as an asset to be expensed against revenues of future periods. Accountants, however, are suspicious that the amounts spent on R&D may not be fully recoverable in future periods. They argue that some R&D expenditures are inevitably wasted, because experimentation by nature implies trial and error. Therefore, rather than permitting managers to record R&D expenditures as assets—and amortize them over the lives of new products and processes—accountants in the U.S. require managers to expense all R&D expenditures in the current period (this practice differs in other countries).

The EVA calculation reverses this thinking. R&D expenditures are put back on the balance sheet as assets and amortized over some estimated life (typically five or 10 years). This has the effect of increasing income by the amount of the R&D expense (less any amount associated with its amortization over time) and increasing the value of the asset or capital base recorded on the balance sheet.

Adjustments to Calculate the Cost of Capital

The next set of calculations summarize the investment base used to generate profit. The cost of capital for EVA is generally calculated by including all forms of financing—both equity and debt. Thus, the investment base closely mirrors what would be used for a standard ROA calculation—that is, by including all of the major accounts on the right side of the balance sheet, we are actually arriving at the value of assets on the left side of the balance sheet.

Once the value of debt and equity are identified (or alternatively, the value of assets employed), the WACC is calculated. For example, if a firm was financed 60% by equity and 40% by debt, the cost of equity financing was 16%, and the after-tax cost of debt financing was 8%, then the WACC would be calculated as follows:

Debt	$ 400,000	×	8% =	$ 32,000
Equity	600,000	×	16% =	96,000
	$1,000,000			$128,000

Equivalently, the rate itself can be calculated directly as:

$$(0.40 \times 0.08) + (0.60 \times 0.16) = \underline{12.8\%}$$

Of course, multiplying this rate (12.8%) by the total amount of debt and equity ($1,000,000) yields an identical $128,000 as the cost of capital.

The following example for a publicly traded biotechnology company will illustrate the effects of these adjustments. The objectives of this calculation are (1) to compute the true value of assets under management's control (which equals exactly the capital base of the firm), (2) to calculate the expected return on those assets based on WACC, and (3) to subtract expected returns from actual profit (after EVA adjustments) to calculate the residual income.

To make these calculations, the following information is needed. This information would be contained in the footnotes of an annual report or, for a smaller business unit or private company, would be available to managers inside the firm.

1. Inventories are stated at the lower of cost or market. Cost is based on the LIFO method. Replacement cost of year-end inventory would be $5,600 higher than the amount reported on the balance sheet. Replacement cost of year-end inventory for the prior year would be $4,800 higher than the amount reported on the previous year's balance sheet.

2. Deferred taxes are due to timing differences in the calculation of depreciation for tax purposes and book purposes.

3. Goodwill results from the purchase of a subsidiary in 20X1, in which the excess of cost over identifiable net asset value equaled $200,000, which is being amortized over 10 years.

4. Research and development costs, related to the investment in prototypes and test machinery for the next generation of product, are being expensed as incurred. Over the life of the firm, $600,000 of R&D expenditures have been written off.

5. The WACC is 12%.

With this information in mind, refer to Exhibit 8–3 for a summary of the analysis to adjust net income and balance sheet accounts for EVA purposes. [*Note:* The top of Exhibit 8–3 presents four columns for the adjustment of balance sheet accounts. The first column is the original accrual balance sheet at 12/31/20X1 with assets equal to liabilities. The next column represents the EVA adjustments. The final two columns represent "Net Operating Assets" and "Adjusted Capital Base," respectively, as computed under EVA. Net Operating Assets total $1,330,600 in net debits (assets minus current liabilities). The Adjusted Capital Base also equals exactly $1,330,600 in net credits (equity plus long-term liabilities). Every line item on the original balance sheet (either a debit or a credit in column one) can be traced across—after adding or subtracting for any EVA adjustments—to either the Asset (debit) or Capital Base (credit) column. Thus, the debits and credits from the original balance sheet stay in balance.]

After making the adjustments shown in Exhibit 8–3, the calculation of EVA is straightforward:

1. Assets = Capital Employed = $1,330,600
2. Expected Return = $1,330,600 × 12% = $159,700
3. EVA = $326,800 − $159,700 = $167,100

Thus, Bio Techno has earned $167,100 more than its cost of capital.

EVA has proven attractive to companies for several reasons. First, it focuses managers on generating returns in excess of the cost of the capital entrusted to them. Positive EVA should result in the creation of wealth and an increase in value for the firm.

EXHIBIT 8–3
Bio Techno Company
Balance Sheet and Income Statement
Year Ended December 31, 20X1

	12/31/20X1	SIMPLIFIED EVA ADJUSTMENTS*	NET OPERATING ASSETS (ASSETS MINUS LIABILITIES)	ADJUSTED CAPITAL BASE (DEBT AND EQUITY CAPITAL)
Assets				
Cash	$ 280,000		$ 280,000	
Accounts receivable	420,000		420,000	
Inventory	300,000	$ 5,600 (1)	305,600	$ 5,600
Plant & equipment	250,000		250,000	
Accumulated depreciation	(140,000)		(140,000)	
Goodwill	180,000	20,000 (3)	200,000	20,000
Capitalized R&D		475,000 (4)	475,000	475,000
	$1,290,000			
Liabilities & Shareholders' Equity				
Accounts payable	$ 145,000		$ (145,000)	
Income tax payable	45,000		(45,000)	
Other current liabilities	270,000		(270,000)	
Long-term notes payable	120,000			120,000
Deferred income taxes	105,000	105,000 (2)	—	105,000
Common stock	305,000			305,000
Retained earnings	300,000			300,000
	$1,290,000		$1,330,600	$1,330,600

Note that ROE for Bio Techno would be calculated as $160,000 ÷ $605,000 = 26.4%—a number somewhat higher than the returns suggested by the EVA analysis. Second, because EVA is not a ratio, it reduces the risk of managers shrinking the asset base (denominator) to bolster ROA or ROCE measures (managers can still increase residual income by reducing the asset base, but the effect of shrinking assets is less pronounced under EVA).

However, EVA does not work well in all companies. As with ROI-type measures, EVA demands that all assets be valued accurately. This remains problematic for knowledge-intensive businesses or any business with intangible resources that do not appear on the balance sheet. EVA is also difficult to calculate for any business that must allocate large-scale production and corporate assets among many different business units. Also, EVA does not work well for financial institutions that must set aside a prescribed amount of capital for regulatory purposes.

EVA has also been criticized as a myopic measure that fails to consider the industry and competitive context in which the firm competes. EVA measures the company's

EXHIBIT 8–3 *(Continued)*

Income Statement		EVA ADJUSTMENTS*	EVA Income
Revenue	$5,200,000		$5,200,000
Cost of goods sold	2,930,000		2,930,000
	2,270,000		2,270,000
Inventory holding gain		800 (1)	800
Selling & administration expenses	1,780,000		1,780,000
Research & development	175,000	115,000 (4)	60,000
Amortization of goodwill	20,000	20,000 (3)	—
Interest expense	10,000	10,000 (5)	—
	1,985,000		1,840,000
Income before taxes	285,000		430,800
Income tax expense—Current	100,000	4,000 (5)	104,000
—Deferred	25,000	25,000 (2)	—
Net income	$ 160,000		$ 326,800

Explanation of Adjustments: [balance sheet adjustments are made simultaneously to both the asset (a debit) and the capital base (a credit)]
(1) $5,600 is added back to inventory for EVA purposes and added to the capital base. $800 is added to income to adjust for the increase in the LIFO reserve.
(2) The deferred income tax reserve is transferred to the capital base. The increase in deferred taxes for the current year is added back to income.
(3) Accumulated amortization is added back to goodwill on the balance sheet and net income is increased by the amount of the current year's amortization.
(4) Accumulated R&D expenses ($600,000) are added back as an asset, less $125,000 accumulated amortization. An amortization schedule indicates that $60,000 of this should be amortized in 20X1.
(5) Because interest is included in the charge for WACC, interest expense (after-tax) is added back to avoid double counting.

ability to earn more than its cost of capital, but it fails to consider how the company has performed relative to its competitors. Shedding underperforming business, repurchasing shares, and slashing costs may increase a company's short-term share price and EVA, but these actions do not necessarily create sustainable wealth.[8]

One might ask why EVA has taken hold in the 1990s, when accountants have had no luck over many generations in selling the idea of residual income. Part of the answer may be in EVA's ability to bring accrual accounting closer to economic cash flows. However, a deeper answer may lie in the extended bull market of the 1990s, during which stock prices have increased dramatically and unceasingly. Investors have come to count on capital appreciation and higher market values as a matter of course. It proved quite hard to sell residual income as a surrogate for market value added during the period 1966 to 1981, when inflation-adjusted stock prices were either falling or flat.

LINKING EXTERNAL MARKETS AND INTERNAL OPERATIONS: BACK TO THE PROFIT PLAN

We have discussed the key performance measures that managers monitor to ensure that they are meeting the expectations of investors, customers, and suppliers. Often, however, these external parties want to understand more details about the prospects of the

---

[8] Gary Hamel, "How Killers Count," *Fortune*, (June 23, 1997): 74.

The Shell Business Model

Top executives wanted Shell Oil Company's 21,000 employees to understand what drives value for the shareholder. With $30 billion in revenue and four major operating companies, Shell managers decided to use performance measurement to communicate the economics of the business.

The Shell Business Model now routinely reports the following indicators:

Revenue Growth	Overall Market Value
ROI	EVA

CEO Philip Carroll reported, "It is not a program that lets me sit at a computer and figure out what the East Chicago revenue is going to be. Rather, it influences the way I can discuss and evaluate the changing business strategies of the business units. We think of it as a financial beacon that supports decision making in a very rigorous way."

Source: Adapted from Joel Kurtzman, "Smart Managing: Is Your Company Off Course?" *Fortune,* February 17, 1997, 128.

firm before they invest, purchase products, or deliver services. Managers need a way of communicating their goals to external markets. Financial markets will be interested in knowing the long-term economic prospects of the firm—based on an evaluation of the likelihood of success of its competitive strategy. Important customers who must make critical sourcing decisions will be interested in understanding the commitment of the business to support its products in the future and its ability to deliver promised goods and services according to specifications. Key suppliers who are asked to be partners in the value-creation process will be interested in the mix of activities the firm is investing in and their role in those activities.

Profit plans are the critical link used by managers to link business strategy with value creation. Figure 8–4 shows the pivotal role of the profit plan in linking the creation of economic value with the strategic goals of the organization.

Profit plans are the principal tools that managers use to price their business and operating plans, make trade-offs between different courses of action, set performance and accountability goals, and evaluate the extent to which business performance is likely to meet the expectations of different constituents. Examples of the types of strategic decisions that are reflected in a firm's profit plan include the following:

**FIGURE 8–4   A Profit Plan Links Economic Value Creation
with Strategic Goals**

CHAPTER 8

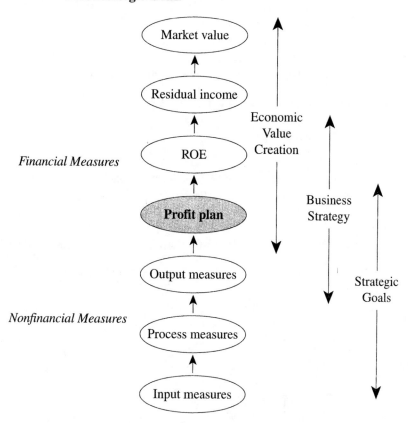

Revenue
   1.   Number of products in product portfolio
   2.   Mix and type of products
   3.   Price points of products (a function of features, quality, and competitive products)
   4.   Changes in any of the above, including
        (a)   new-product introductions
        (b)   product deletions

Cost of Goods Sold
   1.   Cost of features
   2.   Cost of quality
   3.   Efficiency of internal processes
        •   production scale and batch sizes
        •   economies of purchasing
        •   economies of distribution
        •   capacity
   4.   Customization

5. Investment in R&D
6. Investment in plant and equipment (through depreciation)

Gross Margin
1. Sustainability of business
2. Success of pricing strategy
3. Market acceptance of product-differentiation strategy

Selling, General, and Administrative Expenses
1. Level of support services
2. Outsourcing

Profit
1. Attractiveness of business for future investment
2. Willingness of stockholders to invest resources

FIGURE 8–5   Using Profit Plan Goals to Communicate with External Markets

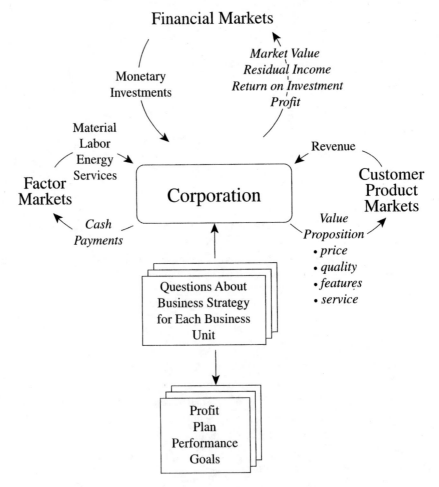

Managers use profit plans to communicate—to analysts, customers, suppliers, and others interested in the prospects of the firm—the strategic choices that have been made and the level of aspirations that have been set as goals (Figure 8–5). This communication—using accounting numbers—can be extremely effective in helping managers reduce the uncertainty of key constituents regarding the prospects and strategy of the firm.

CHAPTER SUMMARY

Profit plans and other performance indicators are linked to markets inside the firm and outside the firm. Any firm that chooses to transfer goods and service internally between autonomous divisions must rely on transfer prices and adjust the profit plans of the divisions involved. Although there are multiple ways of setting transfer prices, there is no simple solution to the transfer pricing problem. Trade-offs among transfer pricing policies must be understood. In the final analysis, success depends on reasonable managers sitting down and negotiating differences so that the firm can benefit from their actions.

Managers must also understand the linkage between internal operations and external markets. These linkages affect capital markets, customer markets, and supplier markets. To communicate effectively with these markets, managers must know how to use accounting-based tools such as profits plans, ROE and residual income measures, and EVA.

In the next chapter—Building a Balanced Scorecard—we study how to extend this analysis beyond financial accounting numbers by building performance measurement systems that focus on intangible resources: key customers, internal processes, and learning and growth.

9

Building a Balanced Scorecard

The emergence of new information technologies and the opening of global markets has changed many of the fundamental assumptions of modern business. No longer can companies gain sustainable competitive advantage solely by deploying tangible assets. The information-age environment for both manufacturing and service organizations requires new capabilities for competitive success. The ability of a company to mobilize and exploit its intangible assets has become decisive in creating and sustaining competitive advantage.[1]

Intangible resources and assets enable an organization to

- develop customer relationships that build loyalty
- serve new customer segments and markets
- introduce innovative products and services
- produce customized high-quality products and services at low cost and with short lead times
- mobilize employee skills for continuous improvements in process capabilities, quality, and response times

In the past, as companies invested in programs and initiatives to build their capabilities, managers relied solely on financial accounting reports. Today, however, the financial accounting model must be expanded to incorporate the valuation of the company's intangible and intellectual assets. As discussed in earlier chapters, these intangible assets include valuable product and service franchises, motivated and skilled employees, distinctive internal capabilities, and satisfied and loyal customers.

If intangible assets and company capabilities could be valued accurately and reliably on a balance sheet, organizations that enhance these assets and capabilities could communicate this improvement to employees, shareholders, creditors, and other constituencies. Conversely, when companies deplete their stock of intangible assets and capabilities, the loss in value could be reflected immediately on the income statement. Unfortunately, difficulties in placing a reliable financial value on intangible assets — like the value of new-product pipelines, process capabilities, employee skills, customer loyalties, and customer databases — will likely preclude them from ever being recognized on a business's balance sheet. Yet, these are precisely the assets and capabilities that are critical for success in today's competitive environment.

---

[1] Hiroyuki Itami, *Mobilizing Invisible Assets* (Cambridge, Mass. Harvard University Press, 1987).

FIGURE 9-1   Translating Vision and Strategy: Four Perspectives

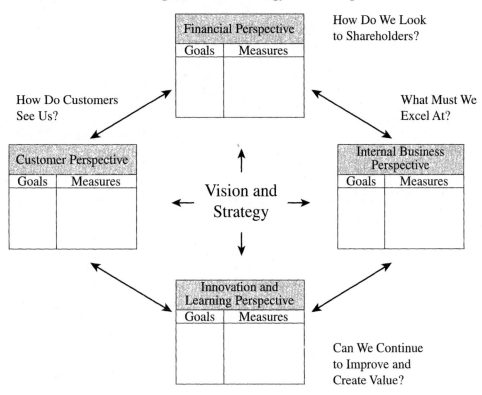

THE BALANCED SCORECARD

The **balanced scorecard** communicates the multiple, linked objectives that companies must achieve to compete based on their intangible capabilities and innovation. The scorecard translates mission and strategy into goals and measures, organized into four different perspectives: financial, customer, internal business process, and learning and growth (see Figure 9–1).

Managers can build a balanced scorecard by following a logical four-step sequence.

Step 1: Develop Goals and Measures for Critical Financial Performance Variables

The balanced scorecard retains the **financial performance perspective** discussed in previous chapters because financial measures are essential in summarizing the economic consequences of strategy implementation. Financial performance measures indicate whether the implementation of plans and initiatives is contributing to profit improvement. As discussed in previous chapters, financial objectives can be measured by operating profit, ROCE, and EVA. Additional financial objectives can relate to any variable on the profit wheel, the cash wheel, or the ROE wheel.

For Boston Retail, the financial goals are set out in the profit plan that we developed in Chapter 5. In particular, Boston Retail set a stretch goal to increase sales and operating income by 150% over the next five years—an ambitious target for a mature, largely saturated industry such as apparel retailing.

Step 2: Develop Goals and Measures for Critical Customer Performance Variables

In the **customer perspective** of the balanced scorecard, managers identify the customer and market segments in which the business desires to compete. Targeted segments could include both existing customers and potential customers. Then, managers develop measures to track the business unit's ability to create satisfied and loyal customers in these targeted segments.

Studies have shown that businesses with satisfied, loyal customers become significantly more profitable over time. Loyal customers typically increase the amount of their purchases, cost less to serve, refer new customers to the business, and are willing to pay a price premium for products or services that they trust. Thus, a 5% increase in customer loyalty can produce profit increases from 25% to 85%.[2]

The customer perspective typically includes several core or generic measures that relate to customer loyalty. These core outcome measures include customer satisfaction, customer retention, new customer acquisition, customer profitability, and market and account share in targeted segments (see Figure 9–2).

FIGURE 9–2   Customer Perspective: Core Outcome Measures

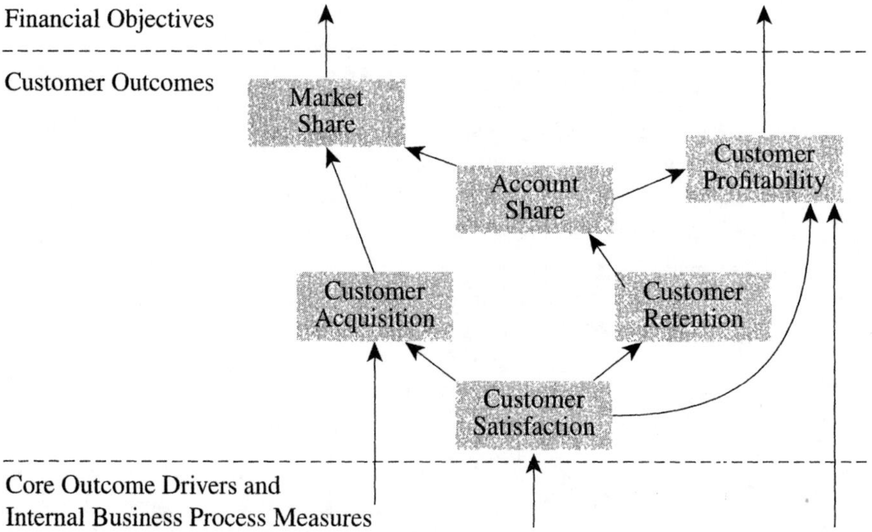

Source Adapted from Robert S. Kaplan and David P Norton, "Linking the Balanced Scorecard to Strategy," California Management Review (Fall 1996).

---

[2] Frederick Reichheld and W. Earl Sasser, Jr. "Zero Defections: Quality Comes to Services," *Harvard Business Review* (September–October, 1990).

Although these customer measures appear to be generic across all types of organizations, they can and should be customized to the targeted customer groups from whom the business expects its greatest growth and profitability. That is, customer satisfaction, customer retention, customer loyalty, and market share should be measured only for those customer or market segments for which the organization desires to be a dominant provider of goods and/or services.

Some common customer-based measures can be developed as follows:

Customer Satisfaction[3]

- Measuring customer satisfaction can take the form of familiar market research tools such as customer response cards and questionnaires.
- Customer satisfaction can also be measured through letters of complaint, feedback from field sales and service representatives, and "mystery shopper" programs. These sources of customer feedback often give a deeper understanding of customer satisfaction issues.

Customer Retention

- Monitoring the average duration of a customer relationship can detect problems with the value proposition. Are new customers defecting because they were the wrong customers for this product or service? Are long-term customers leaving because of changes in quality, a better price elsewhere, or a combination of both?
- Surveying defecting customers to understand where defectors go and why they left provides critical feedback on the validity of the firm's strategy.

Customer Loyalty

- Measuring the number of new customers referred by existing customers can quantify the degree of customer loyalty to a firm. A customer must be highly satisfied before recommending a firm to others.
- Measuring the "depth of relationship" with customers can also provide insight into customer loyalty. For example, a fast-food restaurant chain could measure how much of an average customer's weekly food budget was captured. A luxury-item retailer could measure how often good customers make purchases at their stores versus competitors' stores.

As we have discussed in previous chapters, an effective strategy is based on a unique value proposition the business delivers to attract and retain customers in its targeted segments. Although value propositions vary across industries and across different market segments within industries, there are a common set of attributes that organize the value propositions in most industries. These attributes fall into three categories (see Figure 9–3):

- product/service attributes
- customer relationship
- image and reputation

Let's consider each briefly.

Product and service attributes of a value proposition encompass desirable product or service features, price, and quality. For companies competing on operational

---

[3] James Heskett et al., "Putting the Service-Profit Chain to Work," *Harvard Business Review* (March–April 1994): 164–174.

**FIGURE 9–3   Customer Perspective: Linking Unique Value Propositions
to Core Outcome Measures**

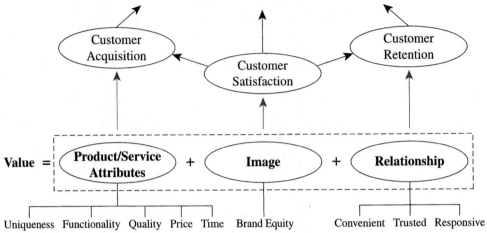

Source: Adapted from Kaplan and Norton, "Linking the Balanced Scorecard to Strategy," p. 62.

excellence, for example, critical performance measures might include the price of the product relative to competitors, the quality perceived by customers (such as defect rates and field failures), and timeliness (such as lead times and on-time delivery). Other companies, competing on uniqueness or particular product features, will choose to measure those product attributes that create value in a different way for their particular customer segment. For example, size is a critical performance variable for implantable medical devices, disk drives, and computer chips. For electronic instruments, accuracy might be highly valued. For automobiles, acceleration, braking capabilities, and engine performance might be dimensions that determine customer preferences. Depending on the value proposition, measures can be developed for each of these critical performance attributes.

The *customer relationship* dimension of a value proposition includes the delivery of the product or service to the customer, including response and delivery time, and how the customer feels about the buying experience. Many companies perform detailed customer surveys or "mystery shopper" programs to assess the quality of the relationship between the customer and the company.

The *image and reputation* dimension of the value proposition enables a company to calibrate and measure the value of its franchise. Advertising and marketing research companies employ techniques to measure the strength of a brand name. These measures can be used to track the effectiveness of the strategy in building franchise value. Other examples of image and reputation measures include the price premium earned by a product compared with an unbranded competitive offering and the willingness of retailers to stock the product because of the consumer demand generated by a strong brand.

Boston Retail could generate a variety of measures for its customer value proposition using all three components of the value equation—product attributes, customer relationship, and brand image—as follows:

Product Attributes
1. Price Benefits
- Average unit retail price (an indicator of a successful product mix)
- Total dollar sales at discounted prices (an indicator of failed merchandise categories)

2. Fashion and Design
- Average annual sales growth in "strategic merchandise" (key items that best exemplify the image Boston Retail is attempting to convey)
- Average mark-up achieved (an indicator of well-received merchandise design and fashion)

3. Quality
- Return rate (an indicator of the consumer's satisfaction with the quality of the product)

Customer Relationship
1. Availability
- Out-of-stock percentage on strategic merchandise
- Data, collected by responses on a "What do you think?" card solicited from each customer, asking about satisfaction with the availability of size and color on selected items

2. Shopping Experience
- "Mystery shopper" audits (An independent, third-party shopper was hired to purchase selected items at each Boston Retail location and evaluate the experience according to criteria established for the "perfect shopping experience.")

Brand and Image
- Market share in strategic merchandise categories
- Premium price earned on branded items (If Boston Retail is successful in communicating an attractive brand image, it should command a higher price over unbranded or generic items of comparable product characteristics and quality.)

Managers at Boston Retail decided that their core customer outcome measures should include market share, account share (e.g., share of wardrobe), and satisfaction for customers in its targeted segment (18- to 30-year-old, college-educated females). Information on market and account share was not available from public sources. Therefore, Boston Retail engaged a market research firm to conduct surveys to estimate its performance with this targeted customer segment.

Step 3: Develop Goals and Measures for Critical Internal Process Performance Variables

In the **internal business process perspective,** managers identify the critical internal processes for which the organization must excel in implementing its strategy (see Figure 9–4). The internal business processes dimension represents the critical processes that enable the business unit to

- deliver the value propositions that will attract and retain customers in targeted market segments, and
- satisfy shareholder expectations regarding financial returns.

Thus the internal business process measures should be focused on the internal processes that will have the greatest impact on customer satisfaction and achieving the organization's financial objectives.

Each business will have a unique set of processes for creating value for customers and producing superior financial results. The **internal value chain** model provides a handy template that companies can use to customize for their own objectives and measures in their internal business process perspective of the scorecard. The generic value chain model encompasses three principal business processes (see Figure 9–4):

1. innovation processes
2. operations processes
3. post-sales service processes

Innovation Processes

In the **innovation process,** managers research the needs of customers and then create the products or services that will meet those needs. Companies identify new markets, new customers, and the emerging and latent needs of existing customers. Then, companies design and develop new products and services that enable them to reach these new markets and customers.

As part of the innovation process, managers perform market research to identify the size of the market and the nature of customers' preferences and price sensitivity for the targeted product or service. As organizations deploy their internal processes to meet these customer needs, accurate information on market size and customer preferences becomes vital to effective resource allocation.

Managers at Boston Retail chose to focus their innovation efforts on *fashion leadership.* Thus, they measured this objective with two key measures:

FIGURE 9–4   The Internal Value Chain

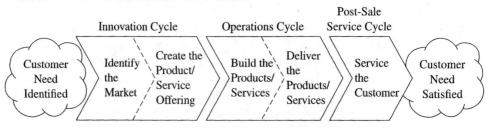

Source: Adapted from Kaplan and Norton, *The Balanced Scorecard* (Boston· Harvard Business School Press, 1996), p 96

- number of key items in which Boston Retail was first or second to the market
- percentage of sales from items newly introduced into stores

Operations Processes

The **operations process,** the second major step in the internal value chain, represents those processes that produce and deliver existing products and services to customers. The operations process starts with receipt of a customer order and finishes with delivery of the product or service to the customer. These processes stress efficient, consistent, and timely delivery of existing products and services to existing customers.

The operations process has historically been the focus of most organizations' internal measurement systems. Today — as always — operational excellence and cost reduction remain important goals. However, as the internal value chain in Figure 9–4 shows, such operational excellence may be only one component — and perhaps not the most decisive component — in the internal value chain.

Existing operations tend to be repetitive. Therefore, scientific management techniques can be readily applied to control and improve production and delivery processes. Traditionally, these operating processes have been monitored and controlled by financial measures such as standard costs, budgets, and efficiency variances. Over time, however, excessive focus on narrow financial measures such as labor efficiency, machine efficiency, and purchase price variances has sometimes led to dysfunctional actions, such as:

- keeping labor and machines busy building inventory not related to current customer orders
- switching from supplier to supplier to chase cheaper purchase prices (but ignoring the costs of poor quality and uncertain delivery times)[4]

In recent years, the influence of the TQM and time-based competition practices of leading Japanese manufacturers has led many companies to supplement their traditional cost and financial measurements with measurements of quality and cycle time.[5]

Quality Measures   Almost all organizations today have quality initiatives and quality programs in place. Measurement is a central part of any quality program. Therefore, most organizations are already familiar with a variety of process-quality measurements, including:

- process parts-per-million (PPM) defect rates
- yields (ratio of good items produced to good items entering the process)
- scrap

---

[4] Robert Kaplan, "Limitation of Cost Accounting in Advanced Manufacturing Environments," Chap. 1 in Robert S. Kaplan, ed., *Measures for Manufacturing Excellence* (Boston Harvard Business School Press, 1990)

[5] Many references could be cited here. A representative sample includes C. Berliner and J. Brimson, "CMS Performance Measurement," Chap. 6 in *Cost Management for Today's Advanced Manufacturing* (Boston: Harvard Business School Press, 1988); C. J. McNair, W. Mosconi, and T. Norris, *Meeting the Technology Challenge. Cost Accounting in a JIT Environment* (Montvale, N J.: Institute of Management Accountants, 1988); and R. Lynch and K. Cross, *Measure Up! Yardsticks for Continuous Improvement* (Cambridge, Mass : Basil Blackwell, 1991).

- rework
- returns
- percentage of processes under statistical process control

Service organizations should also identify any defects in their internal processes that could adversely affect costs, responsiveness, or customer satisfaction. They can then develop customized measures of quality shortfalls. One bank, for example, developed an index to indicate the defects in its internal processes that lead to customer dissatisfaction. The index included items such as:

- long waiting times
- inaccurate information given to customers
- access denied or delayed
- request or transaction not fulfilled
- financial loss for customer

Cycle Time Measures   Many customers place a high value on short and reliable lead times, measured as the time elapsed from when they place an order until the time when they receive the desired product or service. Accordingly, the value proposition delivered to targeted customers often includes short response time for the delivery of goods and services as a critical performance attribute.

Manufacturing companies generally have two ways of offering short and reliable lead times to customers. One way is to have efficient, just-in-time (JIT), short-cycle order fulfillment that can respond rapidly to customer orders. The other way is to produce and hold large stocks of finished-goods inventory so that any customer request can be met by shipments from inventory stocks. Rapid response through JIT processes potentially enables the company to be a low-cost and timely supplier. The second way—based on large inventory stocks—can lead to high inventory carrying and obsolescence costs, as well as an inability to respond quickly to orders for nonstocked items (because the manufacturing processes are typically busy building inventories for normally stocked items). When manufacturing companies attempt to shift away from high inventories (producing large batches for "just-in-case" inventory) to the JIT approach, reducing cycle or throughput times of internal processes becomes a critical internal process objective.

Cycle or throughput times can be measured in different ways. The start of the cycle can correspond to the time that

1. a customer order is received
2. a production batch is scheduled
3. raw materials are ordered for the order or production batch
4. production on the order or batch is initiated

Similarly the end of the cycle can correspond to the time that

1. production of the order or the batch has been completed
2. an order or batch is in finished goods inventory, available to be shipped
3. an order is shipped
4. an order is received by the customer

The choice of starting and ending points is determined by the scope of the operating process for which cycle-time reductions are being sought. The broadest definition, corresponding to an *order fulfillment cycle,* starts the cycle with receipt of a customer order and ends when the customer has received the order. A much narrower definition, aimed at improving the *flow of physical material* within a factory, could correspond to the time between when a batch is started into production and when the batch has been fully processed. Whatever definition is used, the organization should continually measure cycle times and set goals for employees to reduce total cycle times.

Several organizations use a metric called manufacturing cycle effectiveness (*MCE*), defined as:

$$MCE = \frac{\text{Processing Time}}{\text{Throughput Time}}$$

This ratio is less than 1 because throughput time, the denominator, can be broken out as follows:

$$\frac{\text{Throughput}}{\text{Time}} = \frac{\text{Processing}}{\text{Time}} + \frac{\text{Inspection}}{\text{Time}} + \frac{\text{Movement}}{\text{Time}} + \frac{\text{Waiting/Storage}}{\text{Time}}$$

To emphasize the importance of reducing throughput time, this equation can be rewritten as:

$$\text{Throughput Time} = \text{Value-added Time} + \text{Nonvalue-added Time}$$

where *value-added time* equals processing time plus the times during which work is actually being performed on the product, and *nonvalue-added time* represents the time the part is waiting, being moved, or being inspected.

Although JIT production processes and the MCE ratio were originally developed for manufacturing operations, they are just as applicable to service companies. If anything, eliminating waste time in a service delivery process is even more important than in manufacturing companies. Consumers are increasingly intolerant of being forced to wait in line for service delivery. In many service companies, studies have indicated that customers experience long cycle times for service, despite actual processing time being quite low. As a result, some automobile rental companies and hotel chains have now automated all aspects of check-in and check-out, enabling repeat customers to bypass all waiting in line when accessing the service and upon completion of the service delivery process.

Thus, companies attempting to deliver products and services on demand to targeted customers can set objectives to have MCE ratios approach 1, thereby dramatically shortening lead times to customer orders.

Cost Measures   Amidst all the attention to process time and process quality measurements, one might lose sight of the cost of these internal processes. Traditional cost accounting systems measure the expenses and efficiencies of individual tasks, operations, or departments. However, these systems fail to measure costs at the *process level of analysis.* Today, with activity-based cost systems, managers can obtain accurate cost measurement of their business processes. Activity-based cost analysis enables organizations to obtain process cost measurements that, along with quality and cycle-time

In addition to the profit plan goals established in Chapter 5, Boston Retail established two critical objectives for its operating processes: (1) sourcing leadership and (2) merchandise availability. It measured these two objectives with two measures each, as shown below:

Sourcing Leadership
- Percentage of items returned to vendors because of quality problems
- Vendor performance rating (incorporating dimensions of vendors' quality, price, and lead time)

Merchandise Availability
- Out-of-stock percentage on selected key items
- Inventory turnover on selected key items (a "compensating" measure to ensure that high in-stock performance was achieved by excellent supplier and distribution performance, not by holding excess inventories)

measurement, provide important parameters to track the effectiveness and efficiency of important internal business processes.

In summary, some aspects of quality, time, and cost measurements will likely be included as critical performance measures in any organization's internal business process perspective on its balanced scorecard.

Post-Sale Service Processes

The third and final stage in the internal value chain is customer service after the original sale or delivery of service. The **post-sale service process** includes warranty and repair activities, treatment of defects and returns, and the administration of payments, such as credit card processing. Some companies have explicit strategies to offer superior post-sale service. For example, companies that sell sophisticated equipment or systems may offer training programs for customers' employees to help them use the equipment or system more effectively. They may also offer rapid response to failures and downtime. Newly established automobile dealerships, like Acura and Saturn, have earned reputations for offering dramatically improved customer service for warranty work, periodic car maintenance, and car repairs. A major element in their value proposition is responsive, friendly, and reliable warranty and service work. Accordingly, these companies measure customer satisfaction each time a customer has his or her car serviced by the dealer.

Another aspect of post-sale service can include the invoicing and collection process. Companies with extensive sales on credit or with branded credit cards will likely apply cost, quality, and cycle-time measurements to their billings, collection, and dispute resolution processes. Several department stores offer value propositions that include generous terms under which customers can exchange or return merchandise. As with the car dealer, these companies can measure the satisfaction of key customers with returns policies and billings and collections.

Companies that deal with hazardous chemicals and materials illustrate a special case of post-sale service. These companies may introduce critical performance measures associated with the safe disposal of waste and byproducts from the production process. For example, one distributor of industrial chemicals developed after-sale disposal services for used chemicals, freeing its customers from this expensive task, which is fraught with liability and subject to intense governmental scrutiny by agencies such as the Environmental Protection Agency and the Occupational Safety and Health Administration. This company measures the percentage of customers that uses its recycling program. This measure signals to the company's employees the importance of soliciting this business and delivering post-sale service in a reliable, cost-effective manner.

For many companies, excellent community relations may also be a strategic objective to ensure the continuing right to operate production facilities. Accordingly, these companies often set post-sale service objectives for environmental performance. Measures such as waste produced during production processes may be more significant for their impact on the environment than for their slight increase in production costs. All of these activities add value to the customers' use of the company's product and service offerings.

We have now reviewed the innovation, operations, and after-sale service components of the internal value chain. The analysis reveals two fundamental differences between traditional and balanced scorecard approaches to performance measurement. Traditional approaches attempt to monitor and improve *existing* business processes. These approaches may go beyond just financial measures of performance by incorporating quality and time-based metrics—but they still focus on improving existing processes. The balanced scorecard approach, by contrast, can identify entirely *new processes* at which the organization must excel to meet customer and financial objectives. For example, as part of a balanced scorecard analysis, the organization may realize that it must develop a process to anticipate customer needs or one to deliver new services that customers value. The balanced scorecard internal business process objectives highlight these processes—several of which it may not be currently performing.

The second departure of the balanced scorecard approach is to incorporate *innovation processes* into the internal business process perspective. Traditional performance measurement systems focus on the processes of delivering today's products and services to today's customers. However, the drivers of long-term financial success may require the organization to create entirely new products and services that will meet the emerging needs of current (and future) customers. The innovation process is, for many companies, a more powerful driver of future financial performance than the short-term operating cycle. The ability to manage successfully a multiyear product-development process or to develop a capability to reach entirely new categories of customers may be more critical for future economic performance than managing existing operations efficiently, consistently, and responsively. The internal business process perspective of the balanced scorecard can incorporate objectives and measures for the innovation cycle as well as the operations cycle.

Step 4: Develop Goals and Measures for Critical Learning and Growth Performance Variables

The fourth balanced scorecard perspective—**learning and growth**—identifies the infrastructure that the organization must build to create long-term growth and improvement. The customer and internal business process perspectives identify the factors most critical for current and future success. However, businesses are unlikely to be able to meet their long-term targets for customers and internal processes using today's technologies and capabilities. Intense global competition requires companies to continually improve their capabilities for delivering value to customers and shareholders.

Organizational learning and growth come from three principal sources: people, systems, and organizational procedures. The financial, customer, and internal business process objectives on the balanced scorecard will typically reveal large gaps between existing capabilities and those required to achieve targets for breakthrough performance. To close these gaps, businesses must invest in training employees, enhancing information technology and systems, and aligning organizational procedures and routines. These objectives are articulated in the learning and growth perspective of the balanced scorecard. As in the customer perspective, employee-based measures can include quantitative outcome measures based on surveys to measure employee satisfaction, employee retention, employee training, and employee skills. Information systems capabilities can be measured by the availability and responsiveness of accurate, critical, customer and internal process information to front-line employees. Organizational procedures can examine alignment of employee incentives with overall organizational success factors and measure rates of improvement in critical customer-based and internal processes.

Studies across multiple industries have shown that employee and customer satisfaction closely track one another.[6] This "satisfaction mirror" occurs for a number of reasons: Positive encounters with customers lead to higher levels of employee job satisfaction, which in turn engender greater employee loyalty. As employee loyalty increases, so does average employee tenure. Over time, employees get to know their job and their customers better. As a result, they can deliver higher levels of service to their customers, potentially at a lower cost. Better service reinforces employee satisfaction, creating a virtuous cycle. Measuring employee skills (through testing and training) and empowerment (evaluating the extent to which employees are given authority to correct customer problems, information systems to support their interactions with customers, etc.) are essential to maintaining the virtuous cycle.

Step 5: Use the Balanced Scorecard to Communicate Strategy

As we have discussed, the balanced scorecard retains important financial measures. Financial measures alone, however, are insufficient for guiding and evaluating how companies create *future* value through investment in customers, employees, processes, and innovation. Financial measures tell the story of tangible assets; the balanced scorecard provides a window into the value created by intangible assets.

---

[6] James Heskett, W. Earl Sasser, and Leonard Schlesinger, *The Service Profit Chain* (New York: The Free Press, 1997): 101.

Using the balanced scorecard, top managers can measure how effective their business units are in creating value for current and future customers, building and enhancing internal capabilities, and investing in people, systems, and procedures necessary to improve future performance. The balanced scorecard captures critical value-creation activities that escape traditional income statements and balance sheets. While retaining an

---

Balanced Scorecard and Strategic Alignment at Cigna

Cigna International Property & Casualty Company applied the balanced scorecard approach as part of its strategic transformation. It took President Gerald Isom and his management team three months to define the four categories of the scorecard: financial, external (customer), internal (business processes), and learning and growth. Isom made it clear that these measures would now be used to define and achieve Cigna's vision of becoming a specialist insurer with financial results in the top 25% of the commercial insurance industry. The plethora of nonfinancial measures was totally new to Cigna managers. According to Isom, in the past the entire focus was on the financial numbers. There was insufficient attention devoted to outcomes or to understanding critical performance variables. To communicate strategy down the three levels of the organization, Isom asked the company's three divisions and 20 business units to devise their own balanced scorecards, which were to be constantly reviewed.

Cigna's balanced scorecard enabled business units to align their business plans with corporate strategy. For example, Cigna set premium growth as an objective at the corporate level, but profitable growth required different plans in each business unit. Some business units chose to measure increases in premiums from new producers (brokers and agents), whereas others measured premiums from new segments or premiums from new products. Cigna also wanted strong relations with brokers and agents. Again, different business units implemented measures appropriate to their circumstances: more flexible underwriting in one unit, faster underwriting decisions in another, a broader array of services in a third, more price competitiveness in a fourth, and so on.

Employees received "position shares," whose face value of $10 per share was to be adjusted according to balanced scorecard performance. At the beginning of the year, employees received a certain fixed number of position shares (based on their job level), and additional shares were awarded as a bonus during the year. This system allowed the heads of strategic business units to reward any employee who influenced the unit's performance measure.

Cigna executives can check business unit performance anytime on the corporate information system. Although each business unit has its own target, all units rate themselves using the same 1 to 5 scale numerical system, enabling easy comparisons. Underperforming units are flagged with yellow or red. Constant feedback is reinforced by the fact that the score of each unit is available to the others.

Source. Adapted from Bill Birchard, "Cigna P&C: A Balanced Scorecard," *CFO* (October 1996): 30–34.

interest in short-term performance—via the financial perspective—the balanced score-card clearly reveals the value drivers for superior long-term financial and competitive performance.

Well-designed scorecards enable both financial and nonfinancial measures to be part of the information system for employees at all levels of the organization. Front-line employees can see the financial consequences from their decisions and actions; senior executives can understand the drivers of long-term financial success. The balanced scorecard represents a translation of a business unit's mission and strategy into tangible goals and measures. The four perspectives of the scorecard permit a balance (1) between short- and long-term objectives, (2) between external measures—for shareholders and customers—and internal measures of critical business processes, innovation, and learning and growth, (3) between desired outcomes and the performance drivers of those outcomes, and (4) between hard objective measures and softer, more subjective measures.

Many people think of measurement as a tool to control behavior and to evaluate past performance. However, the measures on a balanced scorecard should be used in a different way. Balanced scorecard measures should be used to articulate the strategy of the business, to communicate this strategy to employees, and to help align individual, organizational, and cross-departmental initiatives to achieve common goals. Used in this way, the scorecard does not strive to keep individuals and organizational units in compliance with a preestablished plan. Rather, the balanced scorecard should be used as part of a larger management system for communication, information sharing, and learning.

The multiplicity of measures on a balanced scorecard may seem confusing, but properly constructed scorecards, as we will see, contain a unity of purpose; all the measures are directed toward achieving an integrated strategy.

TESTING THE LINKAGE OF MULTIPLE SCORECARD MEASURES TO A SINGLE STRATEGY

The multiple measures on a properly constructed balanced scorecard should consist of a linked series of goals and measures that are both consistent and mutually reinforcing. In other words, the balanced scorecard should be viewed as the instrumentation for a *single* strategy. The integrated system of scorecard measures should incorporate the complex set of cause-and-effect relationships among the critical variables that describe the trajectory and the flight plan of the strategy. The linkages should incorporate both outcome measures and performance drivers.

Cause-and-Effect Relationships

Good measurement systems should make the relationships among goals and measures explicit so they can be managed and validated. The chain of cause and effect should pervade all four perspectives of a balanced scorecard. For example, ROCE may be a scorecard measure in the financial perspective. The driver of this financial measure could be repeat and expanded sales from existing customers, the result of a high degree of loyalty. Customer loyalty is included on the scorecard (in the customer perspective) because it is expected to have a strong influence on ROCE, but how will the organization achieve customer loyalty? Analysis of customer preferences may reveal that on-time delivery of orders is highly valued by customers. Thus, improved on-time delivery is expected to lead to higher customer loyalty, which, in turn, is expected to lead to higher financial performance. Therefore, both customer loyalty and on-time delivery are incorporated into the customer perspective of the scorecard.

The process continues by asking what internal processes must the company excel at to achieve exceptional on-time delivery. To achieve improved on-time delivery, the business may need to achieve short cycle times in operating processes and high-quality internal processes, both factors that could be scorecard measures in the internal perspective. How do organizations improve the quality and reduce the cycle times of their internal processes? By training and improving the skills of their operating employees, an objective that would be a candidate for the learning and growth perspective. In this manner, an entire chain of cause-and-effect relationships can be established as a vertical vector through the four balanced scorecard perspectives:

Financial	ROCE
	⇑
Customer	Customer Loyalty
	⇑
	On-Time Delivery
	⇑ ⇑
Internal Business Process	Process Quality Process Cycle Time
	⇑ ⇑
Learning and Improvement	Employee Skills

Thus, a properly constructed balanced scorecard should tell the story of the business unit's strategy. It should identify and make explicit the sequence of hypotheses about the cause-and-effect relationships between outcome measures and the performance drivers of those outcomes.

Performance Drivers

A good balanced scorecard should have a mix of outcome measures and performance drivers (i.e., critical input and process measures). Outcome measures without performance drivers do not communicate how the outcomes are to be achieved. They also do not provide early warning about whether the strategy is being implemented successfully. Conversely, performance drivers based on inputs and processes alone—such as cycle times and PPM defect rates—enable the business unit to achieve short-term operational improvements. However, these measures fail to reveal whether the operational improvements have been translated into expanded business with existing and new customers, and, eventually, into enhanced financial performance. Thus, a good balanced scorecard should have an appropriate mix of outcomes (lagging indicators) and performance drivers (leading indicators) of the business unit's strategy. In this way, the scorecard translates the business unit's strategy into a linked set of measures that define the long-term strategic objectives, as well as the mechanisms for achieving those objectives.

Strategic Measures

Most organizations today already have hundreds, if not thousands, of measures to keep themselves functioning and to signal when corrective action must be taken. However, most of these measures are not drivers of a business's competitive success. They are necessary for ongoing operations, but they do not define or measure success in achieving key strategic goals.

A simple example clarifies this point. Many aspects of our bodily functions must perform within fairly narrow operating parameters if we are to survive. If our body temperature departs from a normal 1°–2° window (away from 98.6° F or 37° C), or our blood pressure drops too low or escalates too high, we have a serious problem for our survival. In such circumstances, all our energies (and those of skilled professionals) are mobilized to restore these parameters back to their normal levels. However, under normal circumstances, we do not devote much energy to optimizing our body temperature and blood pressure. Being able to control our body temperature to within 0.01° of the optimum will not be one of the strategic success factors that will determine whether we become a chief executive of a company, a senior partner in an international consulting firm, or a tenured professor. Other factors are much more decisive in determining whether we achieve our unique personal and professional objectives. Are body temperature and blood pressure important? Absolutely. If these measurements fall outside predetermined limits, we have a major problem that we must attend to and solve immediately. Although these measurements are *necessary,* they are not *sufficient* for the achievement of our long-run goals.

The balanced scorecard is a complement, not a replacement, for an organization's other performance measurement and control systems. The measures on the balanced scorecard are chosen to direct the attention of managers and employees to those factors where high performance levels can be expected to lead to competitive breakthroughs. Although the cockpit of a Boeing 747 has hundreds of gauges and dials, the pilot monitors only a handful of these gauges actively—using that information to balance the critical performance variables of the aircraft relative to its destination. The other indicators are essential only if a basic function fails to perform and a warning buzzer sounds. Like body temperature and blood pressure, they are hygiene factors. In a business, hygiene factors are not the basis for competitive breakthroughs. If these factors do not meet acceptable standards, they can prevent the organization from meeting its objectives—but they are not the foundation for successful strategy.

For example, in the 1980s, product and process quality of many Western companies were so poor compared with their Japanese competitors that the companies had to put quality improvements at the top of their priorities. After years of hard and diligent work, many U.S. companies have achieved excellent quality and are now at parity with their foreign competitors. At this point, quality has been neutralized as a competitive factor. Of course, companies need to maintain existing quality and continue to make continuous improvements, but quality is no longer a critical factor for determining strategic success. In such a situation, quality is monitored diagnostically, and the company needs to find other dimensions in its value proposition to distinguish itself from competitors. These other dimensions are at the core of the balanced scorecard.

FOUR PERSPECTIVES: ARE THESE SUFFICIENT?

The four perspectives of the balanced scorecard should be considered as a template, not a straitjacket. No mathematical theorem exists to prove that four perspectives are both necessary and sufficient. The owners and capital contributors to the organization appear on every scorecard through goals and measures in the financial perspective. Customer measures also appear on every scorecard (in the customer perspective) because customers are essential for meeting the financial goals. Goals and measures for employees appear on the balanced scorecard when outstanding performance along this dimension will lead to breakthrough performance for customers and shareholders.

Companies rarely use fewer than four perspectives but, depending on industry circumstances and a business unit's strategy, one or more additional perspectives may be needed. For example, some managers incorporate the interests of other important stakeholders, such as suppliers and the community. When strong supplier relationships are part of the strategy leading to breakthrough customer and/or financial performance, then outcome and performance driver measures for supplier relationships should be incorporated within the organization's internal business process perspective. When outstanding environmental and community performance is a central part of a company's strategy, then objectives and measures for that perspective also become an integral part of a company's scorecard.[7]

CHAPTER SUMMARY

In rapidly changing, highly competitive global markets, companies succeed by investing in and managing their intangible assets and capabilities. Functional specialization must be integrated into customer-based business processes. Mass production and delivery of standard products and services are being replaced by flexible, responsive, and innovative products and services that can be customized to targeted customer segments. Innovation in products, services, and processes must be created by highly trained employees, superior information technology, and aligned organizational procedures.

As organizations invest in acquiring these new intangible capabilities, their success cannot be motivated or measured solely by the traditional financial accounting model. The balanced scorecard integrates measures at the core of implementing strategy. While retaining key financial measures, the balanced scorecard introduces the drivers of future financial performance. These drivers—encompassing customer, internal business process, and learning and growth perspectives—are derived from an explicit and rigorous translation of the organization's strategy into tangible goals and measures.

---

[7] See comments of D. W. Boivin, President and COO Novacor Chemicals, "Using the Balanced Scorecard," letter to the editor, *Harvard Business Review* (March–April 1996): 170.

PART III

Achieving Profit Goals and Strategies

10

Using Diagnostic and Interactive Control Systems

To achieve financial and nonfinancial goals, managers must rely on the efforts and initiative of employees. Employees throughout the organization must understand the business's strategy and their role in achieving strategically important goals. As businesses grow larger, communication of strategic goals and measures becomes both more important and more difficult. Managers face increasing demands on their time and must use their scarce resources wisely. Using performance measurement and control systems effectively becomes critical to success.

Step back in time to the initial start-up of Boston Retail. The founders had an idea that they believed could be built into a successful business. At first, they rented one retail store and started as most entrepreneurs do—by doing everything themselves. They tested their value proposition, focusing on the youthful college fashion market. Feedback from customers was encouraging. The entrepreneurs worked diligently to build up the scale of the business and attract a loyal customer base. Early profits were plowed back into the business and additional resources were acquired—new store furnishings, warehouse facilities, and additional inventory. A few temporary employees were hired to help out in the evenings and during the busy holiday seasons.

In the day-to-day operation of the store, all important decisions were reserved for the founders. They were always on hand and could be consulted for any issues that required a judgment call. The owners signed all checks and monitored carefully the flow of inventory, paperwork, and cash receipts to ensure that all receipts were safely deposited in the bank, all inventory was properly handled, and all sales transactions were accurately recorded. Because of their constant oversight, few errors occurred and those that did were caught early and rectified.

As Boston Retail prospered, additional stores were opened and new employees were hired to staff the stores. The founders tried, as much as possible, to give new employees the training and information needed to effectively perform their jobs. However, as time passed, it became increasingly difficult to directly monitor the work of the employees. The business had grown too large and dispersed. The founders were experiencing limits as to what they could accomplish single-handedly. There were now too many employees and too many stores to watch everything themselves; besides, the entrepreneurial founders wanted to devote more of their time to pursuing expansion opportunities. If the business was to continue its profitable growth, the founders would have to change their focus. For the first time in the history of the young company, success would

FIGURE 10–1   Two Levers of Control: Diagnostic and Interactive Control Systems

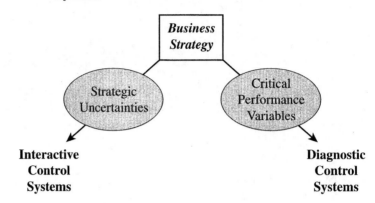

Source: Adapted from Simons, *Levers of Control,* p. 7.

be determined by the founders' ability to effectively *communicate* strategy to employees and *control* strategy implementation.

To understand how to communicate and control strategy effectively, we differentiate between two different types of control systems: diagnostic control systems and interactive control systems. Managers rely on both types of systems, but for different purposes. Diagnostic control systems are used as levers to communicate critical performance variables and monitor the implementation of intended strategies. Interactive control systems are used to focus organizational attention on strategic uncertainties and provide a lever to fine-tune and alter strategy as competitive markets change (Figure 10–1).

We should, however, make a critical point at the outset of our analysis. The difference between diagnostic and interactive control systems is not in their technical design features. A diagnostic control system may look identical to an interactive control system. The distinction between the two is solely in the way that managers *use* these systems. For example, the same profit planning system or balanced scorecard can be used *either* diagnostically *or* interactively. As we shall see, this choice has profound implications for maximizing ROM and the effective implementation of strategy.

DIAGNOSTIC CONTROL SYSTEMS

When driving your car, the speedometer is part of a diagnostic control system. You can use information from the dial on your dashboard to compare your actual speed with the posted speed limit. If there is a significant deviation, you can accelerate or slow down to bring the car in line with the desired speed of travel.

Many of the control systems in businesses operate in much the same way. For example, managers set annual profit plan and balanced scorecard goals and then receive monthly statements that report actual accomplishments for the period. Variance analysis highlights significant differences. If any deviations threaten the achievement of key goals, managers can initiate actions to get things back on track.

We define **diagnostic control systems** as the *formal information systems that managers use to monitor organizational outcomes and correct deviations from preset standards of performance.*[1] Any formal information system can be used diagnostically if it is possible to (1) set a goal in advance, (2) measure outputs, (3) compute or calculate performance variances, and (4) use that variance information as feedback to alter inputs and/or processes to bring performance back in line with preset goals and standards. Diagnostic control systems are the prototypical cybernetic feedback systems described in Chapter 4.

Although profit plans are a common diagnostic control system, managers can use most performance measurement and control systems diagnostically, including:

- balanced scorecards
- expense center budgets
- project monitoring systems
- brand revenue/market share monitoring systems
- human resource systems
- standard cost-accounting systems

Why Use Control Systems Diagnostically?

Managers must be selective about which control systems they should personally monitor. After all, there are literally thousands of measures in any organization that could be reported to senior managers. Managers cannot review and monitor every possible measure. To understand how managers choose among these systems, we must discuss the two principal reasons for using a system diagnostically: to implement strategy effectively and conserve scarce management attention.

Implementing Strategy

Managers are interested primarily in monitoring diagnostic control systems that report variance information about **critical performance variables**—*those factors that must be achieved or implemented successfully for the intended strategy of the business to succeed.*[2] In essence, diagnostic control systems are the top-down monitoring tools for implementing strategy as plan (Figure 10–2). They link strategy with critical performance goals and targets and monitor their successful implementation. Without diagnostic control systems, managers could neither communicate nor implement strategy effectively in large complex organizations.

Because of the importance of these systems, managers must ensure that (1) critical performance variables have been analyzed and identified, (2) appropriate goals have been set, and (3) feedback systems are adequate to track performance.

Conserving Attention

When driving for long distances, watching the speedometer and constantly adjusting the accelerator can be tiring. This activity consumes energy and attention. Thus, automobile

---

[1] Robert Simons, *Levers of Control* (Boston: Harvard Business School Press, 1995): 59.
[2] For a full discussion of critical performance variables, see Chapter 11.

FIGURE 10–2   **Linking Strategy to Diagnostic Control Systems**

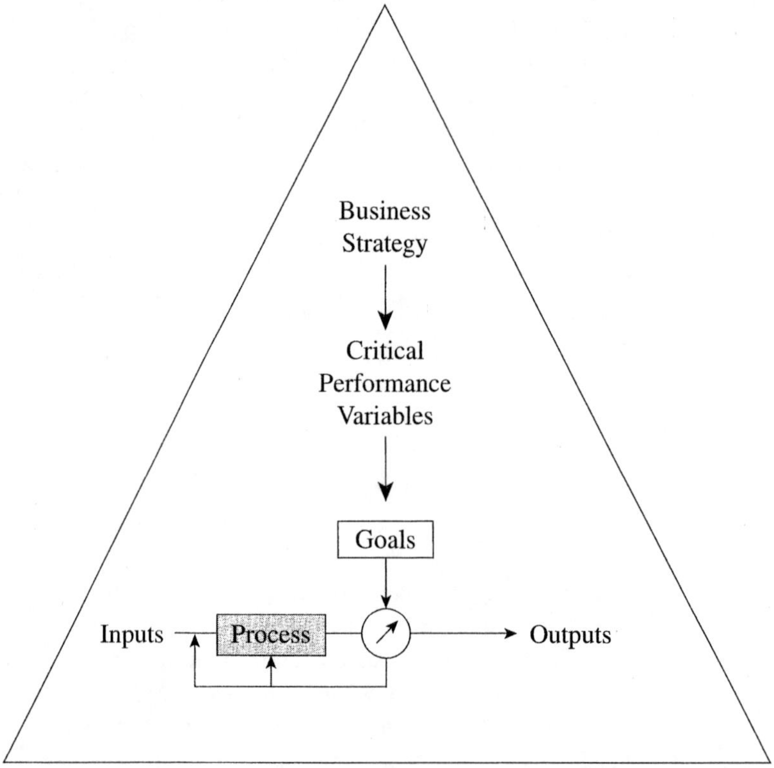

Source: Adapted from Simons, *Levers of Control,* p. 63.

companies offer automatic speed controls that automate this diagnostic process. You can set the desired speed, and the computer keeps the automobile's speed within tight bounds. The speed controller frees up your attention to concentrate on other things (day-dreaming, talking with your spouse, or worrying about your next appointment).

In organizations, managers can do the same thing with performance measurement and control systems. They can use them to put the organization on automatic pilot. Instead of constantly monitoring a variety of internal processes and comparing results with preset targets and goals, managers receive periodic exception reports from staff accountants. If everything is on track, the reports can be reviewed quickly and managers can move on to other issues. If, on the other hand, significant deviations are identified, then—and only then—do managers need to invest the time and attention to investigate the cause of the deviation and initiate appropriate remedial actions. This process is called *management by exception.*

Using Diagnostic Control Systems Effectively

Using the automatic speed control in your car conserves attention, but you must know how to use the device effectively. Just as the automobile driver must know how to set the device's speed and adjust it from time to time, so, too, must business managers know how to set key targets and make adjustments as circumstances warrant.

To operate diagnostic control systems effectively, managers must ensure that they devote sufficient attention to five areas: setting goals, aligning performance measures, designing incentives, reviewing exception reports, and following up significant exceptions.

1. Setting and Negotiating Goals   Performance goals are the hallmark of diagnostic control systems. They are critical to the effective implementation of strategy because they define where subordinates should devote their energy. Because of the importance of goal setting, managers must personally ensure that goals are appropriate both in terms of desired direction and level of achievement.

When making a long trip in your car, you must initially set the target speed, but then you do not need to adjust it for long periods. In a similar way, managers need only set critical performance goals infrequently—usually once per year. If these goals are properly set, they should not require any additional adjustment or attention. Managers can monitor progress during the operating period by a quick scan of exception reports.

2. Aligning Performance Measures   Diagnostic control measures define the span of accountability—that is, the performance variables for which a manager is accountable. Therefore, if managers wish to rely on diagnostic control systems for assurance that strategy is on track, they must ensure that performance measures truly reflect strategic goals and priorities. Techniques such as balanced scorecards are important to assure that these measures align correctly with intended strategy. Again, this need only be done infrequently, but it is extremely important.

3. Designing Incentives   The speed control in your car is powered by an internal electrical system. Diagnostic control systems in a business must also be powered up by some energy source. Managers who wish to maximize their ROM use formula-based incentives as a way of powering up, or motivating, goal achievement. Bonuses, promotions, and merit increases can be made contingent upon performance reported in diagnostic control systems. Then, incentives provide extrinsic motivation so that managers do not have to monitor the day-to-day activities of subordinates to be sure that they are working toward desired goals. Diagnostic performance measures and formulas that link rewards with results are sufficient to keep everyone focused on strategy implementation.

4. Reviewing Exception Reports   With diagnostic control systems in place, managers can review monthly and quarterly exception reports as soon as they are released to gain confidence that strategy implementation is on track. If measurement systems and incentives are well-designed and aligned, this review can be conducted very quickly and efficiently, thereby increasing ROM. Managers need only scan reports for evidence of large, significant exceptions, or indications that problems may be looming.

5. Following Up Significant Exceptions   Although managers use diagnostic control systems to conserve attention, when a significant deviation appears, they must initiate action quickly to get things back on track. Subordinates are monitoring the same

The Budget Brigade

In an article in *Financial Executive,* managers at The Interpublic Group of Companies (IPG)—a New York-based advertising organization—described their profit planning and budgeting process:

> Complete reviews of each system's business and financial results begin with the budget process in December. The managements of [our three major businesses] meet with the financial and operating managers of every local agency. The managements of all three agency systems then make presentations to IPG in an agreed-on format, which includes a mission statement, business outlook and business strategy, such as new business opportunities. Every year, we give each agency goals for revenue, profit margin, operating profit and net-income growth, based on IPG objectives and historical performance, and we provide salary guidelines and headcount goals. At the budget meetings, we work with the management of each agency system to ensure the goals and guidelines are realistic and achievable.

> We also review financial-trend data on a consolidated basis with each agency's management, emphasizing major markets and problem markets. Each review covers cash, dividends, receivable management, capital-expenditure requirements and technology needs. When we finish going over the budgets with the agencies, we consolidate the reviews so we can present them to the board of directors every February, along with our corporate-earnings target and our plans for achieving it.

> Each April and September, IPG holds follow-up or update meetings with the agency systems' management to measure performance against budget and objectives. These are thorough and frank reviews of the agency's business and client relationships, designed to ensure agency management is fully aware of business trends, new business opportunities, cash and capital requirements and possible merger or acquisition candidates. These update meetings are crucial to the overall management process and enable IPG to interact with the operating and financial managers of the agencies and keep the lines of communication open, which is so vital in a global business.

Source: Thomas J. Volpe and Alan M. Forster, "Ruling With A Firm Hand," *Financial Executive* 11 (January/February, 1995): 43–47.

measures as their bosses (remember, these measures define span of accountability and potential reward incentives), so remedial steps may have already been taken to rectify problems by the time the superior picks up the exception in a diagnostic report. Managers then need only initiate brief discussions to confirm that problems have already been identified and resolved.

Risks in Using Diagnostic Control Systems

Putting the business on automatic pilot and powering up the system through performance measures and incentives is not without risk, just as putting your car on speed control introduces special risks. All managers who use diagnostic control systems must guard against the following:[3]

---

[3] These risks are enumerated in Simons, *Levers of Control,* pp 81–84.

Measuring the Wrong Variables   Setting your car's automatic speed control keeps the vehicle at the right speed but gives no assurance that the car is pointed in the right direction. It does little good to get the speed right if you are traveling south when you want to go north. Similarly, misaligned control systems in businesses can do more harm than good. As the old saying goes, "What gets measured, gets managed." Attention is limited, and people must make choices about where they will spend their time. Sometimes, misaligned diagnostic measures can cause the strategy to go off track.

- In the late 1980s, Dun & Bradstreet's Credit Services Division was accused of overcharging clients. Diagnostic control system measures caused this problem. Measures and incentives rewarded salespeople for increasing sales of subscription units regardless of a client's actual usage patterns. As a result, salespeople failed to inform clients of their true usage patterns in an attempt to sell them more units than they needed.[4]

Building Slack into Targets   When performance is a function of achieving preset goals, employees will naturally want to increase the probability of meeting those goals. One way of doing this, of course, is to start with a relatively easy goal. Accordingly, employees may try to build slack into their performance targets. If managers do not compensate for this tendency by ensuring that goals are set at challenging levels, it can lead to serious problems.

- In the 1980s, General Motors measured quality defects on a scale of 1 to 100. To the dismay of plant managers, cars were coming off the assembly line with an average of 45 defects, causing quality scores to fall to a dismal 55 points. To make scores look better, managers changed the rating scale so that scores would now be compared to a target of 145 points. Quality did not improve, but scores under the new system generally exceeded 100, which seemed more acceptable than scores of 50 or 60. During this time, continuing quality problems eroded GM's franchise with customers.[5]

Gaming the System   Bonuses tied to diagnostic measures release energy and creativity. People will generally work hard to achieve what they are measured on. However, this energy may focus on ways of enhancing the measure, even if increasing the measure does not lead to advancement of the underlying goal or strategy. This misdirected effort is called gaming.

- To build customer focus, IBM sales representatives were awarded sales commissions for all the IBM products sold in their districts, even if these sales were made by independent retailers. As a result, some reps spent their time traveling around their districts trying to identify retail sales for which they could claim bonus credits. The time spent searching for credits—which was completely unproductive—could have been better spent trying to sell new products to new customers.[6]

---

[4] J.L. Roberts, "Credit Squeeze—Dun & Bradstreet Faces Flap Over How It Sells Reports on Business," *Wall Street Journal* (March 2, 1989): A1.

[5] M. Keller, *Rude Awakening: The Rise, Fall, and Struggle for Recovery of General Motors* (New York: Morrow, 1989): 29–30.

[6] Robert Simons and Hilary Weston, "IBM: Make It Your Business," Harvard Business School Case No. 90–137 (1990).

Other common distortions when relying on diagnostic control systems for goal achievement include:

- *Smoothing* — This occurs when an individual alters the timing and/or recording of transactions to show better performance. This may happen, for example, when a manager has achieved the maximum bonus in one accounting period. Rather than book additional sales that are not eligible for additional bonus in the current period, he or she may defer booking the new revenue until the next accounting period to apply those sales to next period's bonus goal.
- *Biasing* — Managers bias information when they attempt to report only good news (e.g., goals that have been achieved) or to hide or downplay bad news (goals that have been missed).
- *Illegal acts* — Sometimes, performance pressures can cause someone to violate laws or organizational policies in an attempt to increase diagnostic measures and achieve related bonuses.[7]

The negative side effects of diagnostic control systems are pervasive but well known. Whenever people are rewarded for achieving performance targets and left alone to figure out how to do this, there is always the risk some may stray out of bounds. In Chapter 1, we described the organizational blocks that can cause well-intentioned people to stray from the path of doing what they know to be right and ethical. Diagnostic control systems and their related incentives create many of the pressures and temptations that are at the root of this dysfunctional behavior. This tension creates a dilemma for managers. On the one hand, managers are forced to rely on diagnostic control tools to motivate goals achievement and allow high ROM. On the other hand, the same tools inevitably risk dysfunctional behavior from employees who might respond inappropriately to pressure or temptation to bend the rules.

Whenever diagnostic control systems are used for evaluation and reward, managers must install good control systems and be alert for the underlying organizational pressures that may cause well-intentioned people to bend the rules to distort diagnostic measures. We study how to design and use these control systems in Chapters 12 and 13.

INTERACTIVE CONTROL SYSTEMS[8]

With diagnostic control systems in place, top managers have effectively put their organization on automatic pilot. If goals, measures, and incentives are properly aligned, the business is like a heat-seeking missile focused intently on achieving profit goals and strategies. These systems give managers the freedom to concentrate on growing the business, enhancing profitability, and positioning products and services in rapidly changing markets.

---

[7] Jacob G. Birnberg, Lawrence Turpolec, and S. Mark Young, "The Organizational Context of Accounting," *Accounting, Organizations, and Society* 8 (1983): 111–29.

[8] The remainder of this chapter draws upon ideas, examples, and concepts enumerated in Simons, *Levers of Control*, Chapter 5.

In the previous section, we used an automobile speed control as an analogy for the management by exception that is the hallmark of diagnostic control systems. However, managers need a different kind of control system to grow the business and search for new ways of positioning products and services in dynamic markets. They need a system more like the one used by the National Weather Service to search for and identify patterns of change. Ground stations all over the country monitor temperature, relative humidity, barometric pressure, and wind velocity and direction. Satellites and aircraft provide additional information about emerging storm patterns. All of this information is fed into a central location where data is gathered and analyzed to predict the likely affects of changing conditions. Based on predicted changes, action plans are adjusted (should we delay our trip?) and preparations can be made for impending threats (do we need to evacuate low-lying shore areas in advance of a strengthening hurricane?).

Strategic Uncertainties

For managers of any business, **strategic uncertainties** are the *emerging threats and opportunities that could invalidate the assumptions upon which the current business strategy is based.* Uncertainty, in general, results from a difference between the amount of information required to perform a task and the amount of information possessed by the organization.[9] Strategic uncertainties relate to *changes* in competitive dynamics and internal competencies that must be understood if the business is to successfully adapt over time. By definition, strategic uncertainties are unknowable in advance and emerge unexpectedly over time.

New technologies may undermine the business's ability to create value, changes in population demographics may decrease the need for specific goods and services, predatory pricing by competitors may put the existing value proposition at risk, product defects may scare away customers, and changes in government policy or regulation may unexpectedly remove vital protection or subsidies. Sometimes, these unexpected changes may also bring opportunities. Changing tariff structures may open up new markets, the unexpected exit of a competitor from the market may offer a chance to serve new customers, or another business may inquire about the possibility of forming a joint venture. Any of these events—either good or bad—may necessitate adjustment of the current strategy and value proposition.

Questions must be asked constantly about how to realign the strategy to take advantage of these emerging opportunities or deflect unexpected threats. Senior managers must energize the entire organization around these issues. Effective managers know that people can be extremely creative and can turn almost any threat or opportunity to advantage—if they can just focus the organization on these uncertainties.

Strategic uncertainties are different than critical performance variables. The critical performance variables enumerated in balanced scorecards or other diagnostic control systems are determined by analysis and embedded in plans and goals. Strategic uncertainties, by contrast, trigger a search for new information and meaning, rather than a

---

[9] Jay R. Galbraith, *Organization Design* (Reading, MA: Addison-Wesley, 1977): p. 36.

TABLE 10–1 Distinction Between Critical Performance Variables and Strategic Uncertainties

	CRITICAL PERFORMANCE VARIABLES	STRATEGIC UNCERTAINTIES
Recurring questions	What must we do well to achieve our intended strategy?	What changes in assumptions could alter the way we achieve our vision for the future?
Focus on	Implementing intended strategy	Testing and identifying new strategies
Driven by	Goal achievement	Top management unease and focus
Search for	Efficiency and effectiveness	Disruptive change

Source: Adapted from Simons, *Levers of Control,* p. 95.

cursory checkup to ensure that plans are on track. Strategic uncertainties focus on questions rather than answers. Table 10–1 summarizes the main differences between the two concepts.

Interactive Control Systems

The challenge for managers in any medium- or large-scale business is finding ways to focus everyone in the organization on these strategic uncertainties. To do so, they rely on a simple but universal fact: *everyone watches what the boss watches.*

To signal where they want people to pay attention, senior managers choose to use one or more control systems in a highly interactive way. **Interactive control systems** *are the formal information systems that managers use to personally involve themselves in the decision activities of subordinates.* Simply stated, interactive control systems are the hot buttons for senior managers. They provide the information that the boss pays a lot of attention to and are used to create an ongoing dialogue with subordinates.

We must now repeat the important point that we made in the introduction to this chapter. Interactive control systems are not defined by their technical design features. Instead, they are defined by how senior managers *use* these systems. Top managers pore over reports as soon as they are received and later use the information to challenge the thinking and action plans of subordinates. Senior managers use the interactive control system to spark information searches throughout the entire organization. This intensive use and focus stands in stark contrast to the management by exception that defines diagnostic control systems.

Figure 10–3 illustrates how an interactive control system focuses organizational attention and stimulates the emergence of new strategies over time.

Business strategy, in the upper left corner of Figure 10–3, reflects how the business currently creates value for customers and differentiates its products and services from competitors. Management's vision for the future—how it sees the business evolving in the marketplace—gives rise to specific *strategic uncertainties.* These are the issues and questions that keep managers awake at night. Depending on the current strat-

FIGURE 10-3   Using the Interactive Control Process for Learning

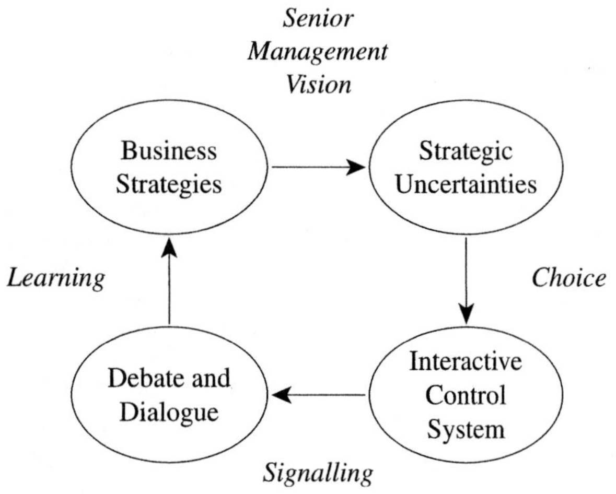

Source: Adapted from Simons, *Levers of Control,* p. 102.

egy and management's vision for the future, strategic uncertainties may relate to changes in customer preferences, competitor actions, new technology, government regulation, or any number of potential threats and opportunities.

To focus the organization on these strategic uncertainties, managers chose one (or more) performance measurement and control system and use it in a highly *interactive* way. Data from the system is used to challenge subordinates and their action plans and force them to attempt to make sense of rapidly changing conditions. This choice signals unequivocally what is important. Remember, everyone watches what the boss watches. In anticipation of the inevitable questioning from their bosses as new data is released, subordinates throughout the business work diligently to gather as much data as they can to be able to respond to questions and suggest action plans that respond to changing circumstances. Interactive *debate and dialogue* takes place at all levels of the organization as new information is studied and analyzed.

This ongoing discussion highlights the need for changing ways of doing things, changing the value proposition, or even changing aspects of the business strategy. The debate and dialogue forces organizational learning, which, in Figure 10-3, loops back to the adjustment of strategy. Thus, *emerging strategy* can be an indirect result of bottom-up action plans and experimentation.

Senior managers at Pepsi describe how they use an interactive control system that reports weekly market share data:

> Pepsi's top managers would carry in their wallets little charts with the latest key Nielsen figures. They became such an important part of my life that I could quote them on any product in any market. We would pore over the data, using it to search for Coke's vulnerable points where an assault could successfully be launched, or to explore why Pepsi slipped a fraction of a percentage point in the game. . . . The Nielsens defined the ground rules of competition for everyone at Pepsi. They were at the epicenter of all we did. They were

the non-public body counts of the Cola Wars. . . . The company wasn't always this way. The man at the front of the table made it so.[10]

A senior manager at Pepsi described how this interactive control system affected the behavior of managers throughout the business:

> No matter where I was at any time of the day, when the Nielsen flash came out, I wanted to be the first to know about it. I didn't mind a problem, but I hated surprises. The last thing I'd want was Kendall [Pepsi's CEO] calling for an explanation behind a weak number without having had the chance to see it myself. I'd scribble the details down on the back of an envelope or whatever else was convenient. Within an hour, some sixty or seventy people at Pepsi also would get the results and begin to work on them.[11]

The discussions surrounding interactive control systems are always face-to-face, involving operating managers directly. Meetings are used to brainstorm and use every possible piece of data to collectively make sense of changing circumstances. The debate focuses on new information, assumptions, and action plans.

The pressure to use a control system interactively is created quite simply by the regular and recurring attention of the highest levels of management. In face-to-face meetings, senior managers probe subordinates to explain any unforeseen changes in their business and offer suggested action plans. This pressure cascades from the top of the organization to the bottom. In response, through a series of interlocking meetings, the new information and learning flows upward, from the bottom of the organization to the top (see Figure 10–4).

In Chapter 2, we discussed how strategies can emerge spontaneously in organizations as employees experiment and replicate small successes in their attempts to create value. This is strategy as emerging *patterns of action.* Interactive control systems provide the principal means by which managers can guide this otherwise serendipitous process. Many of the best strategies come from unexpected ideas that originate with employees close to customers and markets. At Pepsi, a local experiment eventually laid the groundwork for a new strategy:

> We fought hard for a meager 7 percent share against Coke's 37 percent. It was hardly a contest. Out of sheer desperation, Larry Smith . . . urged an advertising effort more powerful than Pepsi's lifestyle approach. Not wanting to tamper with our hugely successful Pepsi Generation campaign, Pepsi advertising executives and [our advertising agency] resisted. Undaunted, Smith hired his own advertising agency in Texas and dispatched his vice president of marketing to help put together something that would represent a radical departure from what we or any other company had ever done before. The result amounted to one of the most devastating advertising and promotional campaigns ever devised. The Texas agency called it the "Pepsi Challenge."

By focusing attention on strategic uncertainties, managers can use the interactive control process to guide the search for new opportunities, stimulate experimentation and rapid response, and maintain control over what could otherwise be a chaotic process.

---

[10] John Sculley, *Odyssey: Pepsi to Apple: A Journey of Adventure, Ideas, and the Future* (New York: Harper & Row, 1987): 6–7.

[11] Sculley, p. 6.

FIGURE 10–4   Top-Down Pressure: Bottom-Up Strategy

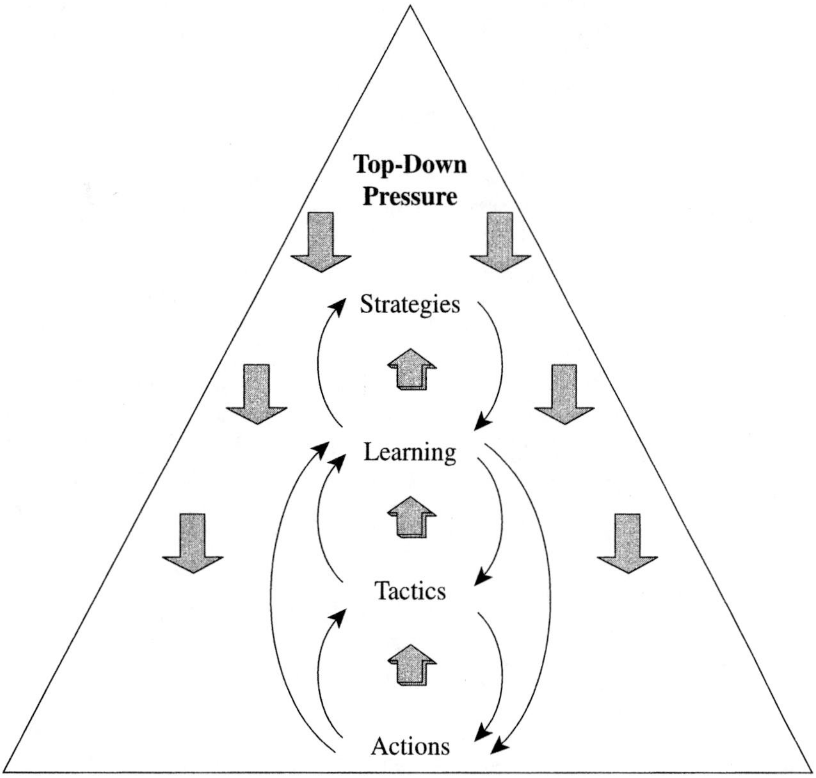

Source: Adapted from Simons, *Levers of Control,* p. 99.

Over time, the debate and dialogue that are the hallmarks of interactive control systems allow a business to adapt and renew its strategy:

> We treated each Challenge as a major event, a battle to be fought in our long-term war against Coke. Weeks before a Challenge would debut, we would begin quality tests on the product. If it failed to measure up, we would improve its taste so that a subgoal of the contest was to upgrade the overall quality of our product.[12]

Design Features of Interactive Control Systems

An interactive control system is not a unique type of control system; any control system can be used interactively by senior managers if it meets certain requirements. For example, managers might choose to use a profit planning system interactively, or a market share monitoring system (like the Nielsen data used at Pepsi), a project monitoring system, or a balanced scorecard. There are countless other systems in any organization that could be used interactively as well.

---

[12] Sculley, pp 43–44, 49.

By way of example, we can look at the U.S. healthcare industry, where senior managers in different firms use *one* of the following five control systems interactively based on their business strategy and unique strategic uncertainties:[13]

- *Profit planning systems* are used interactively when strategic uncertainties relate to the development and protection of new products and markets (e.g., highly innovative consumer products).
- *Project management systems* that report information about the discovery and integration of new technology projects are used interactively in businesses where changes in product technology are strategic uncertainties (e.g., high technology medical devices).
- *Brand revenue budgets* that report revenue, market share, and shipment data by brand or product category are used interactively in businesses where strategic uncertainties relate to extending the attractiveness of mature products (e.g., branded consumer goods such as hair coloring).
- *Intelligence systems* that report information about social, political, and technical business issues are used interactively when there is significant uncertainty concerning changes in regulation and government policy (e.g., prescription drug companies).
- *Human resource systems* that report information on skill inventories, manpower planning, and succession planning are used interactively when strategic uncertainties relate to acquiring new skills to meet competitive needs (e.g., in new and/or rapidly growing businesses).

Figure 10–5 illustrates how these system choices are determined by strategy and strategic uncertainties.

For a system to be eligible for use as an interactive control system, four criteria must be satisfied:

1. *The information contained in an interactive control system must be simple to understand.* If debate and dialogue are to be productive, everyone must be working from the same data and have faith in its accuracy. Managers cannot afford to waste their time arguing about the validity of complex algorithms or calculations that determine how data is compiled. The market share indicators used by managers at Pepsi satisfy this condition. They provide simple and unambiguous data; there is little uncertainty or debate about how the numbers were constructed or their internal validity.

2. *Interactive control systems must provide information about strategic uncertainties.* This condition is at the heart of why interactive control systems are so important— they focus attention unerringly throughout the organization. Everyone watches what the boss watches. Accordingly, it is critical that an interactive control system collect data on the strategic uncertainties of the business. Determined by a business's unique strategy, these uncertainties may relate to customers, technology, government regulation, or any number of other factors that are critical underpinnings of the current value proposition and strategy.

3. *Interactive control systems must be used by managers at multiple levels of the organization.* Managers use control systems interactively to stimulate subordinates to search for, analyze, and discuss new information. Thus, for any system to be used interactively, the information system must be available widely and used by a broad array of subordinate managers. This condition is met by a profit plan; it is not met by a long-range strategic plan that does not leave the executive suite.

---

[13] Robert Simons, "Strategic Orientation and Top Management Attention to Control Systems," *Strategic Management Journal* (Vol. 12, 1991): 49–62.

4. *Interactive control systems must generate new action plans.* An interactive control system focuses attention on patterns of change. Just as the National Weather Service predictions are used to change action plans, the critical questions asked over and over again by senior business managers using an interactive control system must be: (1) What has changed? (2) Why? and—most importantly— (3) What are we going to do about it? Interactive control systems are used above all else to adjust emerging strategy on a real-time basis.

FIGURE 10–5   Interactive Control System Choices: A Function of Strategy and Strategic Uncertainties

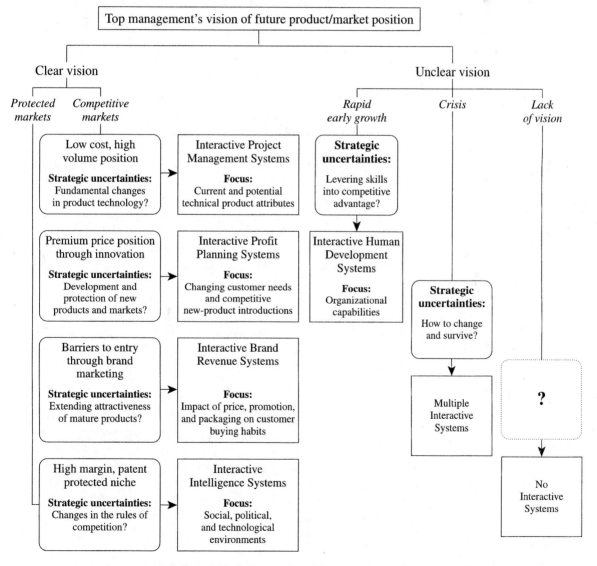

Source: Adapted from Simons, "Strategic Orientation and Top Management Attention to Control Systems," *Strategic Management Journal* 12 (1991): p. 54.

TABLE 10–2 Factors Affecting the Design and Choice of Interactive Control Systems

STRATEGIC UNCERTAINTY	IF UNCERTAINTY IS *HIGH*, THEN INTERACTIVE CONTROL SYSTEM	IF UNCERTAINTY IS *LOW*, THEN INTERACTIVE CONTROL SYSTEM
Technological Dependence	Focuses on emerging new technologies	Focuses on changing customer needs
Regulation and Market Protection	Focuses on sociopolitical threats and opportunities	Focuses on competitive threats and opportunities
Value Chain Complexity	Uses accounting-based measures	Uses input/output measures
Ease of Tactical Response	Uses short planning horizon	Uses long planning horizon

Source: Adapted from Simons, *Levers of Control,* p. 112.

Choosing Which System to Use Interactively

Given the many systems in an organization that could be used interactively, we can analyze the factors that influence which systems managers select. At least four factors influence the choice of systems to which managers devote their attention (see Table 10–2):

Technological Dependence The more a business is dependent on a specific technological base (such as an aircraft manufacturer), the more critical it becomes for managers of that business to protect their competitive advantage by focusing attention on new ways of applying technology. Managers use interactive project-management systems in these circumstances to focus the organization on emerging technologies and their potential effects on the current strategy of the business. Failure to do so can result in technological obsolescence, as occurred with Encyclopedia Britannica's failure to anticipate the effects of CD-ROM technology on the delivery of encyclopedia information.

Conversely, when technological dependence is low (e.g., household cleaning products), customers are not locked into any one product or product concept. In these cases, senior managers focus organizational attention on finding ways of responding to changing customer needs through new products or marketing programs. In these circumstances, interactive brand-revenue systems or interactive profit-planning systems that can model business trade-offs are often used.

Regulation Managers operating in regulated or semiregulated industries, such as public utilities and research-based pharmaceutical companies, must pay special attention to public sentiment, political pressures, and emerging regulations that could affect their businesses. For these firms, interactive intelligence systems are essential for gathering data to understand and influence the complex social, political, and technical environment of their businesses. Accordingly, managers make these systems interactive to force everyone in the organization to continually scan the environment for signs of impending change in regulations or political processes.

Complexity of Value Creation Managers of businesses with complex value chains — for example, businesses that compete through product innovation in multiple markets such as high-technology consumer electronics—must monitor complex trade-offs across product lines and markets. In these businesses, R&D, production, distribution, and marketing tend to be linked in complex and dynamic ways. Accounting-based measures, such as interactive profit-planning systems, are effective tools for building business models that highlight how changes in one variable are likely to affect the business.

In contrast, managers of businesses with stable, well-understood value chains—for example, mature consumer brands such as Coca Cola—have fewer complex trade-offs to manage. Their businesses are relatively simple. They can, therefore, reduce the level of complexity by focusing attention on simpler input and output measures, such as brand volume and market share. Therefore, these businesses often use brand-revenue budget systems interactively.

Ease of Tactical Response   Finally, if copying a competitor's tactics is relatively easy (e.g., the cola wars between Pepsi and Coke), the planning horizon will be extremely short. Tactical responsiveness becomes the key to competitive success. In these circumstances, interactive brand-revenue systems give rapid feedback about the effects of pricing, promotion, and packaging tactics. Conversely, if emulating the strategic initiatives of competitors is difficult due to technological or market constraints (e.g., automobile manufacturing), planning horizons will be substantially longer and interactive project-management systems or interactive profit-planning systems will be more effective.

To test these predictions, consider Johnson & Johnson, which competes with premium-price products and a high level of product innovation. Managers at Johnson & Johnson use their profit planning system interactively to focus attention on the development and protection of new products and markets. Periodically during the year, Johnson & Johnson managers reforecast the predicted effects of competitive tactics and new product rollouts on their profit plans for the current and following year. They also adjust five- and 10-year plans.[14]

Reference to Table 10-2 suggests that their choice of an interactive profit-planning system fits their strategy and strategic uncertainties. The technological dependence of the business is relatively *low,* suggesting that the interactive system should focus on changing customer needs, and there is *little* government regulation in most parts of its business, so the system can be designed to focus on competitive threats and opportunities. Also, the emphasis on innovation and product diversity results in *high* complexity, suggesting the appropriateness of accounting-based measures to monitor trade-offs, and the relative *ease* of tactical response by competitors indicates the need for a planning horizon longer than weeks but shorter than years.

Choosing How Many Control Systems to Use Interactively

Any medium- to large-size business has a multitude of formal performance measurement and control systems—profit planning systems, budgeting systems, cost accounting systems, balanced scorecards, project monitoring systems, and so on. Most of these systems are used diagnostically. At the extreme, if there are (*n*) control systems in a

---

[14] Robert Simons, "Codman & Shurtleff: Planning and Control System," Harvard Business School Case No. 187–081, 1987.

business, managers will generally use only *one* of these systems interactively and $(n - 1)$ of those systems in a diagnostic, management-by-exception way. Managers choose to use only one system interactively for three reasons: economic, cognitive, and strategic.

Economic   Management attention is a scarce and costly resource. By definition, interactive control systems demand frequent management attention throughout the organization and, therefore, exact high opportunity costs by diverting attention from other tasks.

Cognitive   The ability of individuals to process large amounts of disparate information is limited. Decision makers suffer from information overload as the amount and complexity of information increases. Attempting to focus intensively on too many things simultaneously risks information overload, superficial analysis, a lack of perspective, and potential paralysis. Thus, effective managers avoid asking subordinates to focus on multiple interactive systems (except during periods of organizational crisis, during which top managers will make *all* control systems interactive for short periods to help redefine strategy).[15]

Strategic   The last reason is also the most important. Managers use a control system interactively to activate learning about strategic uncertainties and generate new action plans. Interactive control systems are primarily signaling and communication devices. Using multiple systems interactively diffuses the signal about what is important. Clarity of communication demands focus.

Interactive Control Systems and Formal Incentives

All control systems must be aligned carefully with incentives. As we discussed in previous sections, the rewards and bonuses tied to the achievement of diagnostic control system goals are generally set by formulas. These formula-based incentives allow managers to "power up" their diagnostic control systems. Recall also, however, that these same formula-based incentive systems can lead to various types of "gaming" behaviors — building slack into targets, smoothing, and biasing of information.

If managers want to use a control system interactively to stimulate information sharing and learning, incentives are necessary but must be designed differently. Linking incentives with predetermined formulas will not work. If formula-based incentives are used, people may attempt to game the system and withhold information, thereby subverting the desired learning.

Incentives for interactive control systems must, therefore, be designed to reward an individual's innovative efforts and contribution. This can only be done by *subjective* assessment. Subjective rewards — relying on the personal judgment of superiors — allow managers to recognize innovative behavior that is difficult to specify in advance and to assess the contribution and effort of individuals in the interactive process. Only subjec-

---

[15] See Simons, "Strategic Orientation and Top Management Attention to Control Systems," 1991, for a discussion of the role of interactive control systems during periods of organizational crisis.

tive rewards provide the flexibility to reward creativity in the face of unanticipated threats and opportunities.

Subjective rewards yield three outcomes that help stimulate organizational learning:

1. Rewarding contribution and effort provides incentives for employees to *make their efforts visible* to their superiors. To demonstrate their contributions, employees will be motivated to communicate information about emerging problems and opportunities to their bosses, as well as to report how they have responded. In this way, they can demonstrate their competence, creativity, and effort through information sharing, analysis, and action planning. Of course, this upward communication feeds the learning process that can lead to better understanding of competitive markets and potential new action plans.

2. Rewarding contribution and effort, rather than results, *reduces information biasing* that is a constant concern in diagnostic control systems. Because rewards are not mechanically tied to uncontrollable events that could affect performance expectations, employees are more likely to share both good news and bad news.

3. Rewarding contribution subjectively demands that superiors have the ability to calibrate the efforts of subordinates accurately. To do so, superiors must themselves have a *sound understanding* of the business environment, decision context, array of possible decision alternatives, and potential outcomes of decisions not taken. Without this knowledge, it is impossible to allocate rewards fairly. However, superiors can only gain this knowledge from a deep understanding of the business and its changing competitive environment. Superiors must, therefore, invest a good deal of their own time and attention to really learn about the business and its changing dynamics.

This last condition also reminds us why most rewards in organizations are based on preset formulas. Although subjective rewards promote learning and information sharing (which are undeniably good), they also demand a disproportionate investment of time up and down the hierarchy. This investment is justified for interactive control systems that focus on strategic uncertainties; but for diagnostic processes where goals are clear, ROM is maximized by using formulas to automate the implementation of approved plans.

Contingencies

There is one special case relating to profit plans that we should mention before we leave this topic. Managers who wish to use a profit plan interactively face a special problem. As we have discussed at length, profit planning systems are a key diagnostic tool for coordination and control. Financial goals must be communicated in all businesses to meet basic obligations to shareholders. Yet, managers at some companies—like those at Johnson & Johnson—may wish to use their profit planning system interactively to stimulate learning about trade-offs among R&D, new-product introduction, advertising, and so on. The question arises, how can a profit plan be used *both* diagnostically and interactively at the same time?

Managers who wish to use their profit plans interactively solve this dilemma by adding contingency buffers to the profit plan to protect key diagnostic targets. These contingencies provide a cushion that allows managers to reforecast profits during the year as part of an interactive process, while at the same time they ensure that key targets are not jeopardized. For example, managers may set a $10 million profit goal for the upcoming year. This target would typically be monitored in a diagnostic fashion, and incentives would be tied by formula to the achievement of this profit plan goal.

If, however, senior managers want to use the profit plan interactively, they can add an additional contingency line that will hold business managers accountable for an initial target of $11 million, with a $1 million contingency fund that can be drawn upon if the business is unable to meet their targets. Monthly meetings will discuss achievement against the profit plan, reasons for unexpected changes, revised estimates based on new-product rollouts and competitor actions, and proposed action plans. As discussed above, bonuses and incentives related to profit plan achievement will be available subjectively.

By mutual agreement, profit plan targets can be adjusted during the year and the contingency can be drawn down if needed to protect the key target of $10 million. Incentives will be determined subjectively based on innovative efforts to expand and seize new opportunities to meet the $11 million goal; the contingency fund can be used as a buffer if necessary to ensure that at least $10 million is achieved.

RETURN ON MANAGEMENT

In taking charge of a business, one of the most important tasks for managers is to find ways to leverage their time and attention effectively. In Chapter 1, we defined *ROM* as:

$$ROM = \frac{\text{Amount of Productive Organizational Energy Released}}{\text{Amount of Management Time and Attention Invested}}$$

To maximize the impact of their efforts, managers must find ways to increase the numerator and decrease the denominator. They must use all the tools and techniques at their disposal to release productive organizational energy. One of the keys for any manager who wishes to maximize ROM is to understand what he or she must do *personally* and what can be *delegated* to staff assistants. Diagnostic control systems act as *attention-conserving* devices for senior managers: they allow the business to operate without constant monitoring and, thereby, increase ROM. Therefore, much of the work in diagnostic control systems can be delegated to staff specialists and accountants. In contrast, interactive control systems are *attention enhancers*. Senior managers assume primary responsibility for interpreting the data contained in these systems. The interpretation of data in interactive control systems is not delegated. Staff groups are used primarily as facilitators in the interactive process.

Table 10–3 provides a recap of the roles and responsibilities for operating managers and staff groups in designing and using diagnostic and interactive control systems.

Diagnostic control systems are critical to the implementation of strategy, so target setting and follow-up are not delegated. Managers should personally set or negotiate performance goals and receive periodic exception reports to ensure that strategy is on track. However, these systems typically require significant expertise to design and substantial resources to maintain. Therefore, profit planning systems, balanced scorecards,

TABLE 10-3 Control System Tasks for Managers and Staff Groups Using Diagnostic and Interactive Control Systems

	MANAGERS	STAFF GROUPS
Diagnostic Control Systems	Periodically set or negotiate performance targets Receive and review exception reports Follow up significant exceptions	Design and maintain systems Interpret data Prepare exception reports Ensure integrity and reliability of data
Interactive Control Systems	Choose which system to use interactively Schedule frequent face-to-face meetings with subordinates to discuss data contained in system Demand that operating managers throughout the organization respond to information contained in the systems	Gather and compile data Facilitate interactive process

Source: Adapted from Simons, *Levers of Control,* p. 170.

and strategic profitability analysis can all be designed and managed by staff experts. Managers should supply key assumptions and set targets, but staff groups can interpret data, do the necessary calculations and variance analyses, and send exception reports to managers for review. With this allocation of duties, the ROM of operating managers can be greatly increased.

Interactive control systems require special care in their design and use. Only top managers can decide which control systems they desire to use interactively, based on their vision of the future for the business and their personal sense of strategic uncertainties. Effective managers will insist on face-to-face meetings with subordinates to discuss data, assumptions, and action plans. They will demand that managers throughout the organization respond to the questions raised by the new data. The role of staff groups should be carefully constrained to gathering and compiling data and facilitating the interactive process. Managers should be careful not to allow staff groups to intrude in the interactive process so that paperwork and forms become more important than face-to-face dialogue and action planning. The overriding objective should be to keep the interactive system simple and accessible to operating managers to ensure that it is used by managers throughout the organization.

BUILDING BLOCK SUMMARY

Appendix 10-1 highlights the essential features of diagnostic and interactive control systems.

APPENDIX 10–1 Building Block Summary for Diagnostic and Interactive Control Systems

---

DIAGNOSTIC CONTROL SYSTEMS

WHAT   feedback systems that monitor organizational outcomes and correct deviations from preset standards of performance

Examples: profit plans and budgets
goals and objectives systems
balanced scorecards
project monitoring systems
brand-revenue monitoring systems
strategic planning systems

WHY   to allow effective resource allocation
to define goals
to provide motivation
to establish guidelines for corrective action
to allow ex post evaluation
to free scarce management attention

HOW   set standards
measure outputs
link incentives to goal achievement

WHEN   performance standards can be preset
outputs can be measured
feedback information can be used to influence or correct deviations from standard
process or output is a critical performance variable

WHO   senior managers set or negotiate goals, receive and review exception reports, follow up significant exceptions
staff groups maintain systems, gather data, and prepare exception reports

---

INTERACTIVE CONTROL SYSTEMS

WHAT   control systems that managers use to involve themselves regularly and personally in the decision activities of subordinates

Examples: profit planning systems
balanced scorecards
project management systems
brand revenue systems
intelligence systems

WHY   to focus organizational attention on strategic uncertainties and provoke the emergence of new initiatives and strategies

HOW   ensure that data generated by the system becomes an important and recurring agenda in discussions with subordinates
ensure that the system is the focus of regular attention by managers throughout the organization
participate in face-to-face meetings with subordinates
continually challenge and debate data, assumptions, and action plans

WHEN   strategic uncertainties require search for disruptive changes and opportunities

WHO   senior managers actively use the system and assign subjective, effort-based rewards
staff groups act as facilitators

Source: Adapted from Simons, *Levers of Control,* pp 179–180.

CHAPTER SUMMARY

In Part II of this book, we reviewed the design principles and technical features of different types of profit planning, performance measurement, and control systems. In this chapter, we introduce an additional dimension—how managers *use* those systems. This choice is about allocating attention—both their own and, by implication, the attention of the managers who report to them.

Diagnostic control systems are the management-by-exception systems that define span of accountability. If designed properly, these systems give top managers assurance that the goals of each work unit will be achieved. Diagnostic control systems are powered up by formal incentives and bonuses that are set in advance by formula.

Interactive control systems supply signals for people to infer what is important in allowing the business to reposition itself over time. Interactive control systems absorb a great deal of management attention, but it is attention well spent, because it is leveraged throughout the whole organization and allows high ROM. Using a control system interactively forces the entire organization to focus on strategic uncertainties—those assumptions about competition and distinctive competencies that keep the boss awake at night.

In tandem, diagnostic control systems and interactive control systems work together to allow the implementation of today's strategy, while at the same time allowing the organization to position itself for tomorrow's changing marketplace.

11

Aligning Performance Goals and Incentives

We have reviewed in detail how to design performance measurement and control systems. Now, we must explore more carefully the impact of these systems on the employees who work in organizations. It is, after all, these employees who will ultimately determine the success or failure of any strategy implementation.

In this chapter, we cover design principles that form the foundation for effective performance goals and incentives. We must consider issues related to the creation of goals, the design of performance measures and targets, and the role of incentives on motivation. Designing performance goals and incentives is like building a house. You start with a series of concepts and a rough idea of what the end product should look like. Then, you make a myriad of choices. The architect reviews plans and discusses design alternatives. The builder discusses options concerning fixtures and trims. The painter offers you more choices for colors, papers, and special effects.

Whether building a house or establishing business goals, we must keep several questions in mind:

- What are we trying to accomplish?
- What are the trade-offs—including costs—explicit in our choices?
- What fundamental aspects of design apply in all circumstances, and what aspects are contingent upon specific strategies and objectives?

THE NATURE OF PERFORMANCE GOALS

In any business, managers are interested—above all else—in how to use goals to implement strategy. Recall our definition of strategy from Chapter 2: strategy focuses on the *choices* that must be made to create value for customers and differentiate products and services. However, successful strategy implementation requires *communicating* these strategic choices to hundreds or thousands of employees. Each individual employee requires guidance about how he or she can contribute. Performance goals provide that guidance. *A goal is a formal aspiration that defines purpose or expected levels of achievement.* Goals specify the *ends* that managers wish to achieve and the *means* by which to achieve them. They communicate to people what it is that managers expect them to do and how they should allocate their time and attention among competing demands.

Goals, Objectives, and Targets

Many companies make a distinction between goals, objectives, and targets. For example, *goals* may relate to general aspirations, such as:

- introduce a new line of sailboats for the cruising market
- improve production efficiency
- become profitable

Objectives or *targets* are more specific. They incorporate measurement standards and time frames against which to gauge progress and success. For example,

- have six firm orders in hand for a new 32-foot cruising sailboat in the next nine months
- reduce the cost of waste and scrap by 10% each quarter over the next year
- earn 15% return on sales in the next year

In practice, there is little consistency in how firms use the terms goals, objectives, and targets. Some firms use goals and objectives as outlined above, but other firms reverse this order, with objectives relating to general aspirations and goals encompassing specific measurable targets that support those objectives.

We will not attempt to say which ordering is preferable. The important point is that goals and objectives can be made actionable only when *measurement* is attached to any set of aspirations. Therefore, in this chapter we focus on understanding how managers create and define business goals — aspirational directions — and how they calibrate, communicate, and support those goals through performance measures and incentives. Thus, we will adopt the term **performance goal** to denote *a desired level of accomplishment against which actual results can be measured.*

Purpose of Performance Goals

Financial goals such as maximizing profit, cash flow, or ROCE cannot — by themselves — supply the necessary guidance to implement strategy. Financial goals do not tell employees how to create value for customers or how to differentiate products and services. Without the *clarity of purpose* that performance goals provide, employees may choose very different ways of generating financial returns. One employee may attempt to cut costs at the expense of customer service, whereas another may boost expenses to build customer loyalty. With everyone pulling in different directions, any strategy is bound to fail.

Moreover, it is important to remember that strategies are only hypotheses: they are assumptions and expectations about cause and effect written down in plans and balanced scorecards. To bring strategies to life, managers must use specific performance goals to communicate business direction to subordinates. Because all employees pay attention to what they are measured on, individuals throughout the organization will attempt to infer the strategy of the business from their performance goals and measures (Figure 11–1).

For example, the manager of a retail chain might be held accountable for different performance goals depending on the strategy of the business. With a growth strategy, he might be accountable for increasing sales revenue per store and opening three new stores in Texas. Alternatively, if the business is following a low-cost strategy, the manager might be held accountable for reducing expenses or for keeping prices below

FIGURE 11–1   **Inferring Strategy from Performance Measures**

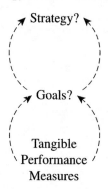

competitors. Each of these *measures* (revenue growth, store openings, expense reduction, price versus competition) will communicate a different set of *priorities* and allow subordinates to *infer* the strategic direction that top managers wish to follow.

Let's revisit Boston Retail. Assume that managers have decided to open three new stores in New York state. Under this strategic alternative, we can recap the key data from the profit plan that we developed in Chapter 5 (See Exhibit 11–1).

By studying the profit plan, it is clear what needs to be done—a vigorous attempt must be made to get the new stores on line and boost revenue by $3.6 million while at

---

EXHIBIT 11–1
Boston Retail
Profit Plan Goals for Expansion Strategy

	20X1 ACTUAL	20X2 WITH EXISTING STORES	20X2 WITH ADDITION OF N.Y. STORES	INCREASE DUE TO ADDITION OF N.Y. STORES
Sales	$9,200	$10,120	$13,800	$3,680
Cost of goods sold	4,780	5,258	7,170	1,912
Gross margin	4,420	4,862	6,630	1,768
Wages	1,530	1,591	2,387	796
Rent	840	882	1,322	440
Advertising	585	644	704	60
Administration	435	478	718	240
Interest	72	65	97	32
Depreciation	57	109	181	72
Training	38	40	59	19
Other	54	56	84	28
Total Expenses	3,611	3,865	5,552	1,687
Profit before tax	$ 809	$ 997	$ 1,078	$ 81

the same time holding down expenses. The owner/president of Boston Retail can set additional performance goals for the manager of the new store, such as:

- hire all new staff by June 1
- launch grand opening on Labor Day weekend
- generate $650,000 revenue in first six months

These performance goals and measures allow systematic and clear communication of what he wants the manager to focus on. Relying exclusively on verbal communication is not enough.

Another reason that performance goals are important is tied to the clarity of communication discussed above. The communication of unambiguous performance goals frees up top management attention to focus on other things, allowing high ROM. Recall our discussion of Chapter 4 in which we enumerated the purposes for which managers use information:

- to improve decision making
- to motivate and evaluate the efforts of subordinates
- to signal preferences about activities and opportunities to pursue
- to promote education, training, and learning
- to communicate to external constituencies

Performance goals play a critical role in enhancing ROM for each of these purposes. Goals, by their nature, signal the preferences of top managers—what is important and where people should be dedicating their time. Moreover, performance goals provide a disciplined approach to management that is the essence of management training: how to run a business successfully and achieve your agendas by working through other people. Goals serve as a reference point for all key decisions. When goal achievement is linked to bonuses and promotions, they provide managers with motivational tools. Finally, performance goals can be shared with stockholders and analysts, when appropriate, to communicate the prospects of the business.

Critical Performance Variables

How do managers select performance goals? In earlier chapters of this book, we studied profit plans, ROE and residual income, and balanced scorecards. Obviously, managers can choose among many performance goals. However, only some of these goals will be *truly* critical to the implementation of their strategy. These are called *critical performance variables*—factors that must be achieved or implemented successfully for the intended strategy of the business to succeed. Managers must identify the critical performance variables for their particular business.

There are two steps in determining critical performance variables for any business. The first is to work deductively to identify potentially important performance drivers. For any strategy, **performance drivers** are variables that either (1) influence the probability of successfully implementing the strategy (an effectiveness criterion) or (2) provide the largest potential for marginal gain over time (an efficiency criterion).

The second step is to identify the critical performance variables from among this list of performance drivers. To do this, managers must ask themselves, If I transported

FIGURE 11-2   **Fear of Failure Determines Critical Performance Variables**

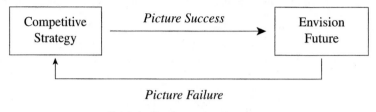

= **Critical Performance Variables**

myself five years forward in time to discover that my business strategy had *failed,* what would I point to as the reasons for this failure? These are the *critical* performance variables—those factors relating to competitive dynamics that are important enough to cause the strategy to fail (Figure 11-2). Depending on the business, these critical performance variables could relate to customer needs, implementing new technology, building new competencies, or the ability to access new markets.

Whatever the critical performance variables for any specific business, the acid test is simple: Any performance variable that could cause the strategy to fail should be on the short list for strategic performance goals.

SELECTING PERFORMANCE MEASURES

To ensure that performance goals are achieved, managers must design *measures* for desired outcomes. *A **measure** is a quantitative value that can be scaled and used for purposes of comparison.* Performance measures may be either financial or nonfinancial. *Financial measures* are stated in monetary terms, usually drawn from a business's accounting systems. Revenue and profit are examples of financial measures. *Nonfinancial measures* are quantitative data created outside the formal accounting system. Weight of scrap metal is quantitative—it can be measured numerically—but, because it is not expressed in dollars and cents, it is classified as a nonfinancial measure.

To determine if a measure is suitable to support a performance goal, it must be subjected to three tests.

Test 1: Does It Align with Strategy?

Measures tell people what is important. If an employee is being measured on customer satisfaction, he is able to infer what is important. If he is being measured on cost reduction, he is likely to infer something different.

The first test of a good measure, then, is to ask the question: If I looked at the measures for which an employee is accountable, could I accurately infer the goals that senior managers want that person to focus on? For example, what would you infer as the goals for a plant employee accountable for the following measures:

- $ cost/unit
- monthly scrap expense
- setup time in hours

Incentive Problems at the Internal Revenue Service

Congressional investigations of alleged taxpayer abuse by the Internal Revenue Service uncovered some flaws in the IRS's performance goals. The study of the tax agency's examination division found that IRS employees were improperly driven by dollar-collection goals. For example, the annual job performance evaluations of three-fourths of IRS group managers were based on such statistics as "dollars assessed on taxpayers per work-hour." This system led IRS employees to perform overly aggressive and sometimes illegal activities to meet seizure quotas.

According to IRS Commissioner Charles Rossotti, a more balanced approach measuring customer satisfaction, inventory management, and case "quality" was being considered, but any new system would not go into effect for two or three years. In the interim, he predicted that IRS managers would be "very unclear about what they're supposed to do and what they're not supposed to do."

Source: Adapted from Judith Bruns, "IRS Chief Promises Changes, But Not Overnight," *Dow Jones Newswires Capital Markets Report,* May 1, 1998; Jacob Schlesinger, "IRS to Review Property Seizures for Wrongdoing," *Wall Street Journal,* July 13, 1998, A3; and Stephen Barr, "IRS Report Says Agents Pursued Assets of Sick, Dying Taxpayers," *Washington Post,* July 11, 1998, A9.

Would your answer change if the same plant employee were accountable for:

- quality failures
- customer-order fulfillment time
- new-product quality satisfaction

Each of these sets of measures tells a different story in terms of priorities, goals, and, ultimately, business strategy. Good measures allow employees to infer and understand intended business strategy.

Test 2: Can It be Measured Effectively?

Ideally, measures should be objective, complete, and responsive (Figure 11–3).

Nature of Measures

An **objective measure** can be independently measured and verified. For example, revenue or cost of goods sold are objective measures because they can be verified by independent auditors. Because objective measures are derived from clear formulas, there is little ambiguity about their meaning or the results that are desired. By contrast, *subjective* measures cannot be independently measured and verified. Instead, they rely on the personal judgment of superiors. The work of an employee can be rated subjectively based on a boss's observation of the salesperson at work. However, the boss must have good information so that he or she can make an informed judgment. In addition, trust must be high, because the subordinate must have confidence that the subjective judgment is fair and will be used appropriately.

FIGURE 11–3   Nature of Measures

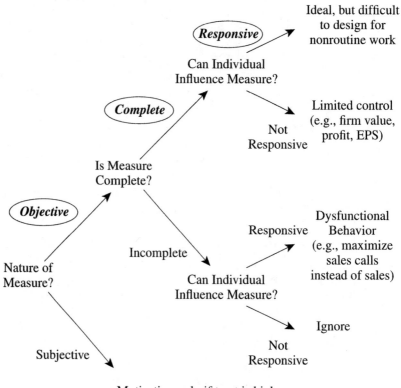

Source: Adapted from Simons, *Levers of Control,* p. 77.

Measures also vary according to their degree of completeness and responsiveness. A **complete measure** captures all the relevant attributes of achievement; a **responsive measure** reflects actions that a manager can directly influence. For example, to measure the rate of progress in driving from Boston to Vancouver, car speed as recorded on the speedometer would provide a responsive, but incomplete, measure. The driver can accelerate or decelerate to influence the measure, but it is incomplete because it does not take into account the number and duration of stops.

In a business, share price is often considered to be a complete measure of top management performance because all managerial actions are eventually reflected in share price.[1] However, share price also reflects economic conditions such as interest rates and other factors outside the control of top managers. Therefore, it is not fully responsive to their actions. On the other hand, profit or ROE measures are responsive to the actions of

---

[1] Share price may not be a complete measure in any single period because it may fail to capture the future period effects of management's decisions, especially if managers have private information that is not available to shareholders or financial analysts.

top managers. However, these measures are less complete because they do not reflect the future value of long-term decisions, such as investing in new technologies.

To increase the responsiveness of performance measures, lower-level employees are usually measured only on those activities within their span of control. However, highly responsive measures sometimes create risk. People may engage in behaviors that increase the measure but that do little to increase the overall value of the firm. For example, a manager might choose to measure the number of sales calls made each week by her salesmen. Using this responsive measure, salespeople can easily increase the number of calls per day, if they disregard the potential for sales at each stop. The measure fails the test of completeness.

Objective, complete, and responsive measures—the upper path of Figure 11-3—can often be achieved for lower-level jobs at the plant floor level or at a front-line customer service desk. For higher-level managerial jobs, however, finding the right balance between objectivity, completeness, and responsiveness requires careful thought and design on the part of managers. Measures—if poorly designed—bring unintended consequences described in the previous chapter, including gaming (attempting to manipulate the measure without achieving the underlying goal), smoothing (adjusting accounting accruals to alter the timing of revenues and expenses between periods), and biasing (reporting only favorable data and suppressing unfavorable data). For example, to encourage efficiency in their customer service operation, managers of a credit card company measured employees on (1) the number of calls answered per day and (2) talk time. Goals and rewards depended on increasing the former and decreasing the latter; and employees did just that. Unfortunately, when a customer asked a difficult question that would take a lot of time to answer, employees merely transferred the call to another department. This gaming behavior achieved high scores on the measures but left customers frustrated and angry.

Test 3: Is the Measure Linked to Value?

As described in earlier chapters, all organizational processes can be segregated according to the *Inputs→Process→Outputs* model. We can measure any number of input variables (information, energy, labor, materials, etc.), process variables (cycle time, quality, usage rates, and so on), or output variables (efficiency and effectiveness).

In our discussion of the balanced scorecard, we made an important distinction between measures that are *leading* indicators of success and those that are *lagging* indicators of success. In building a house, for example, a *lagging* indicator of success—one that tells the story after the fact—might be the profit that you realize in selling the house five years after its completion, perhaps as contrasted with other similar-sized houses. A high resale value indicates that the house was well constructed, aesthetically pleasing, and located in a desirable neighborhood. In this case, profit on sale would be a good lagging indicator of your success in building a good house. In a business setting, break-even time for a new-product introduction would be an example of a lagging indicator.

However, when you are building the house, you probably do not want to wait five years to find out if your house is any good. Instead, you might look at *input* indicators, such as published ratings of neighborhood desirability, the reputation of the architect with whom you will work, and testimonials from other clients who have hired the builder you are considering. In addition, you can also rely on *process* indicators: visiting the site often, checking on critical construction details before they are hidden by finishing walls, monitoring costs to ensure that construction is within your overall budget constraints, and ensuring that top quality fixtures are being installed. These are *leading* indicators.

In business, managers may choose to measure leading variables, such as employee training, process quality controls, and work-in-process costs, as well as lagging variables, such as profit or customer satisfaction. To rely on leading indicators, however, we must remember the critical assumptions about cause-and-effect relationships that we discussed in Chapter 4. Assume a situation where managers believe that highly trained employees (*A*) cause high levels of customer satisfaction (*B*), which in turn leads to repeat sales (*C*), which leads to profit. This could be modeled as follows:

$$A \Rightarrow B \Rightarrow C \Rightarrow \text{Profit}$$

$$\text{where } A = \text{employee training}$$

$$B = \text{customer satisfaction}$$

$$C = \text{repeat sales}$$

How much confidence do we have that any or all of these variables lead to economic value? Profit—the lagging indicator—is likely to be highly correlated with economic value. The more profit the business makes, the more economic value it creates, but is the same equally true for the other three variables?

As we move from right to left, our confidence in the ability of the variable to create economic value decreases. Repeat sales (*C*) *probably* leads to more profit, but not necessarily. Certain customers, because of their buying habits, lot size, or discounts, may in fact generate losses. Customer satisfaction (*B*) *may or may not* lead to increased profit. Even though our customers are satisfied, they may still choose to buy from a competitor if that competitor's current product offering more closely meets their current needs. Finally, with employee training, (*A*), the link to economic value becomes even more tenuous. Although it is probably a good thing to have well-trained employees, it may be *difficult to prove* that training expenditures will generate economic value for the firm—especially when choices must be made about the different types of training to be offered, and employee turnover is high.

Thus, when designing performance measures, output measures (that is, lagging indicators) give the highest confidence that economic value is being created. Input and process measures (i.e., leading indicators) are valid only if managers are confident that they understand cause-and-effect relationships.

(In addition to these three tests of a good measure, the reader may wish to revisit the discussion of Chapter 4 where we describe criteria for choosing to monitor inputs, processes, or outputs. These criteria include technical feasibility of monitoring, understanding of cause and effect, cost, and the desired level of innovation.)

Changing Performance Measures in the Public Sector

U.S. government agencies have been revamping their diagnostic control systems to ensure that they are measuring the right performance variables.

The U.S. Coast Guard, for example, used to measure the number of inspections and certifications performed by its officers. However, it realized that its primary goal was to save lives and it should, therefore, measure its performance by reductions in the marine fatality rate. The main culprit in marine accidents is human error, not equipment failures, which were previously the subject of the inspections. Focusing on sectors with the highest death rates, like the towing industry, the Coast Guard began helping them change the training for new workers, who are most vulnerable to mishaps. In five years, using fewer people at lower cost, the Coast Guard reduced the fatality rate in the towing industry from 91 per 100,000 to 27 per 100,000.

The Federal Emergency Management Agency (FEMA) also took a new tack in its performance measurement. Instead of concentrating on handing out checks and warm blankets after a disaster, it believed that the more buildings that survived a catastrophe, the less aid the agency would have to provide. It began measuring the level of flood insurance in flood-prone areas and the number of inspections in high-risk areas to help local authorities strengthen building codes. As a result of implementing this change in measurement, FEMA has seen reductions in the amount of aid spent per disaster.

The National Oceanic and Atmospheric Administration (NOAA) used to measure the number of weather predictions as a performance indicator. In an effort to improve the effectiveness of its short-term warning and forecast services, it now measures the lead time for tornado warnings. Deploying a new Doppler radar system, NOAA increased the national average for warning time from seven to nine minutes—a short but critical edge for people in the path of a dangerous storm.

Source: Adapted from Douglas Stanglind, "What Are You Trying to Do?" *U.S. News & World Report* (March 3, 1997), 36–37.

How Many Measures for Each Employee?

To implement strategy effectively, people throughout a business must focus their energies on a small number of variables that are truly critical to success. To be effective as communication devices, managers must use measures to focus attention. As we all know, what gets measured, gets managed.

An important design decision for managers, therefore, is deciding how many measures to assign to each subordinate. As a rule of thumb, effective managers provide focus and impact by insisting that individuals be accountable for no more performance measures than they can recall from memory. How many measures is that?

Professor George Miller gave us the answer in the 1950s in his famous article: "The Magic Number Seven, Plus or Minus Two."[2] Think of all the things in our life that are configured in sevens:

- digits of a telephone number
- days of the week
- notes on the musical scale
- colors in the rainbow
- wonders of the world

In business,

- seven steps of quality
- seven "S" analysis
- seven habits of highly effective people

Why seven? Because individuals can remember, recall, and work creatively with seven bits of information. With 10 or more bits of information, individuals suffer from information overload. Moreover, if people are asked to do too many things concurrently, no single initiative will receive enough attention to assure success. Using this rule of thumb, managers should assign no more than seven to nine performance goals to any single individual. Of course, as managers cascade goals and measures down their organizations, different people will be accountable for different measures. This is to be expected as measures are aligned with specific job responsibilities.

SETTING THE PERFORMANCE BAR

As part of any goal setting process, managers must choose the target or desired level of achievement. Consider the following historical performance data for the Cambridge store of the Boston Retail chain:

	20X0	20X1	20X2
Sales goal	$1,300	$1,550	*$1,450 or $1,550 or $1,750?*
Actual sales	$1,275	$1,450	

What is the correct sales goal or target for 20X2? Should the sales goal be set at last year's actual ($1,450) or some higher amount? If higher, by how much should the performance goal be increased? To answer this question, several factors must be considered; foremost is the importance of any given performance goal to the successful implementation of business strategy. For example, a business strategy may require successfully introducing a new product line to generate an incremental boost in revenue of $50,000 in the first quarter, $75,000 in the second quarter, and $100,000, in both the

[2] George A. Miller, "The Magic Number Seven, Plus or Minus Two: Some Limits in Our Capacity for Processing Information," *The Psychological Review* 63 (1956): 81–97.

third and fourth quarters. If failure to meet these performance goals could jeopardize the successful implementation of the strategy, then there is little choice about the right level.

Benchmark Comparisons

In each facet of business operations—material acquisition, production, logistics, marketing, R&D, distribution, customer service, and corporate support—some firms or business units do a better job than others. To set performance goals effectively, managers need to know which firms set the standard for the most effective utilization of resources. Then, they must calibrate their own efforts against this "best of class" yardstick. This technique is called *benchmarking*.

For example, the chief financial officer may wish to know what the "best of class" standard is for transaction processing (for example, the number of clerical staff needed to process 10,000 transactions per month), financial statement preparation (e.g., the number of days elapsed between the month-end close and the distribution of monthly financial statements), and information technology (e.g., the optimum level of IT expenditure for each 1,000 employees). To answer these questions, a study can be conducted to determine which firms do the best job on these dimensions and what their relative levels of efficiency and effectiveness are on various indicators. These studies are often conducted by consultants who specialize in this type of work. Gathering this type of information provides top managers with data that can be used to calibrate performance goals related to the effective and efficient use of resources within their own firm.

Businesses with multiple production or distribution sites can also benchmark best *internal* practices by collecting data and comparing performance across units. For example, McDonald's collects statistics from all franchisees on the amount of each sales dollar spent on labor, food, nonfood supplies, and so forth. These data are compiled and

---

John Browne at British Petroleum

John Browne, CEO of The British Petroleum Company, commented on how to motivate people to excel at learning:

> To get people to learn, you need to give them a challenge. Setting a target is crucial even if you don't actually know whether it's fully achievable—because in times of rapid change, you have to make decisions and get people to step outside the box.

> One process that we employ to promote learning and drive performance is not that unusual. It involves understanding the critical measures of operating performance in each business, relentlessly benchmarking those measures and their related activities, setting higher and higher targets, and challenging people to achieve them.

> We've worked with the managers of each business unit to create an annual performance contract that spells out exactly what they're expected to deliver, and we review their progress quarterly.

Source: Steven E. Prokesch, "Unleashing the Power of Learning: An Interview with British Petroleum's John Browne," *Harvard Business Review* 75 (September–October 1997): 146–168.

FIGURE 11–4   Relationship Between Motivation and Goal Difficulty

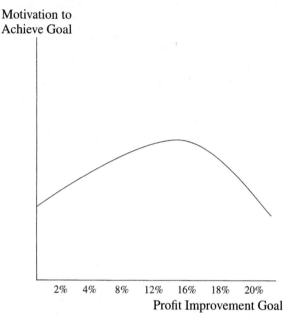

Motivation to
Achieve Goal

2%   4%   8%   12%   16%   18%   20%
Profit Improvement Goal

sent out to all McDonald's franchisees to enable then to benchmark their individual operations.

Motivating Effort

In thinking about the motivational effects of performance goals, two issues must be addressed. First, how do aspirational goals affect individual work habits? In other words, how do individuals respond to goals that are either easy or difficult? The second question is, Who should be involved in setting the performance bar? Is this something reserved for senior managers, or should subordinates be involved in jointly setting the goals and targets that will affect them?

Level of Difficulty

Behavioral research suggests that individual creativity and initiative can be maximized when people are under some reasonable amount of pressure to perform; remove the pressure, and performance and creativity slow to a more relaxed pace.[3] Therefore, performance goals should be challenging, but not perceived as either too easy or unreasonably difficult. An increase in profit of 4% may be relatively easy to achieve; an increase in profit of 25% may be extremely difficult.

As shown in Figure 11–4, if a goal is too easy to achieve—say 4%—people will not be challenged and the motivational effects will be dampened. As the goal is made

---

[3] For a review of the literature relating to goal difficulty and performance, see chap. 2 in Edwin A. Locke and Gary P. Latam, *A Theory of Goal Setting and Task Performance* (Englewood Cliff, N.J.: Prentice–Hall, 1990).

more difficult, effort increases. Many individuals rise to the challenge and stretch to find ways of meeting the goal. At 15%, employees are working at their full potential to do whatever it takes to get the job done. A certain point is reached, however, where the goal seems unreasonably difficult, and, at this point, individuals begin to give up. They believe that achieving the goal is either impossible or not worth the effort. We see in Figure 11–4 a tailing off in motivation and effort as the goal passes 18%.

Deciding Who Should Participate in Setting Goals

The previous discussion about goal difficulty begs the question, Who should participate in setting the difficulty level of performance goals? Should this be a top-down process, driven entirely by superiors who establish goals and hand them down to subordinates for implementation? Or, should subordinates have some say in the level of goals that affects them?

Recent research has looked at the degree of employee participation in planning and budgeting processes. Researchers were trying to understand why some organizations encouraged subordinates' participation in these future-looking processes, whereas others imposed top-down objectives for the coming year without input from subordinates.

The results of these studies suggest that the desire for information sharing explains a big portion of the puzzle. When organizations face uncertain environments and the information that may be relevant to address these changes is dispersed throughout the organization, then the planning and budgeting processes are used interactively with intense participation. This participation helps people exchange information and better understand the changes that are happening around them. As a result, performance improves.

On the other hand, companies in stable environments do not need to exchange information about profit plan goals because managers at the top already know what to expect in the future. In these cases, the planning and budgeting processes are not used to exchange information but to challenge people in the organization to achieve challenging objectives and ensure that the objectives are met.[4]

Thus, the decision about who should participate in setting performance goals depends on managers' beliefs about where the relevant information is located in the organization. If managers believe that the information needed to set performance goals is dispersed widely throughout the organization, then a participative style is appropriate. If information is held at the top, then little consultation is needed.

The decision on who should participate in setting performance goals also depends greatly on the assumptions that managers make about human behavior in organizations. For example, in the typical model of human behavior used in economics, subordinates are viewed as rational, self-interested, utility-maximizing individuals who typically are risk averse and dislike effort. These "agents" work under hire for "principals"—the owners or superiors who have the power to set performance goals for subordinates,

---

[4] Leslie Kren, "Budgeting Participation and Managerial Performance: The Impact of Information and Environmental Volatility," *The Accounting Review* 67 (1992): 511–526; Peter Brownell and Alan S. Dunk, "Task Uncertainty and Its Interaction with Budgeting Participation and Budget Emphasis: Some Methodological Issues and Empirical Investigation," *Accounting, Organizations and Society* 16 (1991): 693–703.

evaluate their efforts, and dispense rewards. In this view, the problem is to minimize the tendency of the agent to engage in behaviors that are not in the best interests of the principal (or boss). Part of the solution for the so-called agency problem is to design top-down contracts (that is, goals) and enforcement mechanisms (i.e., performance measures and control systems) linked to rewards and punishments. In this view, subordinates are *not* invited to participate in setting goals because it is expected that subordinates will attempt to bias the goal-setting process in their favor to minimize future effort.

An alternative view, prevalent in organization behavior, is that most individuals inherently enjoy achievement for its own sake and will become self-motivated to achieve the goals of the organization if they (1) believe the goal is legitimate and (2) become committed to the goal through a process that includes their input and participation. Thus, subordinates are invited to participate in goal setting to increase commitment and, ultimately, motivation.

Which of these views is correct? There is probably a little truth in each, and managers will make different choices depending on what the goal-setting process is designed to achieve, who possesses relevant information, and the level of trust in the organization.

Multiple Purposes of Performance Goals

The goal-setting process is complicated because performance goals are used simultaneously for a variety of purposes. Performance goals are used for communicating strategy and motivation, as described above, but also for planning and coordination, early warning of potential problems, and ex post evaluation of managers and businesses.

Performance goals are important for *planning and coordination* to ensure (1) adequate levels of resources and (2) workflow coordination among interdependent units. Plans must be coordinated and discrepancies worked out in advance. For example, the production department needs to know the marketing department's sales estimates so that it can plan for adequate capacity. If the production department can build 1,500 units per month at full capacity, it will make a big difference if the marketing department's sales forecast calls for 1,200 units per month or 1,800 units per month.

Performance goals also provide managers with standards that can act as *early warning* signals when operations begin to run off track. Performance goals, by their nature, are established before work actually occurs. As the work unfolds, shortfalls and problems can be identified by comparing actual results with the performance goals. Shortfalls on key indicators provide diagnostic early warning indicators for managers to investigate problems and develop remedial actions.

Finally, performance goals are often an important ingredient in ex post *evaluation* of accomplishment. Managers and their units are judged on the extent to which they met, exceeded, or fell short of their performance goals.

Using performance goals for all of these purposes—motivation, planning and coordination, early warning, and evaluation—invites problems because the level of the goal must be adjusted to best serve each different purpose. For example:

- For *planning and coordination,* performance goals should be set at levels that represent management's best judgment about the *most likely* levels of output. To secure and dedicate scarce production resources, it is important that accurate predictions are reflected in performance goals and operating plans.

- For *motivation,* managers may wish to *stretch* performance levels to create pressures for extra performance. For example, a performance increment of 10% may be added to the "best-guess" goal in the hope of motivating better performance.

- For ex post *evaluation,* managers may wish to adjust the original performance goals by *factoring out unforeseen or uncontrollable events* that were outside the manager's span of attention. Although managers predicted selling 1,600 units per month to a major customer, should they be held accountable for lower sales due to a lightning strike that disabled the factory of that customer? [5]

In practice, managers are aware of these tensions and walk a fine line in choosing performance goals that are a compromise in meeting these conflicting objectives. Therefore, when setting performance goals, managers must use their judgment to find the right balance between information accuracy and motivational impact.

ALIGNING INCENTIVES

In general, there are two ways of motivating people to work toward the goals of an organization. The first occurs when people believe that goals are legitimate and, therefore, exert effort willingly to achieve them. This is "intrinsic" motivation—motivation from within. Intrinsic motivation occurs naturally when people voluntarily join benevolent organizations such as churches, synagogues, and charities where they believe inherently in the goals of the organization. Effort is given willingly because individuals believe in the mission that institution is pursuing. Economists call this the "first-best" solution to motivation.

Managers can enhance intrinsic motivation in a variety of ways. First, as discussed in Chapter 1, they can emphasize the positive ideals and beliefs of the business so that employees want to contribute to its overall mission. In other words, they can make people proud of where they work. Second, they can involve subordinates in the goal-setting process to increase the likelihood that subordinates will see the goals as legitimate. If subordinates are included in the process of setting goals—asked to provide input and information—they are more likely to feel that the goals are legitimate and work more diligently to achieve them. (The risk, of course, is that if given the chance, individuals may attempt to lower expected achievement levels to make goals more attainable and predictable.) Also, managers can communicate the cause-and-effect linkages that underlie the current strategy so that employees can understand better their roles in helping the organization achieve its goals.

The second way that business managers can ensure attention to goal achievement is through a formal **incentive**—that is, a reward or payment that is expected to motivate performance. Financial incentives are an essential element in the design of most performance measurement systems. These mechanisms create "extrinsic motivation"—motivation from outside. To enhance extrinsic motivation, financial performance awards— typically in the form of bonuses—can be linked explicitly to the achievement of goals

---

[5] M. Edgar Barrett and Leroy B. Fraser, "Conflicting Roles in Budgeting for Operations," *Harvard Business Review* 55 (1977): 137–146.

and targets. This is done either by paying a percent of profits or by linking bonuses to the achievement of predetermined outcomes.

For example, a salesman may earn a 7% commission on all revenue with no upside limit: sell more, earn more. This approach might also be used for a division manager who is paid a fixed percentage of division profits. Although this approach is sensible for some employees such as salesmen, it becomes problematic when multiple products and multiple goals—financial and nonfinancial—must be balanced. Thus, if a manager's performance goals include EVA, market share, product quality, and customer satisfaction, it would not be prudent to pay incentives only as a percentage of profit—ignoring the other goals.

Thus, incentives for managers are usually tied to predetermined levels of accomplishment against specific goals or outcomes. If a key target is hit (e.g., increase market share in Europe to 5%), then a bonus is paid. With this approach, goals can be set at varying levels of achievement to reflect the benchmarking data, strategic imperatives, and motivational effects discussed in previous sections.

There are three major design decisions that must be made in designing contingent incentives: (1) the bonus pool, (2) the allocation formula, and (3) the type and mix of incentives.

Performance Pay Pitfalls at Lantech

Lantech was a small (325 employees, 1995 revenues of $65 million), privately held Kentucky-based manufacturer of machines that wrap retail shipments in plastic film. In the late 1970s managers tried to introduce incentive-based pay by asking workers to rate their peers' performance; the resulting tension among workers killed the plan. The next attempt a decade later was to give each of the company's five manufacturing divisions a bonus based on the profit generated by that division, which could comprise as much as 10% of a divisional employee's regular pay.

As the company's founder Pat Lancaster recalled, "By the early Nineties, I was spending 95% of my time on conflict resolution instead of on how to serve our customers." The problem was that Lantech's divisions were so interdependent that it was difficult to determine how to fairly allocate costs and revenues for determining bonuses. Instead of working harder to increase the company profits, employees tried to rig the division profit numbers in their favor. The goal of managers in each division was to gain revenue from other divisions and hand off as much cost as possible. This behavior was costly both in excess inventory (as one division tried to ship as much as possible to other divisions) and technological delay (it took several years to decide to purchase an expensive crane for the shop floor because no one could agree on cost allocations). The ultimate silliness was an argument over whether to allocate the cost of toilet paper by gender.

CEO Lancaster eventually replaced the performance-based system with a profit-sharing system based on salary.

Source: Adapted from Peter Nulty, "Incentive Pay Can Be Crippling," *Fortune* (November 13, 1995): 235.

The Bonus Pool

The term "incentive" implies that individuals are paid more when performance exceeds some base or threshold. In other words, higher performance generates higher pay; lower performance, lower pay. Although this seems simple enough, the mechanics can become quite complicated and, in all cases, require careful design.

Bonus incentives, defined as additional rewards or payments for successful achievement of a task, are usually paid out of a **bonus pool**—a pot of money that is reserved for the payment of incentive and recognition awards. This pool is typically determined by reference to business or corporate-level performance. For example, 15% of annual corporate profits may be set aside in a bonus pool to fund incentive payments.

The bonus pool for Boston Retail may be computed as:

Revenue	$9,200,000
Pretax profit before bonuses	952,000
Percent reserved for bonus pool	15%
Bonus pool to be allocated among designated employees	143,000
Pretax profit after bonuses	809,000

The Allocation Formula

Once the bonus pool has been determined, the next decision is the allocation of the bonus pool to individuals. There are generally three categories of performance that can be used to allocate bonuses: individual performance, business performance, and corporate performance. For example, a manager at General Electric may receive bonus compensation based on his personal goal achievement, the performance of the lighting business of which he is a member, and the performance of the overall corporation.

For any manager, a decision must be made about how to allocate weights across these three performance variables. In general, *the wider the span of control of an individual manager within a single business, the higher the weight given to business performance relative to personal performance.* Also, the more the business interacts with other business units in the same corporation, the higher the weight given to corporate performance relative to either types of performance. For example, consider the following alternative weighting schemes:

	MANAGER A	MANAGER B
Corporate Performance	20%	40%
Business Performance	20%	40%
Individual Performance	60%	20%
	100%	100%

Manager A's weighting scheme—which gives a relatively high weight to individual performance—is likely to be more appropriate for a lower-ranking employee with a narrow span of control. Manager B's weighting scheme, by contrast, gives primary weight to corporate and business performance and may be appropriate for a senior-level business manager operating a unit that has significant interactions with other units in the corporation.

Within each of these percentages, a further decision must be made about how to calculate the actual amount of the payment. For example, if 40% is allocated to business performance and 20% to personal goal, how do we assess levels of achievement? There are two basic methods: by formula and by subjective judgment.

A formula may be of the following type:

If profit = X,	then bonus = Y
If X < profit < X + 10%,	then bonus = Y + $20,000
If X + 10% ≤ profit < X + 20%,	then bonus = Y + $50,000
If profit ≥ X + 20%,	then bonus = Y + $75,000

Formula-based allocation systems have two distinct advantages. First, there is no ambiguity about what results are desired or how they will be measured. Thus, employees are clear about what they will be rewarded for. Second, and related to the first, bonus allocation schemes can be set infrequently—typically once per year—and do not then require much attention from managers. Thus, a formula-based allocation system allows high ROM—set the goal, determine the bonus formula, and then concentrate on other things, confident that employees are pursuing the goals that are mirrored in the bonus calculation.

The other alternative is to allocate performance rewards based on subjective evaluation of performance. To do this, managers must use their knowledge, experience, and judgment to determine the contribution of a subordinate. This requires not only a high degree of trust, but also a large investment of time on the part of the boss, who must gather sufficient information to determine the performance of the subordinate. Subjective evaluation is a hallmark of the interactive control systems described in the previous chapter.

Payout formulas can be based on any of the goals discussed to date: profit, cash flow, and ROCE, as well as balanced-scorecard goals such as market share, new-product development, and personal goals such as mentoring and training. Sometimes, compensating goals may be created to try to overcome the limitations of specific measures and goals that we have discussed in earlier chapters. For example, if an important goal is to increase ROCE, senior managers may wish to devise a payout formula that will pay increasing rewards as ROCE increases. There is risk here, however, because there are two ways of increasing any ratio. The first—and desired outcome—is to increase the numerator—net income. But there is also a second way—decreasing the denominator. Thus, there is some risk that, to increase their bonus compensation, managers may be motivated to underinvest in assets or even sell off assets that have future value to the business.

To compensate for this risk, managers can create a payout matrix like the one shown in Figure 11–5. In this matrix, bonus formula payouts are increasing in both ROCE and asset growth, thereby eliminating the incentive for managers to shrink the denominator. The message is now straightforward—increase returns on capital and grow the size of the business.

Eli Lilly Links Compensation to EVA

The pharmaceutical giant Eli Lilly & Company is among a number of companies that have linked senior management compensation to EVA. Lilly decided in 1994 to use EVA as a performance measure for two reasons: EVA aligns well with shareholder value and it forces managers to focus critically on capital expenditures. The pharmaceutical business is highly capital-intensive, so EVA reinforces the concept that managers are accountable for ROCE.

In the past, executive pay at Lilly had been tied to sales and net income, but Lilly found that these measurements did not correlate well to shareholder value. By rewarding managers who deliver continuous, year-to-year improvements in EVA, Lilly hopes that managers will be motivated to continue to raise shareholder value.

Lilly adopted a top-down approach to rolling out EVA. Although lower-level employees do not have their compensation tied to EVA, they know what drives senior officers' bonuses, resulting in a rapid change in attitudes toward capital throughout the business. To promote greater understanding of EVA among employees, Lilly has run stories about EVA in employee publications, and managers talk with their employees about how EVA works. Lilly estimates that teaching EVA concepts to managers requires several days. Implementing this scheme outside the United States requires significantly more training.

Lilly decided to pay bonuses based on EVA calculated at the corporate level, rather than business-unit EVA, for two reasons: Lilly was experiencing a significant reorganization into global business units at the time (and introducing a new compensation system might overwhelm employees), and Lilly wanted to avoid the possibility of individual business-unit managers making decisions that suboptimized corporate EVA.

Lilly also recognized that, because EVA is calculated annually, managers may make shortsighted decisions without regard for long-term shareholder value. For example, lowering the asset base and depleting inventory would increase EVA in one year but leave Lilly with nothing to sell in the following year. To guard against this kind of behavior, Lilly pays out only a portion of a manager's EVA bonus and places the rest in a "bonus bank." Managers can withdraw from the bonus bank only if EVA improves annually. On the other hand, if a manager makes an investment in year one that reduces EVA in year three, Lilly deducts money from the bonus bank. There are no annual caps on EVA bonuses, reducing the potential for distortion to avoid bonus limitation rules.

Source: Adapted from Justin Martin, "Eli Lilly Is Making Shareholders Rich. How? By Linking Pay to EVA," *Fortune* (September 9, 1996): 173.

FIGURE 11–5   ROCE Matrix

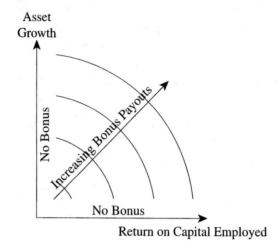

Types and Mix of Incentives

The final design decision concerns what types of incentives to provide to employees to recognize their achievements. We normally think of bonuses as cash payments, but in fact there is a wide range of options concerning the types of financial incentives that can be provided. In addition to cash, some of the more common are:

- gifts and prizes
- deferred cash payments
- awards of company stock
- grants of options for the future purchase of company stock

We can think this array of incentives as analogous to assets on a balance sheet. On a balance sheet, we start with the most liquid asset — cash — and then progress through a listing of other assets, ranked in order of decreasing liquidity. With incentives, we start with liquid incentives — cash payments — and then move through other categories that move further away from cash: gifts and prizes, deferred cash payments, stock awards, and the granting of stock options.

The incentive value of cash is clear. However, other incentives may provide additional benefits. Gifts and prizes can often be used to great effect as ways of celebrating accomplishment. For example, the ceremonial awarding of a trip to Hawaii in recognition of outstanding accomplishment may create more excitement among employees than the payment of a $3,000 cash bonus. Public recognition is a powerful motivator (just ask any university professor!). This technique — public recognition and rewards — is used extremely effectively by many direct-selling companies such as Mary Kay Cosmetics.

Incentives that have longer-term payouts — for example, deferred cash payments — may force managers to think more carefully about the trade-offs between the short term and the long term in their decision making. For example, the payment of cash bonuses based on sales revenue growth may be deferred for a 12-month period to reflect adjustments for uncollectable customer accounts. Thus, a salesperson who might be inclined to generate quick revenue by selling goods or services to customers with poor credit ratings would think twice about this practice because any bad debts would reduce his or her ultimate bonus payment.

Finally, we may choose to offer payment of incentives in terms of stock or stock options. Stock ownership helps motivate employees to make decisions and act in ways that will enhance shareholder value and, therefore, stock price. Employee incentives are aligned with those of the stockholders. Stock options add an additional dimension. An option is the right to purchase stock at a specified price (known as the strike price). As an incentive payment, we might give employees stock options valued at today's current share price. Holders of these options may choose, at any time in the future, to exercise their right to buy shares in the company at the strike price. Of course, the options only have value if the price of the company's stock rises.

For example, as a bonus, we may give a manager 10,000 stock options valued at today's closing stock price of $23 per share. If share price falls to $20, then the manager is holding worthless options—no rational person would pay $23 to buy a share that is only worth $20. However, if the share price rises to $40, then the manager may choose to purchase the 10,000 shares at the strike price of $23 per share for $230,000. He or she could either hold them or immediately sell them on the open market for $400,000, thereby generating a gain of $170,000. The effect of this award, of course, is to give managers the incentives to do whatever is within their power to increase share price.

It will come as no surprise that stock awards and stock options are among the most popular forms of incentive compensation when stock markets are rising. During the 1990s—the longest U.S. bull market in history—stock awards and options have flour-

---

Compensating Pilots at Southwest Airlines

In most airline companies, pilots are paid a flat salary. This salary rewards the valuable inputs that pilots bring to the company, that is, their skills and abilities to fly airplanes. This salary structure assumes that selecting the right pilots, paying competitive wages, and giving them a flight schedule for the year will result in the desired level and quality of flight service.

However, not all companies think the same way. In 1995, pilots at Southwest Airlines Company, agreed to give up salary increases for the next five years in exchange for 1.4 million shares in the company per year at a predefined price. The move was not only good for the cash flow of the company, it also acknowledged that pilots bring more than just flying skills to their job: They bring leadership, customer service, and reputation through their daily actions. By accepting a stake in the equity of Southwest, the pilots gained a stake in the long-term performance of the company. Southwest not only rewarded the input that pilots brought (their skills) but also gave them a piece of the output, so that they would act in line with Southwest's ultimate objectives.

Source: Adapted from Thomas P. Flannery et al. *People, Performance & Pay.* The Hay Group. (New York: The Free Press, 1996): 112.

ished. A 1997 survey suggests that 45% of large companies with option plans grant stock options to all their employees. In contrast, only 10% did so in 1994.[6] By contrast, from 1966 to 1981, when the stock market actually declined in inflation-adjusted terms, there was little interest in this type of compensation.

EXECUTIVE COMPENSATION AT FORD MOTOR COMPANY

Ford's executive compensation plan illustrates how one company links management and stockholder interests and ties compensation to the achievement of profit goals and strategies.[7] Many large U.S. companies follow similar compensation schemes.

Like all successful companies, Ford must offer competitive compensation to attract and retain talented top managers. Each year, Ford's board of directors commissions an outside consultant to survey executive compensation in the worldwide auto industry and at major U.S. companies. After adjusting the results for company size, performance, reputation, and business complexity, Ford sets its compensation levels to match the average compensation levels reported from the survey.

Ford then divides compensation into two categories: annual compensation and long-term compensation. Annual compensation includes salary and annual bonuses; long-term compensation includes stock options and outright grants of company common stock. Annual bonuses are based on a formula to reward individual or group performance over the past year. Ford ties annual bonuses to EVA by setting the bonus pool for a given year at 6% of pretax residual income. Residual income is computed by taking pretax accounting income and subtracting a cost of capital equal to 10% of capital employed in the business.

Recognizing that decisions made by Ford's executives will affect the company for many years, Ford ties long-term compensation to the achievement of long-term goals and stock price. Stock options and stock grants (the right to receive a prespecified number of shares of stock) are the primary elements of Ford's long-term compensation. Ford's stock-option awards vest (that is, are irrevocably transferred to recipients) over ten years, motivating executives to remain with the company and focus on long-term stock performance.

Depending on market conditions, stock options may not always align executive incentives with shareholder incentives. For example, if an executive's incentives are "out-of-the-money" (i.e., current stock price is lower than option price), then the executive might be motivated to make risky decisions in the hope of boosting performance and stock price. To balance this risk, Ford also makes outright stock grants to its executives as part of their long-term compensation. By owning stock (and not just stock options), executives are fully invested in the downside risk of their decisions. In 1994, the Ford board of directors set goals for all Ford executives at the vice president level and above to own Ford common stock worth a specified multiple of their salary. By 1998, most key managers had achieved this goal.

---

[6] Gretchen Morgenson, "Stock Options Are Not a Free Lunch," *Forbes* (May 18, 1998): 213. In the survey, a large company was defined as one with 5,000 or more employees.

[7] Ford Motor Company Proxy Statement, April 14, 1998.

Ford awards stock grants on a retrospective basis. For example, in 1992 and in 1994, each executive received a number of "contingent stock rights" that were awarded depending on how well Ford met goals in the following areas over a five and three year period, respectively:

1992–1996	1994–1996
Product quality and worldwide acceptance (35%)	Product quality and worldwide acceptance (35%)
Cost reduction (25%)	Corporate ROE (25%)
Product programs (25%)	Product programs (25%)
Relationship with employees (15%)	Relationship with employees (15%)

Each quarter, Ford's top 5,200 managers receive reports on their progress toward these goals.[8]

In 1997, Ford's board of directors evaluated the extent to which managers had achieved goals in each of these areas. They concluded that Ford achieved 80% of these goals in the 1992–1996 period and 83% of its goals in the 1994–1996 period. As a result, Ford executives received in stock the same percentage, respectively, of their 1992 and 1994 contingent stock rights.

In 1998, Ford's board of directors continued its balanced scorecard approach to performance goals and incentives by linking future stock-grant awards to goals in the following areas:

- ROE versus nonoil Fortune 50 companies
- product programs
- customer satisfaction
- selected internal financial measures
- product quality
- relationship with employees

CHAPTER SUMMARY

Setting performance goals and incentives is a key and vital responsibility of management. All managers must set goals for subordinates and for the functions and businesses that they manage. At higher management levels, failure to set goals is a failure of leadership. As Philip Selznick has argued,

> The failure . . . to set goals stems partly from the hard intellectual labor involved, a labor that often seems but to increase the burden of already onerous daily operations. In part, also, there is the wish to avoid conflicts with those in and out of the organization who would be threatened by a sharp definition of purpose, with its attendant claims and respon-

---

[8] Alex Taylor III, "The Gentlemen at Ford Are Kicking Butt," *Fortune* (June 22, 1998): 75.

sibilities. Even business firms find it easy to fall back on conventional phrases, such as that "our goal is to make profit," phrases which offer little guidance in the formulation of policy.[9]

As this quote suggests, setting goals is not easy. It is a skill that must be acquired, combining knowledge of the technical aspects of performance measurement with a grasp of the process flows that are required to cascade performance goals through the organization. Because performance goals and their related incentives determine success (and failure) for individuals, this topic cannot be satisfactorily considered without consideration of the interaction of goals and measures with human behavior.

[9] Philip Selznick, *Leadership in Administration* (New York: Harper & Row, 1957): 62–64.

12

Identifying Strategic Risk

C ompeting in any industry entails risk. However, the more aggressive and fast-paced the business and its management, the greater the potential for a misstep. In this chapter, we consider the different types of strategic risks that can imperil the firm. Then, we illustrate how to use the risk exposure calculator—a diagnostic tool to identify organizational pressure points that could cause these risks to rise to dangerous levels. Finally, we discuss the conditions that could cause individual employees to willfully expose the business to risk.

After identifying the sources of strategic risk, we study the control tools and techniques that managers employ to manage these risks.

SOURCES OF STRATEGIC RISK

A dictionary defines risk as "the possibility of suffering harm or loss."[1] In a business setting, managers must be sensitive to conditions that can cause specific categories of risk to become dangerous. These conditions are a function of the business strategy chosen by top managers.

To effectively manage their business, all managers must assess **strategic risk,** which is *an unexpected event or set of conditions that significantly reduces the ability of managers to implement their intended business strategy.* Figure 12–1 highlights the focus of our analysis. Business strategy—at the center of the figure—is our starting point. Working outward from the center, we consider three basic sources of strategic risk that potentially affect every business: operations risk, asset impairment risk, and competitive risk. If the magnitude of any of these risks becomes sufficiently large, the firm becomes exposed to franchise risk.

Operations Risk

Operations risk results from the consequences of a breakdown in a core operating, manufacturing, or processing capability. All firms that create value through manufacturing or service activities face operations risk to varying degrees. Things can (and do) go wrong in the operating core of the business. Defective products can be shipped, maintenance can be neglected leading to breakdowns, customer packages can be lost, and transactions can be erroneously processed. Any operational error that impedes the flow

---

This chapter is reprinted with permission from Robert Simons, "Identifying Strategic Risk," Harvard Business School Note No. 199-031, 1998. Copyright © 1998 by the President and Fellows of Harvard College.

[1] *The American Heritage Dictionary of the English Language,* 3rd ed. (Boston: Houghton Mifflin, 1992).

FIGURE 12–1   **Sources of Business Risk**

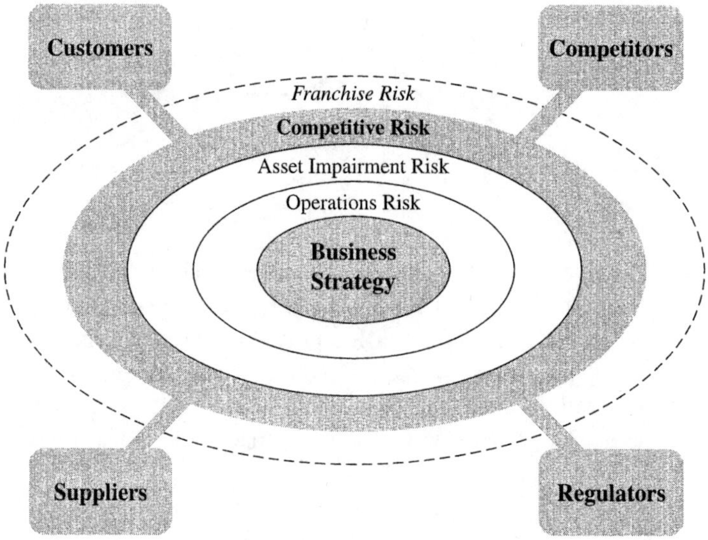

of high-quality products and services has the potential to expose the firm to loss and liability.

Operations risk becomes a strategic risk in the event of critical product or process failures. In a food or drug manufacturer, for example, operations risk is encountered if a toxic substance is inadvertently mixed in with a product formulation. For a financial institution, operations risk is encountered if trades are not executed properly or if a transactions clearing system fails. Fidelity Investment Company, for example, processes more than one million transactions each day in its mutual funds business. With more than $400 billion invested, customers expect their transactions to be processed promptly and accurately. Any failure of processing technology would be devastating to the business.

Basic business strategy affects any firm's exposure to operations risk. For example, AOL has followed an aggressive growth strategy, lowering its prices and providing free access software to capture market share from competitors. However, failures in the ability of its server network to handle growing demand, caused by insufficient modem and network processing capacity, resulted in lawsuits and embarrassing public scrutiny of its service capability. In the food-products industry, Odwalla, a manufacturer of bottled apple juice, attempted to differentiate its products through superior freshness and flavor. To ensure maximum flavor, managers made a strategic decision not to pasteurize their juice. Unfortunately, the operations risk resulting from this strategy led to severe consequences when the company inadvertently shipped tainted products that resulted in sickness and death. Operations risk exposed the business to criminal charges, lawsuits, and loss of confidence by consumers. The company's survival was placed in jeopardy.[2]

---

[2] Pam Belluck, "Juice Maker Pleads Guilty and Pays $1.5 Million in Fatal Poisoning Case," *The New York Times* (July 24, 1998): A12.

In most industries, there are some competitors who knowingly choose strategies in which the safety and/or quality of operations are critical to success—thereby assuming significant operations risk. This is true for an electric utility that chooses to generate power using nuclear power, instead of purchasing bulk power from another provider. The strategy of entering the generation business—backward integrating—coupled with the decision to generate power using nuclear energy rather that fossil fuels, increases operations risk significantly.

In high technology businesses, where certain aspects of operations are "mission critical" to the implementation of strategy, any error or downtime can be sufficiently serious to threaten the viability of the business. We have discussed already the substantial operations risk at large financial institutions like Fidelity Investments. Consider the operations risk at the John F. Kennedy Space Center. Any failure in operations can imperil the safety of the space shuttle and its crew. Because managers rely on complex technologies, NASA has assumed significant operations risk.

The consequences of operations risk are often triggered by employee error. Most of these errors are unintended and/or accidental. Occasionally, however, employees may consciously decide to cut corners in quality or safety to meet performance targets or receive bonuses. For example, the horrific nuclear accident at Chernobyl in the former Soviet Union was caused by operators and managers who intentionally falsified performance indicators to ensure that they would achieve production targets and earn desired bonuses.

Applying the Inputs → Process → Outputs Model

Applying the inputs → process → outputs model is critical for identifying and controlling operations risk, especially when technology failure can lead to inefficiencies and breakdowns.

Analyzing operations according to the inputs → process → outputs model provides guidance about what key processes should be standardized and controlled tightly to assure safety and quality. This is a first step in the assessment of operations risk. As discussed in Chapter 4, standardization and scalability are appropriate for critical internal processes that lie at the core of a business's operations. The inputs → process → outputs model should be used in all critical parts of the value chain to identify points where system errors could damage key operations or impair important assets. Standardization and practices such as TQM based on best practice, benchmarking, and engineering studies can then be used to ensure that inefficiencies and breakdowns do not create significant operating risks for the business.

Asset Impairment Risk

Moving outward from the core of Figure 12–1, the second source of strategic risk is **asset impairment risk.** An asset is a resource owned by the firm to generate future cash flows. An asset becomes *impaired* when it loses a significant portion of its current value because of a reduction in the likelihood of receiving those future cash flows. Like other risks, asset impairment risk is largely a function of the way that managers have chosen to compete.

Asset impairment can become a strategic risk if there is deterioration in the financial value, intellectual property rights, or the physical condition of assets that are important for the implementation of strategy.

Financial Impairment

Financial impairment results from a decline in the market value of a significant balance sheet asset held for resale or as collateral. An asset becomes impaired when the future cash flows accruing to the firm are no longer sufficient to support the asset's balance sheet valuation (computed as the NPV of those future cash flows). For example, firms holding significant Mexican assets found those assets impaired when the government devalued the peso in late 1994. Russian assets became impaired in the same way in 1998. In both of these cases, currency devaluation decreased the expected value of future cash flows. Similarly, the value of a long-term bond portfolio may sink dramatically with a rise in market interest rates (which increases the discount rate used in the NPV calculation).

All firms that sell goods or services on credit face the possibility that accounts receivable—a financial asset on the balance sheet—will prove uncollectable. *Credit risk* occurs when a creditor becomes bankrupt or insolvent and is unable to pay contractual obligations as they become due. All businesses that extend payment terms are exposed to credit risk, although some strategies expose the business to more credit risk than others. Managers must balance risk and reward as they choose the conditions and terms under which they are willing to grant credit. Most businesses can increase sales and revenues if managers are willing to offer more liberal credit terms to customers who are poor credit risks. Long payback periods coupled with low levels of collateral increase the risk and cost of default. Alternatively, managers can minimize credit losses by turning away sales on account, but at the cost of forgone revenue. Similarly, they can insist on marketable collateral to secure loans or withhold the legal transfer of title until payment is made in full.

Depending on the strategy of the firm, creditors may be individuals, businesses, or even governments. At the extreme, a business may be exposed to risk at the national level (called *sovereign risk*) when a foreign government becomes unable or unwilling to repay its debts. Sovereign risk is greatest, of course, when a business follows a strategy that results in significant cross-border financial exposure in politically unstable countries. Instability in Indonesia and other Asian countries in 1998 increased sovereign risk for many firms.

Financial trading firms—those that routinely buy and sell financial securities—often enter into agreements to buy or sell assets on specified dates in the future. These agreements are called forward contracts. Such firms are exposed to a special type of credit risk known as *counterparty* risk—the risk that the other party to the agreement may be unable to honor its contractual obligation due to insolvency or inability to deliver what was promised. This risk can become substantial if a large number of transactions and forward contracts are concentrated with a small number of counterparties or if failures of specific financial institutions lead to a general market insolvency.

For financial trading businesses such as banks, retail stockbrokers, and mutual funds, specific business strategies determine how much financial impairment risk the business is exposed to. Firms following high-risk strategies often hold unhedged assets such as global derivatives and other highly leveraged securities whose value can change rapidly and erratically. More conservative competitors may choose strategies that limit their financial impairment risk: they eschew highly leveraged instruments in favor of more easily controlled investments.

Financial impairment is often due to unpredictable changes in financial market variables. However, like operations risk, assets may sometimes become impaired by the willful actions of employees. Consider these examples:

- A bank vice president wished to improve the asset position of her balance sheet at year-end. Accordingly, she sold a portfolio of mortgage loans to a friendly bank. She did not inform anyone of the agreement to repurchase the mortgage portfolio in six months.
- A bond trader lost $1 million on currency market trades. He instructed accounting personnel to post the loss to a suspense account. He explained that he would offset the loss against an open position that was guaranteed to generate a sizable profit.

In cases such as these, employees expose a business to asset impairment risk in their attempts to achieve performance targets a nd/or cover up previous losses.

Manufacturing and service firms are not immune from financial impairment risk. When excess cash is invested in short-term financial assets, any business may be exposed to financial impairment risk. For example, managers of industrial or consumer-products companies may be tempted to bolster their short-term profitability by taking unhedged financial positions that pay off if financial markets move in predicted directions. As a result of this type of gamble, Procter & Gamble lost millions of dollars in highly leveraged derivative positions. This financial speculation also caused the much publicized municipal insolvency of Orange County, California in the mid 1990s.

Bank Lending Risks

Employees sometimes decide to step out of bounds to take advantage of certain situations. The manager of a bank's branch did precisely this. One of his customers was a construction company that was having problems obtaining a loan from other banks. The bank officer agreed to give the company a loan if, in exchange, the construction company did some work at his house for free. Apparently, the bank officer thought that this was a mutually satisfactory arrangement: the company received the credit that it was looking for, and he was able to have his house remodeled. The bank officer then decided to use the same approach with two other customers, also in the construction sector, who approached the bank for loans. In due course, the regional manager noticed the increased credit risk that the branch was taking with these customers and decided to investigate. He quickly discovered the reasons for their credit approvals and fired the branch manager.

Impairment of Intellectual Property Rights

For many companies today, intangible resources such as intellectual property and proprietary customer information are far more valuable than the tangible assets on the firm's balance sheet. Many software and Internet firms are good examples. The huge market value of firms such as Microsoft Corporation, Amazon.com, and Netscape Communications is not a function of the size of their balance sheets, but rather reflects the estimated value of future cash flows related to their intangible intellectual resources. Similarly, the value of ethical drug manufacturers such as Merck & Company and Pfizer resides primarily in their research capabilities, patents, and trade secrets.

For these firms, the potential for loss or impairment of these intellectual property rights creates significant strategic risk. Impairment may be due to unauthorized use of intellectual property by competitors (e.g., patent infringement), unauthorized disclosure of trade secrets to a competitor or third party (such as leaking of proprietary computer code, manufacturing procedures, or formulas), and failure to reinvest in intellectual capital as asset quality deteriorates over time (e.g., failure to upgrade information-based assets or invest in employee training).

Physical Impairment

Assets can also become impaired by the physical destruction of key processing or production facilities. This impairment may be due to fire, flood, terrorist action, or other catastrophe. Managers whose business depends on large-scale data centers must ensure that processing can be switched to backup facilities without significant loss of operating capacity. Risk managers are typically responsible for ensuring adequate coverage for insurable physical destruction risks and the implementation of fail-safe backup plans to protect against mission-critical processing failures.

Competitive Risk

So far, we have considered strategic risks due to defective transaction flows (operations risk) and impaired value of significant balance sheet assets and intangible resources (asset impairment risk). The third source of strategic risk has to do with the risks inherent in market competition. **Competitive risk** results from changes in the competitive environment that could impair the business's ability to successfully create value and differentiate its products or services. Examples of competitive risks that could impair the ability of a business to create value include the actions of *competitors* in developing superior products and services (for example, compact disks displacing vinyl records); changes in *regulation* and public policy (e.g., regulators requiring electric utilities to sell off their generation facilities); shifts in *customer* tastes or desires (such as fashion fads); and changes in *supplier* pricing and policies (e.g., preferential pricing for "super" retailers) (Figure 12–1).

Competitive risk, by definition, is faced by all businesses that compete in dynamic markets. Regardless of the industry in which a business competes, so long as it has active competitors and demanding customers, it is exposed to competitive risk. The five-forces analysis, covered in Chapter 2, provides a starting point to consider the direction from which these risks can emanate:

- Intense rivalry from existing competitors can change the basis of value creation.
- Demanding customers may choose to switch suppliers.
- Suppliers may choose to limit availability or increase the cost of critical inputs.
- New competitors may enter the industry with new technologies and products.
- Substitute products or services may become available with superior costs or attributes.[3]

Managers must be constantly alert to the risk that they will fail to anticipate and react to these competitive risks quickly, thereby allowing the rules of the competitive game to turn against them. However, competitive risk can also be created by the actions of employees. Employees can inadvertently damage the franchise in their attempts to maximize short-term profit. These kinds of risk are created when employees act inappropriately in dealing with customers, suppliers, and competitors. For any given strategy, a series of questions can reveal those employee behaviors that could imperil the strategy.

Customers: *What employee actions could drive customers away?*
- A small consulting firm competed by offering specialized services to an elite group of demanding clients. Employees in a branch office provided consulting services to the competitor of a large and important client. As a result of a perceived conflict of interest, the large client severed relationships with the firm.

Suppliers: *What employee actions could cause important suppliers to stop supplying the firm?*
- A beer distributor relied on a national brewer for the majority of its business. Employees became complacent and allowed relationships with the supplier to deteriorate. Because of poor service, the brewer awarded distribution rights to a competing wholesaler.

Substitute Products: *What employee actions could cause customers to switch to competing products or services?*
- To obtain commission bonuses in an electronic-instrumentation business, salespeople pushed obsolete products that were stockpiled in inventory. Customers wishing to purchase the latest technology placed orders with new suppliers who were trying to build market share.

New Entrants: *What employee actions could cause new competitors to enter the industry?*
- In a cable television business, abuses in customer service caused regulators to increase competition by licensing new competitors.

Interactive controls systems are essential to monitor competitive risks in a culture that could potentially create barriers to impede the free flow of information about emerging threats and opportunities.

---

[3] Michael E. Porter, *Competitive Strategy* (New York: The Free Press, 1980).

Franchise Risk

Unlike the three sources of risk enumerated above (operations, asset impairment, and competitive risk), franchise risk is not in itself a *source* of risk. Instead, it is a *consequence* of excessive risk in any one of the three basic risk dimensions. **Franchise risk** occurs when the value of the entire business erodes due to a loss in confidence by critical constituents. Franchise risk occurs when a problem or set of problems threatens the viability of the entire enterprise. In the worst case, customers stop buying a business's products or services because they lose confidence in the company's ability to deliver what it has promised. However, loss of confidence by other constituents—suppliers, regulators, or business partners—can be equally devastating (Figure 12–1).

Loss of confidence in either a brand or the entire corporation—the hallmark of franchise risk—can result from any of the risks previously enumerated. Consider the following examples:

- *Operations risk*—After a well-publicized fatal crash in Florida, AirTran Holdings (formerly ValuJet Airlines) managers were unable to restore public confidence that flight operations and safety procedures at the airline were adequate. The market share of other discount-fare regional competitors also eroded as the public lost confidence in the safety and reliability of low-cost operators.
- *Asset impairment risk*—During the savings and loan crisis, the public lost confidence that besieged banks, reeling from losses in real estate collateral, had sufficient resources to repay depositors. The "run on the banks" that occurred at several institutions required federal agencies to step in and guarantee deposits as a means of restoring confidence.
- *Competitive risk*—The disastrous slide in market share at Apple Computer, reflecting competitive forces and eroding technological leadership, caused many in the industry to lose confidence in Apple's ability to support its products. As a result, software suppliers declined to invest in Apple applications and customers abandoned Apple computers in favor of competitors' products.

Franchise risk—sometimes known as *reputation risk*—occurs when business problems or actions negatively affect customer perceptions of value in using the business's goods or services. The intrinsic value of a business (i.e., its value proposition) is based on customers' willingness to pay for a known set of attributes and quality. Any significant breakdown in operations, impairment of assets, or erosion of competitive strength can negatively influence public perception and drive away customers.

For any firm operating in a competitive market, reputation is critical to the ongoing ability to create value. When customers have a choice about which firms' products to buy, reputation risk must be a major concern for managers. Franchise risk is acute, however, for any firm that depends on its reputation for integrity as a critical competitive resource in attracting and maintaining customers. For example, public accounting firms, defense contractors, airlines, and pharmaceutical firms (among many others) hold a public franchise that depends fundamentally on the public's faith in the integrity and trustworthiness of their business. What are the effects of a story that appears in the morning newspaper describing how managers of a mutual fund have been manipulating published figures to deceive investors? How long will the franchise of that business last? A damaged reputation can destroy the franchise—and ultimately the business—literally overnight.

Restaurant Risk Management

Dining out in restaurants is a significant part of the modern lifestyle, with patrons' concerns ranging from the politeness of service to safety implications from widely publicized outbreaks of foodborne bacteria. Because of these factors, Debra Smithart, CFO of Brinker International, a $1.2 billion casual-dining company with 600 restaurants, decided to establish an internal audit function to address risk issues. "When we did our own risk audit, we realized we had business risks in areas that you couldn't financially engineer or where you couldn't go out and buy something to protect yourself."

She then decided to automate and build in preventive processes in all the group's operations, even if this meant involving financial personnel in nonfinancial areas. Restaurant managers' bonuses were changed to reflect how well they controlled losses, and accident costs were reported on restaurants' monthly financial statements. Cash registers were modified to identify every transaction in more than 140 ways; kettle designs were changed to prevent hot water burns. The company examined every possibility for preventing any contamination by *e. coli* bacteria because no insurance could be bought for such an occurrence and operational cleanliness measures were not foolproof. Accordingly, Brinker's auditors visited slaughterhouses before deciding on which suppliers would be willing to work with them to develop testing procedures.

Brinker's management team also assumed responsibility in managing potential risks to its reputation. Customer complaints were answered by top management within 24 hours. In 1993, when a polo accident put the chairman and CEO Norman Brinker in a (temporary) coma, the board of directors appointed an interim successor within two days. The company received kudos from the press not only for its management of the potential succession crisis, but also for its response two years later to a fire that burned down a restaurant in Jackson, Mississippi: Brinker found every employee another job (mostly in other Brinker restaurants).

Source: Adapted from Stephen Barr, "Redefining Risk," *CFO* (August 1996): 61–66.

Many of the pitfalls of risk management can be avoided if early warning systems are in place to warn managers of impending problems. Diagnostic exception reports that focus on key indicators can alert managers if risk levels are unacceptable. Examples of some common risk indicators are:

Operations Risk
- system downtime
- number of errors
- unexplained variances
- unreconciled accounts
- defect rates/quality standards
- customer complaints

Asset Impairment Risk

- unhedged derivatives on balance sheet
- unrealized holding gains/losses
- concentration of credit or counterparty exposure (e.g., total debt due from specific financial institutions)
- default history
- dropoff in product sales

Competitive Risk

- recent product introductions by competitors
- recent regulatory changes
- changes in consumer buying habits reported in trade journals
- changes in distribution systems

Franchise Risk

- customers/bids lost to competitors
- unfavorable news coverage
- pending lawsuits/legal actions
- system downtime
- competitor business failure

ASSESSING INTERNAL RISK PRESSURES

We have now outlined the types of strategic risk that all firms potentially face. Managers must assess their exposure to these risks based on their specific business strategy.

Now we move to the second step of the analysis by attempting to understand how strategic risks may be exacerbated by the context in which the organization operates. Based on a variety of factors, firms competing in the same product markets may be exposed to very different levels of risk. The **risk exposure calculator** (illustrated in Figure 12–2) analyzes the pressure points inside a business that can cause strategic risks to "blow up" into a crisis. Some of these pressures are due to *growth,* some are due to management *culture,* and some are due to *information management.* Collectively, these forces can "surprise" managers in the form of operating errors, impairment of assets, and crises of customer confidence.

The risk exposure calculator is a diagnostic tool to estimate the magnitude and type of "pressures" that might lead to a substantial failure or breakdown. As suggested by Figure 12–2, the nine pressure points that we discuss are additive. One pressure feeds upon the other. If the pressure builds too high, operations risk, asset impairment risk, and competitive risk can cause irreparable damage. Let's look at each of the pressure points in turn.

Risks Pressures Due to Growth

Growth is a fundamental goal of most high-performing businesses. Yet, success in achieving market-driven growth can bring risk for three reasons. The first reason relates to the *unrelenting pressure for performance* that is a hallmark of high-growth compa-

FIGURE 12–2   The Risk Exposure Calculator

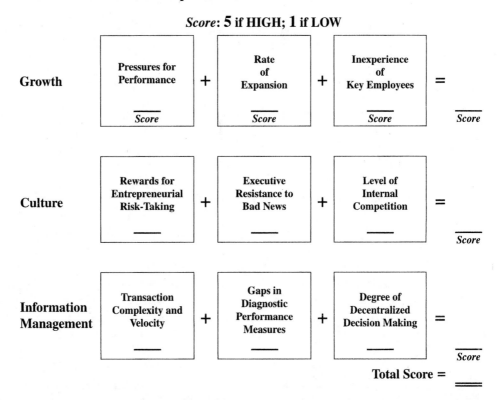

Score: **5** if HIGH; **1** if LOW

nies. High-growth companies typically have very high performance expectations for their managers and employees. Goals are set at demanding levels. Employees are informed that they are expected to deliver results (or else risk punishment or possible replacement). Incentive rewards and bonuses are linked directly and explicitly to performance. Under these circumstances, some people may feel intense pressure to succeed at all costs and may, therefore, engage in behaviors that invite risk. They may, for example, take unacceptable credit risks by selling goods and services to customers with poor credit ratings; they may cut corners to speed operations; or, they may be tempted to bend revenue-recognition rules to book profits before full completion of a sale. If pushed hard enough, some employees may even consider misrepresenting their true performance to cover up any temporary shortfalls.

Rapidly expanding scale of operations is another sign of successful growth. Successful companies grow bigger. However, rapidly increasing scale can also bring undesirable levels of risk. Resources become strained to the limit as people and systems work beyond their normal capacity. Infrastructures designed for a small operation quickly become inadequate. New production, distribution, and service facilities must be brought on line and integrated into overall operations. As a result of rapidly expanding operations, mistakes and breakdowns may occur. Operations errors are likely to creep into the system. New customer accounts may increase credit risk. Product or service quality may suffer, increasing franchise risk.

Growth also means hiring large numbers of new people to staff operations. Competitive advantage cannot be achieved by waiting until all the right people are in place before launching new products and services. Sometimes, in the rush to staff new positions, background checks may be waived and minimum performance standards and educational qualifications may be lowered. Newly hired employees may lack adequate training and experience and, as a result, not fully understand their jobs. *Decreasing experience* can, therefore, result in increased possibility for inadvertent error. Bad business decisions may expose the firm to asset impairment risk and franchise risk.

These risks are increased significantly when a business *lacks consistent values.* Consistent and strong core values are an essential foundation in any highly competitive business. In new, start-up businesses that have not had time to allow consistent values to emerge and take hold, managers and employees may make very different assumptions about organizational purpose and acceptable behaviors. In larger, more-diversified businesses, different business units within the same firm may have very different core values. This occurred, for example, when General Electric — an industrial company — purchased and attempted to manage Kidder Peabody, a financial brokerage firm. The core values in these businesses were so different that it was difficult to communicate a consistent set of corporate-wide beliefs about acceptable risks and behaviors. What was seen as an acceptable credit or operations risk in one business was completely unacceptable in another business, and vice versa. Confusion about values and beliefs invites individuals under pressure to engage in behaviors that increase risk — especially impairment risk and franchise risk.

These three pressure points — unrelenting drive for performance, expanding scale of operations, and decreasing experience and shared values — operate together in an additive fashion to increase the possibility of *errors of omission and commission.* Quite simply, people under pressure make mistakes. An **error of omission** occurs when an employee inadvertently omits to perform an action that is necessary to protect the franchise and/or assets of the business. An **error of commission** occurs when an employee purposefully follows a course of action that increases risk, impairs assets, or otherwise endangers the business.

Paradoxically, it is success and growth that create the potential for errors of omission and commission. Performance pressure, increasing size, and the hiring of new people generally indicate a healthy, vibrant company. Yet, these same forces can easily become catalysts for significant risk and error.

Risks Pressures Due to Culture

The culture of an organization — determined by its history and top-management leadership style — is the second major cause of risk pressures in many businesses. For example, many organizational cultures encourage *entrepreneurial risk taking.* Individuals are motivated to be as creative as possible in finding and creating market opportunities. Although this is usually healthy, there is always the danger that individuals may pursue or create opportunities that significantly increase strategic risk. In a culture of entrepreneurial risk taking, investments may be made in risky assets, deals may be struck with counterparties who have a limited ability to honor their contracts, commitments may be made that are difficult to fulfill, or employees may engage in behaviors that damage the reputation of the business.

Culture also influences the willingness of subordinates to inform superiors about potential risks in the business. Early warning signs about impending problems are often evident to employees who are in day-to-day contact with operations, customers, suppliers, and competitive markets. Too often, however, this critically important early warning information is not communicated upward to senior managers. In some organizations, this reluctance arises from a well-founded *fear in bearing bad news.* In businesses where senior managers have a low tolerance for dissent, or are known for "shooting the messenger," information barriers are inevitable. People become afraid to voice their concerns for fear of sanction or other personal repercussions. As a result, the communication of early warning information breaks down, and top managers can be caught off guard when problems surface unexpectedly.

Additionally, some cultures foster a spirit of *internal competition,* which brings a unique set of issues relating to risk. In these cultures, top managers often knowingly foster a sense of competition among subordinates vying for bonuses and/or promotion. Private information often brings power and rewards to the holder, so individuals jealously guard information. This tendency is exacerbated in a culture where advancement is perceived as a zero-sum game. To advance their own careers, employees may increase business risk by gambling with business assets, credit exposure, and firm reputation in attempts to enhance short-term performance. Unfortunately, the payoffs and costs from these behaviors are asymmetric. If the gamble pays off, the individual is rewarded with large bonuses and promotions. If the gamble results in a substantial loss for the firm, however, the worst that can happen to the employee is losing his or her job. The business is forced to absorb the sometimes significant financial or reputation loss.

These three cultural factors—entrepreneurial risk taking, fear of bearing bad news, and internal competition—feed off each other to create forces that lead to *incomplete management information.* In organizations where these pressures are intense, managers may, as a result, be uninformed about dangers that lurk in their businesses. Employees will take unwarranted risks, hold back bad news, and resist sharing information. Accordingly, managers may unknowingly increase performance pressures and ramp up the scale of the business with little understanding of the potential risks.

Risks Pressures Due to Information Management

The final category of risk is due to information management, which can create risk in several ways. First, *transaction velocity*—created by high transaction volume and increased processing speed—can increase the possibility of operations risk. In 1991, for example, Fidelity Investments processed 250,000 transactions per day; by 1998, the business processed more than one million transactions per day. If information technology had failed to keep pace with this intense increase in processing demand, operational errors would have been inevitable. Accordingly, Fidelity has made massive investments in technology to ensure that support is adequate as the business grows. Still, operations risk is a continuing concern for Fidelity's managers. America Online, by contrast, suffered the consequences of information processing risk related to increased transaction velocity when its processing infrastructure was unable to keep pace with increased demand.

Transaction complexity also increases risk. As transactions become more complex, fewer people may fully understand the nature of these transactions and how to control them. Crossborder agreements in international operations, creative financing of customer purchases, and elaborate consortium arrangements can all produce highly complex contracts. Without full understanding of contractual obligations and the nature of contingent cash flows, asset impairment risk increases substantially. The increase in complexity due to highly leveraged derivative financial products (i.e., financial instruments whose value fluctuates based on changes in the values of other underlying assets) has caused more than one well-managed firm to sustain substantial losses.

Gaps in diagnostic performance measures also increase risk. If managers are unaware of potential problems, they cannot take remedial action to contain the risk. All types of risk need appropriate diagnostic systems to track current risk levels and serve as warning indicators. Operations risk indicators, financial and credit risk indicators, and systems that provide early warning about changes in competitive risk and franchise risk should be in place (we discuss these indicators later in the chapter). These diagnostic indicators often require specialized information processing systems that can consolidate information across dispersed operations; if these systems are fragmented or inadequate to supply information about problems, the consequences of risks can become greatly magnified.

Finally, highly *decentralized decision making* can increase risk. In decentralized businesses, individuals are encouraged to make decisions autonomously and create opportunities without constant monitoring and oversight by superiors. As we discussed in Chapter 3, this structural configuration is appropriate when top managers wish to focus attention and decision making on local markets. Because of the freedom created by decentralized structures, however, fewer operating rules and constraints are likely to be imposed on operating managers. Consequently, they may be able to engage in activities that increase risk without requiring approval from corporate-level managers. Moreover, when several separate businesses within the same firm are acting independently, understanding the aggregation of risk across business units becomes important. For example, aggregating credit risk across several businesses in the same firm may be important if those businesses are all making risky loans to the same customer. By decentralizing credit approval, the concentration of credit risk is greatly magnified.

These three pressure points—transaction complexity and velocity, gaps in diagnostic performance measures, and decentralized decision making—can lead to lapses in diagnostic information and *inefficiencies and breakdowns* in transaction processing. Such inefficiencies and breakdowns can, in turn, significantly increase operations risk, asset impairment risk, and franchise risk.

The nine pressure points listed in Figure 12–2 provide a window into a business to calibrate the potential for significant risk and loss due to employee or management error, systems breakdown, and bad information. Once identified, managers can estimate the magnitude of the strategic risk exposure and ensure that organizational attention is devoted to controlling significant risks.

MISREPRESENTATION AND FRAUD

So far in this chapter, we have discussed strategic risks and the pressures that heighten these risks. However, there is one special case—misrepresentation and fraud—that must be considered separately. Sometimes, because of the pressures identified previously, managers and/or employees may knowingly subject the firm to unacceptable levels of risk. Employees may misrepresent their performance (or that of their business) or misappropriate company assets. Bad decisions can be covered up and expose the firm to loss of valuable assets. In most instances, the amounts involved are small. Sometimes, however, these actions have severely damaged—or even destroyed—the businesses in which these people worked.

In Part I of this book, we made some heroic assumptions about the inherent nature of people in high-performing organizations: we assumed that individuals want to contribute, achieve, innovate, do competent work, and will choose to do what is right based on socialized personal values (learned through family and religious teaching, laws, organizational norms, and so on). However, we also identified organization blocks that can overturn these tendencies and lead to dysfunctional behaviors: confusion about how to contribute, temptation and pressures, conflicting demands with too few resources, and fear of failure. We must now confront the consequences of these organizational blocks.

In all too many of these cases, senior managers were unaware of the risks to which employees had exposed the business. Employees had either covered up their actions (to the extent they had contravened stated policies) or failed to report information to superiors that would have given early warning about potential problems. The destruction of Barings Bank by trader Nick Leeson was a chilling reminder to all managers of the types of risks that they must guard against.

Accordingly, we must analyze the forces that can cause individuals to willfully misrepresent or alter data, engage in fraud, or otherwise expose the business to unacceptable levels of risk.

A Dangerous Triad

Generally, people employed by business and nonprofit organizations do not start out to do bad things. Most often—even in blatant cases of misrepresentation and fraud—an individual starts down a "slippery slope," starting with a small misdeed that, over time, gains momentum and grows in magnitude. Soon, the subterfuge becomes too large for the employee to control. The risk that employees may engage in wrongful acts that expose the business to risk—including misrepresentation and fraud—is greatest *if three conditions exist simultaneously.* These three conditions—pressure, opportunity, and rationalization—are illustrated in Figure 12–3. As we shall discuss, all three conditions are necessary before most individuals will start down the slippery slope.[4]

---

[4] These prerequisites for fraud have been eloquently described by Peter A. Humphery, vice president at Fidelity Investments, in his presentations on risk management.

FIGURE 12–3   A Dangerous Triad

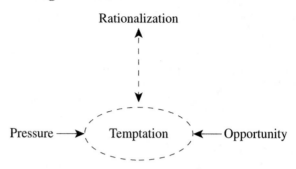

1. Pressure

The pressures to achieve profit goals and strategies are intense in any high-performing organization. The risk calculator highlights many of these pressures. Sometimes, the combination of extrinsic and intrinsic forces will create pressure to manipulate accounting records and/or misuse company assets for personal gain. Extrinsic pressures are due largely to the *performance goals and incentives* that were the subject of the previous chapter. As we discussed there, high-performing organizations are typically high-pressure organizations. Employees are often under significant pressure to meet difficult performance goals. Success in meeting these performance goals can bring substantial financial rewards, including salary increases, bonuses, and possible promotion. Pressure to meet goals may be enhanced by the desire for recognition of success—by superiors, subordinates, and peers. Correspondingly, failure to meet performance goals can often result in loss of prestige, reduction in compensation, and, sometimes, dismissal. Together, the potential for rewards and the fear of failure can create a high level of pressure to succeed, sometimes at all costs.

Pressures to bend the rules or otherwise misuse company assets or resources for personal gain can also be due to *personal problems* that originate outside the workplace. Debts, addictions, or other personal crises may create severe pressures to engage in fraud or misrepresentation to take advantage of an employer or misappropriate company assets.

2. Opportunity

The second necessary condition for willful error and fraud is *opportunity*. Even if someone is under great pressure to bend the rules to achieve performance goals and/or misappropriate assets, they can only engage in wrongful acts if the opportunity to do so exists. In other words, they must have access to valuable assets and/or be able to manipulate accounting and performance measurement systems to their advantage so that their actions are undetected. Thus, control systems must be sufficiently flawed that any misdeeds will not be detected.

We must remember from Chapter 1, however, one of the fundamental tensions of management: there is too much opportunity and too little management attention. Employees are surrounded with opportunity, especially in high-innovation organizations that rely on the creativity of empowered employees. Yet management attention is limited; there is simply not enough time or attention to monitor all the activities of every employee.

When performance pressure is coupled with opportunity to use company assets for personal gain or inflate performance measures, a dangerous situation is created. Any individual in these circumstances will feel *temptation*—temptation to secure rewards and/or use weaknesses in control systems to their advantage. Notwithstanding this great temptation, however, there is one additional prerequisite that must occur before most people will engage in wrongful acts or misdeeds that put the company at risk. They must believe that what they are doing is not really creating risk for themselves or the business.

3. Rationalization

Employees—even those experiencing great temptation and pressure—are unlikely to succumb and engage in wrongful actions unless they can find rationalizations for their aberrant behavior. Employees know the difference between right and wrong and typically will not engage in actions that contravene generally accepted moral codes of our society. A variety of studies has shown that when employees engage in damaging or unethical behaviors, they will do so only if they can justify their actions with one or more of the following excuses:

- The action is not "really" wrong—Employees may convince themselves that many other people do similar things, and/or the action is not serious enough to warrant concern. For example, an auditor may routinely underreport the hours worked by subordinates in an attempt to meet client budget targets.
- The likelihood of being caught is small—Because people often have the opportunity to manipulate company records to cover up their acts, they often believe that they will never be found out. Thus, they may have little fear that their behavior will ever be discovered.
- The action is in the organization's best interest—Employees may convince themselves that misrepresenting performance or manipulating data can advance the firm's interest. For example, an employee may lie to a government investigator because she believes that the investigator is an "enemy" of the business and is trying to hurt it.
- If exposed, senior management would condone the behavior and protect the individuals involved—To the extent that employees believe they are working to protect or further the company's interests, then their rationalization often takes the next logical step. They convince themselves that if they are caught and forced to explain what they did and why they did it, their superiors would understand, support them, and stand by them.[5]

Managers of all high-performing businesses—where there is typically a great deal of both performance pressure and freedom—must ensure that employees cannot easily fall back on these rationalizations.

All three of these conditions—pressure, opportunity, and rationalization—must be present before employees or managers can be expected to abuse their access to infor-

---

[5] Saul W. Gellerman, "Why 'Good' Managers Make Bad Ethical Choices," *Harvard Business Review* 64 (1986): 85–90.

mation or assets for personal gain. If only two of the three prerequisites are present, there is unlikely to be significant risk. For example, opportunity and pressure without rationalization will cause most employees to avoid actions that they know to be wrong,

---

Corporate Fraud at Kurzweil Applied Intelligence

Senior executives at Kurzweil Applied Intelligence, a manufacturer of voice-recognition software, were able to commit fraud despite the scrutiny of its auditors, directors, and the underwriter of its August 1993 initial public offering. Most astonishing was how this could happen under the reign of CEO Bernard Bradstreet, characterized by former Harvard M.B.A. classmates as conservative and clean-living. Some observers suggested that Bradstreet's increasing personal expenses might have pressured him to boost the value of his 35% stake in the company. Others concluded that Bradstreet was so obsessed with posting six consecutive quarters of improving results, so that he could take the company public, that he would stop at nothing.

Kurzweil posted its first profit of $110,000 on revenues of $10.5 million in 1991. During that time, Bradstreet allowed the company to book several transactions a few days prior to customer shipment to meet quarterly goals. By 1992, the accrual rules were further relaxed and some sales were booked as much as two weeks early. By the following year, the treasurer testified that "the whole [revenue recognition] policy basically went out the window and we did whatever was necessary to book the revenue."

A turning point came at the end of 1992, when Kurzweil's sales vice president pressured a sales representative to close $220,000 in sales to meet a quarterly goal. The sales rep forged his customers' signatures on a bogus order with the full knowledge of the vice president. As part of Kurzweil's annual audit, its accountants sent confirmation letters to these customers. Again, the sales representative forged his customers' signatures on the auditor's forms. Kurzweil booked similar questionable transactions in 1993. In August 1993, Kurzweil went public at $10 per share and a market capitalization of $68 million.

As the next yearly audit approached in early 1994, the treasurer ordered her staff to purge files of compromising materials. The scheme was detected in April 1994, when an auditor uncovered an invoice for nine months of storage for products that were supposedly shipped to customers. After reexamining Kurzweil's books, auditors found that at least $6.3 million of 1994's $18.4 million in sales should not have been booked.

Kurzweil's CEO, sales vice president, treasurer, accounting staff, and most of the sales force were fired. The treasurer received immunity from prosecution in exchange for her testimony. The CEO and sales vice president were tried, convicted, and sentenced to jail.

Source: Adapted from Mark Maremont, "Anatomy of A Fraud," *Business Week* (September 16, 1996): 90–94.

even in the face of temptation. Their conscience will intervene. Similarly, rationalization and opportunity by themselves are unlikely to lead to problems if there are no external or internal inducements to bend the rules. Why take any risks if there are no pressing reasons? Finally, pressure and rationalization—a potentially dangerous combination—can be contained effectively if employees do not have the opportunity to engage in actions that could put the business at risk. Control systems and safeguards must be sufficient to deny unauthorized access to accounting records and/or valuable assets.

Thus, to control the risks that employees may engage in willful misrepresentation or fraud, managers must remove at least *one* of the three prerequisites. We discuss how effective managers do this in the next chapter.

LEARNING WHAT RISKS TO AVOID

Unfortunately, the most common, but painful, way of learning about risk is to suffer the consequences firsthand. For example, the manipulation of revenue numbers to hit performance targets can cause acute embarrassment and even lawsuits. The reputation damage can be substantial. If misstatements are material, financial statements must be restated and the indiscretion must be reported to regulatory authorities (and will likely be picked up by the business press). In these cases, two results are almost certain. First, the managers involved in the indiscretion will be disciplined—probably fired along with their superiors, who will be held accountable for poor leadership and oversight. Second, top managers will install new controls—clearly specifying the consequences to those who are tempted to cross the line—to ensure that this damaging behavior will never happen again.

Vicarious learning occurs when managers witness a failure or mishap in another business and realize that the same thing could easily happen in their own business ("There, but for the grace of God, go I"). For example, when brokerage firm Kidder Peabody & Company and Barings PLC were fatally damaged because of the unsupervised activity of individual traders, managers of similar Wall Street firms rushed to install new control systems in an attempt to avoid the actions that had caused the demise of these businesses.[6]

To determine strategic risk, a look at failures can be revealing. One technique—followed by a successful U.S. construction company—is to annually review all projects that have *failed*—that is, those that were significantly over budget or failed to meet client expectations. A series of intense meetings is then devoted to discussing the causes for these failures and attempting to learn from them to ensure that they will not recur. Thus, over time, managers have learned that there are certain types of projects that do not fit their core competencies and should be subject to special controls and management attention. For example, they have learned that they have a poor track record at successfully building sewage treatment plants and have, accordingly, declared these types of projects out-of-bounds.

---

[6] John R. Dorman, "Brokerage Firms Take Action to Detect Potential Rogue Trades in Their Midst," *The Wall Street Journal* (November 29, 1995): Cl.

CHAPTER SUMMARY

Strategic risk comes in many different forms. Managers must assess the nature of the risks facing their business based on the ways that they have chosen to compete in the market. The primary forms of risk are operations risk, asset impairment risk, and competitive risk. If any of these risks becomes severe, the franchise of the entire business may be at stake.

There are nine pressure points that managers should analyze in determining the potential level of risk inside their businesses. These pressures are due to growth, culture, and information management. In combination, these pressure points can lead to errors, incomplete management information, and inefficiencies and breakdowns.

Risk often leads to adverse consequences because of the actions or inactions of employees. Most often, these actions are inadvertent. Sometimes, however, they may be willful. Whatever the cause, employee actions are more likely to cause risk when pressure is high inside the organization.

Individual employees may sometimes create risk by engaging in wrongful acts—either misrepresentation or fraud. This is most likely if three conditions exist: (1) pressure to bend the rules, (2) opportunity to access valuable assets and/or manipulate accounting records, and (3) rationalization that these actions are "not really wrong."

In the next chapter, we discuss how to control strategic risks. Managing risk effectively means utilizing specialized control tools and techniques. All managers must understand how to control these risks, because nothing less than the survival of the business may be at stake.

13
Managing Strategic Risk

In the previous chapter we identified various types of risk, their linkage with business strategy, and the pressure points that aggravate exposure to risk or increase the possibility of loss. In this chapter, we discuss how managers can proactively manage these risks as they work to achieve profit goals and strategies.

Much of the risk that we have described is created by management's use of aggressive performance goals and incentives to get the organization up to speed, just like a driver who steps hard on the gas pedal. In this chapter we look at another set of systems—the brakes that managers employ to control businesses operating at high speeds. High-performing businesses need good brakes, just like high-performing cars. Cars have brakes for two reasons. First, and most obvious, they allow the driver to slow the car down and stop safely. However, cars have brakes for another reason. They give the driver the confidence to go very fast. Imagine a high-performance racing car on a speedway. The driver can operate at top speeds only if he knows that he can rely on excellent brakes to control the car on tight turns. Like the fastest cars, managers of high-performing businesses need the best brakes to control strategic risks that are an inevitable consequence of driving their businesses to their maximum potentials.

Strategic risks are managed primarily by communicating effective boundaries—both business conduct and strategic—and installing good internal control systems. Boundary systems are designed to communicate risks to be avoided and to remove any ability to rationalize actions that could expose the firm to undesirable levels of risk. Internal control systems are designed to protect assets and to remove the opportunity for inadvertent error or willful wrongdoing in transaction processing and performance measurement. Together, these two systems supply the necessary control to ensure that accidental or willful error does not harm the ability of the firm to create value for customers, stockholders, and employees.

BELIEFS AND BOUNDARIES

Empowered employees—those who are asked to make decisions and assume responsibility for their work—must make choices every day about how to create value. They must balance tensions between profit, growth, and control, tensions between short-term and long-term goals, and tensions between self-interest and the desire to contribute to organizational success. If properly managed, these tensions can result in innovation that enhances the value and strategy of the firm. Think back over the past 10 years to all the innovations that businesses have brought to market and the new markets that individuals have created: cellular telephones, global-positioning satellite systems, derivative financial products, the Internet, and geographical expansion in China and eastern Europe. The list goes on and on. The potential for people to identify and create opportunities in changing markets is virtually limitless.

Sometimes, however, as we discussed in the previous chapter, people may pursue opportunities in a way that actually harms the firm. They may pursue opportunities that do not align with the intended strategy of the business. They may attempt to take advantage of a loophole in the law that causes the firm embarrassment when reported in the press; they may engage in insider trading to personally benefit from knowledge of an upcoming business transaction; or they may decide to ship substandard products in the mistaken belief that no one will be hurt by their actions. Whenever employees are asked to make choices, good brakes are needed to ensure that a business does not crash and burn.

To ensure that employees engage in the right type of activities, managers must first inspire commitment to a clear set of core values. **Core values** *are the beliefs that define basic principles, purpose, and direction.* Often rooted in the personal values of the founders, core values provide guidance about responsibilities to customers, employees, local communities, and stockholders. They explicitly define top management's views on trade-offs such as short-term performance versus long-term responsibilities. Core values provide guidance to employees where rules and standard operating procedures alone cannot suffice.

We know from work in organizational behavior that inspirational leaders (1) articulate a vision that addresses the values of the participants, (2) allow each individual to appreciate how he or she can contribute to the achievement of that vision, (3) provide enthusiastic support for effort, and (4) encourage public recognition and reward for all successes.[1] Employees will go the extra mile and work diligently for the best interest of organizations to which they are committed and proud. For example, commitment to mission and purpose allows successful nonprofit and charitable organizations to attract talented individuals at little or no cost. Without commitment to organizational purpose, people will not be able to fully participate in the decisions that affect growth and profitability.

In small companies, communication of core values can be accomplished informally. As organizations become larger, however, managers must formalize this process by articulating and communicating *formal* beliefs systems. **Beliefs systems** *are the explicit set of organizational definitions that senior managers communicate formally and reinforce systematically to provide basic values, purpose, and direction for the organization.*[2] Using the mission statements and credos discussed in Chapter 2, managers attempt to give all employees who work for the business a sense of pride and purpose. Core values and statements of purpose are actively communicated to provide a compass for action. This is strategy as perspective—one of the four Ps of strategy.

---

[1] John P. Kotter, *A Force for Change* (New York: The Free Press, 1990): 63.
[2] Robert Simons, *Levers of Control,* 34.

Managers should never delegate the preparation of missions and credos. Managers should take every opportunity—both written and verbal—to personally reinforce core values and their importance. To increase ROME, however, the work of distributing documents, designing educational programs, and conducting organizational surveys to test awareness can, and should, be delegated to staff groups.

Because missions and credos are designed to appeal to all levels of the organization—from truck drivers to company presidents—they must be written at high levels of abstraction and generality. Therefore, they can never be specific enough to tell people facing difficult choices how to compete or how to choose appropriate actions in novel situations. These inspirational beliefs are typically too vague to provide much concrete guidance. How, then, can managers avoid those specific employee actions that could expose the business to risk?

In Chapter 4, we discussed two basic ways of controlling human behavior. The first is to tell people *what to do*—to dictate which opportunities to pursue and to specify in detail how to create value and overcome obstacles along the way. This is the "command and control" approach followed by the military in its tactical operations. Mission and objectives are defined by the highest level of command. Surveillance and intelligence data are fed to field commanders, giving them a unique view of emerging threats and opportunities. Tactical and strategic decisions are restricted to those with the proper authority. Commanders issue explicit orders that subordinates are expected to follow faithfully.

In a business that relies on empowered employees to continually innovate, the military model does not work very well. As we discussed, telling people what to do drives out innovation and creativity. Strict orders about how someone must do their job precludes creative experimentation in attempting to find new approaches and ways of doing things. Unlike the military, specific knowledge about threats and opportunities, as well as new ideas about products and markets, is widely dispersed throughout the organization; it is not all in the hands of business "commanders." It is just not possible to transmit all of the knowledge possessed by employees—who are closest to markets and customers—back to senior managers.

The second possibility for controlling human behavior, again covered in detail in Chapter 4, is to hold people *accountable for outcomes* and leave it up to their initiative and creativity to figure out how to do their jobs most effectively. This is the approach used by managers who wish to rely on their subordinates to help them implement strategy in rapidly changing, highly competitive markets. However, it is precisely this approach that carries the most risk. Employees may make widely different assumptions about the types of opportunities to pursue. They may engage in activities that are wasteful or do not support the current business strategy. Sometimes, they may engage in activities that put the business at risk. It is in these circumstances—when individuals are accountable for high levels of performance *and* asked to be creative—that managers need the best brakes.

Managers of high-performing businesses face a dilemma in deciding how to control the opportunity-seeking behavior of employees. On the one hand, opportunism is at the heart of innovation in highly competitive markets. In these fast-moving markets, managers must encourage subordinates to constantly search for new ideas and new ways of creating value. On the other hand, this same opportunism poses considerable risk. Employees may choose to pursue or create an opportunity that exposes the business to consequences that senior managers would choose to avoid.

Therefore, in high-performing businesses, managers must go one step beyond missions and inspirational beliefs. They must also install brakes by communicating clearly to all employees the behaviors and opportunities that are off-limits. In other words, managers must tell subordinates what *not to do* and then encourage them to innovate and seek all possible opportunities—to drive as fast as possible—within those clearly defined boundaries.

The idea of imposing limits or boundaries on opportunistic behavior is not new. This concept is deeply rooted in the Ten Commandments of the Judeo-Christian experience:

1. You shall have no other gods.
2. You shall not make any graven images and bow down.
3. You shall not take the name of the Lord in vain.
4. Keep the Sabbath holy—You shall do no work on that day.
5. Honor your father and mother.
6. You shall not kill.
7. You shall not commit adultery.
8. You shall not steal.
9. You shall not bear false witness against your neighbor.
10. You shall not covet anything that is your neighbor's.

The Ten Commandments do not tell people what to do; they decree what *not* to do. They create boundaries that clearly delineate behaviors that are off-limits.

This turns out to be a simple, but extremely powerful, principle for all business managers. Ask yourself the question, If managers want their employees to be innovative, creative, and entrepreneurial, are they better to tell them *what* to do, or what *not* to do? What happens if managers tell employees what to do? Quite simple, they do it. They arrive at work, follow orders and procedure manuals, and go home at night. But are they likely to innovate? Will they be entrepreneurial and creative? The answer, of course, is no.

Instead, to implement strategy, effective managers inspire their employees to maximum effort and innovation by (1) creating shared beliefs and mission, (2) setting challenging goals, (3) linking incentives to accomplishment, and (4) *declaring certain actions off-limits*. Then—and only then—can employees respond creatively, but safely, to the opportunities they encounter, limited only by their abilities and imagination.

The relationship of beliefs and boundaries to business strategy, which we will explore in the remainder of this chapter, is illustrated in Figure 13–1.

BUSINESS CONDUCT BOUNDARIES

Based on a business's unique strategy, boundary systems communicate specific *risks to be avoided*. The most basic **business conduct boundaries** are those that define and

FIGURE 13–1   Two Additional Levers of Control: Beliefs Systems and Boundary Systems

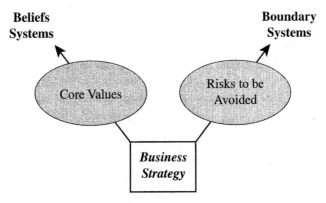

Source: Adapted from Simons, *Levers of Control*, p. 7.

communicate standards of business conduct for all employees. These are commonly called *codes of business conduct.* Like the Ten Commandments, codes of business conduct are stated in negative terms; they specify actions that are forbidden. Off-limit behaviors typically include:

- conflicts of interest—such as, employees are forbidden from owning a significant stake in a business that supplies goods or services to the business
- activities that contravene anti-trust laws—for example, employees are forbidden from colluding to fix prices with competitors
- disclosure of confidential company information—employees are forbidden from revealing private company information to anyone not entitled to know it
- trading in company securities based on nonpublic information—for example, employees are forbidden from buying or selling shares of the company in anticipation of market price reactions when private information becomes available to the public ·
- illegal payments to government officials—such as, employees are forbidden from making any payments in contravention of local laws to expedite services or receive preferential treatment

More than 75% of medium and large companies—defined as those with net worth in excess of $100 million—have formal codes of business conduct.[3] Some of these proscriptions are aimed at any employee who might be tempted to engage in a wrongful activity for personal enrichment. Other activities are illegal under statute, and it is clear why managers would forbid them. Managers must remember, however, that employees may sometimes be tempted to engage in harmful or unethical activities if they believe that what they are doing is helping the company achieve its goals or protecting the business from adverse consequences. For example, a respected senior vice president of an electric utility company was caught lying under oath to state regulators in a public

---

[3] Robert B. Sweeney and Howard L. Siers, "Survey: Ethics in Corporate America," *Management Accounting* 71 (1990): 34–40.

hearing. He did so not for personal gain, but because he believed that the regulators' line of inquiry could be harmful to the company's legitimate interests.[4]

In their zeal to achieve performance goals and/or protect the company, well-meaning employees sometimes make decisions that can damage the long-term health of the business. The utility vice president was fired, but in the ensuing public scandal, the CEO was also forced to resign. It took a new CEO several years to repair the damage to the company's reputation and restore trust with the regulators.

The Ten Commandments remind all of us of lines that must not be crossed as we attempt to deal with the pressures and temptations that are an inevitable part of daily life. Pressure and temptation can also be substantial in high-performing businesses. Surveys have repeatedly revealed that a majority of managers and employees feel pressure at some time in their careers to compromise personal standards of integrity to achieve company goals.[5] For example, a 1997 study on the sources and consequences of workplace pressure found that more than half (56%) of the 1,300 managers and employees surveyed felt immense pressure at work to act unethically. Sixty percent of survey participants believed that pressure had increased noticeably in the past five years.[6]

As we discussed in the previous chapter, people are more likely to succumb to pressure and temptation if they can find reasons to rationalize their own behavior. Managers of all high-performing businesses—where there is typically a great deal of both performance pressure and freedom—must ensure that employees cannot fall back easily on these rationalizations. Unambiguous codes of conduct must be used as a communication device to eliminate ambiguity about how employees are expected to respond in the face of pressure and temptation.

The need for codes of business conduct is especially critical in any business whose strategy is built upon trust and a reputation for quality and integrity. Managers of these businesses must install business conduct boundaries to protect their franchise. Such businesses include consumer products companies that market health products (e.g., Johnson & Johnson), food manufacturers (General Mills), pharmaceutical companies (Merck), automobile manufacturers (Ford), and countless others. In these companies, any employee action that could undermine a reputation for integrity in the marketplace is potentially catastrophic to the value of its franchise. Shipping tainted product, lying about product attributes, failing to follow required safety testing—any action that could compromise health or safety jeopardizes the trust that is the foundation of these competitive franchises.

A damaged reputation can do serious, sometimes irreparable, harm to the ability of the business to implement its strategy. Think of the consequences when the news media picked up the story that ValueJet was cutting corners on safety checks, or when managers at Denny's restaurants were accused of discrimination in its hiring practices.

---

[4] Ken Goodpaster, "Witness for the Corporation," Harvard Business School Case No. 384–135, 1983.

[5] Archie B. Carroll, "Managerial Ethics: A Post-Watergate Review," *Business Horizons* 18 (1975): 75–80.

[6] Alison Boyd, "Employee Traps—Corruption in the Workplace," *Management Review* 86 (1997): 9. The survey was sponsored by the American Society of Chartered Life Underwriters and Chartered Financial Consultants, and the Ethics Officer Association.

Franchise risk (i.e., reputation risk) is particularly acute for any firm that relies on its reputation for trust and integrity to secure new business. Strategy consulting firms and auditors, for example, invariably set strict codes of business conduct concerning misrepresentation and confidentiality of client data. There is good reason for this. Imagine how long McKinsey & Company or PricewaterhouseCoopers could retain their market franchises if clients suspected that key strategic data, gathered during a consulting assignment or audit, was being leaked to competitors. Their franchise—and their ability to attract and retain clients—would be significantly impaired. Accordingly, in these firms any activity that could jeopardize their reputation for integrity is declared off-limits.

Similarly, professions that depend on public trust always insist upon compliance with a code of business conduct as a condition of membership. Accountants, lawyers, physicians, and other professions diligently safeguard their reputation by codifying rules of professional conduct. These boundaries articulate the types of behavior that could damage the image of the profession and, therefore, must be avoided by its members. For example, the Standards of Ethical Conduct for Management Accountants state in part that members must:

- avoid actual or apparent conflicts of interest and advise all appropriate parties of any potential conflict
- refrain from engaging in any activity that would prejudice their ability to carry out their duties ethically
- refuse any gift, favor, or hospitality that would influence or would appear to influence their actions
- refrain from either actively or passively subverting the attainment of the organization's legitimate and ethical objectives
- recognize and communicate professional limitations or other constraints that would preclude responsible judgment or successful performance of an activity
- refrain from engaging in or supporting any activity that would discredit the profession[7]

In a survey of profit center managers to investigate the types of situations that lead people to engage in unethical activities, managers reported that they were more likely to manipulate profit figures when competitive environments were highly uncertain.[8] In terms of installing brakes, managers must understand that the *greater the performance pressures and temptations in their business, the greater the need for business conduct guidelines.* Many of the recent frauds and control breakdowns—such as Barings Bank and Kidder Peabody—have been caused by intense performance goals coupled with lucrative incentive performance bonuses. In the trading environments in which money managers and equity traders work, there is always the risk that loosely supervised traders will engage in unethical activities to increase their bonus payouts. In these situa-

---

[7] Institute of Management Accountants (formerly National Association of Accountants), "Statement on Management Accounting: Standards of Ethical Conduct for Management Accountants," Statement No. 1C (New York, 1983).

[8] Kenneth A. Merchant, "The Effects of Financial Controls on Data Manipulation and Management Myopia," *Accounting, Organizations, and Society* 15 (1990): 297–313.

tions, managers must install codes of business conduct that stipulate—in no uncertain terms—the types of behavior that are forbidden. Managers must reduce ambiguity and make it difficult for employees to rationalize dangerous behaviors.

The techniques that we studied in previous chapters—profit plans, balanced scorecards, diagnostic and interactive control systems, performance goals and measures, and incentives—are the tools that managers use to implement strategy. However, they are also precisely the means by which performance pressures and temptations are created. This pressure is generally healthy, because performance pressure breeds innovation. (As a counterpoint, consider how little innovation exists in business settings with no performance pressure, such as protected industries, monopolies, or any government agency that does not face market pressures.) But the harder that managers step on the gas pedal, the more important it becomes to have confidence in the quality and robustness of the business's brakes and boundary systems.

Incentives for Compliance

Like any other control system, rewards and punishments must be aligned with business conduct boundaries, but how should incentives be designed? Is a carrot or stick approach most appropriate for enforcing adherence to boundaries of behavior? (Readers with children will implicitly know the answer to this question.)

In most business situations, there is little reason to reward employees for acting with integrity. Managers should expect nothing less than complete integrity from all subordinates. In fact, the vast majority of employees will, as a matter of personal principle, choose to do what is right without the need for explicit incentives or rewards. To reward integrity would incur costs without any increase in organizational performance.

Therefore, instead of rewarding good behavior, managers generally choose to punish the rare, but significant, instances of noncompliance. For sanctions to be effective, the threat of punishment must be communicated as an inherent part of the business conduct guidelines. Employees must understand that violating these guidelines is grounds for disciplinary action up to and including dismissal. Managers must be clear that sanctions will be enforced on a "no exceptions" basis. In strategy consulting firms, for example, divulging confidential client information brings automatic dismissal with no chance of reprieve. At PricewaterhouseCoopers, the well-known official accountants responsible for tallying the votes for the annual Academy Awards, the rules for staff members are unambiguous: "Discuss the tally with anyone besides your supervisor, and you're fired."[9] Moreover, managers often choose to make an example of people who, through their actions, put the business franchise at risk, so that there can be no mistake about the type of behaviors that are unacceptable.

Business Conduct Boundaries and Organizational Freedom

Like brakes on a car, boundary systems in organizations can be thought of as either constraining (i.e., bringing the car to a stop) or liberating (allowing the car to travel at high

---

[9] Ed Brown, "The Most Glam Job in Accounting," *Fortune* (March 31, 1997): 30.

speed). We have discussed the constraint side of the coin, but we must now turn the coin over to see the other side. In a perverse way, constraint provides the freedom in which creativity can flourish.

Imagine a situation in which you start a new retail sales job at a Boston Retail store. Your first morning on the job, your new boss tells you that there are no rules: "Just do whatever it takes to satisfy a customer," he says. On your first day on the job, you accept a return from a customer who purchased the item two months ago. Later, the store manager berates you and tells you not to accept any returns beyond a 30-day limit. The next day, you do something else—in this case, telling a customer to try a nearby competitor for a desired item that your store does not carry. Again, your boss is disapproving and admonishes you never to do that again. And so on . . . one incident follows the next: when you try something new, the boss is often upset. Soon, you avoid any behavior that could expose you to the risk of embarrassment and sanction. Because you are unsure about the boundaries of acceptable behavior, innovation comes to a halt.

Compare this to another situation in which, on your first day, you are given a sales manual with clear rules as to what is *not* acceptable—return policies, customer service, and so on. After studying the guidelines to ensure familiarity with all store policies, you are confident that you can engage in any practice or innovation that does not contravene a stated policy. Now, when your boss tells you to "do whatever it takes to satisfy a customer," you have the confidence to be creative within a defined sphere of activity. Like the Ten Commandments, once the rules are understood and internalized, they do not seem onerous. The guidelines do not substantively infringe on important freedoms because there is still so much opportunity to act independently and create value for customers *within the stated boundaries.*

Effective business conduct boundaries are often very simple. At Sears, incoming CEO Arthur Martinez has led the drive to replace 29,000 pages of policies and procedures with two very simple booklets called "Freedoms" and "Obligations." Says Martinez, "What you want to preserve are the great qualities of a corporation. Some would define that as tradition, a sense of integrity, or doing what's right. We're trying to tell our managers what they're responsible for, what freedoms they have to make decisions, and where to turn for help. But we don't want to codify every possible situation."[10]

Business conduct boundaries are a powerful way for managers to communicate their beliefs about the importance of integrity. Such guidelines can empower employees to refuse to do what they believe to be wrong—even if ordered to do so by a superior. Mid-level supervisors are themselves often under intense performance pressures and can apply pressure on subordinates to bend the rules to ensure that key diagnostic targets are achieved (e.g., "let's not book that expense until the start of the new fiscal year"). Business conduct boundaries, if published and communicated widely, provide an incontestable defense against these misguided overtures by superiors.

Appendix 13–1 on page 297 summarizes the essential features of beliefs systems and boundary systems.

---

[10] Patricia Sellers, "Sears: In With the New," *Fortune* (October 16, 1995): 98.

INTERNAL CONTROLS

Beliefs systems and boundary systems delineate core values and proscribed behaviors, but management must still guard against both willful violations and unintentional errors in company processes (that is, errors of omission and commission). Data from profit statements, ROI and EVA measures, balanced scorecards, and other measurement systems can be relied upon only if managers have faith in the accuracy of the numbers. However, managers of every business must confront the possibility that errors can creep into accounting and measurement systems. Errors can occur in many ways: untrained staff may process transactions incorrectly, or experienced employees may make unintentional errors in the rush of day-to-day work demands. In rare but potentially costly cases, employees may misappropriate company assets for personal gain and then falsify accounting records to avoid detection.

Because of these inevitable risks, managers of even the smallest business must install controls and safeguards to ensure that all transaction information (e.g., sales receipts) is accounted for properly and that employees are denied the opportunity to inappropriately divert assets to personal use. These systems and procedures are called *internal controls,* which are defined as *the policies and procedures designed to (1) ensure reliable accounting information and (2) safeguard company assets.*

Internal controls can be segregated into three categories of safeguards: **structural safeguards, system safeguards,** and **staff safeguards** (see Figure 13–2). Each of these safeguards is essential in any business where a manager or owner delegates custody of assets and/or the processing of accounting transactions to subordinates.

Structural Safeguards

Structural safeguards—the first category of internal controls—are designed to ensure clear definition of authority for individuals handling assets and recording accounting transactions. Structural safeguards encompass the following:

Segregation of Duties   The cardinal rule of internal control is that one person should never handle all aspects of a transaction involving valuable company assets. In particular, the *accounting* for assets should be done by someone other than the person who has *physical custody* of those assets. **Segregation of duties** requires one person to check or reconcile the work of another. Then, if someone makes an error (or purposely misstates a transaction), the second person will catch the inconsistency when he or she reconciles accounting records with assets on hand or transaction receipts.

Most employee frauds are perpetrated when an individual has access to either cash or securities *and* the ability to record accounting transactions for those assets. Without segregation of duties, an unscrupulous person could manipulate accounting records (e.g., post transactions to the wrong account) to hide the misappropriation of funds. Lack of basic segregation of duties allowed Nick Leeson to make unauthorized security trades and hide his trading losses by making false entries in the accounting records at Barings Bank. Over time, his fraud destroyed a 200-year-old institution.

FIGURE 13–2   Internal Controls: The Foundation of Every Business

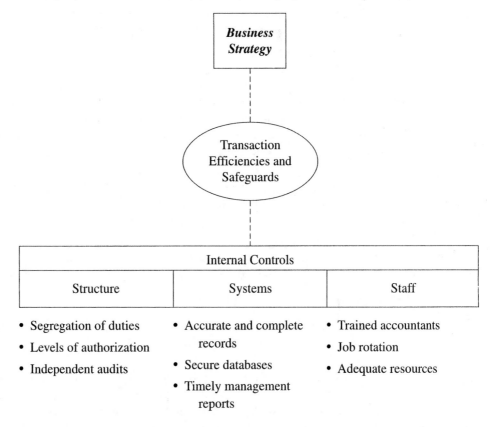

- At Boston Retail, one person deposits daily check receipts in the bank; a second person reconciles bank deposits with check receipt records to ensure that all receipts have been properly deposited.

Defined Levels of Authorization   This principle requires that an individual's access to company funds be commensurate with their level of responsibility, thereby limiting exposure to error or fraud.

- At Boston Retail, check-signing authority permits store managers to sign checks up to $500. Checks for larger amounts must be signed by a company officer.

Physical Security for Valuable Assets   Valuable assets subject to theft should always be protected by vaults, gates, and locked storerooms. Access to these assets should be restricted to those employees accountable for any loss. Many companies, for example, hold bearer bonds in bank vaults. The bank is typically given instructions to open the vault only if two designated company officials are present so that each official can independently verify that bonds are properly handled and accounted for.

When valuable assets cannot be easily counted and reconciled, direct surveillance becomes necessary to ensure that individuals are adequately safeguarding the assets. Thus, highway toll collectors are watched by camera surveillance in their toll booths.

- At Boston Retail, cash receipts are collected every two hours and deposited in a locked safe in the back of each store.

Independent Audit All firms should use external auditors—certified public accountants (called chartered accountants in Commonwealth countries)—to examine the integrity of the firm's internal controls. As part of their review, auditors examine asset security and the integrity of accounting information. Their findings are reported to senior managers and the board of directors, who are responsible for correcting deficiencies.

The board of directors is ultimately responsible to shareholders for the integrity of internal controls. In larger companies, directors typically choose their most experienced members to form an audit committee to oversee the work of the independent auditors.

- Boston Retail employs a respected accounting firm to audit its financial statements and annually review the adequacy of its internal controls. As part of their review, the auditors provide recommendations to management on how to improve internal controls.

Systems Safeguards

Systems safeguards are designed to ensure adequate procedures for transaction processing, as well as timely management reports. Systems safeguards encompass the following:

Complete and Accurate Record Keeping Procedures must ensure that all transactions are recorded accurately and promptly in the accounting records. Accounting data becomes worthless for management purposes if it is not accurate and timely. To allow verification and reconciliation of data, there must be an adequate trail of documents (or electronic entries) so that it is possible to track each transaction back to its source. Thus, it should be possible to trace a customer payment back to an accounts receivable statement, which in turn can be traced back to a sales invoice and shipping record.

- Boston Retail's controller balances the general ledger each month and reconciles the bank account and accounts receivable ledger to ensure that all double-entry accounting transactions are accurate.

Restricted Access to Information Systems and Databases Integrity of accounting data can only be assured if access to information systems is restricted to those who have a legitimate right to change or view accounting transaction records. In an electronic age, this requires secure databases that prevent unauthorized access or tampering. Several years ago, Citibank's computer systems were infiltrated by a hacker based in Moscow. Using illicitly obtained access codes, he was able to shift money among bank accounts. Passwords, data encryption, and internal verification routines are necessary to ensure the integrity of information.

- The ability to access accounting systems and to process adjustments in each of Boston Retail's stores is limited by password to the store manager. Passwords are changed monthly.

Timely Management Reporting   Managers should receive accounting and control reports soon after the data is processed. If reports are not timely, feedback may be too late to act upon, and the business may be vulnerable to losses and/or poor management decisions based on faulty information.

- The founders at Boston Retail receive an income statement and balance sheet by the eighth working day after each month's end. In addition, they receive sales figures from each store on a weekly basis (daily during the critical holiday season). Bank reconciliations are reviewed monthly.

Staff Safeguards

Staff safeguards are designed to ensure that accounting and transaction-processing staff have the right level of expertise, training, and resources. Staff safeguards encompass the following:

Adequate Expertise for Accounting and Control Staff   The design and operation of good internal controls requires significant technical expertise. This expertise is offered by accounting professionals such as certified public accountants (CPAs) and certified management accountants (CMAs), who are trained in the design of effective internal control systems.

- Managers at Boston Retail are struggling with a decision regarding the possible replacement of the firm's controller, who was hired when the business was small. The increasing complexity of growing operations has outstripped his skills and abilities. The founders have engaged an accounting search firm to identify a candidate with professional accounting certification to assume a newly created position of vice president finance.

Rotation in Key Jobs   If an employee is hiding accounting irregularities, an independent person who is asked to take over that job for a period of time will usually discover the discrepancies. Accordingly, it is good practice to insist that employees with access to critical accounting records take regular vacations. During their absence, someone else should assume their responsibilities. The $1.1 billion fraud at Daiwa Bank was concealed when an employee, with access to company bonds, sold the bonds to cover his trading losses. Because he had entered false accounting transactions to cover his trail, he did not take an extended vacation for more than 11 years. Why? He could not afford the risk that someone would take over his work and discover the irregularity. During this time, senior management praised his dedication to the company.[11]

- Managers at Boston Retail rely on their auditors to verify the probity of the accounts. Because of the business's small size, they believe that it is impractical to rotate employees between key accounting jobs.

Sufficient Resources   Internal controls cost money. Accounting professionals must be hired, systems installed, and clerical staff trained to perform reconciliations and checks.

---

[11] Jathon Sapsford et al., "How Daiwa Bond Man in New York Cost Bank $1.1 Billion in Losses," *The Wall Street Journal* (September 27, 1995): A6.

Segregation of duties requires two people to perform a job that could be done by one person alone. Yet, the additional work of reconciliation and checking does nothing to increase the output efficiency of the business; it only provides assurance that assets are secure and information is accurate.

Accounting firms have reported a greatly increased number of material errors and frauds over the past decade as many firms have reengineered their internal processes. Reengineering and downsizing often eliminate redundancy and middle management positions that would otherwise provide an independent check of transaction processing accuracy. Accordingly, great care must be taken to ensure that internal controls remain adequate as businesses streamline processes to become more efficient.

- The founders at Boston Retail have devoted additional staff resources to internal controls after their bank manager told them how a business similar to theirs was forced into bankruptcy by the misappropriation of more than $1 million by a dishonest employee who was stealing money to cover gambling debts.

Responsibility for Internal Controls

Internal controls guard against errors of all kinds. Good internal controls provide the checks and balances to assure managers that errors will not creep into critical operating systems and unauthorized actions will not be allowed to impair assets. They also deny the opportunity to anyone who might be tempted to misrepresent data or misappropriate assets. Although essential in any business, internal controls are especially important where operations risk and asset impairment risk interact with rapid growth. In these situations, errors of omission and commission are both more likely and more costly.

Business managers typically spend little time either designing or overseeing internal control systems. Instead, they delegate this responsibility to trained accountants and auditors. Managers should be aware, however, that if there is ever a significant financial or operating loss due to poor internal controls, they must shoulder the responsibility. Because internal control systems are essential for the security of assets and the integrity of performance information, managers are accountable for ensuring these controls are in place. Thus, business managers must be sure that sufficient resources are devoted to operating these controls effectively.

In large firms, failures in internal controls can lead to financial loss, embarrassment, and, sometimes, the end of promising careers. (Look at the front page of *The Wall Street Journal* to see how many business failures are due to failed internal controls.) In small start-up entrepreneurial firms, inadequate internal controls are sometimes enough to propel the business into bankruptcy. As a result of these risks, large public accounting firms are increasingly refusing to audit businesses with weak internal controls or those where they believe that managers may choose to circumvent controls because of performance pressures.[12]

---

[12] Elizabeth McDonald, "More Accounting Firms Are Dumping Risky Clients," *The Wall Street Journal,* (April 25, 1997).

Assumptions Underlying Internal Controls

Appendix 13–2 on page 298 analyzes the assumptions that are critical to the effective functioning of internal control systems. A self-assessment tool is also provided in the appendix for you to test your own beliefs about the nature of human activity in organizations and the implications of these assumptions for effective internal controls. Appendix 13–3 on page 300 summarizes the essential features of internal control systems for reference purposes.

STRATEGIC BOUNDARIES

Beliefs systems, business conduct boundaries, and internal controls deal primarily with the risks that people will make errors or the wrong choices in balancing profit, growth, and control. However, there is another kind of risk that is just as dangerous for long-term profitability and growth—the risk of wasting scarce resources on initiatives that do not support the business's strategy. Does it make sense, for example, to have the managers of an electric utility spend their time trying to build a database business for libraries? Or, for a consumer products company to attempt to run an airline or hotel business? If managers constantly encourage people to look for new opportunities, how can they ensure that subordinates will not waste their time pursuing initiatives that senior managers have no desire or intention of supporting? The dilemma comes back to one of the basic tensions of high-performance organizations: there are too many promising opportunities in the market and too little management attention to go around. The worst thing that managers can do in these situations is to sprinkle a little attention and resources over so many opportunities that no single initiative gains sufficient momentum and resources to allow success.

The basic principle underlying strategic boundaries is straightforward and should be familiar from our earlier discussion. Because managers cannot anticipate all the opportunities that employees can identify or create, it does not make sense to try to enumerate in detail *how* individuals throughout the business should create value in the marketplace. Let them exercise their initiative and creativity to figure out the best way of responding to customer needs and/or configuring internal processes for maximum efficiency and effectiveness. However, managers must recognize that unfocused initiatives can waste both financial resources and management attention—both scarce resources. Therefore, to ensure that individuals throughout the organization are engaged in activities that support the basic strategy of the business, senior managers should state what types of business opportunities should be avoided, thereby drawing a "box" around the opportunities that individuals are encouraged to exploit. The resulting **strategic boundaries** implicitly define the desired *market position* for the business.

More than fifty years ago, Chester Barnard, an influential management theorist, wrote, "The power of choice is paralyzed in human beings if the number of equal opportunities is large. . . . Limitation of possibilities is necessary to choice. Finding a reason why something should *not* be done is a common method of deciding what should be done. The processes of decision . . . are largely techniques for narrowing choice."[13]

Consider the following strategic boundaries that managers of different businesses have installed to focus opportunity-seeking behavior:

- Jack Welch, CEO of General Electric, communicated clearly to all employees that he will not support investment in any business that cannot attain a number one or number two competitive position in its market.
- A large computer company developed a matrix of all anticipated business opportunities that might be pursued during the coming planning cycle. Opportunities were then color coded as "green space" or "red space." Green space represented opportunities that were to be pursued aggressively; those colored red were declared off-limits.
- Automatic Data Processing, the largest U.S. payroll processing company, maintained a list of key requirements for investment in any business opportunity. The requirements related to revenue and growth potential, competitive position, product attributes, and management strength. Failure to meet the necessary minimum requirements for any of these "hurdles" resulted in divestment of the business.
- During Chrysler's dramatic turnaround, CEO Lee Iacocca decided to refocus the firm's resources on North American auto and truck manufacturing. All European, African, and nonautomobile businesses were declared off-limits. As a result, international and tank businesses were sold off, and the firm exited its leasing business.

Each of these examples illustrates how managers used strategic boundaries to communicate direction and maximize their ROM. Effective managers want to make all organizational energy as productive as possible by ensuring that people are devoting their full attention to implementation of intended strategy. At the same time, senior managers do not want to spend all their time looking over the shoulders of subordinates to ensure that initiatives fit with the strategic direction. Therefore, based on their unique strategy—how they want to create value for customers and differentiate their products and services—effective managers specify the opportunities that do not align with the strategy and declare them off-limits.

Strategic Boundaries at Microsoft

Even Bill Gates, founder and CEO of Microsoft—and one of the world's richest men—is clear in terms of business opportunities that are off-limits:

> To be very clear, we are not going to own any telecommunications networks—phone companies, cable companies, things like that. We're not going to build hardware—the computer makers and consumer electronics companies will do that. We're not going to do system integration or consulting for corporate information systems . . . . I don't think companies like Andersen Consulting or EDS will see us as competing in that domain.

Source: Brent Schlender, "What Bill Gates Really Wants," *Fortune* (January 16, 1995): 40.

---

[13] Chester I. Barnard, *The Functions of the Executive* (1938; reprint, Cambridge, Mass.: Harvard University Press, 1968): 14.

Consider a bank that attempted to implement a new strategy focusing on private banking services for wealthy individuals. Senior managers segmented their market to focus resources on clients who could generate at least $5,000 in recurring annual net revenue. Existing clients who did not meet this profile were to be pruned so that all energy could be focused on the target market segment. In a meeting with branch managers to discuss the implementation of the new strategy, a branch manager asked, "What happens if an individual who we will never see again walks into my branch and wants to do a one-time foreign exchange transaction that will generate fees of $2,000? Do you really want me to send that customer away?"

The answer to the question was "Yes!" Above all else, senior managers wanted to avoid the myriad day-to-day distractions that could sap organizational attention from the new strategy. Managers worried that each transaction might look attractive on its own merits, but at the end of the day, employees would have been so distracted that they failed to devote enough attention to the clients who were critical to the new strategy. Each decision to pursue an opportunity—as good as that short-term opportunity might appear—has costs in terms of drawing away scarce attention. When attempting to implement a clear strategy, these "opportunity costs" are extremely high, but they may not be obvious to employees faced with what appears to be an easy way to create some short-term value.

Harold Geneen, the legendary CEO of ITT, described how he created a strategic boundary that forbade work on any initiative having to do with the development of computers:

> The road you don't take can be as important in your life as the one you do take. In the very early sixties, when computers were seen as the wave of the future, many of our engineers, particularly those in Europe, were eager to surge into this new, phenomenal field. Our German company, which was far ahead of the others in computer development, outbid IBM and won a contract to build a computerized reservation system for Air France. We lost $10 million on that contract. I called a halt to further computer development.
>
> I withstood a great deal of pressure at the time to enforce my early prohibition against the development of general-purpose computers at ITT. Not only our engineers but our investment advisors favored computer development. Everyone who could was going into computers, they said. The mere announcement would send our stock up, they promised. I stood firm.[14]

Communicating Strategic Boundaries

Managers usually find it relatively easy to define what they want their organization to achieve in terms of high quality, excellent customer service, superior products, and new markets. However, effective managers know that attempting to be all things to all people in every market is a surefire recipe for lackluster profitability and growth. Choices must be made—in fact, *choice is the essence of strategy.* If there is no choice, there is no strategy.

---

[14] Harold Geneen, *Managing* (New York: Avon Books, 1984): 219–220.

Strategic Boundaries at Daimler-Benz

Jürgen Schrempp, chairman of Daimler-Benz, the holding company of Mercedes, has built a reputation as a tough manager since he took over in May 1995. At the time, Daimler-Benz was a diverse conglomerate with businesses from cars to aerospace, electronics, and software development. Several divisions were reporting losses and ROCE was dismal.

When Schrempp took over the conglomerate, he started by focusing management attention on those businesses where it had a competitive advantage and sold off the rest. For the divisions that Daimler-Benz kept, he established a cutoff point: for a business to stay inside Daimler-Benz, it would have to earn at least 12% return on its capital employed. Divisional managers would be required to meet this target if they wanted to keep their position. In addition, he negotiated with unions an incentive program for each of the 140,000 employees based on their contribution to the overall performance of the company.

Source: Adapted from *Fortune* (November 10, 1997): 144–152.

The hard work of strategy is deciding what *not* to do. Effective strategic boundaries clarify and communicate strategic choice in terms of desired market position. In small firms, this communication can be informal. At Boston Retail, the communication was simple: We will not support any products that we would not own and wear ourselves.

As businesses grow larger and more dispersed, however, the communication must be formalized. Senior managers must be willing to bear direct scrutiny of their choices regarding strategic boundaries and the opportunities that are to be left behind. For example, the following strategic boundaries are often communicated as part of a formal planning process:

1. Minimum Levels of Financial Performance   Employees throughout the business are informed about the minimum financial requirements that are prerequisites for continued investment in a business. Recalling our discussion of the profit wheel, cash wheel, and ROE wheel, key financial indicators can include, for example:

- revenue potential
- profit and profitability
- asset utilization ratios
- cash flow and payback

2. Minimum Sustainable Competitive Position   Employees throughout the firms should know in advance the types of market positions that senior managers will not support. Jack Welch will not fund any business that cannot reach a number one or number two share position. In a smaller entrepreneurial business, managers may insist that no business opportunity be funded unless it can sustain a critical growth rate.

3. Products and Services That Do Not Draw on Core Competencies   Successful managers understand their business's distinctive competencies and seek to exploit these capabilities. Strategic boundaries enumerate the types of products and services that do not exploit core competencies so that employees can avoid opportunities that will distract attention from the core strengths and strategy of the business.

4. Market Positions and Competitors to be Avoided   In many industries, certain competitors with powerful resources and deep pockets dominate segments of the market (e.g., Microsoft in operating systems). Managers of smaller firms know that they cannot win an open battle with these competitors. Often, managers will set strategic boundaries that warn employees to avoid market positions that will result in head-on competition with these competitors.

It is important to understand that strategic boundaries such as those listed above stipulate necessary—but not sufficient—conditions for investing in or continuing to support a business opportunity. If a boundary condition is met, this does not imply that top managers will necessarily support the initiative—only that it has passed the basic hurdle. Before any final decision to commit resources, managers must apply the analytic techniques covered earlier in the book (SWOT analysis, asset allocation analysis, profit wheel analysis, and balanced scorecard analysis) to ascertain whether investment is justified.

Boundary Systems and Staff Groups

Boundaries—both business conduct and strategic—are established by senior managers who are in a unique position to appreciate the risks that derive from innovation and high-performance strategies. To ensure that these boundaries achieve their desired effect, however, managers must rely on staff groups for two critical tasks: communication and monitoring.

Staff specialists are usually assigned responsibility for codifying codes of business conduct (often with the help of legal counsel) and distributing them widely on a periodic basis. Managers should review drafts to be sure they are adequate and insist on modifications based on past or anticipated franchise risks. In addition, dedicated staff specialists often set up procedures whereby recipients of business conduct guidelines are required to periodically sign a document confirming that they understand the guidelines and are abiding by them.

Information contained in these codes of conduct and planning guidelines is communicated regularly, and feedback is received by staff specialists for processing. Deviations can be acted upon, and it is here that staff groups serve a second important role—as policemen. Some firms employ special staff members known as *ombudsmen,* who are responsible for receiving formal complaints dealing with potential infringement of codes of business conduct. These staff groups follow up on all leads and allegations and ensure that the business franchise is not being compromised by the actions of any employee.

Strategic boundaries are different. These boundaries are at the heart of establishing market positions. They implicitly define strategy. Therefore, strategic boundaries are invariably set by top managers, not by staff assistants. However, staff groups can be given

TABLE 13–1 Tasks for Managers and Staff Groups in Communicating Beliefs and Boundaries

	MANAGERS	STAFF GROUPS
Beliefs Systems	Personally prepare substantive drafts of beliefs statements Communicate message and importance	Facilitate awareness and communication through distribution of documents, education programs, and organizational surveys
Boundary Systems	Personally prepare strategic boundaries Review business conduct boundaries compiled by staff groups Mete out punishment personally to offenders	Prepare business conduct boundaries Communicate both strategic and business conduct boundaries Educate organization about important boundaries Monitor compliance

Source: Adapted from Simons, *Levers of Control,* p. 170.

responsibility to communicate the types of strategic initiatives that top managers will not support—minimum levels of financial performance, minimum sustainable competitive position, and products, service, and markets to be avoided. Most commonly, these boundaries are formalized and distributed as part of an annual strategic-planning process. Staff groups are also asked to police compliance with these boundaries to ensure that no one is surreptitiously pursuing opportunities that have been declared off-limits. Harold Geneen described how he relied on staff assistants to monitor compliance with his strategic boundary forbidding work on computers:

> Others continued to work on computer development for us on the sly. When I learned of this, I hired two very competent engineers and gave them a special assignment which lasted for several years: to roam at will through our worldwide engineering and new products laboratories and to root out, stamp out, and stop all incipient general-purpose computer projects by whatever code name they were called; and if they were given any trouble to call us at headquarters and we would stamp them out for them.[15]

Table 13–1 provides a summary of the roles and responsibilities for operating managers and staff groups in designing and using beliefs systems and boundary systems.

Risks in Setting Strategic Boundaries

As stated previously, the hard work of strategy is not in specifying what you want to do, the hard work is deciding and communicating what you do *not* want to do. Managers find it easy to use broad generalizations for strategy that focus on such things as "excel-

---

[15] Geneen, p. 220.

lence" or "delighting customers." No one is likely to object or disagree with these expansive strategy statements contained in mission statements or other beliefs systems.

On the other hand, it is much more difficult to specify "we will turn away a customer who cannot generate $5,000 in annual fee revenue," or "we will not fund any products that cannot be mass-produced." With these types of statements there can be no ambiguity in specifying the types of opportunities to avoid. In setting strategic boundaries, managers are forced to make explicit their choices in guiding the strategic direction of the business.

However, there is also significant risk in specifying in stark terms the opportunities that are to be avoided without periodically revisiting that decision. History is littered with businesses where managers were slow in seeing changes in their competitive environments and, accordingly, did not adjust their strategic boundaries in a timely fashion. Wang Computers, for example, maintained a clear strategic boundary that it would not compete in any part of the computer market where IBM was a dominant player. During its formative years, this strategic boundary allowed Wang to build a profitable niche franchise in the dedicated word-processing market, where IBM had chosen not to compete. However, as technology evolved, Wang failed to adjust its strategic boundary. Advancements in hardware and software allowed personal computers to host word-processing software, and Wang's fortunes declined rapidly, resulting ultimately in bankruptcy.

The implication is not that strategic boundaries are inappropriate. They are *essential* to achieve maximum performance potential, but any static strategy is doomed to failure over time. The brakes must be adjusted periodically to ensure that they are properly aligned with changes in technology, industry dynamics, and new ways of creating value in the marketplace.

CHAPTER SUMMARY

Effective managers attempt to eliminate opportunities that could bring unwanted levels of risk. To do so, managers should communicate formal beliefs and business conduct boundaries. Beliefs and core values—enumerated in missions, credos, and statements of purpose—are the essential foundations for any high-performance organization. Boundary systems linked to clear, enforceable sanctions are especially important when difficult performance goals are set and rewards are linked tightly to performance. It is in these challenging circumstances that individuals may be tempted to bend the rules to achieve difficult targets.

Also, managers of all businesses, large and small, install internal controls—the formal procedures that protect assets and the integrity of management information. Internal controls provide the checks and balances to ensure that errors of omission and commission cannot slip undetected into the transaction processing stream. Effective structural safeguards (such as segregation of duties), system safeguards (e.g., accurate record keeping and documentation), and staff safeguards (for example, adequate expertise and rotation in key jobs) limit the possibility that someone might make an unintentional error—or worse—that could expose the business to risk.

Finally, managers often impose boundaries on strategic activity. The objective of strategic boundaries is to limit the areas in which employees will look for opportunities and commit scarce resources. To ensure adequate controls on creativity and entrepre-neurial activities, managers must also communicate the types of behaviors and opportu-nities that do not align with the strategy and are, therefore, off-limits. Like boundaries on business conduct, the focus is on enumerating how the business will *not* compete and the kinds of opportunities that subordinates must *avoid*.

Creating boundaries involves choice—but choosing is the essence of strategy. It is often uncomfortable for managers to take the risks of declaring clear intentions, but it is the only sustainable path to effectively balancing profit, growth, and control.

APPENDIX 13–1 Building Block Summary for Beliefs Systems
and Boundary Systems

BELIEFS SYSTEMS	
WHAT	explicit set of beliefs that define basic values, purpose, and direction, including how value is created, level of desired performance, and human relationships
WHY	to provide momentum and guidance to opportunity-seeking behaviors
HOW	mission statements vision statements credos statements of purpose
WHEN	opportunities expand dramatically top managers desire to change strategic direction top managers desire to energize workforce
WHO	senior managers personally write substantive drafts staff groups facilitate communication, feedback, and awareness surveys

BOUNDARY SYSTEMS	
WHAT	formally stated rules, limits, and proscriptions tied to defined sanctions and credible threat of punishment
WHY	to allow individual creativity within defined limits of freedom
HOW	codes of business conduct strategic planning systems asset acquisition systems operational guidelines
WHEN	Business Conduct Boundaries: when reputation costs are high Strategic Boundaries: when excessive search and experimentation risk dissipating the resources of the firm
WHO	senior managers formulate with the technical assistance of staff experts (e.g., lawyers) and personally mete out punishment staff groups monitor compliance

Source: Adapted from Simons, *Levers of Control,* p. 178.

APPENDIX 13–2 Behavioral Assumptions About Internal Controls

Successful managers understand the importance of hiring the right people—those who have natural drives to achieve, contribute, and act with integrity. However, businesses often create confusing tensions and conflicting motivations. Performance pressures, unclear accountabilities, and temptation sometimes cause good people to engage in behaviors that can damage the business.

Internal controls are designed to catch unintentional errors and discourage behaviors that could lead to misappropriation of assets and fraud. In designing these systems, managers must understand the assumptions that accountants make about the interaction of human behavior and internal controls.[16] If any of these assumptions prove false, then internal controls may be rendered ineffective. You can test your own beliefs regarding these assumptions by completing Table 13–2 on the opposite page. The assumptions underlying internal control systems are the following:

1. *Individuals have inherent moral weaknesses; therefore, internal controls are necessary to safeguard assets and ensure reliable information.* Although managers may believe the best of people—that they want to contribute, achieve, and do right for the business—internal controls assume the worst. This is not to say that everyone will do careless work or take advantage of a situation to steal assets or enter false information. However, internal controls are designed for the exception—those rare, but potentially costly, situations where an individual may fall victim to temptation or pressure.

2. *By the threat of exposure of wrongdoing, an effective internal control system will deter an individual from committing fraud.* Designers of internal controls assume that people will not steal if they risk being caught.

3. *An independent individual will recognize and report irregularities that come to his or her attention.* This assumption—that a second person will uncover and report irregularities—is critical to effective segregation of duties. If irregularities, once discovered, are not reported to senior management, then any independent check will be useless.

4. *Asking someone to assist in defrauding a business is so risky that the probability of collusion between two or more people is low.* Internal control systems assume that employees will report the errors or misbehavior of others. However, if individuals collude to steal assets—for example, if the individual who controls inventory colludes with the person who accounts for that inventory—then no system of internal control can be relied upon to reveal those irregularities.

5. *Formal titles and accountability, as shown on an organization chart, determine who has power in the organization.* Designers of internal control systems assume that power and influence come from the top of the organization. Accordingly, subordinates will pass information about control weaknesses and irregularities up to their bosses.

6. *Records and documentation provide proof of actions and transactions.* Internal controls rely on documents and electronic records for evidence of actual transactions. If documents and records prove to be false or inaccurate, then there can be no assurance that transactions were recorded properly.

7. *There is no inherent conflict between performance goals and the production of reliable information.* Accountants assume that both of these goals—high levels of performance and reliable information—can be achieved simultaneously in organizations.

---

[16] Douglas R. Carmichael, "Behavioral Hypotheses of Internal Control," *The Accounting Review* 45 (April 1970): 235–245. Although this article is almost 30 years old, these behavioral assumptions still underpin all internal control systems.

TABLE 13-2 Assumptions Underlying Internal Controls

These are the common assumptions underlying internal controls in organizations.[a] Do you agree or disagree with each?

1. Individuals have inherent moral weaknesses; therefore, internal controls are necessary to safeguard assets and information.

   ☐ **I agree**

   > **But I would qualify this assumption as follows:**

   ☐ **I disagree**

2. By threat of exposure of wrongdoing, an effective internal control system will deter fraud.

   ☐ **I agree**

   > **But I would qualify this assumption as follows:**

   ☐ **I disagree**

3. An independent individual will recognize and report irregularities.

   ☐ **I agree**

   > **But I would qualify this assumption as follows:**

   ☐ **I disagree**

4. The probability of collusion to commit fraud between two or more people is low because asking someone to assist in collusion is too risky.

   ☐ **I agree**

   > **But I would qualify this assumption as follows:**

   ☐ **I disagree**

5. Formal titles and accountability are the primary source of power in organizations.

   ☐ **I agree**

   > **But I would qualify this assumption as follows:**

   ☐ **I disagree**

6. Records and documentation provide proof of actions and transactions.

   ☐ **I agree**

   > **But I would qualify this assumption as follows:**

   ☐ **I disagree**

7. There is no inherent conflict between performance goals and the production of reliable information.

   ☐ **I agree**

   > **But I would qualify this assumption as follows:**

   ☐ **I disagree**

---

[a] Adapted from Douglas R. Carmichael, "Behavioral Hypotheses of Internal Control," *The Accounting Review* 45 (April 1970): 235–245.

APPENDIX 13–3 Building Block Summary for Internal Control Systems

INTERNAL CONTROL SYSTEMS	
WHAT	systems that safeguard assets from theft or accidental loss and ensure reliable accounting records and financial information systems
WHY	to prevent inefficiency in transaction processing, flawed decisions based on inaccurate data, and fraud

HOW	Structural Safeguards
	    segregation of duties
	    defined levels of authorization
	    restricted access to valuable assets
	    independent internal-audit function
	    active audit committee of the board
	Systems Safeguards
	    complete and accurate record keeping
	    restricted access to information systems and databases
	    relevant and timely management reporting
	    adequate documentation and audit trail
	Staff Safeguards
	    adequate expertise and training for all accounting, control, and internal-audit staff
	    rotation in key jobs
	    sufficient resources

WHEN	at all times in all businesses
WHO	staff professionals (trained accountants, independent auditors) managers usually should not spend much time designing or reviewing the details of internal controls

Source: Adapted from Simons, *Levers of Control,* p. 181.

14

Levers of Control
for Implementing Strategy

I n this final chapter, we recap and summarize the performance measurement and control system tools that are available to managers as they work to achieve their profit goals and strategies. In so doing, we can draw an analogy between a manager and a physician. The physician—through training, internship, and experience—is expected to (1) know how to diagnose the health of a patient, (2) understand the range of treatments and medications that are available for any problems, and (3) possess the skill to apply those treatments and remedies to ensure the ongoing health of the patient. For any manager, his or her business is the patient. Like the physician, the manager is expected to know how to diagnose the health of a business, understand the array of performance measurement and control tools that are available to achieve desired goals, and possess the skill to apply those solutions in different circumstances.

In the sections to follow, we organize the performance measurement and control system tools covered so far in the book into a coherent model called the **levers of control.** Then, we illustrate how a manager, like a physician, can diagnose an organization to determine when and how to apply these levers in differing circumstances to achieve specific profit goals and strategies.

LEVERS OF CONTROL[1]

We have now laid out basic assumptions, built a "tool chest" of performance measurement and control techniques, and illustrated how top managers can use these tools to achieve specific objectives. Each control system or technique was differentiated as much as possible to highlight its unique characteristics and attributes. Now that we have considered each separately, an important proposition can be stated: Control of business strategy is achieved by *integrating the four levers* of beliefs systems, boundary systems, diagnostic control systems, and interactive control systems. The power of these levers in implementing strategy does not lie in how each is used alone, but rather in how they complement each other when used together. The interplay of positive and negative forces creates a dynamic tension between opportunistic innovation and predictable goal achievement that is necessary to stimulate and control profitable growth.

---

[1] The first two sections of this chapter draw from Chapter 7 of Robert Simons, *Levers of Control: How Managers Use Innovative Control Systems to Drive Strategic Renewal* (Boston: Harvard Business School Press, 1995).

Using the Levers of Control to Guide Strategy

Before focusing on the dynamics of the four levers of control, we must revisit the nature of the strategy process. As discussed in Chapter 2, strategy can be described as a plan, a pattern of actions, a product-market position, or a unique perspective. To be effective, the levers of control must recognize the roles of each of these types of strategy.

To aid in the analysis, consider briefly the distinction between intended strategies, emergent strategies, and realized strategies.[2] *Intended strategies* are the plans that managers attempt to implement in a specific product market based on analysis of competitive dynamics and current capabilities. These are the strategies that managers want to achieve. *Emergent strategies,* by contrast, are strategies that emerge spontaneously in the organization as employees respond to unpredictable threats and opportunities through experimentation and trial and error. These are the strategies that were unplanned. **Realized strategies** are the outcome of both streams—that is, what actually

FIGURE 14–1   Relationship Between Levers of Control and Realized Strategies

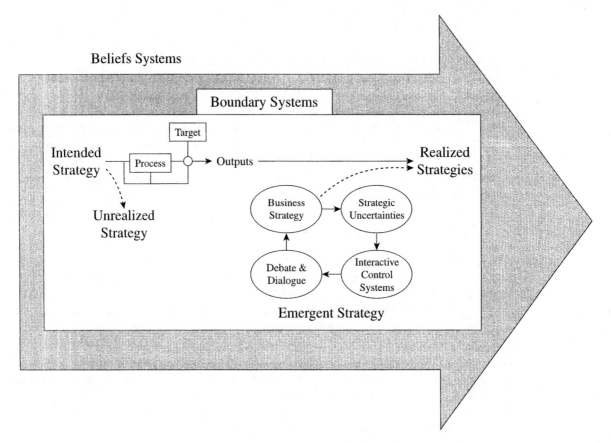

Source: Adapted from Simons, *Levers of Control,* p. 154.

---

[2] Henry Mintzberg, "Patterns in Strategy Formation," *Management Science* 24 (1978): 934–48.

happened. Realized strategies are the combination of intended strategies that were actually implemented and unplanned emergent strategies that occurred spontaneously. This distinction will prove to be important in understanding how the levers can be used to control business strategy (see Figure 14–1).

Diagnostic control systems are the essential management tools for transforming intended strategies into realized strategies: they focus attention on goal achievement for the business and for each individual within the business. Diagnostic control systems relate to *strategy as a plan.* Diagnostic control systems allow managers to measure outcomes and compare results with preset profit plans and performance goals. Without diagnostic control systems, managers would not be able to tell if intended strategies were being achieved.

Some intended strategies, however, may go unrealized; goals may be set inappropriately or circumstances may change, making goal achievement either impossible or less desirable. Some intended strategies are never implemented because unanticipated roadblocks are encountered or resources are insufficient. Again, diagnostic control systems are needed to monitor these situations.

Interactive control systems are different than diagnostic control systems. They give managers tools to influence the experimentation and opportunity-seeking that may result in emergent strategies. At the business level, even in the absence of formal plans and goals, managers who use selected control systems interactively are able to impose consistency and guide creative search processes. These systems relate to *strategy as patterns of action.* Tactical day-to-day actions and creative experiments can be welded into a cohesive pattern that responds to strategic uncertainties and may, over time, become realized strategy.

The beliefs systems of the organization inspire both intended and emergent strategies. Management's vision, expressed in mission statements and credos, motivates organizational participants to search for and create opportunities to accomplish the overall mission of the firm. These systems relate to *strategy as perspective.* Beliefs systems appeal to the innate desires of organizational participants to belong and contribute to purposive organizations. The beliefs systems create direction and momentum to fuse intended and emergent strategies together and provides guidance and inspiration for individual opportunity-seeking.

Boundary systems ensure that realized strategies fall within the acceptable domain of activity. Boundary systems control *strategy as position,* ensuring that business activities occur in defined product markets and at acceptable levels of risk. Without boundary systems, creative opportunity-seeking behavior and experimentation can dissipate the resources of the firm. Boundary systems make explicit the costs that will be imposed on participants who wander outside the boundaries to engage in proscribed behaviors. Table 14–1 summarizes the relationship between the four levers of control and strategy.

Dynamic Interplay of Forces

Strategic control is not achieved through new and unique performance measurement and control systems, but through beliefs systems, boundary systems, diagnostic control sys-

TABLE 14–1 Relating the Four Levers of Control to Strategy

CONTROL SYSTEM	PURPOSE	COMMUNICATES	CONTROL OF STRATEGY AS
Beliefs Systems	Empower and expand search activity	Vision	Perspective
Boundary Systems	Provide limits of freedom	Strategic domain	Competitive position
Diagnostic Control Systems	Coordinate and monitor the implementation of intended strategies	Plans and goals	Plan
Interactive Control Systems	Stimulate and guide emergent strategies	Strategic uncertainties	Pattern of actions

Source: Adapted from Simons, *Levers of Control,* p. 156.

tems, and interactive control systems working together to control both the implementation of intended strategies and the formation of emergent strategies. The dynamic energy for controlling strategy derives from inherent tensions among and within these systems (see Figure 14–2). Two of the control systems—beliefs systems and interactive control systems—motivate organizational participants to search creatively and expand opportunity space. These systems create intrinsic motivation by creating a positive informational environment that encourages information sharing and learning. Beliefs systems and interactive control systems are the positive systems—the yang of Chinese philosophy. The other two systems—boundary systems and diagnostic control systems—are used to constrain search behavior and allocate scarce attention. These systems rely on extrinsic motivation by providing explicit goals, formula-based rewards, and clear limits to opportunity-seeking. Boundary systems and diagnostic control systems are the negative systems—the opposing yin.

As noted earlier, each system is *used* in different ways to leverage scarce management attention and maximize ROM. Diagnostic control systems conserve management attention; interactive systems amplify management attention. Beliefs and boundary systems ensure that core values and rules of the game are understood by everyone in the organization.

Strategic control is achieved, therefore, when the tension between creative innovation and predictable goal achievement is transformed into profitable growth. This tension implies that managers of effective organizations must know how to achieve both high degrees of learning and high degrees of control.

The levers of control are capable of reconciling the tensions between innovation and efficiency. Boundary systems are weighted heavily to control and limits. However, they also reflect learning, because past mistakes and the tactical moves of competitors dictate the adjustment of business conduct and strategic boundaries. Diagnostic control systems clearly emphasize control and efficiency, but setting goals, measuring outcomes, remedying variances, and assigning rewards involve elements of innovation and learning. It is mostly single-loop learning, but, occasionally, double-loop learning

FIGURE 14–2   Levers of Control

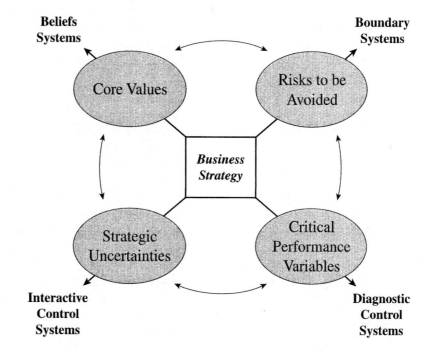

Strategy as "Perspective"
Obtaining Commitment to
    the Grand Purpose

Strategy as "Position"
Staking Out the Territory

*Strategy as
    "Patterns in Action"*
Experimenting and Learning

Strategy as "Plan"
Getting the Job Done

Source: Adapted from Simons, *Levers of Control,* p. 159.

occurs.[3] Interactive control systems also involve both control and learning, although learning and innovation dominate as senior managers use the interactive control process as a catalyst to force the organization to monitor changing market dynamics and motivate debate about data, assumptions, and action plans. Over time, the information and learning generated by interactive control systems can be embedded in the strategies and goals that are monitored by diagnostic control systems.

Not only is there an interplay of motivational forces between the four systems, there is also a tension of motivational forces within each system. Boundary systems, for

---

[3] Chris Agyris and Donald A. Schön, *Organizational Learning* (Reading, Mass.: Addison-Wesley, 1978): 18–20.

example, are powered by both direct threats of punishment and innate desires to do right. Diagnostic systems are motivated by wealth-enhancing economic rewards and innate desires to achieve and be recognized by others. Interactive systems are powered by the personal intervention of senior managers, as well as participants' innate desires to innovate and create.

For any organizational participant at any point in time, countervailing forces are at work. The creative tensions between learning and control, between guidance and proscription, between motivation and coercion, and between rewards and punishment become the yin and yang—the dynamic forces that simultaneously foster both stability and change.

LEVERS OF CONTROL AND HUMAN BEHAVIOR

Managers of any high-performing business know that people are the key to success. Finding, hiring, training, and motivating innovative, opportunity-seeking, entrepreneurial employees is the only way to achieve and sustain competitive advantage in dynamic markets. However, we must also remember the organizational blocks that we identified in Chapter 1. These blocks can easily inhibit the release of productive energy from even the best employees. The organizational blocks to human potential are due primarily to people (1) being unsure of the purpose of the organization and how they can contribute, (2) being subject to pressure and temptation, (3) lacking focus and/or resources, (4) lacking opportunity to innovate, and (5) fearing to challenge the status quo. The levers of control can be used to overcome these blocks if managers are clear about the assumptions they are making about human behavior in organizations.

Assumptions about human behavior entail real risks, risks that flow from the assumptions themselves and risks that the assumptions are wrong. This is the Type I and Type II error problem familiar to students of statistical inference. A Type I error occurs when we reject a hypothesis that is true; a Type II error occurs when we accept a hypothesis that is false.

Suppose that a manager must choose between two models of human behavior and treat subordinates accordingly. The first model postulates that subordinates are honest, hardworking, and fulfill their commitments to the best of their abilities. In this model, subordinates represent potential to be unleashed. The second model views subordinates as inherently dishonest, lazy, and eager to avoid work that involves effort. In this model subordinates require careful monitoring and control.

If a manager chooses the first model when, in fact, subordinates are honest and hardworking, then the manager can unleash the potential of subordinates, who will respond to the opportunity that is provided to them to achieve and contribute.

If a manager chooses the second model when subordinates are actually hardworking and honest, then a Type I error has been made. In this case, subordinates will be denied the opportunity to participate in key decisions for fear that their self-interested behavior will be detrimental to the firm. As subordinates recognize the lack of trust, they will become unwilling to commit and work toward the goals of the organization. Gaming or other dysfunctional behavior will result. Thus, the Type I error becomes a self-fulfilling prophecy that blocks the contribution of subordinates and may lead to negative consequences for the firm.

On the other hand, if the manager believes the first model to be true when subordinates are in fact lazy and adverse to effort, a Type II error has been committed. The actions (or inactions) of the manager will provide an opportunity for subordinates to shirk and potentially misappropriate assets. In this case, the lack of controls and monitoring will allow the self-interested behavior of subordinates to displace organizational goals.

These examples, although clearly stylized and simplistic, illustrate the potential cost and pitfalls of incorrectly specifying human behavior. The assumptions a manager makes about human behavior are critical to the choices that must be made to control strategy.

Of course, there is evidence of both models of behavior in most organizations. Humans value contribution and commitment but also exhibit traits of self-interest. In the absence of leadership and purpose, individuals will inevitably become self-interested and work for their own benefit with little regard to the goals of the organization. Therefore, effective controls must deal with both models.

The model of human behavior adopted in this book reconciles these two views by assuming that people desire (1) to achieve and contribute, (2) to do right, and (3) to create and innovate. We assume lapses in these behaviors are due primarily to organizational blocks, rather than a misspecification of the basic nature of people working inside organizations.

Table 14–2 illustrates the links between these assumptions and managerial action. The first column specifies key behavioral assumptions; the second column lists the organizational blocks that often hinder human potential in organizations. The final two columns provide remedies—both in managerial actions and the levers of control.

Our model of human behavior assumes that people desire to contribute but that organizations often make it difficult for individuals to understand the larger purpose of their efforts or how they can add value in a way that matters. Effective managers recognize these organizational blocks and try to remove them by actively communicating core

TABLE 14–2 Human Behavior, Organizational Blocks, and the Levers of Control

ORGANIZATION MAN/WOMAN DESIRES TO	ORGANIZATIONAL BLOCKS	MANAGERIAL SOLUTIONS	RELEVANT CONTROL LEVER
Contribute	Unsure of purpose	Communicate core values and mission	Beliefs systems
Do right	Pressure or temptation	Specify and enforce rules of the game	Boundary systems
Achieve	Lack of focus or resources	Build and support clear targets	Diagnostic control systems
Create	Lack of opportunity or afraid of risk	Open organizational dialogue to trigger learning	Interactive control systems

Source: Adapted from Simons, *Levers of Control,* p. 173.

values and mission. In small organizations, this can and should be done informally whenever senior managers interact with subordinates. In larger organizations, managers must rely on formal systems (i.e., beliefs systems) to inspire organizational commitment and reduce organizational blocks.

Our model assumes that people desire to act in accordance with the moral codes of our society but that temptations and pressures always exist in organizations, which may lead to cutting corners, diverting assets, or otherwise choosing courses of action that are in conflict with stricter codes of behavior. Managers try to remove these blocks by clearly specifying and unambiguously enforcing the rules of the game. Some behaviors are never tolerated. The firing of the manager who inflated his or her expense report by $100 is a familiar story in many organizations. This action signals that the consequences of stepping over ethical and moral boundaries, even in small ways, are severe and non-negotiable. In larger organizations, managers must rely on formal boundary systems to ensure that these boundaries are communicated and understood.

Our model assumes that people desire to achieve, both for tangible economic benefits and because the satisfaction from achievement can be an end in itself. Unfortunately, organizations can make achievement and the resulting sense of accomplishment difficult. Individuals may not be given the opportunity to focus their energies in ways that permit goals to be achieved and recognized. Often, resources are not available to allow people to rise to their potential. Effective managers attempt to remove these blocks by communicating clear targets and providing the necessary resources for achieving those targets. As organizations grow larger, managers use diagnostic controls to achieve these ends.

Finally, our model assumes that individuals want to innovate and create but that organizations often stifle this innate desire. Individuals either are denied the opportunity to experiment or fear the organizational risks that accompany challenges to the status quo. Effective managers remove these blocks by opening up channels for organizational dialogue and encouraging a learning environment that values dissent and new ideas. When organizations are small, this can be done informally. As organizations grow larger, interactive control systems are the necessary catalyst for learning, experimentation, and information sharing.

Assumptions about human nature are at the core of using the levers of control effectively. Use Table 14–2 to test your own assumptions of human behavior. Do you agree with the assumptions that underlie this theory? If not, what are your assumptions concerning human behavior? What are the implications of your behavioral assumptions for strategy formation and implementation? For empowerment? What are the effects of Type I and Type II errors if your assumptions are incorrect? For any manager, confronting and reconciling unstated assumptions of human behavior are the starting points for realizing human potential in organizations.

APPLYING THE LEVERS OF CONTROL

Now that we have recapped how the levers of control can be used to implement strategy and release productive energy, we will illustrate in the final two sections how managers can use these levers to achieve profit goals and strategies in two different contexts. Performance measurement and control systems are not created equal, and their application at any given point in time depends—like the physician—on diagnosing the life cycle of the business and applying the right control tools and techniques. In the first example, we review how the levers of control can be applied over time as the firm grows and matures. In the second example, we review how newly appointed managers can use the levers of control to take charge of a business and implement their agendas and strategies.

Levers of Control and Organizational Life Cycle

As businesses evolve and grow over time, they progress through a series of predictable life cycle stages. The levers of control must be phased in over the life cycle of the firm to effectively balance profit, growth, and control. As we shall see, the ability to apply the levers of control at the appropriate stage of a business's growth is essential to building a sustainable franchise.

Managers who run small entrepreneurial firms, such as Boston Retail in its early years, can and should control the 4Ps of strategy informally. Formal information systems, with their requirements for staff experts, technology support, and management training, are not necessary. Core values can be communicated effectively by the actions of the founders and reinforced through day-to-day discussions about what they believe to be important. Risks to be avoided can also be communicated easily as the owners learn firsthand—through actions of employees or watching other firms—what kinds of behavior can put the business at risk. Critical performance variables—both financial and nonfinancial—can be monitored informally, without reliance on formal reports and measures. Information about strategic uncertainties can be gathered from a variety of informal sources: customers, trade shows, suppliers, and competitors. This information consists largely of trade gossip and news of emerging developments in the industry. Internal controls can be minimal and yet still be adequate to meet the requirements of auditors and bankers. Any weaknesses in controls can be compensated by the owner's careful scrutiny of most transactions.

As the business grows larger, however, these informal processes become inadequate. Regular face-to-face contact with employees is reduced due to time pressures. More people, more locations, more customers, and more products all pull top managers in too many directions. As a result, it becomes increasingly difficult for managers to communicate information about strategies and plans to employees. It also becomes increasingly difficult for top managers to stay informed about progress in meeting goals and become aware of emerging threats and opportunities.

Breakdowns in control are often the first sign of problems. Errors, bad decisions, missed opportunities, and confusion slowly sap the energy of the organization. Profit margins erode and competitive position worsens. For the business to survive, the informal controls—once sufficient—must now be formalized.

We next discuss three stages in the life cycle of a typical firm: start-up, rapid growth, and maturity. To achieve profit goals and strategies over the different life cycle stages of the firm, managers must learn how to integrate the techniques and tools that we studied in this book. Figure 14–3 presents a simplified view of how the levers of control can be successfully implemented as a business grows and matures.

FIGURE 14–3 Introduction of Control Systems over the Life Cycle of a Business

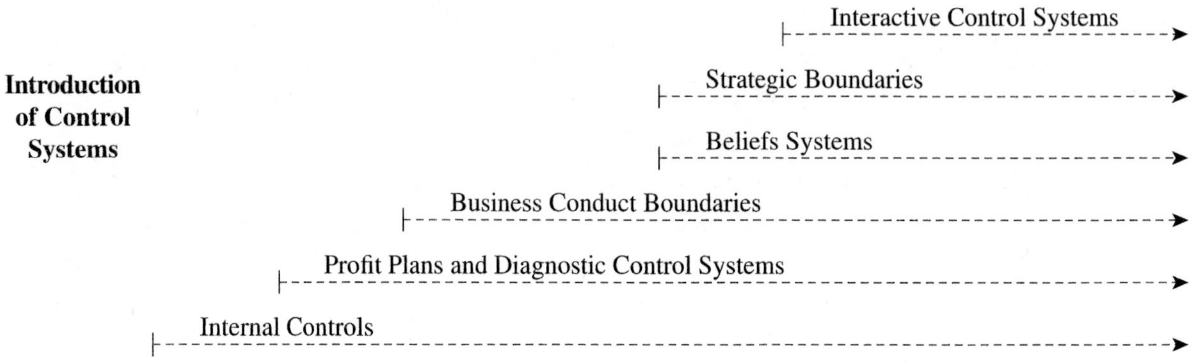
Introduction of Control Systems
Interactive Control Systems
Strategic Boundaries
Beliefs Systems
Business Conduct Boundaries
Profit Plans and Diagnostic Control Systems
Internal Controls

Life Cycle	Small Start-up	Growing		Mature
Organization Structure	Informal	Functional Specialization	Market-Based Profit Centers	Product/Regional/Customer Groupings

Source: Adapted from Simons, *Levers of Control,* p. 128.

Stage 1: Start-Up

In the first stage in any organization's evolution—the start-up period—an intimate sense of purpose pervades the business: commitment is achieved by a sense of enthusiasm about the new product or service. Key measures revolve around revenue growth and cash flow as the business struggles to survive. If the value proposition finds appeal in the marketplace, additional employees are hired to bring products and services to a broader market. Threats and opportunities are acted on quickly as people share ideas and action plans. Everyone pulls together by sharing roles and responsibilities to get the job done.

During the early years of an entrepreneurial firm, there is little need for formal control systems. In even the smallest firm, however, managers must install internal control systems to ensure that assets are secure and accounting information is reliable.

> *At Boston Retail, internal control systems have been put in place by the firm's accountant. The system of internal controls is reviewed and tested each year as part of the annual audit conducted by a firm of independent CPAs hired by the board of directors.*

As discussed previously, as the firm prospers and grows, sooner or later it becomes too large to manage informally. Communication between hierarchical levels and geographic locations becomes increasingly difficult. The founders are no longer able to involve themselves in all key decisions. Without effective performance measures and controls, inefficiencies build and market opportunities are missed.

To sustain growth, entrepreneurs must first install effective profit plans to support management needs for decision making and control. Other diagnostic control systems linked to critical performance variables must also be established, and incentives should be tied formally to the achievement of diagnostic targets. Top managers can then rely on exception reports and strategic variance analysis to monitor the achievement of key outputs and profit plan targets.

As managers introduce these new systems, however, they must also be aware of the risks that they are creating. The imposition of formal performance-evaluation systems linked to incentive rewards has increased the likelihood that some employees might cut corners or misuse company assets. Accordingly, effective managers soon install clear business-conduct boundaries to proscribe behaviors that could expose the firm to business risk.

> *Managers at Boston Retail have built profit plans and set cash flow and ROE objectives. They have established goals for a limited number of nonfinancial performance variables such as store openings and market share. They have used their profit plans to communicate with bankers, shareholders, and important customers. They have analyzed the sources of profitability to ensure that the implementation of their strategy is on track. These plans and goals represent the financial and nonfinancial milestones to be achieved over the coming year.*

Stage 2: Rapid Growth

As the pace of growth increases, new offices are opened and new product lines are launched. To reduce redundancy and increase efficiency, managers create functional work units, each with its own area of specialization. Manufacturing, R&D, marketing, and finance are set up as separate cost centers. Top managers set detailed performance goals, budgets, and incentives for the functional managers who report to them and monitor these systems carefully.

With increasing specialization, efficiencies improve and gross margins increase, allowing both growth and profitability. Unfortunately, the success in driving functional efficiency throughout the business begins to stifle the creativity and initiative that were the hallmarks of the original entrepreneurial business. With narrow specialization and tight functional performance goals, employees find it increasingly difficult to respond creatively to local market conditions. The business begins to lose its vitality and its ability to adapt quickly to market threats and opportunities.

To restore responsiveness and growth at this critical juncture in a firm's life cycle, senior managers must decentralize decision making by creating decentralized accountability structures, such as market-based profit centers. Under the new decentralized structure, profit center managers must be given considerable freedom to run their own businesses to meet local customer needs. They are now responsible for setting business strategy, staffing, and acquiring assets to support local R&D, production, and marketing of their products and services. With empowered profit center managers and an increased focus on local markets, the firm regains its ability to respond quickly to threats and opportunities. Growth again takes hold.

With so much independence in the hands of autonomous profit center managers, however, several additional controls are now needed. First, top managers must create and communicate their core values using formal beliefs systems. Mission and vision statements must be created and communicated to motivate, empower, and supply direction. These formal beliefs systems become critical in instilling shared values among increasingly dispersed employees. Second, managers must clarify and communicate strategic boundaries. With increased delegation of decision rights comes the risk that subordinates will squander scarce resources on opportunities that do not support the overall strategy of the business. Top managers must, therefore, declare certain activities off-limits to avoid distraction, bad investments, and failed projects. Third, accounting measures must focus not only on profitability (i.e., net income as a percent of sales), but also on the assets used to generate those profits. Thus, ROCE and residual income (e.g., EVA) become key measures for evaluating managers and their decentralized businesses. These measures should be augmented by balanced scorecards to communicate corporate strategy and strategic initiatives throughout the business.

The founders of Boston Retail have attempted to define the values and direction of the business by asserting uniqueness, providing prestige to group membership, and using the mission as a symbol to define what the organization represents. Top managers have articulated their core values and beliefs in a simple mission statement:

Boston Retail Clothing was founded to offer young-at-heart customers
the best in fashion, value, and fun. Our employees work together as a team
to listen, learn, and serve to the very best of our ability.
We will not sell products that we would not be proud to own and wear ourselves.
We anticipate fashion trends and ensure that our products lead the way.

The founders have also communicated a concise, yet clear, boundary as part of their mission statement: "We will not sell products that we would not be proud to own and wear ourselves." *By communicating clearly the types of market opportunities that will not be supported, managers hope to be successful in ensuring that Boston Retail's business stays focused on the fashion market that is at the core of its value proposition. Other opportunities, even those that could generate short-term profit, are to be passed over.*

Stage 3: Maturity

The business is now large, mature, and complex—perhaps a Fortune 500 company traded on the New York or NASDAQ stock exchanges. The company has several divisions and competes in multiple product markets. To align span of control, span of accountability, and span of attention, managers group together the disparate business units to form larger market-based sectors, grouping similar businesses by product, region, or customer. New staff groups are created to manage the increasingly important planning systems and to design new asset allocation systems to allocate scarce resources among businesses. Staff specialists ensure that strategic criteria are consistent across the corporation and that appropriate financial hurdles are being consistently met.

In the large, mature firm, senior managers must learn how to rely on the opportunity-seeking behavior of subordinates for innovation and new strategic initiatives. At this point, managers should make one or more control systems interactive. These interactive control systems signal where debate and learning should occur. As a result of top management's interest, the entire organization focuses on strategic uncertainties and their potential effects on the implementation of strategy. Staff groups assist in gathering and facilitating information flows, but, to avoid unneeded bureaucracy, the role of staff groups is carefully constrained.

The transition from one life cycle stage to another, outlined briefly, is not always smooth. In the absence of effective performance measurement and control systems, organizations will often drift into a crisis that can imperil managers, employees, and ultimately the entire business. In some cases, the crisis leads to the hiring of new executives, who are asked to make fundamental changes and restore the business to profitable growth. We can consider this situation next.

TAKING CHARGE OF A BUSINESS

At any point during the life cycle of a business, a new top manager may be hired to take over—either to replace existing managers who failed to achieve profit goals and strategies, or as a result of normal succession planning (i.e., retirement of the previous top manager). In some cases, the mandate of the new managers will be to continue a trajectory of profitable growth. In other cases, they will be hired to turn the business around and restore profitability and growth. To take charge and implement their strategic agenda effectively, managers must know how to use the levers of control. Table 14–3 summarizes how these levers can be used to drive either strategic turnaround or strategic renewal.[4]

Using the Levers of Control to Drive Strategic Turnaround

If the business has failed to achieve profit goals and strategies in the past, the board of directors or executive committee will expect a new manager to turn the business around quickly and set it on a new course of profitable growth. A new manager must act with determination to change routines and strategies that had previously caused the business to underperform. In these circumstances, a new manager can use the levers of control to (1) overcome organizational inertia, (2) communicate the substance of the new agenda, (3) establish implementation timetables and targets, and (4) ensure continuing attention

---

[4] For a complete discussion of how newly-appointed managers use the levers of control, see Robert Simons, "How New Top Managers Use Control Systems as Levers of Strategic Renewal," *Strategic Management Journal 15* (1994): 169–189.

TABLE 14–3 How Newly Appointed Managers Use the Levers of Control

PURPOSE	STRATEGIC TURNAROUND	STRATEGIC RENEWAL
First Twelve Months:		
1. Overcome organizational inertia ↓	Formalize and communicate strategic boundaries	Use diagnostic controls to: • Link bonuses to financial targets • Raise minimum performance levels for financial targets
2. Communicate substance of new agenda ↓	Formalize new strategy and communicate through new mission statements (beliefs systems) Use diagnostic control systems in presentations to superiors	Issue planning guidelines to subordinates outlining new strategic initiatives
3. Establish implementation timetable and targets ↓	Based on commitments made to superiors, fix accountability targets with subordinates Link diagnostic control system targets to critical performance variables	Use diagnostic control system targets to teach and test new agenda Link diagnostic control system targets to critical performance variables
4. Ensure continuing attention through incentives ↓	Alter bonus incentives to be subjectively determined based on allegiance to new strategic agenda	Alter bonus incentives to be formula-based and linked to new, more-demanding financial targets Institute business conduct boundaries in response to control system manipulation
Second Twelve Months:		
5. Focus organization learning on strategic uncertainties associated with vision for the future	Begin using one control system interactively to signal priorities and motivate debate and dialogue	Begin using one control system interactively to signal priorities and motivate debate and dialogue

Source: Adapted from Simons, *Levers of Control,* p. 150.

through incentives. A new manager can use the levers of control to accomplish these objectives as follows:

To Overcome Organizational Inertia
- Strategic boundaries can be crafted and communicated to inform employees that the old strategy and assumptions will no longer be tolerated.

To Communicate the Substance of the New Agenda
- A new manager can draft and communicate a new mission and statement of core values to give employees a renewed sense of purpose and direction.
- New managers taking charge can use performance goals to communicate to superiors (that is, the board of directors) the level of achievement that can be expected and the timeframe in which profit goals and strategies will be achieved.

To Establish Implementation Timetables and Targets
- To drive this sense of urgency through the organization, managers can use diagnostic control system goals and targets to communicate to subordinates what is expected of them and the timeframe in which they must achieve key objectives.
- To ensure the implementation of strategic objectives, managers can link diagnostic control system targets to the critical performance variables that underly the strategy (i.e., those performance variables that could cause the new strategy to fail).

To Ensure Continuing Attention Through Incentives
- To gain allegiance to the new agenda, bonus compensation can be determined subjectively, based on the new top manager's perception of the commitment and allegiance of each subordinate to support and work toward the new strategic agenda.

Using the Levers of Control to Drive Strategic Renewal

The issues are different—but no less difficult—for a manager taking over a successful business. He or she will likely want to introduce new strategic initiatives to allow the business to adapt to changing competitive realities. At the same time, because of the success of previous management in achieving profit goals and strategies, employees may be complacent and resist the changes desired by the new manager.

Yet, if a company is to succeed in the future and adapt to changing market conditions, strategic renewal will be necessary. As in the case of strategic turnaround, managers can use the levers of control to: (1) overcome organizational inertia and create a sense of urgency, (2) communicate the new agenda for strategic renewal, and (3) establish implementation timetables and targets.

To Create a Sense of Urgency
- A new manager can break complacency and create a sense of urgency by raising minimum levels of achievement for diagnostic goals and targets—often by benchmarking leading firms in similar industries.
- In addition, management bonuses can be linked by formula to financial targets and critical performance variables that support new strategic initiatives.

To Communicate the New Agenda for Strategic Renewal
- New managers can communicate expectations using top-down performance goals and balanced scorecards.
- Managers can then use the goal-setting process to review and revise the bottom-up goals and initiatives submitted by subordinates. This process can be used to teach subordinates about the new agenda and then test the adequacy of their understanding and response.

To Establish Implementation Timetables and Targets
- To support these actions, managers must ensure that diagnostic control systems are adequate to monitor progress in achieving the new profit goals and strategies. If they are deficient, new systems can be installed.

Focusing on Strategic Uncertainties

Regardless of the mandate of any new top manager—that is, strategic turnaround or strategic renewal—after the new agenda is in place, he or she will want to focus the attention of the entire organization on the strategic uncertainties related to the new strategy. Therefore, top managers can make one or more control systems interactive. These interactive control systems will be used throughout the organization to monitor changes in competitive dynamics and communicate new developments back to senior management. Over time, interactive control systems will allow managers to guide and focus organizational attention and debate so that creative experiments can be welded into a cohesive pattern of action that responds to emerging threats and opportunities.

ACHIEVING PROFIT GOALS AND STRATEGIES

To achieve profit goals and strategies, managers must manage the inherent tensions found within all high-performing organizations. These are the tensions between:

- profit, growth, and control
- intended and emergent strategies
- unlimited opportunities and limited attention
- self-interest and the desire to contribute

Managers must know how to use various performance measurement techniques in combination with the levers of control to overcome these blocks and manage these tensions.

Effective top managers use the levers of control to inspire commitment to the organization's purpose, to stake out the territory for experimentation and competition, to coordinate and monitor the execution of today's strategies, and to stimulate and guide the search for strategies of the future. Managing the tension between creative innovation and predictable goal achievement is the key to profitable growth.

The levers of control, coupled with the performance measurement techniques of Part II—profit planning, variance analysis, corporate performance measures, balanced scorecards, and resource allocation systems—allow managers to effectively take charge and manage a business. Taken as a whole, these performance measurement tools and control systems provide the motivation, measurement, learning, and control that allow efficient goal achievement, creative adaptation, and profitable growth over the life cycle of the firm.

FURTHER READING

Chapter 1: Organizational Tensions to be Managed

1. Argyris, C. 1985. *Strategy, change and defensive routines.* Marshfield, Mass.: Pitman.

2. Argyris, C. 1990. *Overcoming organizational defenses: Facilitating organizational learning.* Needham, Mass.: Allyn and Bacon.

3. Ashforth, B. E., and F. Mael. 1989. Social identity theory and the organization. *Academy of Management Review* 14 (1): 20–39.

4. Deci, E. L., and R. M. Ryan. 1985. *Intrinsic motivation and self-determination in human behavior.* New York: Plenum.

5. Ferris, K. R., and J. L. Livingstone, eds. 1989. *Management planning and control: The behavioral foundations.* Columbus, Ohio: Publishing Horizons, Inc.

6. Herzberg, F. 1966. *Work and the nature of man.* Cleveland, Ohio: World Publishing.

7. Hopwood, A. 1974. *Accounting and human behavior.* Englewood Cliffs, N.J.: Prentice–Hall.

8. Kuhn, R. L., ed. 1988. *Handbook for creative and innovative managers.* New York: McGraw-Hill.

9. Langfield-Smith, K. 1997. Management control systems and strategy: A critical review. *Accounting, Organization and Society* 22 (2): 207–232.

10. Leonard-Barton, D. 1995. *Wellsprings of knowledge: Building and sustaining the sources of innovation.* Boston, Mass.: Harvard Business School Press.

11. Lorange, P., M. S. Morton, and S. Ghosal. 1986. *Strategic control systems.* St. Paul, Minn.: West Publishing.

12. Maslow, A. H. 1954. *Motivation and personality.* New York: Harper & Row.

13. McGregor, D. 1960. *The human side of enterprise.* New York: McGraw-Hill.

14. Merchant, K. A., and R. Simons. 1986. Research and control in complex organizations: An overview. *Journal of Accounting Literature* 5: 183–203.

15. Simons, R. 1995. *Levers of control.* Boston: Harvard Business School Press.

16. Simons, R., and A. Dávila. 1998. How high is your return on management? *Harvard Business Review* 76 (1): 70–80.

17. Stevenson, H. H., and J. C. Jarillo. 1990. A paradigm of entrepreneurship: Entrepreneurial management. *Strategic Management Journal* 11: 17–27.

18. Stevenson, H. H., and D. E. Gumpert. 1985. The heart of entrepreneurship. *Harvard Business Review* 63 (2): 85–94.

19. Vancil, R. F. 1973. What kind of management control do you need? *Harvard Business Review* 51: 75–86.

Chapter 2: Basics for Successful Strategy

1. Andrews, K. R. 1987. *The concept of corporate strategy.* 3rd ed. Homewood, Ill.: Irwin.

2. Burgelman, R. 1996. A process view of strategic business exit: Implications for an evolutionary perspective on strategy. *Strategic Management Journal* 17: 193–214.

3. Collins, J. C., and J. I. Porras. 1994. *Built to last.* New York: Harper Business.

4. Collis, D. J., and C. A. Montgomery. 1998. Creating corporate advantage. *Harvard Business Review* 76 (3): 70–83.

5. Collis, D. J., and C. A. Montgomery. 1997. *Corporate strategy: Resources and scope of the firm.* Chicago: Irwin.

6. Ghemawat, P. 1991. *Commitment: The dynamic of strategy.* New York: Free Press.

7. Itami, H. 1987. *Mobilizing invisible assets.* Boston, Mass.: Harvard University Press.

8. Mintzberg, H. 1987. The strategy concept I: Five Ps for strategy. *California Management Review* 30 (1): 11–24.

9. Mintzberg, H. 1987. Crafting strategy. *Harvard Business Review* 65 (4): 66–75.

10. Mintzberg, H., and J. Waters. 1985. Of strategies, deliberate and emergent. *Strategic Management Journal* 6 (3): 257–272.

11. Porter, M. E. 1980. *Competitive strategy: Techniques for analyzing industries and competitors.* New York: Free Press.

12. Porter, M. E. 1985. *Competitive advantage.* New York: Free Press.

13. Quinn, J. B., and H. Mintzberg. 1991. *Strategy process.* Englewood Cliffs, N.J.: Prentice–Hall.

14. Quinn, J. B. 1980. *Strategies for change: Logical incrementalism.* Homewood, Ill.: Irwin.

15. Rumelt, R. P., D. E. Schendel, and D. J. Teece, eds. 1994. *Fundamental issues in strategy: A research agenda.* Boston, Mass.: Harvard Business School Press.

16. Teece, D. J., G. Pisano, and A. Shuen. 1997. Dynamic capabilities and strategic management. *Strategic Management Journal* 18 (7): 509–533.

17. Wernerfelt, B. 1984. A resource based view of the firm. *Strategic Management Journal* 5 (2): 171–180.

Chapter 3: Organizing for Performance

1. Baiman, S., Larcker, D. F., and Rajan, M. V. 1995. Organizational design for business units. *Journal of Accounting Research* 33 (2): 205–29.

2. Chandler, A. D., Jr. 1962. *Strategy and structure: Chapters in the history of American industrial enterprise.* Cambridge, Mass.: MIT Press.

3. Bruns, W. J., and J. H. Waterhouse. 1975. Budgeting control and organizational structure. *Journal of Accounting Research* 13: 177–203.

4. Bruns, W. J., Jr., and S. M. McKinnon. 1993. Information and managers: A field study. *Journal of Management Accounting Research* 5: 84–89.

5. Chappe, E. D., and L. R. Sayles. 1961. *The measure of management.* New York: Macmillan.

6. Cyert, R. M., and J. G. March. 1963. *A behavioral theory of the firm.* Englewood Cliffs, N. J.: Prentice–Hall.

7. Galbraith, J. 1973. *Designing complex organizations.* Reading, Mass.: Addison-Wesley.

8. Gordon, L. A., and V. K. Narayanan. 1984. Management accounting systems, perceived environmental uncertainty and organizational structure: An empirical investigation. *Accounting, Organizations and Society* 9 (1): 33–47.

9. Lawrence, P. R., and J. W. Lorsch.

1969. *Organization and environment.* Homewood, Ill.: Irwin.

10. March, J. G., ed. 1988. *Decisions and organizations.* New York: Basil Blackwell.

11. March, J. G., and H. A. Simon. 1958. *Organizations.* New York: Wiley.

12. Miles, R. E., and C. C. Snow. 1978. *Organizational strategy, structure, and process.* New York: McGraw-Hill.

13. Mintzberg, H. 1979. *The structuring of organizations.* Englewood Cliffs, N.J.: Prentice–Hall.

14. Nadler, D. A., and M. L. Tushman. 1997. *Competing by design.* New York: Oxford University Press.

15. Ouchi, W. G. 1977. The relationship between organizational structure and organizational control. *Administrative Science Quarterly* 22: 95–113.

16. Perrow, C. 1986. *Organizations: A critical essay.* 3rd ed. New York: Random House.

17. Thompson, J. 1967. *Organizations in action.* New York: McGraw-Hill.

18. Vancil, R. F. 1979. *Decentralization: Management ambiguity by design.* Homewood, Ill.: Dow Jones-Irwin.

Chapter 4: Using Information for Performance Measurement and Control

1. Amey, L. R. 1979. *Budget planning and control systems.* Marshfield, Mass.: Pitman.

2. Anthony, R. N. 1988. *The management control function.* Boston: Harvard Business School Press.

3. Anthony, R. N., and V. Govindarajan. 1998. *Management control systems.* 9th ed. Burr Ridge, Ill.: Irwin McGraw-Hill.

4. Ashby, W. R. 1970. *Design for a brain: The origin of adaptive behavior.* London: Chapman and Hall.

5. Barrett, M. E., and L. B. Fraser. 1977. Conflicting roles in budgeting for operations. *Harvard Business Review* 55 (July–August): 137–146.

6. Eccles, R. G. 1991. The performance measurement manifesto. *Harvard Business Review* 69 (1): 131–37.

7. Eisenhardt, K. M. 1985. Control: Organizational and economic approaches. *Management Science* 31 (2): 134–149.

8. Feldman, M. S., and J. G. March. 1981. Information in organizations as signal and symbol. *Administrative Science Quarterly* 26 (2): 171–86.

9. Itami, H. 1977. *Adaptive behavior: Management control and analysis.* Studies in Accounting Research 15. Sarasota, Fla.: American Accounting Association.

10. Lawler, E. E., III, and J. G. Rhode. 1976. *Information and control in organizations.* Santa Monica, Calif.: Goodyear.

11. Locke, E. A., G. P. Latham, and M. Erez. 1988. The determinants of goal commitment. *Academy of Management Review* 13 (1): 23–39.

12. McKinnon, S. M., and W. J. Bruns, Jr. 1992. *The information mosaic.* Boston: Harvard Business School Press.

13. March, J. G. 1994. *A primer on decision making: How decisions happen.* New York: Free Press.

14. Merchant, K. A. 1985. *Control in business organizations.* Marshfield, Mass.: Pitman.

15. Merchant, K. A. 1997. *Modern management control systems: Text and cases.* Upper Saddle River, N.J.: Prentice–Hall.

16. Ouchi, W. G. 1979. A conceptual framework for the design of organizational control mechanisms. *Management Science* 25 (9): 833–48.

17. Thompson, J. D. 1967. *Organizations in action: Social science bases of administrative theory.* New York: McGraw-Hill.

18. Tushman, M., and D. Nadler. 1978. Information processing as an integrating concept in organizational design. *Academy of Management Review* 3 (3): 613–624.

19. Vancil, R. F. 1979. *Decentralization: Managerial ambiguity by design.* Homewood, Ill.: Dow Jones-Irwin.

Chapter 5: Building a Profit Plan

1. Brownell, P. 1985. Budgetary systems and the control of functionally differentiated organizational activities. *Journal of Accounting Research* 23 (2): 502–512.

2. Brownell, P. 1982. Participation in the budgeting process—When it works and when it doesn't. *Journal of Accounting Literature* 1: 124–53.

3. Govindarajan, V., and A. K. Gupta. 1985. Linking control systems to business unit strategy: Impact on performance. *Accounting, Organizations and Society* 10 (1): 51–66.

4. Kaplan, R. S. 1994. Flexible budgeting in an activity-based costing framework. *Accounting Horizons* 8 (2): 104–109.

5. Hongren, C. T., G. Foster, and S. M. Datar. 1997. *Cost accounting: A managerial emphasis.* 9th ed. Upper Saddle River, N.J.: Prentice–Hall.

6. Emmanuel, C. R., D. Otley, and K. Merchant. 1990. *Accounting for man-*

agement control. London; New York: Chapman and Hall.

7. Lorange, P. 1980. *Corporate planning: An executive viewpoint.* Englewood Cliffs, N.J.: Prentice–Hall.

8. Shields, J. F., and M. D. Shields. 1998. Antecedents of participative budgeting. *Accounting, Organizations and Society* 23 (1): 49–76.

9. Simons, R. 1987. Accounting control systems and business strategy: An empirical analysis. *Accounting, Organizations and Society* 12 (4): 127–43.

10. Simons, R. 1987. Planning, control, and uncertainty: A process view. In *Accounting & Management: Field study perspectives,* eds. W. J. Bruns and R. S. Kaplan. Boston: Harvard Business School Press.

11. Steiner, G. A. 1979. *Strategic planning: What every manager must know.* New York: Free Press.

12. Umapathy, S. 1987. *Current budgeting practices in U.S. industry: The state of the art.* New York: Quorum Books.

Chapter 6: Evaluating Strategic Profit Performance

1. Abarbanell, J. S., and B. J. Bushee. 1998. Abnormal returns to a fundamental analysis strategy. *Accounting Review* 73 (1): 19–45.

2. Barrett, M. E., and L. B. Fraser. 1977. Conflicting roles in budgeting for operations. *Harvard Business Review* 55 (4): 137–146.

3. Garrett, K. 1990. Variance analysis: Uses and abuses. *Accountancy* 106 (1168): 90–91.

4. Hofstede, G. 1968. *The game of budget control.* London: Tavistock.

5. Hunter, K. 1993. Various ways to analyze variance. *Accountancy* 112 (1203): 84–86.

6. Kaplan, R. S. 1994. Flexible budgeting in an activity-based costing framework. *Accounting Horizons* 8 (2): 104–109.

7. Kaplan, R. S. 1983. Measuring manufacturing performance: A new challenge for managerial accounting research. *Accounting Review* 58 (4): 686–705.

8. Kaplan, R. S., and A. A. Atkinson. 1989. *Advanced management accounting.* 2nd ed. Englewood Cliffs, N.J.: Prentice–Hall.

9. Kloock, J., and U. Schiller. 1997. Marginal costing: Cost budgeting and cost variance analysis. *Management Accounting Research* 8: 299–323.

10. Mak, Y. T., and M. L. Roush. 1996. Managing activity costs with flexible budgeting and variance analysis. *Accounting Horizons* 10 (3): 141–146.

11. Mak, Y. T., and M. L. Roush. 1994. Flexible budgeting and variance analysis in an activity-based costing environment. *Accounting Horizons* 8 (2): 93–103.

12. Shank, J. K., and V. Govindarajan. 1993. *Strategic cost management.* New York: Free Press.

13. Shank, J. K., and N. Churchill. 1977. Variance analysis: A management-oriented approach. *The Accounting Review* 5: 950–57.

14. Walsh, F. J., Jr. 1987. Measuring business-unit performance. *Research Bulletin No. 206.* New York: The Conference Board.

15. Shank, J. K., and V. Govindarajan. 1993. *Strategic cost management.* New York: Free Press.

Chapter 7: Designing Asset Allocation Systems

1. Baldwin, Y. C., and K. B. Clark. 1992. Capabilities and capital investment: New perspectives on capital budgeting. *Journal of Applied Corporate Finance* 5 (2): 67–82.

2. Baldwin, Y. C., and K. B. Clark. 1994. Capital-budgeting systems and capabilities investments in U.S. companies after the Second World War. *Business History Review* 68 (1): 73–109.

3. Boquist, J. A., T. T. Milbourn, and A. V. Thakor. 1998. How do You win the capital allocation game? *Sloan Management Review* 39 (2): 59–71.

4. Bower, J. L. [1970] 1986. *Managing the resource allocation decision.* Boston: Harvard Business School Press.

5. Bromiley, P. 1986. *Corporate capital investment: A behavioral approach.* Cambridge: Cambridge University Press.

6. Haka, S. F., L. A. Gordan, and G. E. Pinches. 1985. Sophisticated capital budgeting selection techniques and firm performance. *The Accounting Review* 60 (4): 651–669.

7. Haka, S. F. 1987. Capital budgeting techniques and firm specific contingencies: A correlational analysis. *Accounting Organizations and Society* 12 (1): 31–48.

8. Hertenstein, J. H. 1988. Introductory note on capital budgeting practices. Boston: Harvard Business School Note 188–059.

9. House, C. H., and R. L. Price. 1991. The return map: Tracking product teams. *Harvard Business Review* 69 (January/February): 92–100.

10. Miller, P., and T. O. Leary. 1997. Capital budgeting practices and complementarity relations in the transition to modern manufacture: A field-based analysis. *Journal of Accounting Research* 35 (2): 257–271.

11. Myers, S. and R. A. Brealey. 1996. *Principles of corporate finance.* 5th ed. New York: McGraw-Hill.

12. Porter, M. E. 1992. Capital disadvantage: America's failing capital investment system. *Harvard Business Review* 70 (5): 65–82.

13. Ross, M. 1986. Capital budgeting practices of twelve large manufacturers. *Financial Management* 15 (4): 15–22.

Chapter 8: Linking Performance to Markets

1. Alles, M., and S. Datar. 1998. Strategic transfer pricing. *Management Science* 44 (4): 451–461.

2. Bushman, R. M, R. J. Indjejikian, and A. Smith. 1996. CEO compensation: The role of individual performance evaluation. *Journal of Accounting and Economics* 21 (3): 161–193.

3. Chalos, P., and S. Haka. 1990. Transfer pricing under bilateral bargaining. *Accounting Review* 65 (3): 624–641.

4. Cassel, H. S., and V. F. McCormack. 1987. The transfer price dilemma—and a dual price solution. *Journal of Accountancy* 164 (3): 166–175.

5. Dearden, J. 1969. The case against ROI control. *Harvard Business Review* 47 (3): 124–35.

6. Dearden, J. 1987. Measuring profit center managers. *Harvard Business Review* 65 (5): 84–88.

7. Dechow, P. M. 1994. Accounting earnings and cash flows as measures of firm performance: The role of accounting accruals. *Journal of Accounting and Economics* 18 (1): 3–42.

8. Eccles, R. G. 1985. *The transfer pricing problem: A theory for practice.* Lexington, Mass.: Lexington Books.

9. Grabski, S. V. 1985. Transfer pricing in complex organizations: A review and integration of recent empirical and analytical research. *Journal of Accounting Literature* 4: 33–75.

10. Kaplan, R. S., D. Weiss, and E. Desheh. 1997. Transfer pricing with ABC. *Management Accounting* 78 (11): 20–28.

11. Kovac, E. J., and H. P. Troy. 1989. Getting transfer prices right: What Bellcore did. *Harvard Business Review* 67 (5): 148–154.

12. Lev, B. 1989. On the usefulness of earnings: Lessons and directions from two decades of empirical research. *Journal of Accounting Research,* Supplement: 153–92.

13. Luft, J. L., and R. Libby. 1997. Profit comparisons, market prices and managers' judgments about negotiated transfer prices. *The Accounting Review* 72 (2): 217–229.

14. Rappaport, A. 1986. *Creating shareholder value.* New York: Free Press.

15. Reece, J. S., and W. R. Cool. 1978. Measuring investment center performance. *Harvard Business Review* 56 (3): 28–49.

16. Sahlman, W. A. 1997. How to write a great business plan. *Harvard Business Review* 75 (4): 98–108.

17. Swieringa, R. J., and J. H. Waterhouse. 1982. Organizational views of transfer pricing. *Accounting Organizations and Society* 7 (2): 149–165.

18. Stewart, G. 1991. *The quest for value: A guide for senior managers.* New York: Harper Business.

19. Wenner, D. L., and R. W. LeBer. 1989. Managing for shareholder value—from top to bottom. *Harvard Business Review* 67 (6): 52–66.

Chapter 9: Building a Balanced Scorecard

1. Berliner, C., and J. Brimson. 1988. *Cost management for today's environment.* Boston: Harvard Business School Press.

2. Boivin, D. W. 1996. Using the balanced scorecard: Letters to the editor. *Harvard Business Review* 74 (2): 170.

3. Burgelman, R. 1983. A process model of internal corporate venturing in a diversified major firm. *Administrative Science Quarterly* 28 (2): 223–44.

4. Burgelman, R. 1983. Corporate entrepreneurship and strategic management: Insights from a process study. *Management Science* 29 (12): 1,349–64.

5. Chandler, A. D. 1977. *The visible hand: The managerial revolution in American business.* Cambridge, Mass.: Harvard University Press.

6. Epstein, M., and J. F. Manzoni. 1988. Implementing corporate strategy: From tableaux de bord to balanced scorecards. *European Management Journal* 16: 190–203.

7. Goldratt, E., and J. Cox. 1986. *The goal: A process of ongoing improvement.* Croton-on-Hudson, N.Y.: North River Press.

8. Itami, H. 1987. *Mobilizing invisible assets.* Cambridge, Mass.: Harvard University Press.

9. Heskett, J. L., W. E. Sasser, and L. A. Schlesinger. 1997. *The service profit chain.* New York: Free Press.

10. Hope, T., and J. Hope. 1996. *Transforming the bottom line.* Boston: Harvard Business School Press.

11. Johnson, T. H., and R. S. Kaplan. 1987. *Relevance lost: The rise and fall of management accounting.* Boston, Mass.: Harvard Business School Press.

12. Kaplan, R. S., editor. 1990. *Measures for manufacturing excellence.* Boston, Mass.: Harvard Business School Press.

13. Kaplan, R. S., and D. P. Norton. 1996. *The balanced scorecard: Translating strategy into action.* Boston, Mass.: Harvard Business School Press.

14. Kaplan, R. S., and D. P. Norton. 1996. Using the balanced scorecard as a strategic management system. *Harvard Business Review* 74 (1): 75–85.

15. Kaplan, R. S., and D. P. Norton. 1993. Putting the balanced scorecard to work. *Harvard Business Review* 71 (5): 134–42.

16. Kaplan, R. S., and D. P. Norton. 1992. The balanced scorecard: Measures that drive performance. *Harvard Business Review* 70 (1): 71–79.

17. Lessner, John. 1989. Performance measurement in a just-in-time environment: Can traditional performance measurement still be used? *Journal of Cost Management:* 22–28.

18. Lynch, R. and K. Cross. 1991. *Measure up! Yardsticks for continuous improvement.* Cambridge, Mass.: Basil Blackwell.

19. McNair, C. J., W. Mosconi, and T. Norris. 1988. *Meeting the technology challenge: Cost accounting in a JIT environment.* Montvale, N.J.: Institute of Management Accountants.

Chapter 10: Using Diagnostic and Interactive Control Systems

1. Austin, R. D. 1996. *Measuring and managing performance in organizations.* New York: Dorset.

2. Argyris, C. and A. Schön. 1978. *Organizational learning: A theory of action perspective.* Reading, Mass.: Addison-Wesley.

3. Birnberg, J. G., L. Turopolec, S. M. Young, and J. W. Buckley. 1983. The organizational context of accounting. *Accounting, Organizations and Society* 8 (2/3): 111–138.

4. Chenhall, R. H., and D. Morris. 1986. The impact of structure, environment, and interdependence on the perceived usefulness of management accounting systems. *The Accounting Review* 61 (1): 58–75.

5. Collins, F., O. Holzmann, and R. Mendoza. 1997. Strategy, budgeting, and crisis in Latin America. *Accounting, Organizations and Society* 22 (7): 669–689.

6. Dent, J. F. 1990. Strategy, organization and control: Some possibilities for accounting research. *Accounting, Organizations and Society* 15 (1/2): 3–24.

7. Keller, M. 1989. *Rude awakening: The rise, fall, and struggle for recovery of General Motors.* New York: Morrow.

8. Levitt, B., and J. G. March. 1988. Organizational learning. *American Review of Sociology* 14: 319–40.

9. Lorange, P., M. S. Scott Morton, and S. Goshal. 1986. *Strategic control.* St. Paul, Minn.: West.

10. McKenney, J. L., M. H. Zack, and V. S. Doherty. 1992. Complementary communication media: A comparison of electronic mail and face-to-face communication in a programming team. In *Networks and organizations: Structure, form, and action,* eds. N. Nohria and R. G. Eccles. Boston: Harvard Business School Press.

11. Mintzberg, H. 1994. *The rise and fall of strategic planning.* New York: Free Press.

12. Nohria, N., and R. G. Eccles. 1992. Face-to-face: Making network organizations work. In *Networks and organizations: Structure, form, and action,* eds. N. Nohria and R. G. Eccles. Boston: Harvard Business School Press.

13. Pascale, R. T. 1984. Perspectives on strategy: The real story behind Honda's success. *California Management Review* 26 (3): 47–72.

14. Sathe, V. 1982. *Controller involvement in management.* Englewood Cliffs, N.J.: Prentice–Hall.

15. Sculley, J. 1987. *Odyssey: Pepsi to Apple . . . A journey of adventure, ideas, and the future.* New York: Harper & Row.

16. Simons, R., and H. Weston. 1990. IBM: Make it your business. Case Study 190–137. Boston: Harvard Business School.

17. Simons, R. 1990. The role of management control systems in creating competitive advantage: New perspectives. *Accounting, Organizations and Society* 15 (1/2): 127–43.

18. Simons, Robert. 1991. Strategic orientation and top management attention to control systems. *Strategic Management Journal* 12: 49–62.

19. Tani, T. 1995. Interactive control in target cost management. *Management Accounting Journal* 6 (4): 399–414.

Chapter 11: Aligning Performance Goals and Incentives

1. Antle, R., and Smith, A. 1986. An empirical investigation of the relative performance evaluation of corporate executives. *Journal of Accounting Research* 24 (1): 1–39.

2. Baber, W. R. 1985. Budget-based compensation and discretionary spending. *The Accounting Review* 60 (1): 1–9.

3. Baker, G. P., M. C. Jensen, and K. J. Murphy. 1988. Compensation and incentives: Practice vs. theory. *Journal of Finance* 43 (3): 593–616.

4. Bruns, W. J., ed. 1992. *Performance measurement, evaluation, and incentives.* Boston, Mass.: Harvard Business School Press.

5. Carroll, S. J., and H. L. Tosi. 1973. *Management by objectives: Applications and research.* New York: Macmillan.

6. Fama, E. F., and M. C. Jensen. 1983. Separation of ownership and control. *Journal of Law and Economics* 26 (2): 301–25.

7. Goldratt, E. M., and J. Cox. 1986. *The goal.* Revised edition. Croton-on-Hudson, N.Y.: North River Press.

8. Henderson, R. I. 1989. *Compensation management: Rewarding performance.* 5th ed. Englewood Cliffs, N.J.: Prentice–Hall.

9. Hofstede, G. H. 1968. *The game of budget control.* London: Tavistock.

10. Ijiri, Y. 1975. *Theory of accounting measurement.* Studies in Accounting Research 10. Sarasota, Fla.: American Accounting Association.

11. Ittner, C. D., D. F. Larcker, and M. V. Rajan. 1997. The choice of performance measures in annual bonus contracts. *Accounting Review* 72 (2): 231–255.

12. Keating, S. 1995. *Performance measurement in diversified firms: An investigation of the factors affecting performance measurement quality and choice.* D.B.A. dissertation, Boston: Harvard Business School.

13. Kerr, Steven. 1975. On the folly of rewarding A, while hoping for B. *Academy of Management Journal* 18: 769–83.

14. Kohn, A. 1993. Why incentive plans cannot work. *Harvard Business Review* 71 (5): 54–63.

15. Locke, E. A., and G. P. Latham. 1990. *A theory of goal setting and task performance.* Englewood Cliffs, N.J.: Prentice–Hall.

16. Locke, E. A., G. P. Latham, and M. Erez. 1998. The determinants of goal commitment. *Academy of Management Review* 13 (1): 23–39.

17. Merchant, K. A. and J. F. Manzoni. 1989. The achievability of budget targets in profit centers: A field study. *Accounting Review* 64 (3): 539–558.

18. Merchant, K. A. 1989. *Rewarding results: Motivating profit center managers.* Boston: Harvard Business School Press.

19. Milkovich, G. T., and J. M. Newman. 1990. *Compensation.* 3rd ed. Homewood, Ill.: BPI/Irwin.

20. Hopwood, A. 1972. An empirical study of the role of accounting data in performance evaluation. *Journal of Accounting Research* 10 (Supplement): 156–182.

21. Selznik, P. 1957. *Leadership in administration: A sociological interpretation.* New York: Harper & Row.

22. Stedry, A., and E. Kay. 1966. The effects of goal difficulty on performance. *Behavioral Science* 11 (6): 459–70.

Chapter 12: Identifying Strategic Risk

1. Bernstein, P. L. 1996. *Against the gods: The remarkable history of risk.* New York: Wiley.

2. Bozeman, B., and G. Kingsley. 1998. Risk culture in public and private organizations. *Public Administration Review* 58 (2): 109–118.

3. Chow, C. W., Y. Kato, and K. A. Merchant. 1996. The use of organizational controls and their effects on data ma-

nipulation and management myopia: A Japan versus U.S. comparison. *Accounting Organizations and Society* 21 (2, 3): 175–192.

4. Froot, K. A., D. S. Scharfstein, and J. C. Stein. 1994. A framework for risk management. *Harvard Business Review* 72 (6): 91–102.

5. Gellerman, S. W. 1986. Why 'good' managers make bad ethical choices. *Harvard Business Review* 64 (4): 85–90.

6. Goodpaster, K. 1983. Witness for the corporation. Case Study 284–135. Boston: Harvard Business School.

7. Hellman, T. 1998. The allocation of control rights in venture capital contracts. *Rand Journal of Economics* 29 (1): 57–76.

8. Jackson, S. E., and J. E. Dutton. 1988. Discerning threats and opportunities. *Administrative Science Quarterly* 33 (3): 370–387.

9. MacCrimmon, K. R., and D. A. Wehrung. 1986. *Taking risks: The management of uncertainty.* New York: Free Press.

10. Noreen, E. 1988. The economics of ethics: A new perspective on agency theory. *Accounting, Organizations and Society* 13 (4): 359–369.

11. Osborn, R. N., and D. H. Jackson. 1988. Leaders, riverboat gamblers, or purposeful unintended consequences in the management of complex, dangerous technologies. *Academy of Management Journal* 31 (4): 924–947.

12. Puschaver, L., and R. G. Eccles. 1996. *In pursuit of the upside: The new opportunity in risk management.* Monograph published by Price Waterhouse LLP.

13. Sitkin, S. B., and L. R. Weingart. 1995. Determinants of risky decision-making behavior: A test of the mediating role of risk perceptions and propensity. *Academy of Management Journal* 38 (6): 1,573–1,592.

14. Sitkin, S. B., and A. L. Pablo. 1992. Reconceptualizing the determinants of risk behavior. *Academy of Management Review* 17 (1): 9–38.

Chapter 13: Managing Strategic Risk

1. Barnard, Chester I. 1938. *The functions of the executive.* Cambridge, Mass.: Harvard University Press.

2. Baruch, H. 1980. The audit committee: A guide for directors. *Harvard Business Review* 58 (3): 174–186.

3. Bowdidge, J. S., and K. E. Chaloupecky. 1997. Nicholas Leeson and Barings Bank have vividly taught some internal control lessons. *American Business Review* 15 (1): 71–77.

4. Carroll, A. B. 1975. Managerial ethics: A post-Watergate review. *Business Horizons* 18: 75–80.

5. Collins, J. C., and J. I. Porras. 1994. *Built to last.* New York: Harper Collins.

6. Dezoort, F. T. 1998. An analysis of experience effects on audit committee members' oversight judgments. *Accounting, Organizations and Society* 23 (1): 1–21.

7. Geneen, H., with A. Moscow. 1984. *Managing.* Garden City, N.Y.: Doubleday.

8. Goold, M. 1991. Strategic control in the decentralized firm. *Sloan Management Review* 32 (2): 69–81.

9. Gorlin, R. A. 1986. *Codes of professional responsibility.* Washington, D.C.: The Bureau of National Affairs.

10. Kendall, R. 1998. *Risk management for executives: A practical approach to controlling business risks.* London: Pitman.

11. McNamee, D. 1997. Risk-based auditing. *The Internal Auditor* 54 (4): 22–27.

12. March, J. D., ed. 1988. *Decisions and organizations.* New York: Basil Blackwell.

13. Merchant, K. 1990. The effects of financial controls on data manipulation and management myopia. *Accounting, Organizations and Society* 15 (4): 297–313.

14. Porter, M. E. 1996. What is strategy? *Harvard Business Review* 74 (6): 61–78.

15. Rich, A. J., C. S. Smith, and P. H. Mihalek. 1990. Are corporate codes of conduct effective? *Management Accounting* 72 (3): 34–35.

16. Simons, R. 1995. Control in an age of empowerment. *Harvard Business Review* 73 (2): 80–88.

17. Simons, R., and A. Dávila. 1998. How high is your return on management? *Harvard Business Review* 76 (1): 70–80.

18. Sweeney, R. B. and H. L. Siers. 1990. Survey: Ethics in corporate America. *Management Accounting* 71 (12): 34–40.

19. Vancil, R. F. 1973. What kind of management control do you need? *Harvard Business Review* 51: 75–86.

20. Watson, T. J., Jr. 1963. *A business and its beliefs: The ideas that helped build IBM.* New York: McGraw-Hill.

Chapter 14: Levers of Control for Implementing Strategy

1. Christensen, C. M. 1997. *The innovator's dilemma: When new technologies cause great firms to fail.* Boston, Mass.: Harvard Business School Press.

2. Greiner, L. E. 1998. Evolution and revolution as organizations grow. *Harvard Business Review* 76 (3): 55–68. Originally published in 1972.

3. Flamholtz, E. 1995. Managing organizational transitions: Implications for corporate and human resource management. *European Management Journal* 13 (1): 39–51.

4. Hopwood, A. 1974. *Accounting and human behavior.* Englewood Cliff, N.J.: Prentice–Hall.

5. Kuhn, A. J. 1986. *GM passes Ford, 1918–1938: Designing the General Motors performance-control system.* University Park, Penn.: Pennsylvania State University Press.

6. Langfield-Smith, K. 1997. Management control systems and strategy: A critical review. *Accounting, Organizations and Society* 22 (2): 207–232.

7. Senge, P. M. 1990. The leader's new work: Building learning organizations. *Sloan Management Review* 32 (1): 7–23.

8. Simons, R. 1994. How new top managers use control systems as levers of strategic renewal. *Strategic Management Journal* 15 (3): 169–189.

9. Simons, R. 1995. *Levers of control: How managers use innovative control systems to drive strategic renewal.* Boston, Mass.: Harvard Business School Press.

10. Simon, W. L. 1997. *Beyond the numbers.* New York: Van Nostrand Reinhold.

11. Tushman, M. L., W. H. Newman, and E. Romanelli. 1987. Convergence and upheaval: Managing the unsteady pace of organizational evolution. *California Management Review* 29 (1): 29–44.

GLOSSARY

Note: Chapter references refer to the first time that a term is introduced or defined.

Accountability (Chapter 3) the outputs that a work unit is expected to produce and the performance standards that managers and employees of that unit are expected to meet

Accounting systems (Chapter 1) procedures and mechanisms to collect information about the transactions of a business. Account balances are ultimately summarized in financial statements such as balance sheets, income statements, and cash flow statements.

Activity-based indirect costs (Chapter 5) costs that cannot be traced directly to a product or service, but change with the level of underlying support activities

Asset (Chapter 2) a resource owned or controlled by the entity that will yield future economic benefits. Examples include plant, equipment, cash on hand, and inventory.

Asset allocation system (Chapter 7) the set of formal routines and procedures designed to process and evaluate requests to acquire new assets.

Asset impairment risk (Chapter 12) the risk of deterioration in the value of an asset because of a reduction in the likelihood of receiving future cash flows from the asset

Asset investment plan (Chapter 5) summary of investment in operating assets and long-term assets needed to support a profit plan

Asset turnover (Chapter 5) sales divided by assets is a ratio measure of asset turnover. This ratio answers the question, How many sales dollars did we generate for each dollar that was invested in assets of the business?

Assumptions (Chapter 5) the starting point for any profit plan is a set of assumptions about the future. These assumptions describe the consensus among managers about how various markets — customer, supplier, and financial — will look in the future.

Balanced scorecard (Chapter 9) the multiple, linked objectives that companies must achieve to compete based on capabilities and innovation, not just tangible physical assets. It translates mission and strategy into objectives and measures.

Beliefs system (Chapter 13) an explicit set of organizational definitions that senior managers communicate formally and reinforce systematically to provide basic values, purpose, and direction for the organization

Benchmark (Chapter 4) a formal representation of performance expectations based on the demonstrated performance of an exemplary work unit or business

Benchmarking (Chapter 6) a technique used to calibrate an organization's efforts against a "best of class" yardstick

Bonus (Chapter 11) additional reward or payment for successful achievement of a task

Bonus pool (Chapter 11) sum of money reserved for the payment of incentive and recognition awards

Boundary systems (Chapter 13) explicit statements embedded in formal information systems that define and communicate specific risks to be avoided. See also *Business conduct boundaries* and *Strategic boundaries*

Budget (Chapter 5) resource plans of any organizational unit that either generates or consumes resources

Business capabilities (Chapter 2) see *Distinctive capabilities*

Business conduct boundaries (Chapter 13) defined standards of business conduct that enumerate forbidden activities and behaviors

Business goals (Chapter 1) the measurable aspirations that managers set for a business. Goals are determined by reference to business strategy. Goals may be financial—for example, to achieve 14% return on sales—or nonfinancial—such as to increase market share from 6% to 9%.

Business strategy (Chapter 1) how a company creates value for customers and differentiates itself from competitors in a defined product market

Capital budget (Chapter 7) see *Asset allocation system*

Capital employed (Chapter 5) the assets within a manager's direct span of control. These assets typically include accounts receivable, inventory, and plant and equipment. Sometimes, corporate-level assets, such as unamortized goodwill, are also allocated to profit centers to be included.

Capital investment plan (Chapter 5) proposed investment in long-term productive assets

Cash wheel (Chapter 5) a model of the operating cash flow through a business. Answers the question of whether the organization has enough cash to remain solvent throughout the year.

Centralized organization (Chapter 3) an organization designed so that unit managers have narrow spans of attention. A decentralized organization, by contrast, is designed so that managers have wide spans of attention.

Committed costs (Chapter 5) expenses determined by previous management decisions and, therefore, not subject to discretion during the current profit planning period

Competitive risk (Chapter 12) changes in the competitive environment that could impair the business' ability to successfully create value and differentiate its products or services

Complete measure (Chapter 11) a measure that captures all the relevant attributes of achievement

Contribution margin (Chapter 6) selling price minus variable costs

Control (Chapter 4) the process of using information to ensure that inputs, processes, and outputs are aligned to achieve organizational goals

Coordination (Chapter 4) the ongoing ability to integrate disparate parts of a business to achieve objectives

Core competencies (Chapter 2) see *Distinctive capabilities*

Core values (Chapter 13) beliefs that define basic principles, purpose, and direction

Corporate performance (Chapter 8) a firm's level of achievement in creating value for market constituents (customers, owners and suppliers)

Corporate strategy (Chapter 2) the way that a firm attempts to maximize the value of the resources it controls. Corporate strategy decisions focus on where corporate resources will be invested.

Cost center accountability (Chapter 3) the narrowest span of accountability encountered in most firms. Managers of cost centers are accountable only for their unit's level of spending relative to goods or services provided. See also *Profit center accountability*

Cost drivers (Chapter 5) activities that consume indirect resources

Critical performance variables (Chapter 10) factors that must be achieved or implemented successfully for the intended strategy of the business to succeed

Current assets (Chapter 2) cash and other assets that will be turned into cash during the course of an accounting cycle—normally one year

Customer perspective (Chapter 9) one of four balanced scorecard categories. Identifies the customer and market segments in which the business unit desires to compete.

Cybernetics (Chapter 4) the study of information and its use in feedback processes

Decentralized organization (Chapter 3) see *Centralized organization*

Diagnostic control system (Chapter 10) formal information system that managers use to monitor organizational outcomes and correct deviations from preset standards of performance

Diffusion of attention (Chapter 3) the constant switching back and forth between tasks that result in wasted time as employees constantly refocus on a new set of activities

Direct method (Chapter 5) technique to estimate cash flows during a period of time; managers project the cash that they

will receive and the cash that they will disburse

Discounted cash flow analysis (Chapter 7) see *Net present value*

Discretionary costs (Chapter 5) expenses that can be increased or decreased at will—almost without constraints

Distinctive capabilities (Chapter 2) special resources and know-how possessed by a firm that give it competitive advantage in the marketplace

Earnings (Chapter 5) see *Profit*

EBIAT (Chapter 5) acronym for earnings before interest and after taxes

EBITDA (Chapter 5) acronym for earnings before interest, taxes, depreciation, and amortization. It is a rough calculation of nonaccrual—or cash-based—operating earnings that can be computed readily from an income statement.

Economic value added (EVA) (Chapter 8) similar to residual income but distinguished by (1) a series of adjustments to eliminate distortions of accrual accounting and (2) the inclusion of both debt and equity sources of capital in the cost of capital

Economies of scale (Chapter 3) reduction in unit costs due to utilization of efficient, large-scale resources and high-volume processing

Economies of scope (Chapter 3) reduction in unit costs due to utilization of the same resources (e.g., distribution channels) across multiple products or activities to increase the throughput for a given fixed amount of that resource

Effectiveness (Chapter 6) the extent to which an activity achieves desired outcomes. Effectiveness focuses on the comparison of actual results with preset expectations or standards.

Efficiency   (Chapter 6) the level of resources that were consumed to achieve a certain level of output. Efficiency focuses on the ratio of inputs to outputs.

Efficiency variance   (Chapter 6) the amount by which profit differs from the original profit plan or budget because of unanticipated changes in the level of inputs used to create outputs

Embedded resources   (Chapter 2) tangible resources that are difficult to acquire and/or replace. Physical plant, distribution channels, and information technology are all embedded assets that represent potential strengths and weaknesses.

Emergent strategy   (Chapter 2) strategy that emerges spontaneously in the organization as employees respond to unpredictable threats and opportunities through experimentation and trial and error

Engineered costs   (Chapter 5) see *Committed costs*

Error of commission   (Chapter 12) error that occurs as a result of an employee knowingly pursuing a course of action that increases risk, impairs assets or otherwise endangers the business

Error of omission   (Chapter 12) error that occurs as a result of an employee omitting to perform an action that is necessary to protect the franchise or assets of the business

EVA   (Chapter 8) widely-used acronym for economic value added (Trademarked by consultants Stern, Stewart, & Co.)

Ex ante   (Chapter 4) set in advance, usually refers to a preset standard

Ex post evaluation   (Chapter 4) comparing actual effort and outcomes against prior expectations

External communication   (Chapter 4) informing financial, supplier, and customer markets about the direction and prospects of the firm

Extrinsic motivation   (Chapter 4) desire to engage in behaviors or actions in anticipation of tangible rewards, such as money or promotion

Fact-based management   (Chapter 4) management that moves from intuition and hunches to analysis based on hard data and facts

Favorable variance   (Chapter 6) the amount by which actual profit is higher than planned profit

Feedback   (Chapter 4) return of variance information from the output of a process to the input or process stages so that adjustments can be made to maintain desired levels of performance or control the stability of a system

Financial impairment   (Chapter 12) decline in the market value of a significant balance sheet asset held for resale or as collateral

Financial leverage   (Chapter 5) the ratio of assets to stockholders' equity focuses on financial leverage by asking, "What percentage of total assets employed are funded by stockholders and what percentage by debt?"

Financial performance perspective (Chapter 9) one of four balanced scorecard categories. Indicates whether the implementation of company strategy is contributing to profit improvement.

Five forces   (Chapter 2) systematic analysis of competitive dynamics to determine the nature and intensity of competition. The five forces are customers, suppliers, substitute products, new markets, and competitive rivalry.

Franchise   (Chapter 2) a business's distinctive ability to attract customers who are willing to purchase the business's products and services based on marketwide perceptions of value. See also *Market franchise*

Franchise risk   (Chapter 12) risk that the value of the entire business erodes due to a loss in confidence by critical constituents. Also known as reputation risk

Full cost transfer price   (Chapter 8) transfer price that includes direct costs plus an allocation for the divisional overhead that would normally be covered by the gross profit margin on goods sold to outside customers

Full cost plus profit transfer price (Chapter 8) the highest accounting-based transfer price that attempts to approach market price by adding an additional markup to the full cost transfer price

Function   (Chapter 3) the most basic organization component, comprising a group of managers and employees who specialize in specific work processes

Functional skills   (Chapter 2) strengths (and weaknesses) in the major functional areas of a business, such as research and development, production and manufacturing, marketing and sales, and administration

Goal   (Chapter 2) a formal aspiration that defines purpose or expected levels of achievement in implementing the business strategy

Hurdle rate   (Chapter 7) the minimum internal rate of return that must be achieved before the acquisition of an asset will be approved

Incentive   (Chapter 11) a reward or payment that is used to motivate performance

Indirect method   (Chapter 5) technique to estimate cash needs over long periods of time; managers start with their pro-

jected income as shown on the profit plan and adjust accruals to reflect actual cash receipts and disbursements

Information   (Chapter 4) the communication or reception of intelligence or knowledge. It is the critical vehicle for profit planning, performance measurement, and management control.

Innovation process   (Chapter 9) component of the internal value chain. Represents the "long wave" of value creation.

Intangible assets   (Chapter 2) Assets that are not physical in nature, such as franchises, copyrights, patents, trademarks, goodwill, valuable licenses (e.g., broadcast rights), and leases.

Intended strategy   (Chapter 2) planned strategy that managers attempt to implement in a specific product market based on analysis of competitive dynamics and current capabilities

Interactive control system   (Chapter 10) formal information system that managers use to personally involve themselves in the decision activities of subordinates

Internal business process perspective (Chapter 9) one of four balanced scorecard categories. Identifies the critical internal processes at which the organization must excel.

Internal control systems   (Chapter 1) the set of policies and procedures designed to ensure reliable accounting information and safeguard company assets

Internal rate of return (IRR)   (Chapter 7) the discount rate applied to any series of cash flows for which the value of the cash inflows exactly equals the value of cash outflows

Internal value chain   (Chapter 9) model of the set of internal processes, for creating value for customers. Includes identifying the market, creating the product/service offering, building products/services, delivering products/services, and post-sale service.

Intrinsic motivation   (Chapter 4) desire to engage in behaviors or actions in anticipation of internally-generated rewards such as personal feelings of accomplishment

Learning and growth perspective (Chapter 9) one of four balanced scorecard categories. Identifies the infrastructure that the organization must build to create long-term growth and improvement.

Levers of control   (Chapter 14) the set of beliefs systems, boundary systems, diagnostic control systems, and interactive control systems used by managers to implement intended strategies and guide emergent strategies

Leveraged business   (Chapter 5) one that relies on a high percentage of debt to fund the productive assets employed in the business to generate revenues

Long-term assets   (Chapter 5) resources held for an extended period of time, such as land, buildings, and equipment

Market capitalization   (Chapter 8) market value of the firm calculated as the product of the total number of ownership shares multiplied by the price per share

Market franchise   (Chapter 2) a business's distinctive ability to attract customers who are willing to purchase the business's products and services based on marketwide perceptions of value. A business is said to "own a franchise" when a brand name itself is an important source of revenue.

Market skills   (Chapter 2) a business's ability to respond to market needs

Market value   (Chapter 8) the total value of ownership claims in the business

as priced by financial markets. Represents the highest, most aggregate, measure of value creation. See *Market capitalization*

Market value added   (Chapter 8) excess of current market value over the amount of capital (i.e., adjusted book value) provided to the firm

Measure   (Chapter 11) quantitative value that can be scaled and used for purposes of comparison. Measures are necessary to ensure that performance goals are achieved.

Mission   (Chapter 2) the broad purpose, or reason, that a business exists

Mission statements   (Chapter 2) Missions (see above) are often written down in formal documents known as mission statements that are designed to communicate the core values of the business and inspire pride in participants

Negotiated transfer price   (Chapter 8) transfer price based on standard direct costs plus some allowance for profit or return on capital employed

Net income   (Chapter 5) see *Profit*

Net present value (NPV)   (Chapter 7) summation of the current value of a series of cash inflows and outflows after adjusting for the time value of money. Also known as *Discounted cash flow analysis*

NOPAT   (Chapter 5) acronym for net operating profit after taxes

Nonvariable costs   (Chapter 5) costs that do not vary directly with the level of sales

Objectives   (Chapter 11) see *Performance goals*

Objective measure   (Chapter 11) a measure that can be independently verified

Operations risk   (Chapter 12) risk of a breakdown in a core operating, manufacturing, or processing capability

Operations process (Chapter 9) component of the internal value chain. Represents those processes that produce and deliver existing products and services to customers.

Organizational blocks (Chapter 1) obstacles that organizations create that inhibit employees from working to their true potential

Organization chart (Chapter 3) a diagram of accountability units within an organization. Organization charts are useful visual reference tools because they allow members of the organization to understand how people and resources are grouped and who is responsible for directing activities and receiving accountability information.

Organizational learning (Chapter 2) the ability of an organization to monitor changes in its environment and internal processes and adjust its processes, products, and services to capitalize on those changes

Organizational structure (Chapter 3) the way in which work units are arranged or put together to form an organization

Output standard (Chapter 4) a formal representation of performance expectations

Payback (Chapter 7) total acquisition cost of an asset divided by the amount of the periodic (that is, monthly or yearly) inflows of cash (or cash savings) that an asset is expected to generate. Expressed in units of time

Performance drivers (Chapter 11) variables that either influence the probability of successfully implementing the strategy or provide the largest potential for marginal gain over time

Performance goal (Chapter 11) a desired level of accomplishment against which actual results can be measured

Performance measurement and control systems (Chapter 1) the formal information-based routines and procedures managers use to maintain or alter patterns in organizational activities

Performance measurement systems (Chapter 1) information systems that managers use to track the implementation of business strategy by comparing actual results against strategic goals and objectives. A performance measurement system typically comprises systematic methods of setting business goals together with periodic feedback reports.

Planning (Chapter 4) the process of preparing an economic and strategic road map for a business. Planning provides a framework for setting aspirations through performance goals and ensuring an adequate level and mix of resources to achieve these goals.

Planning systems (Chapter 1) recurring procedures to routinely disseminate planning assumptions, gather market information, provide details about relevant analyses, and prompt managers to estimate resource needs and performance goals and milestones

Plans (Chapter 4) a road map for the business. See *Planning*

Position of a business (Chapter 2) provides the answer to the following two questions: How do we create value for our customers? and How do we differentiate our products and services from those of our competitors?

Post-sale service process (Chapter 9) final stage of the internal value chain. Includes warranty and repair activities, treatment of defects and returns, and administration of payments

Price premium (Chapter 6) unit price that is higher than profit plan estimate.

Due to effective differentiation and successful market positioning.

Product mix   (Chapter 6) percentage of total sales that is generated by each product in a business's product line

Product division   (Chapter 3) a separate work unit dedicated to producing and marketing a set of products

Product market   (Chapter 2) a defined competitive market for a specific product or category of products

Product mix variance   (Chapter 6) the amount by which profit differs from the original profit plan or budget because of unanticipated changes in the sales mix of products with different contribution margins

Productive assets   (Chapter 2) assets used to produce goods and services for customers. These assets are usually recorded on a balance sheet.

Profit   (Chapter 5) the residual economic value after interest expense and income taxes (both of which are nondiscretionary payments). Based on accounting assumptions, profit is the economic value that is available for distribution to the residual claimants—equity holders—or for reinvestment in the business.

Profit center accountability   (Chapter 3) A profit center manager has a broader span of accountability than a cost center manager. He or she is not only accountable for costs, but also for revenues and, sometimes, for assets. See also *Cost center accountability*

Profit plan   (Chapter 1) a summary of future financial inflows and outflows for a specified future accounting period. It is usually prepared in the familiar format of an income statement.

Profit wheel   (Chapter 5) a model of the flow of operating profit through a business. Answers the question of whether the organization's strategy creates economic value

Profitability   (Chapter 5) the ratio of net income to sales. Profitability indicates how much profit was generated for each dollar of sales.

Realized strategy   (Chapter 14) strategies that were actually implemented. The outcome of intended and emergent strategy.

Reengineering   (Chapter 5) streamlining work flows to accomplish the same work with fewer resources

Regional business   (Chapter 3) regionally based work units that focus on specific geographic regions

Residual income   (Chapter 8) a measure of how much additional profit remains for investment in the business or distribution to owners after allowing for expected returns on investment. See also *Economic value added*

Resource   (Chapter 2) a strength of the business embodied in the tangible or intangible assets that are tied semipermanently to the firm

Responsive measures   (Chapter 11) a measure that reflects actions that a manager can influence

Return on capital employed (ROCE) (Chapter 5) a percentage calculated as the product of net income divided by sales and sales divided by capital employed. See also *Capital employed*

Return on equity (ROE)   (Chapter 5) a ratio calculated as net income divided by shareholders' equity

Return on investment (ROI)   (Chapter 5) a ratio measure of the profit output of the business as a percentage of financial investment inputs. This accounting measure is one of the single best surrogates for overall financial performance.

Return on management (ROM)
(Chapter 1) the amount of productive organizational energy released divided by the amount of management time and attention invested

Risk exposure calculator (Chapter 12) a tool to analyze the pressure points inside a business that can cause otherwise manageable risks to "blow up" into a crisis

ROE wheel (Chapter 5) a model of the flow of equity capital through a business. Answers the question of whether the organization creates enough value to attract the financial resources that it needs to invest in new assets.

Segregation of duties (Chapter 13) key structural aspect of internal control. Ensures that one person never handles all aspects of a transaction involving valuable company assets.

Sensitivity analysis (Chapter 5) estimates of profit changes when the underlying assumptions about the environment or other predictions prove to be under or overstated. Companies often develop three different scenarios: worst-case scenario, most likely scenario, and best-case scenario.

Signaling (Chapter 4) when managers send cues throughout the organization about their values, preferences, and the type of opportunities that they want employees to seek and exploit

Span of accountability (Chapter 3) the range of performance measures used to evaluate a manager's achievements. At a most basic level, span of accountability defines the financial statement items for which a manager is accountable.

Span of attention (Chapter 3) the domain of activities that are within a manager's field of view. Span of attention defines what an individual will attempt to gather information on and influence. In simple terms, it's what people care about and pay attention to.

Span of control (Chapter 3) how many (and which) subordinates and functions report to a manager. Span of control describes the resources—in terms of people and work units—directly under a manager's control.

Specialization (Chapter 3) the focusing of individuals and resources on specific tasks that require expertise, training, and dedicated resources

Spending variance (Chapter 6) the amount by which profit differs from the original profit plan or budget because of unanticipated changes in the actual unit cost of inputs

Staff safeguards (Chapter 13) internal controls designed to ensure that accounting and transaction processing staff have the right level of expertise, training, and resources

Standard (Chapter 4) a formal representation of performance expectations

Strategic boundaries (Chapter 13) set of opportunities declared "out of bounds" by senior managers after evaluating a firm's strategy and its unique risks. Implicitly defines the desired market position for the firm.

Strategic profitability (Chapter 6) sum of profit (or loss) from competitive effectiveness and the profit (or loss) from operating efficiencies

Strategic profitability analysis (Chapter 6) variance analysis techniques to evaluate the success of a business in generating profit from the implementation of its strategy

Strategic risk (Chapter 12) unexpected event or set of conditions that significantly reduces the ability of managers to implement their intended business strategy

Strategic uncertainties (Chapter 12) emerging threats and opportunities that could invalidate the assumptions upon which the current business strategy is based

Structural safeguards (Chapter 13) internal controls designed to ensure clear definition of authority for individuals handling assets and recording accounting transactions

SWOT (Chapter 2) an acronym for strengths, weaknesses, opportunities, and threats. A SWOT analysis determines the potential for effective strategy based on an assessment of competitive dynamics (see the *Five forces*) and the resources and capabilities of a business.

System safeguards (Chapter 13) internal controls designed to ensure adequate procedures for transaction processing and timely management reports

Total Quality Management (TQM) (Chapter 4) a management approach that standardizes and streamlines key operating processes to ensure high levels of quality and/or low defect rates

Transfer price (Chapter 8) an internally set transaction price to account for the transfer of goods and services between divisions of the same firm

Unfavorable variance (Chapter 6) the amount by which actual profit is below planned profit

Value proposition (Chapter 8) the mix of product and service attributes that a firm offers to customers in terms of price, product features, quality, availability, image, buying experience and after-sales warranty and service

Variable cost transfer price (Chapter 8) lowest accounting-based transfer price based on only variable costs with no administrative overhead included in the price

Variable costs (Chapter 5) costs that vary proportionally with the level of sales or production outputs

Variance analysis (Chapter 6) the difference between an item estimated on a profit plan or budget prepared prior to the start of an accounting period and the actual income or expense as reflected on accounting statements prepared after the accounting period has ended

Variance information (Chapter 4) the difference between actual outputs and pre-set standards of performance. Used as feedback for corrective action by managers.

Weighted average cost of capital (WACC) (Chapter 7) the average cost of capital calculated by weighting the cost of each source of funds by its proportion of the total market value of the firm. This discount rate represents the minimum rate of return on an investment to meet capital providers' expectations.

Work unit (Chapter 3) represents a grouping of individuals who utilize the firm's resources and are accountable for performance

INDEX